An Introduction to Camp Administration

Basic Camp Management

American Camping Association®

Copyright 1979, 1987, 1990, 1995, 2000, 2004 by American Camping Association, Inc. Available in Russian from the Union of Children Associations of St. Petersburg. Previous editions have been translated into Russian and Japanese.

Printed in the United States of America

Cover design by Joyce Koeper
Text design by IBJ Contract Publishing
Editorial services by BooksCraft, Inc.

Photo credits: (left to right) ACA File Photo; Echo Lake Southwood; © Girl Scouts of Limberlost Council, 2002

American Camping Association
5000 State Road 67 North
Martinsville, Indiana 46151-7902
765-342-8456
800-428-CAMP
www.ACAcamps.org

ISBN 0-87603-188-2

A CIP catalog record for this book can be obtained from the Library of Congress.

Contents

Disclaimer

The purpose of this book is to provide an overview of issues with which camp directors should be familiar. It should be recognized that camp directors and others who run camp operations will require further education and experience in each of the areas covered herein. Neither the publisher nor the authors of this book undertake to verify that individuals who use this book are trained appropriately. Nor do the publisher or authors assume any responsibility for liability for any consequences of the use of information in this book. Further, the American Camping Association, Inc., and the authors hereby expressly disclaim any responsibility, liability, or duty to camp administrators, operators, personnel, any program participants or their families, for any such liability arising out of injury, illness, or loss to any person or organization, by the failure of such administrators or camp personnel to seek further training.

*Dedicated to Kathy and Robin, who found a love of
people and of the world outdoors while growing up at camp.*

*The Staff of YMCA Camp Widjiwagan,
St. Paul, Minnesota, 1963-1974,
who will always be a part of our lives.*

Preface

When the first edition of Basic Camp Management was published in the mid-seventies the idea was to provide a short and simple manual for the very new camp director. With each revision, further information and topics have been added, changing the manual from the rather elementary volume we had originally visualized. One major factor in this evolution has been the growing complexity of the management of camps and conference centers. The other has been the continued use of the book as a text in college courses and the American Camping Association's Basic Camp Director Courses, which required the expansion of information.

Some of the terms we use in the book should be thought of in the broadest sense and may require some explanation.

As we have used it, the term *camp* encompasses many many types of operations beyond the sites that run their own camp programs, including conference/retreat centers or camp sites that also rent their facilities for conference/retreat use or for the use of an environmental education program; camp programs using rented sites, the rented sites themselves..

The term *director* is used to refer to the administrator of the camp, conference/ retreat center, or program. The director is responsible for the site most of the time.

The terms *operator* or *owner* both refer to the entity (whether individual(s) or organization) that owns the operation. In some cases, the ownership involves the property and site and/or the program operated on the site. In other cases, it involves only the program operated in a rented facility.

Independent camp refers to one ordinarily organized for profit, sometimes identified as a private-independent camp or for-profit camp.

The term *not-for-profit* describes camps that operate under a 501 (c) (3) Internal Revenue Service classification or that are operated by a government body. This would include agency, organizational, public, and religiously affiliated camps, as well as a number of camps that were at one time for-profit camps that now operate under a board of directors in compliance with 501 (c) (3) regulations.

The term *core areas* refers to the fourteen topics that make up the body of knowledge for the camping profession, as defined by the American Camping Association. We've addressed all of the core areas . Since this is an introduction, you will want to pursue a more in-depth study of each as you gain experience. The core areas are:

- Leadership
- Target population and diversity
- Mission/purpose
- Participant development and behavior
- Program design and activities
- Human resources
- Risk management

- Health and wellness
- Business and finance
- Marketing
- Site and facilities
- Food service
- Transportation
- Strategic planning

Finally, rather than using "he" as the universal gender denoting both male and female, we have used the rather awkward form *he or she* (in the tradition of John Ledlie), to ensure equal billing for the many female camp directors and staff members, as well as the spouses of male directors and staff members.

Listed at the end of each chapter are references to the *American Camping Association's Accreditation Standards for Camp Programs and Services*, the self-assessment tool "Additional Professional Practices" that is part of that volume, and the *Guidelines for Conference and Retreat Centers* on CD. Though these are modern documents, they have been developed through a professional review process over fifty-plus years. It is likely that these tools will continue to be updated after this book is published, so be sure you are referring to the most recent edition.

We wish to express our thanks to the staff of the American Camping Association; Ed Schirick of Schirick and Associates Insurance Brokers, Inc.; Linda Ecerg, RN, of Concordia Language Camps and the Association of Camp Nurses; and Dr. Dwight Jewson of Strategic Frameworking, Inc., for their assistance in reviewing relevant materials. We also express our appreciation to Connie Coutellier and the training teams of the Basic Camp Director's Courses for their leadership in revising the Basic Camp Director Course curriculum, which, to a large degree, we are trying to parallel in the outline of this edition.

We hope this book will be a practical help to persons just entering our field as well as to experienced directors and that it will inspire *better camping for all*.

Armand and Beverly Ball
Sanibel Island, Florida

The Tradition of Camp

Camping needs the imaginative, the picturesque, the romantic; needs it for its own attractiveness and for the sake of young America, for whom the imaginative will be the only enduring type of play. . . . The . . . camp, if it is worthy, is one of the greatest socializing, humanizing, civilizing factors which can enter the life of a boy or girl.[1]

Organized camping began in North America in the mid-nineteenth century. No accurate record exists of the exact location of the first actual camp. To gain a better understanding of the growth of the organized camp movement during its first one hundred years, one should read *History of Organized Camping: The First 100 Years* by Eleanor Eells and *Blue Lake & Rocky Shore* by the Ontario Camping Association. However, a brief summary of that history is provided here as a background for the person new to the field.

Historical Overview

The Beginnings

The Ontario Camping Association Committee reports that in 1840 a church camp group met for summer camping under canvas at Hogg's Hollow (since renamed York Mills), just north of Toronto's present city limits. It appears that other camps did not come into existence in Canada until the late 1800s.

The first recorded organized camp experience in the United States occurred in 1861, when Frederick William Gunn, the headmaster of the Gunnery School for Boys, Washington, Connecticut, led a group of students on a forty-mile trek to Milford on Long Island Sound. After the two-day hike, the boys camped out for ten days and then hiked back to the school. This experience was stimulated by the interest of youth at that time in the Civil War and the encampments and campfires common to the soldiers of that day. A plaque commemorates that camp at Welch's Point near Milford. Mr. Gunn continued to offer such camp experiences until 1879.

In 1876, the first private independent camp was organized by Dr. Joseph Rothrock, a practicing physician in Wilkes-Barre, Pennsylvania. The camp was designed to improve the health of children, and there was emphasis on physical fitness and health; the camp was short lived. In 1880, Camp Chocorua for boys aged twelve to sixteen was organized on Asquam Lake, New Hampshire, by Ernest Balch. This camp continued for eight years and focused on sports activities and the actual daily living chores of cooking, cleaning, and dishwashing. A decidedly spiritual emphasis was given to the camp. In both of these camps, fees were charged to cover the costs. These fees were, however, not very realistic because both camps closed with deficits.

The first youth camp run by an organization was founded in 1885 by Sumner F. Dudley as a YMCA (Young Men's Christian Association) camp near Newburgh, New York. The camp, which still bears his name, later moved to Lake Champlain near Westport, New York, and is the oldest continuously operating camp in the United States. The oldest camp continuously operating on the same site is Keewaydin Camps, operated by the Keewaydin Foundation and founded as an independent camp in 1894.

In Canada, the first organizational camp and first independent camp were both organized in the same year, 1894: YMCA Kamp Kanawana in Quebec and Camp Keewaydin (formerly Kamp Kah Kiou) in Ontario.

All of these camps were camps for boys; it was not until 1892 that an independent camp, called Camp Arey, reserved a summer session for girls. By 1902 three camps exclusively for girls began: Kehonka in New Hampshire and Wyonegonic Camps and Pinelands Camps in Maine.

It was not until 1922 that the first independent girls' camp was organized in Canada, Camp Glen Bernard in Ontario. This delay in camping for girls was to some degree the result of Victorian attitudes toward young women's dress, decorum, movement, careers, and education.

During this same period, organizational camping was growing rapidly with the development of Fresh Air Camps, designed to serve inner-city youth. These camps sprang up in Connecticut (1886), Wisconsin (1887), and New York City (1892), as did Life Camps (1887) in Connecticut and New Jersey. The YWCA opened a vacation camp for industrial women workers in Asbury, New Jersey in 1874, which was likely the first camp for adults. Settlement houses sprang up during this period and established camps attached to such urban centers as Boston, Pittsburgh, New York City, and Chicago (1898-1908). A camp for children with disabilities began in Chicago in 1899-1900. National youth organizations came into being in the early 1900s with their own camping programs: Boy Scouts of America (BSA) in 1910, Camp Fire Girls (now Camp Fire USA) in 1910, and Girl Scouts of the U.S.A. in 1912.

Camps throughout this period of history primarily focused on getting young people out of the city into a healthy, rural environment and providing recreational activities. However, much of the experience was related to activities necessary to daily living (e.g., cooking, cleaning). Boys' camps tended to place value on rugged outdoor living. Girls' camps also included hiking and aquatics, with a strong emphasis on the creative arts. There was a strong spiritual influence, often with Bible study, in most of the camps of this era. Moral or character development was a key element. Camps were often small and quite rustic during this period and placed much emphasis on small-group living.

The emergence of national youth organizations and local social service organizations and the continued growth and success of independent camps stimulated the growth of camps in a number of areas. Camps began to spread westward, with camps springing up in Pennsylvania, West Virginia, Illinois, Missouri, and California. Local governments started camps in Los Angeles in 1914, Detroit in 1915, and Kansas City in 1920.

With the expansion of camps from around 1910 onward, a more open emphasis on the educational values of the camp experience was seen. Activities such as arts and crafts, music, and dance were added to the curriculum. The progressive education movement began to make its philosophy felt during this period. The training of camp staff began to be accepted as a necessary part of camp planning. By the 1920s, many camps were much more structured with greater emphasis on competition, awards, and scheduled activity. They stressed good character, spiritual attainment, and a good personality. The natural sciences became part of the instructional activities in many camps.

International Expansion

The greatest expansion of camps into other countries occurred through the efforts of several youth organizations in the United States and Canada that were international in scope, as well as through the missionary efforts by various Christian denominations. The world headquarters of various international youth organizations such as Boy Scouts, Girl Scouts (Girl Guides in most other parts of the world), YMCA, and YWCA provided some guidance in the development of camp programs in their movements in other countries.

Missionaries from various Christian denominations simply replicated the camp model utilized in the United States of America, as they were prone to do with church, church school, and educational programs. Consequently, these camps were not always successful in meeting the needs of the indigenous people in these countries. Models adapted to the needs and culture of these people gradually emerged.

The governments of France and Russia developed camp models that they used to provide services to their youth. The camps began in France in the late nineteenth century, whereas they began in Russia in the early 1900s. In Russia, camps were primarily operated in canvas tents prior to World War II. After that war, camps began to spread and to upgrade their facilities, and by the 1980s, Russia represented the largest camping movement in the world.

In Japan, camps began in the early 1900s. In Australia, camps began in the 1940s and developed primarily as facilities for schools to conduct outdoor education. Camps began in Venezuela in the mid-1900s.

Professional Associations

As camps grew in numbers early in the twentieth century, camp directors began to meet together to discuss common problems and to learn from each other. A professional association for directors of boys' camps, the Camp Directors Association of America, was begun in 1912. By 1916, an association of directors of girls' camps, the National Association of Girls' Private Camps, emerged. These associations merged in 1924 into the Camp Directors Association and published a new journal, *Camping*, in 1926. Concerns about health and safety were emerging, and directing a camp began to be taken more seriously as a profession, assuming the same recognition level as teaching or social work. Conventions or training conferences began for camp directors during this period. Camp directors in Ontario and Quebec were also attending many of the professional meetings in the United States. In 1933, the Ontario Camping Association was formed, and for a period it became part of the American Camping Association.

The emphasis on structured or regimented education in camp began to lessen in the thirties as the White House Conference on Child Health and Protection, coming at the beginning of the Great Depression, focused the camp's attention on youth and health. One of the significant findings of that conference was the demand for an inclusive national organization to articulate the needs and interests of the growing camping movement in the United States.

The next several years led to the reorganization in 1935 of the Camp Directors Association (CDA) into the American Camping Association (ACA), with locally operated sections based upon geographical boundaries. This organization began to evolve a set of health and safety standards, which eventually became the set of accreditation standards accepted throughout the United States. The American Camping Association remains today the only professional organization for directors of all types of camps and the nationally recognized accrediting body.

The Canadian Camping Association (CCA) was formed in 1947, and it included the Ontario and Quebec Camping Associations, as they moved out of the American Camping Association. Gradually each Canadian province formed associations as part of the CCA.

Camps Increase

Following World War II, there was a rapid expansion of camp paralleling the increased population of youth in the country. Camp was widely accepted as an appropriate summer experience for youth. The numbers of camps and campers expanded rapidly. As Nelson Wieters, then of George Williams College, pointed out, many camps with generally global objectives began because of that broad acceptance and a ready marketplace, while other camps began for very specific purposes, either philosophical or instructional in nature. The latter objective led to the specialty camp boom in the sixties. Parents and educators raised more and more questions about the specific impact of the camp experience on character development, physical skills improvement, or spiritual growth.

School camping or outdoor education began to come into its own in the early 1940s. Large programs were begun in Michigan, under the auspices of the Kellogg Foundation; Tyler, Texas; and San Diego. Though early efforts began in the early thirties, it did not begin to grow rapidly until the fifties. Colleges and universities began teacher education programs in this field. The Outdoor Education Council of the American Association of Health, Physical Education, Recreation and Dance (AAHPERD) also began during this period and gave leadership to much of the professional development in this field. Other organizations formed in the 1970s and 1980s to promote environmental education and supported the work of environmental educators. These include the North American Association for Environmental Education (NAAEE) and the Coalition for Education in the Outdoors.

Camps for very specific spiritual objectives grew beyond church-sponsored camps to interdenominational and nondenominational camps and conference settings, many privately operated. Out of this growing segment of camps emerged CCI/USA (Christian Camping International/USA) in 1963, which initially required the signing of a statement of personal Christian faith for membership. Its national offices are in Colorado Springs, Colorado.

In the past twenty years, the number of experientially based outdoor programs, primarily involving adventure and stress/challenge activities, has grown. The expansion of this type of program accelerated greatly with the establishment of Outward Bound, an adventure program that began in England and spread to the United States and other countries. Variations of the Outward Bound methods have spread to many settings, including work with at-risk youth, adjudicated youth, and even business executives. In 1972, the Association for Experiential Education (AEE) began as a professional organization to bring together people interested in this discipline. Concern about the impact on the environment spurred organizations such as the Wilderness Education Association, founded in 1977 by leaders from the academic community concerned with excellence in the development of outdoor leadership and the role of education in the preservation of this country's wildland areas.

Camps and camping associations are now operating around the world. There are national camping associations in at least eleven countries: Australia, Canada, Colombia, Greece, Japan, Malaysia, Mexico, Russia, Taiwan, United States, and Venezuela. With the help of the Canadian Camping Association and the American Camping Association, three international conferences have been held: in Toronto in 1983; in Washington, D.C., in 1987; and in

Toronto in 1994. In 1987, an International Camping Fellowship was organized to provide information sharing among individuals interested in international education and exchange. This group publishes a newsletter and promotes international events. Since its formation, the International Camping Congress has held international camping conferences on a three-year cycle: St. Petersburg, Russia (1997); Tokyo, Japan (2000); and Melbourne, Australia (2003). Future Congresses are scheduled for Mexico City and Athens, Greece.

Types of Camps

C amps are almost as varied as people; however, there are basically two types of camps: day and resident. The day camp operates only during a portion of the day, typically morning and afternoon, usually for five successive days of the week, Monday through Friday. Nevertheless, some day camps operate only three days a week, others operate in the evening hours, and many others include at least one overnight experience as part of the camp period. Resident camps bring participants to a setting in which housing is provided for a period of days. The typical resident camp provides lodging and meals. However, the resident camp experience may also take the form of travel or trip camping, in which the housing may be tents, shelters, or hotels and motels, and the campers move every day. Camp sessions vary in length from three to sixty days.

The camp program is operated and staffed by the camp, and supervision of individual campers is a camp responsibility. Camps may be operated with paid or volunteer staff, or a combination thereof. Many camps operate twelve months a year, involving a more typical summer camp experience, as well as school camps, conference groups, retreat groups, and adult education groups. A camp may also be a program operated by a given group for only one or two weeks a year on property owned by an individual, public park, or another camp. Camps may serve youth, adults, senior adults, or families.

Camps are generally recognized as for-profit or not-for-profit. The for-profit camp or entrepreneurial camp may be operated by an individual, partners, or a corporation to return a profit to the owner, including some return on the capital investment made in property and facilities. While for-profit camps are commonly known also as independent camps, some not-for-profit camps also use the term independent because they are not connected to any national organization.

The not-for-profit camp may be operated by an organization such as the YMCA, Girl Scouts, Boy Scouts, a settlement house, a health-related association, a religious entity, or a government body. Public camps are operated by a government body, such as a parks-and-recreation department, school systems, or 4-H. Funding comes from fees and tax dollars. A number of camps that were formerly independent for-profit operations have preserved their identity as a private tax-exempt corporation or foundation. In all these cases, the camp has a tax exemption under article 501(c)(3) of the federal tax code or is operated by a governmental body. In the last two decades, a number of independent camp owners have moved from for-profit to not-for-profit corporations and secured 501(c)(3) status from the federal government. The camp is owned by a corporation and is provided tax breaks, and, as a result, the camp is preserved for the future. This change frequently occurs when second or third generations of the family are no longer interested in running the camp.

The mission, outcomes and/or goals of many not-for-profit camps and for-profit camps are parallel. The facilities in some not-for-profit camps may, in fact, be more expensive than in some for-profit camps because they have the advantage of securing tax-deductible contributions for development. The for-profit camp generally charges higher fees for many reasons, including the need to recover income from the capital investment made by private parties, as well as the need to pay a number of taxes that not-for-profit camps do not have to pay. Therefore, the for-profit camp's clientele tend to come from a socioeconomic level that can pay such fees. Both types of camps may provide financial assistance for those who cannot afford the fee and thus provide a more diverse camper group. The for-profit camp has most often offered longer sessions (three to eight weeks) than the not-for-profit camp, though many have changed to shorter sessions in recent years. Not-for-profit camps have tended to have shorter sessions (one or two weeks) than have for-profit camps, though some camps offer four- or eight-week sessions in order to offer special programs or address child-care needs.

Few generalizations can be made about one type of camp or the other concerning wages, clientele, program, outcomes and goals, objectives, and facilities. Peter Drucker suggests that "The task of the not-for-profit manager is to try to convert the organization's mission statement into specifics." The task of any camp director is to try to bring the camp's purpose/mission into practical accomplishments, and that purpose/mission may be very similar in both for-profit and not-for-profit camps.

In both cases, it is essential that the camp operate in a fiscally sound fashion and that the director earn a decent living. In the not-for-profit camp and in some independent for-profit camps, where the owner is director, the director receives a set salary. In other independent for-profit camps, the director receives a bonus or a portion of the profit (if any) as salary. A not-for-profit camp may have a hard time offering a competitive salary; however, it will be difficult to retain a good director if the salary is not consistent with other comparable professions. The camp cannot long continue to operate in today's competitive climate (however lofty the stated purpose or mission of a camp is) if it does not have as a parallel purpose to be financially accountable.

One of the growing complexities of the camp world is the increase in camps providing a variety of services and serving a variety of audiences. Many camps operate twelve months a year, a portion of which is devoted to the more traditional camp experience; the other portion is devoted to short-term programs run by the camp or by rental or user groups. These include weekend retreats, school environmental education classes, and parent-child programs. When a camp is accredited, the public assumes that all programs on the site are accredited. In 1998, the American Camping Association, addressing this trend and perception, changed its standards to affect all the camp-related programs and services of the organization throughout the year. A separate set of guidelines for conference and retreat centers is available from ACA on CD. Many of the principles in the management of camps, short-term and year-round programs, and conference centers are the same. This text identifies some of the differences wherever possible.

What Is Camp?

Because the early camps were primarily directed toward getting youth out of the city into a healthy and moral environment, little energy went into defining a camp. By 1929, a special committee of the New York Section of the Camp Directors Association reported the essential functions of the camp as being "education for: physical health, emotional integration, an understanding of primitive processes, enlightened social participation, the acquisition of tastes and appreciations, and spiritual growth."

The "primitive processes" referred to outdoor experiences. By the late forties, Hedley S. Dimock identified that the "characteristic elements, blended together in the right proportion, of an organized camp included: (1) people, (2) outdoor life, (3) living in groups, (4) a camp community, and (5) leadership and conditions designed to satisfy personal needs and interests, and to stimulate wholesome personal, social and spiritual development."[2]

He goes on to underline the importance of experiences that are "indigenous to group living in the out-of-door setting." The American Camping Association offers as its definition: "A sustained experience which provides a creative, recreational and educational opportunity in group living in the outdoors. It utilizes trained leadership and the resources of the natural surroundings to contribute to each camper's mental, physical, social, and spiritual growth."

With all of the words that have flowed from experts, it is still difficult to draw narrow lines around what a camp is and what a camp is not. There is substantial support for the definition that characterizes a camp as an institution that provides a group living experience, with trained leaders who facilitate that group and community experience and utilize the outdoor surroundings to accomplish the mental, physical, social, and spiritual outcomes and goals of the sponsoring body or owner.

As Bernard Mason suggests in the opening quotation for this chapter, camps must be imaginative to interest individuals in the outdoor experience. Camp owners and directors have not always been the best source for interpreting the value and meaning of the camp to the general public, relying more often upon the voice of previous campers to propagate the camp.

The commonalties among all types of camps, resident or day, for-profit or not-for-profit, are far greater than the differences. The basic similarities are easily discovered when the directors of camps take the opportunity to sit down together, get to know each other, and get beyond labels, terminology, and preconceptions. Regardless of the type of camp and program, the similarities bind camps together because they all work for an ultimate developmental experience for each camper.

Generic Values of Camping

If one reviews the literature in the camp field concerning how others perceive the value of the camp experience, the lists will be varied and idealistic because camp directors tend to be idealistic people. However, several values can be found on almost any list.

Understanding the Outdoor Environment. The camp environment should be a key factor in determining program and objectives. Being outdoors is one of the distinctive features of the camp experience, and youngsters have few other opportunities to learn about the natural world and recognize their responsibility as stewards of its resources.

A Group Living Experience. The learning experience involved in living in a group of one's peers provides opportunities for teachable moments not easily encountered elsewhere.

Fun. Camp should be fun. Play is a natural growing experience of children and a lifelong need of adults. Gaining leisure skills and attitudes that can be used throughout life is a valuable experience.

To these, Betty Lyle would add:

Experience in Democracy. "With campers from various backgrounds, children may for the first time have an opportunity to live in a really democratic community."

Participation in Program. Programs need to be "related to the interests and needs of the camper," and "campers must have an active share in planning what the camp life and program shall be."

Understanding and Guidance. "The relationship with a counselor is a new kind of relationship with an adult for most campers . . . a good counselor (is) one who likes his campers, understands them as individuals, helps, suggests, listens, guides."[3]

Reynold E. Carlson would add to that list:

Experiencing Individual Growth and Development. "Camp should offer children a chance to discover their own potentialities, to exercise their personal initiative, and to earn respect for what they do as individuals."

Practicing Health and Safety. In camp, children should be "practicing . . . good personal health habits . . . [and] practicing rather than talking about health and safety."

Developing New Skills and Interests and Perfecting Old Ones. "Many of the camp activities have a high carry over value into later years."

Developing Spiritual Meanings and Values. "Many of these insights are caught as well as taught."[4]

James C. Stone, in a 1986 study, found that "campers made a statistically significant gain overall, and increases in the following characteristics:

Responsibility. Skill in being accountable for one's own behavior.

Decision Making. Skill in thinking for one's self.

Self-concept. Skill in getting along with others.

Interpersonal Relations. Skill in making friends and being accepted.

Citizenship. Skill in respecting the rights of others.

Environmental Concern. Skill in appreciating one's natural surroundings."[5]

In 2001, the American Camping Association began an ambitious four-year effort to quantitatively assess the youth development outcomes and goals of the camp experience. According to ACA Executive Director, Peg Smith, "For many years, ACA has recognized the important benefits that the camp experience contributes to youth development and education. Through a Lilly Endowment gift, we will have tangible evidence that will identify the program elements common to the most successful programs and allow us to provide training concerning the developmental value of the camp experience."[6]

The youth development outcomes will be measured through surveys of 5,000 campers and their parents, staff observational checklists, camp questionnaires, and focus groups with a sample of participating camps. The outcomes under study include:

- Increased positive identity

- Increased social skills

- Enhanced positive values and spiritual growth

- Enhanced cognitive and psycho-motor skills

Upon completion of the study, ACA will publish the results and plans to provide materials and training on outcome measurement.

What Are Conference/Retreat Centers or Outdoor Centers?

As camps have moved to year-round operations and facilities designed and improved for multiseason use, many have had to reevaluate their purpose. Most operations that desire to provide programs or lease facilities to other groups for camp-style programs focus primarily on outdoor and recreation activities, and the improved facility allows the operation to provide year-round services. Some camps have changed their name from camp to outdoor center to encompass both the summer camp and the year-round operation.

Some camps design multipurpose facilities and/or may operate a conference/retreat center along with other camp-style programs. Designing one facility that serves both a camp-style group and an adult-conference group and that focuses primarily on indoor meetings utilizing the outdoors for release from the thought process is a challenge. Many operations that desire to serve both groups have both kinds of facilities on one piece of property. As a camp moves into more year-round use and develops its statement of purpose and subsequent outcomes and goals, these client and usage differences should be kept in mind.

The American Camping Association defines a conference/retreat center as "a residential facility designed for adults and other groups who come together for meetings, training sessions, and educational or inspirational programs. Such a facility generally operates at least three seasons of the year and is designed to minimize outside distractions. It provides dedicated meeting space, food service, hospitality and support services, access to facilities and natural environments for release and diversion, and housing styles appropriate to the target clientele."[7]

Kathleen M. Trotter illustrates these conceptual differences in an article for *Camping Magazine* and through her camp consultancy firm, KALEIDOSCOPE, Inc. The myriad of camp and conference center programs for people of all ages takes place in a variety of natural settings and styles of accommodations. Notice in *illustration 1.1* that the spectrum from rustic

Illustration 1.1

Both camps and conference/retreat centers offer opportunities for holistic growth for youth and adults. However, they differ in their relationship to the outdoors and the role played by facilities and services. *(Used by permission)*

| Most Adult Retreats and Conferences | Rustic Conferences | Rustic Resident Camps | Wilderness Camps |

Indoor Focus/Outdoor Release
- "Home-like" comfort and convenience prevent distraction of learning.
- Personal, private space helps facilitate comfort, study, and reflection
- Learning usually begins conceptually and then is applied "experientially"

Outdoor Focus/Indoor Release
- Rustic accomodations help teach simplicity and creativity
- The outdoors becomes a focal point of the curriculm
- Facilities and activities are designed to foster community participation and group independence
- Learning usually begins experientially, then is conceptualized

camps to refined centers is, indeed, wide, and it is sometimes difficult to see common ground among these diverse facilities and programs.

Facilities and program styles differ because of what we want to accomplish. We increase our effectiveness with our clients and with each other when we remember that we share similar values but offer different environments in order to implement our various programs.

"All of us as camp and conference center leaders strive to positively influence our clients in holistic ways so that they leave camp healthier, stronger, more skilled, and mature. Some of us facilitate this process by designing *educational activities* for our campers or guests.

"Others among us provide the context for the experience by creating comfortable, caring *residential environments* that free campers or guests to fully engage in learning and growth. Regardless of the focus, the very nature of our enterprise calls for two essential ingredients: some kind of structured experience, usually called a *program*, and the group living accommodations, which can be referred to as *hospitality* services. Neither of these is dispensable if we are to truly accomplish our mission."[8]

Many camps have increased their year-round staff and are providing environmental education programs to schools and special programs for an existing or new client group. Program staff may switch from outdoor education instructors to camp counselors or program specialist roles in the summer. Often the program looks and feels like camp with a stronger environmental emphasis and the staff skills needed are very similar. Some camps provide services for rental groups whose needs range from strictly facility use to food service and optional program services such as challenge activities or winter sports. This may be the first step toward a year-round operation or provide additional income for the camp to better serve their primary client group.

There may be specific outcomes and goals that deal separately with each type of operation. Any program or service could contribute to the overall purpose of the camp and/or conference center. As long as the decision concerning facilities and program styles is a conscious part of the planning process and is consistent with the mission, there should be few problems that cannot be worked through. However, to slip into one style or the other for expediency in meeting number, dollar, or other goals without being a part of the purpose of the camp can only lead to severe problems in setting priorities and serving clientele. There are additional considerations about budgeting for a year-round operation in chapter 14.

Checkpoints

1. Compare your camp history to the historical overview of camp.

2. What are the overall generic values of camps? How do your camp values compare?

3. How would you determine whether the camp is for-profit or not-for-profit?

4. What are some of the differences between camps and conference/retreat centers?

Related Standards and Guidelines

Listed at the end of most chapters are references to specific standards from the American Camping Association's *Accreditation Standards for camp programs and services*. These are the accepted industry standards. References are also made to the "Additional Professional Practices," a section in the *Accreditation Standards for Camp Programs and Services* and *Guidelines for Conference & Retreat Centers* on CD.

Accreditation Standards for Camp Programs and Services: HR-1

[1] Bernard S. Mason. 1930. *Camping and Education*. New York: The McCall Company.

[2] Hedley S. Dimock. 1948. *Administration of the Modern Camp*. New York: Association Press (YMCA of the USA).

[3] Betty Lyle. 1947. *Camping: What Is It?* Martinsville, IN: American Camping Association. pp. 4–5.

[4] Reynold E. Carlson. 1975. *The Values of Camping*. Martinsville, IN: American Camping Association. p. 4.

[5] James C. Stone. 1986. "Kids Learn Responsibility." *Camping Magazine*, Vol. 59, No. 1, September/October. p. 21.

[6] Peg Smith. 2003. *ACA Launches a World Class Research Project* Martinsville, IN: American Camping Association Press release (cited on 1 October 2003) www.ACAcamps.org

[7] American Camping Association. 1993. *Standards for Conference and Retreat Centers*. Martinsville, IN: American Camping Association. p. 5.

[8] Kathleen M. Trotter. 1989. "Getting Out of the 90-Day Mentality." *Camping Magazine*, Vol. 61, No. 7, May. pp. 28–29.

What is the Camp Director's Job?

Chapter 2

The philosophy under which a camp functions, the morale of staff and counselors, the contributions the camp makes to the lives of youngsters, the adequacy of physical equipment–all are reflections of the insight, character, and competency of the camp director. His/her executive ability, together with a sense and appreciation of justice, needs to be at a high level. He/she needs insight, a world of patience, physical stamina, and ability to command the respect as well as the friendship of those associated with him/her in the camping enterprise.[1]

If you were to line up ten experienced camp directors and ask them what the job of a camp director is, you would probably get ten different answers. To survive, a camp director must possess a smattering of many skills and must combine many roles: cook, bookkeeper, plumber, minister, teacher, nurse, electrician, mechanic, risk manager, salesperson, lawyer, politician, corporate executive, naturalist, and eternal optimist. Every camp director will discover new dimensions at the end of each session.

Job Description

A new camp director's first task, if a thorough job description is not supplied, should be to develop such a description, in consultation with various people at the particular camp. Each camp owner will have different expectations. For example, in one camp, the bookkeeping may be handled entirely by a centralized organization office, while the bookkeeping may be part of the director's job in another. A summer day camp director's duties and concerns will differ from those of a year-round residential camp director. Therefore, it is difficult to outline one model job description for a camp director.

However, there are aspects of the job in any camp that are somewhat uniform and require specific duties depending upon the administrative situation. A camp director's job might include all of the following responsibilities:

- Develop and implement the mission/purpose and the youth development outcomes and goals of the camp and/or year-round operation.

- Determine the constituencies or target populations to be served by the camp.

- Design a program based upon the desired outcomes and goals and various constituencies to be served.

- Develop and implement a risk management system to protect the participants, the camp, and the staff.

- Develop and implement a marketing plan for the camp. Recruit participants.

- Design and implement a staff organization based upon the program and target population; develop job descriptions and personnel policies.

- Design and implement a plan for the development and maintenance of the camp site and facilities and a security plan that protects the camp from intruders.

- Develop and implement a health care plan that provides for the health and emotional and physical safety of the campers and staff.

- Develop and implement a nutritious and sanitary food service program.

- Develop and implement a safe transportation system to meet the needs of program, maintenance, and safety.

- Design a financial development program that includes not only fund-raising but also a sound business plan and budget that is monitored regularly.

- Recruit and train staff.

- Develop and implement an evaluation system that allows campers, parents, staff, and the like to assess program facilities, operations, the staff structure, and youth development outcomes and goals.

- Develop a plan for supervision of staff including training for supervisors, staff structure, expectations for behavior, job responsibilities, and guidelines for dealing with performance issues.

- Maintain relationships with the local community near the camp and the broader community served by the camp.

- Maintain the director's own professional growth through study, peer relationships, and conferences.

- **For Not-for-Profit Camps Only.** Serve as the principal staff member to the managing board or committee, working to ensure the strongest, most effective board or committee possible, and provide the staff support to help that group define the philosophy and policies governing the long-term stability of the operation.

After a job description for the camp director is created, it is vital for a new director to have a clear understanding with his or her supervisor about the priorities of the job. All things are not possible immediately so the supervisor's expectations need to be clarified. The plan of work for the upcoming months should reflect the priorities of both the supervisor or camp owner and those of the camp director.

Administrative Roles

The camp director is an administrator and needs a clear understanding of the principles of administration that shape the day-to-day jobs that are encountered. Here are some of those principles.

Developing Outcome and Goal Statements. This principle will be discussed in more detail in chapter 3.

Planning. This tenet involves securing facts about the present operation, looking ahead to what is predictable based on those facts, and examining the unusual or unpredictable events that could occur. With this information, a short-term and/or a long-range or strategic plan for action should be developed. In the not-for-profit camp or conference center the long-range or strategic plan may be incorporated into the organization plan and approved through the board of directors.

Organizing. One can't do everything simultaneously, even if one has the time. The plan should be broken into units of work and delegated to people who are given clear tasks and timetables with adequate physical support and supervision.

Developing and Managing Resources. This responsibility entails pulling together anything that is needed to accomplish the plan you have organized: people, materials, and finances. It also involves maintaining those resources for the future whether it is land, buildings, staff, campers, or contributors. This principle will probably be the most time-consuming of the administrative roles.

Directing. After the plan is in place and its components delegated to people with adequate resources, the administrator must become the overall resource for implementing and keeping the plan on course. This involves consultation, supervision, communication, coordination, and decision making. An aspect of directing is the control of the overall plan, making sure the outcomes and goals are being met. Day-to-day supervision comes into play at this point.

Evaluating. This principle is actually the first step in starting over, for here the director examines whether outcomes and goals were met, whether there need to be adjustments in the outcomes and goals another time, and where to begin again.

Reporting. In the not-for-profit camp, one aspect of evaluation is reporting to the board or committee and the constituency of the organization.

The camp director must gain skills in each of these administrative areas. It is far more important that these skills be mastered than that he or she become certified in aquatic skills, learn medical information, or be an expert in building repair. The director is a manager, and management is complex and demanding. Success in camp management is built upon being a generalist in a community of specialists and generalists.

Leadership Styles

Beyond asking what the job is, it may be more important for the new director to determine what kind of director he or she wishes to be. The attitude with which a director begins work may well affect his or her ultimate job performance. Only careful thought can prevent a new director from being cast in stereotypic roles like the following ones.

- **Joe Doer.** He is the only one who knows how a thing is to be done; consequently, he does everything. Others may assist him, but ultimately, he must be in the forefront and do it.

- **Jane Delegator.** She delegates everything. Everyone else does the work; she simply makes assignments and gives out gold stars.

- **Happy Mary**. She wants to make everyone happy and cannot operate if anyone is unhappy with her or does not like her decisions.

- **Mike Fix-It.** He loves to fix anything that goes wrong: plumbing, locks, typewriters, motors, cars. He leaves the program and other areas of camp to the rest of the staff.

- **Alice Waterfront.** She was always a great swimmer and directed waterfront when she was a camp staff member. You will always find her at the waterfront; she personally plans the water carnival.

- **Uncle Henry.** He is the father figure of camp. Everyone calls him "Uncle"; he loves to sit by the fireplace and spin tales.

- **Office Sam.** He spends all day in the camp office, signing checks and letters and writing to parents. He lets the program directors walk around camp and check on activities, the kitchen, or the health service. You know where to find him anytime you need him — behind his desk.

- **Easy Millie.** What do you want to do? The decision is yours. Do it in whatever way you would like. Any way suits her, and she seldom expresses an opinion.

- **Bossy Mac.** He will tell you how to do it. He makes the ultimate decision on anything in camp — from where the hiking trip is going to when camp is having roast beef. There is no question about who is boss.

It is hoped you will not be any one of these directors, but they do exist.

Select Your Own Style

There are three areas of skill which, in combination, make a leader effective. Before selecting a personal leadership style as a camp director, look at the three areas: technical skills, interpersonal skills, and conceptual skills.

1. **Technical skills.** A camp director plans, implements, and evaluates programs and services — but is also responsible for logistics, safety, legal issues, and office routines.

2. **Interpersonal skills.** These techniques involve working with people. A camp director must understand the dynamics of a group and be able to resolve conflicts. To accomplish this, he or she also needs to value and respect every individual and be able to communicate with infinite varieties of people.

3. **Conceptual skills.** Probably the most difficult skills to develop, conceptual skills are essential tools for a successful director. They involve evaluative thinking, the capacity to solve problems, and an ability to see the whole picture. Central to the leadership role of a camp director is the conceptual ability to relate a camp's philosophy to program and to see its impact upon his or her style of leadership.

In an article in *Camping Magazine*, Debra Jordan describes six styles of leadership: democratic, benevolent autocratic, consultative, participative, laissez-faire, and coaching. She also points out the importance of understanding the appropriate style of leadership necessary for different situations.[2]

Being a Leader or a Manager?

As one examines leadership styles, the differences between being a leader and a manager begin to appear. A director is employed to be a manager and is consciously evaluated on the results of managing. On the other hand, a camp director is also expected to be a leader and many times is unconsciously evaluated on his or her ability to lead staff or volunteers. The administrative roles identified earlier in this chapter align with managerial responsibilities in that they lead a director to

- Confine discussion to current problems and options
- Focus on the desired outcomes and goals and accountability
- Control change and evolution
- Monitor staff uniformity according to known procedures
- Determine actions and decisions based on rules and policies
- Plan for the future

A leader will also move to

- Investigate and discuss diverse ideas openly
- Focus on people to obtain outcomes and goals
- Strive to make change happen
- Empower others and encourage decision making
- Build actions and decisions around values
- Have a vision for the future and make plans to attain it

Being a good manager can be learned by study and evaluation. Being a leader comes with self-examination and observation of others in leadership roles and is more natural for some than for others. The two are not mutually exclusive, and the most successful directors are able to blend the two.

Camp as a Community

One of the unique aspects of administration in the camp setting is that the camp is a community. Hedley S. Dimock points out that

the camp community possesses most of the elements of a normal community, but in a simplified form. Here may be found the functions of government, home, health, employment, recreation and religion. Because of the relative simplicity and immediacy of the camp community, these basic functions can be concretely visualized, participated in, and shared by the camper. Here, further, may be found in concrete, visible, and manageable form the inner and informal aspects of community life common purposes and aspirations, traditions, customs, cohesiveness, and control.[3]

Although many businesses or institutions develop a sense of family among their employees, the opportunity for developing a community relationship does not exist. This can be a distinct advantage of the camp setting and experience. However, it can also create problems and tensions for the camp administrator that would not ordinarily arise in other situations. The camp community is interdependent and to some degree isolated from the outside. There is little opportunity for relief from the twenty-four-hour-a-day intense environment. Building on the sense of community can have great educational benefits as well as aid in developing relationships and loyalty that endure for many years.

In this context, one of the primary tasks of the camp director is to be an enabler. In her book, *Social Group Work: A Helping Process*, Gisela Konopka characterizes the leadership role as one of enabling, trying to discover the way in which one can enable others to achieve their best performance.[4] To be an enabler, one must consciously outline the outcomes and goals an individual wishes to attain and then analyze that individual's abilities and capacity to reach those outcomes and goals. Where a person's abilities are inadequate for the task, an enabler must consider what can be done to help that person accomplish the task.

To be an enabler requires confidence in what the person can do or become. Often, the enabler must look beyond an individual's immediate abilities or failures to see his or her potential for future accomplishments. The effective enabler sees potential and seeks to provide opportunities for the individual to grow and fulfill that potential. Such an approach to leadership will necessarily cause some disappointments but may also provide many moments of shared pleasure.

Ultimate Responsibilities

The director cannot escape responsibility for some aspects of camp life. These are ultimate responsibilities that belong only to the director and cannot be totally delegated to anyone else. However, in some situations the owner, executive, or camp administrator may keep the responsibility and not delegate it to the on-site camp director. The director's ultimate responsibilities include

- Adhering to the mission
- Maintaining the outcomes and goals and camp policies
- Setting the standards for operation and health and safety
- Relating to the committee or board, if there is one
- Handling legal obligations
- Protecting the investment in property, reputation, and assets
- Managing the bottom line financially
- Supervising personnel administration

To make sure that these ultimate responsibilities are met, the camp director must understand the basics of every area of camp life. He or she must observe these areas firsthand at regular intervals and use checkpoints to help evaluate performance. The supervision of areas in which the director has expertise can easily be delegated and checked informally. Areas in which the director has little experience require the employment of people with skills and experience in those areas and close supervision from the director until he or she is sure that the essentials are being covered.

Certainly the camp director should enjoy and be fulfilled by his or her job. If a director is skilled in a particular area, there is no reason why he or she should not utilize those skills as long as the director's ultimate responsibilities are not neglected. On the other hand, if staff and campers are to feel that all parts of the camp program are equally valid, the director must exhibit an understanding and appreciation of all areas of camp life.

By the very nature of a camp director's responsibilities, the director cannot readily avoid being the key person in camp. However, many tasks may be delegated or responsibilities shared, and the director's role will change as his or her comfort level and experience increases. For the camp director to be such a dominant figure is not necessarily undesirable, but the ultimate effect of such dominance will depend on the role the director takes on and his or her ability to enable other staff to reach their greatest potential.

Checkpoints

1. What are the administrative roles of the camp director?

2. What are the ultimate responsibilities of the camp director?

Related Standards and Guidelines

Accreditation Standards for Camp Programs and Services: HR-1

Guidelines for Conference and Retreat Centers: II-31–33

[1] John A. Ledlie, ed. 1961. *Managing the YMCA Camp.* New York: Association Press (YMCA of the USA).

[2] Debra Jordan. 1996. "Leadership Styles, Which One Is Right for You?" *Camping Magazine*, Vol. 68, No. 4, March/April. pp. 19–21.

[3] Hedley S. Dimock. 1948. *Administration of the Modern Camp.* New York: Association Press (YMCA of the USA). p. 29.

[4] Gisela Konopka. 1983. *Social Group Work: A Helping Process.* Englewood Cliffs, NJ: Prentice Hall.

Where does the Program Begin?

Chapter 3

In no other educational enterprise can the child have such continuous exposure to approved leadership, experience living closely with a small group of people where qualities of cooperation and consideration for others are the type of behavior that pays off, and be exposed to young adults who serve as models for the development of positive ideas and attitudes.[1]

After gaining a clear understanding of the requirements of his or her new job, a director's next step should be to learn as much about the current operation of the camp as possible and, particularly, about the camp's philosophy, purpose, outcomes, and goals. Though not necessarily recent or accurate, old camp literature can give a clue to the expectations of the parents of previous campers and, it is hoped, to the intentions of previous administrators.

Vision, philosophy, purpose, mission, goals, objectives, outcomes, outputs, targets, and values are common terms used in almost any organization. Strategic or long-range planning adds another set of terms (including strategic goals, operational plan, checkpoints, benchmarks, and action plans) that are or should be intertwined with the first set. However, the definitions of these terms and their uses vary greatly depending on the organization, trends in youth development, funding sources, and so on. The process of reaching consensus on outcomes and goals is more important than how they are defined. To help sort through these inconsistencies, the following terms and definitions will be used in this book:

Vision — a mental image of what the organization will look like in the future.

Philosophy/Values — the critical examination of fundamental principles on which the camp desires to operate and an analysis of the basic concepts in the expression of those principles.

Mission/Purpose — a statement of the essential reason for the existence of an organization and/or camp.

Outcomes — the desired results or benefits that contribute to the achievement of the mission.

Goals — statements that define the specific elements that contribute to the accomplishment of the outcomes; a more precise statement.

Evaluation/Indicators — the measure of success in reaching outcomes, that are used to adjust goals and targets for the remainder or next period of time.

Strategic Planning — a process to evaluate periodically the camp's philosophy and mission and to design a comprehensive or long-range plan outlining goals for that future period of time.

Developing a Philosophy

A camp must determine for itself which values will be the most important. This determination is often spoken of as the philosophy of a camp. *Webster's Third New International Dictionary of the English Language* defines philosophy as "the critical examination of the grounds for fundamental beliefs and an analysis of the basic concepts in the expression of such beliefs."[2]

By its nature, philosophy is theoretical and difficult to measure. Despite its abstract nature, the philosophy is the overall operational grounding of how one works with people in the camp setting. In the context of this book, the term philosophy is used to encompass the stated purpose, outcomes, and goals. It is a question of the basic values that will always hold true regardless of how the camp or conference/retreat center facility, program, or services may change. It is more than a physical setting. That philosophy should be determined by the camp's owners, if owned by an individual or group of individuals, or by the camp's board or governing committee, if owned by a corporation.

A camp director may have his or her own philosophy or values about working with people in a camp environment. This is likely to be evident in his or her leadership style and is likely to evolve over a period of time. If there is a major philosophical difference between the camp director's philosophy and that of the owner/operator, it is well for the director to discuss these discrepancies with his or her supervisor and, ultimately, with the operating committee/board. The owner/operator should not be expected to change the underlying philosophy or values of the camp with the arrival of each new camp director. Such changes should really come only after experiences in operation or the marketplace can be used to document a need for change.

For a camp's philosophy to be meaningful in its operation, the philosophies of the camp owner and the camp director must be compatible and symbiotic.

Mission

Before a new camp director can move on to program, he or she must first find a way to define in words the basic philosophy and underlying reason for the existence of the organization or camp. There should be a general overriding purpose or mission statement that can be broken down into several specific outcomes and goals that express how the mission will be accomplished.

If the camp is owned by a larger organization such as a youth agency, school, or religious organization, the basic values and mission may be that of the organization so that the camp is a way to accomplish the mission in a unique outdoor setting. The outcomes and goals will be specific to the camp and describe the contribution the camp makes to the organization's mission. For example, the mission of Camp Fire USA is "to build caring, confident youth and future leaders."[3] The YMCA's mission is "to put Christian principles into practice through programs that build healthy spirit, mind and body for all."[4] Their camps may provide a variety of programs that contribute to the achievement of the organization's mission. Some services the camp chooses to provide may not directly contribute to the mission. Rental services, in some cases, may only contribute financially and enable the camp to continue providing their primary services.

The basic philosophy or values of a camp rarely change. Mission statements usually change drastically only if the mission or purpose has been accomplished. The language may be changed from time to time to make it clearer to the current generation, but the essence rarely changes. The changes most often take place in outcomes and goals, which are more responsive to current trends, emerging youth development needs, and demographics. To simply change the program activities and staff of a camp without carefully tying them to the mission, outcomes, and goals can lead to considerable confusion on the part of staff and parents of campers.

The approval of the camp's mission, outcomes, and goals in organizational-type camps may follow a time-consuming process of boards and committees, but it is an essential part of that board's educational and ownership experience. Though the owner/director of an independent camp has greater latitude to change its philosophy and stated purpose and goals more readily than organizational-type camps, he or she should give no less careful thought to developing purpose/mission statements.

The new camp director may need to research a variety of sources to discover a camp's purpose or mission statement. If not found in the camp's brochure, examination of other camp documents will be necessary. In some cases, the mission of the sponsoring organization becomes the mission of the camp. Perhaps an overriding purpose or some specific goals have been defined by previous directors. If not written in specific documents, they may be discovered in a number of different places:

- In camp brochures
- In previous minutes, if the camp is operated by a board or committee
- In the articles of incorporation, if the camp is incorporated
- In conversation with a previous director or staff or with the executive of the organization or long-time board members
- In reports from previous summers
- In staff manuals

After the director has collected statements of purpose and various outcomes and goals (whether verbal or written), he or she may find it useful to write them out as clearly as possible and then to examine them carefully. The director should examine them for clarity, appropriateness to current community patterns and attitudes, and consistency with the operator's expectations. He or she should examine these statements with a supervisor to see if that person interprets the purpose in a similar fashion. If possible, the director should also examine them with an operating committee or board, the executive committee, or another small responsible group from the board.

When he or she clearly understands the stated purpose as it was defined in the past and as it is now perceived by the operator (committee, board, executive), the camp director should determine if any parts of the purpose are in conflict with his or her own personal philosophy. Regardless, it is wise for the new camp director to operate under the stated purpose for at least one year before making or suggesting any significant changes. Operation is a test of the validity and relevance of a camp's purpose, outcomes, and goals. A director should never hesitate, however, to seek clarification of the meaning of purpose or outcomes and goals.

Statements of Purpose or Mission

The purpose or mission states the essential reason for the camp's existence and may not necessarily be easily measured. The purpose along with its clarifying goals brings the more intangible philosophy or values of the camp into more concrete terms. Here are some examples:

Camp A — The principal purpose is to help young people of all backgrounds to grow into responsible maturity through the application of Christian principles in an outdoor setting.

Camp B — The mission of the camp is to provide an outdoor setting for group living where people can design programs to meet their group's needs and to provide a regular opportunity for youth to gain a deeper understanding of their relationships to their fellow man and the natural environment.

Camp C — The purpose of this camp is to help each individual camper gain skills that help him or her achieve a strong self-concept, a sense of responsibility, and an ability to get along with his or her peers.

Camp D — The (name of organization)'s mission is to provide quality developmental programs to help disadvantaged youth become productive adults and citizens.

The focus of each of these purposes is quite different. Camps A, C, and D focus on the individual camper, but Camp A is directed more toward applying Christian principles and outdoor living, whereas Camp C and D focus on developing interpersonal skills. Camp B focuses both on the facility and provision of program (i.e., where a camp or conference center rents facilities as well as operates camp sessions). Camp D's mission is the same as that of the larger organization that owns the camp.

If a camp serves a narrow age group or a specialized clientele, the developmental needs of that group should be considered in designing a mission statement. One may not be able to address all the developmental needs here, but certainly many of them will be the foundation for the mission, outcomes, and goals. Human growth and development are discussed in more detail in chapter 4. Peter Drucker states that "a mission statement has to be operational, otherwise it's just good intentions. A mission statement has to focus on what the institution really tries to do and then do it so that everybody in the organization can say: This is my contribution to the goal."[5] Therefore, the statement should be simple, clear, and concise — something others can remember and to which they can relate. A starting point is to write a statement, cut it to fifteen or twenty words, and then test it on others.

At this point, a director should pause and ask if this mission statement identifies the essence of the camp. What is the essential being or identity of the camp? Does one word or phase clearly identify what the camp is about? For the moment, shed the multiple words that identify the good things the camp wishes to accomplish in the lives of people and focus on the camp's clear identity. For one camp it may be "wilderness adventure," another "fun outdoors," another "personal growth," and yet another "aquatic skills." Now go back and evaluate that essence phase with the mission statement. Are the two compatible? For example, camp B's mission is lengthy and may include phases that would be better outcomes or goals than a description of the essential qualities of the camp. A better statement might be — the mission of the camp is to provide an outdoor setting for a quality experience in group living.

Desired Outcomes

Outcomes are the desired change. The dictionary defines an outcome as "the result or consequence" of an action. In other words, outcome statements are an effort to define the result the camp wishes to achieve in a given period of time and, in the youth development context, the benefits for the participants during and after the experience. Outcome statements may be developed for a variety of purposes:

Operation. These outcomes could deal with administrative areas such as completing facility construction, improving quality of food, lowering food costs, and balancing the budget. These are primarily measured in quantities, deadlines, and quality.

Hospitality. These outcomes come into play when a camp rents its facilities to other groups and becomes the host. They might deal with providing resources for the groups, developing facilities specifically for such groups, or adding services.

Training. These outcomes would be developed for the precamp staff training week and, where there is year-round staff, for each person annually.

Personnel Performance. These outcomes would be developed by a staff person in conjunction with his or her supervisor for a given time period; they relate to the successful performance of job functions.

Programmatic and/or Youth Development. These outcomes are the desired benefits to the participant during or after the experience at camp, and they are measurable attainments for the participant.

The camp director will find it important to examine each of these outcomes and to determine how and when they are to be developed, what the specific goals will be, and how they will be evaluated. With respect to the mission, camps like most human service organizations are in business to provide programs and services to people; therefore, outcomes must ultimately help to accomplish these benefits rather than compete with them. For example, if an operational outcome is a new building, the need should be based on how the design and use contribute to the accomplishment of the outcome or benefit for the participants. Is it the best use of resources to accomplish the mission and achieve desired participant outcomes? Training outcomes should include knowledge of and achievement of participant outcomes; on the other hand, personnel performance outcomes should be evaluated on the success of the staff in helping participants benefit from the program as promised.

For the purpose of illustration and because participant outcomes are so important to the mission, discussion here focuses on the development of camp program and/or youth development outcomes. Here are some examples of youth development outcomes relating to each of the previous mission statements.

Camp A — The principal purpose is to help young people of all backgrounds to grow into responsible maturity through the application of Christian principles in an outdoor setting.

Outcome 1: Increased personal and social skills.
Outcome 2: Increased knowledge of man's impact on the natural environment.
Outcome 3: Increased ability to apply certain Christian principles to daily life experiences.

Camp B — The mission of the camp is to provide an outdoor setting for group living where people can design programs to meet their group's needs and to provide a regular opportunity for youth to gain a deeper understanding of their relationships to their fellow man and the natural environment.,

Outcome 1: Increased participant decision making.
Outcome 2: Increased interpersonal skills.
Outcome 3: Increased responsibility for the natural environment.

Camp C — The purpose of this camp is to help each individual camper gain skills that help him or her achieve a strong self-concept, a sense of responsibility, and an ability to get along with his or her peers.

> **Outcome 1:** Improvement in skill level.
> **Outcome 2:** Increased social skills.
> **Outcome 3:** Increased self-reliance.

Camp D — The (name of organization)'s mission is to provide quality developmental programs to help disadvantaged youth become productive adults and citizens.

> **Outcome 1:** Demonstrated progression in knowledge and personal skills.
> **Outcome 2:** Increased interpersonal skills.
> **Outcome 3:** Increased sense of belonging.

Goals

The goals are more precise than either purpose statements or outcomes; they more clearly define specific things that will accomplish the outcomes in a given time period. Goals should be realistic and achievable. Some organizations set goals when they do strategic planning. Through that planning process, they determine the length of time for the plan (usually five years or less) and then develop specific action plans. Some goals take more than one planning period to achieve and are therefore renewed or continued. Some goals are specific to one outcome and some contribute to more than one. Here are some examples of goals relating to the mission and desired youth development outcomes stated previously.

Camp A — The principal purpose is to help young people of all backgrounds to grow into responsible maturity through the application of Christian principles in an outdoor setting.

> **Outcome 1:** Increased personal and social skills.
> **Outcome 2:** Increased knowledge of man's impact on the natural environment.
> **Outcome 3:** Increased ability to apply certain Christian principles to daily life experiences.

Outcomes and Goals for Years 1–3

> **Goal 1:** To provide new opportunities within the program for the development of personal and social skills.
> **Goal 2:** To use no-impact outdoor skills training throughout the environmental education program.
> **Goal 3:** To identify one Christian principle each day at morning watch and at the end of the day ask each living group to identify where it had an impact on their lives that day.

Camp B — The mission of the camp is to provide an outdoor setting for group living where people can design programs to meet their group's needs and to provide a regular opportunity for youth to gain a deeper understanding of their relationships to their fellow man and the natural environment.

Outcomes and Goals for Years 1–2

Outcome 1: Increased participant decision making.

Goal 1: To provide decision-making opportunities by organizing living groups into small groups with a trained counselor.

Outcome 2: Increased interpersonal skills.

Goal 2: To provide a new summer camp session where teens can participate in activities designed around interpersonal relationships.

Outcome 3: Increased responsibility for the natural environment.

Goal 3: To provide a well-cared-for natural environment where activities naturally encourage a better understanding of and responsibility for the natural environment.

An example of an operational outcome and goal for Camp B might be:

Operational Outcome 1: Increased year-round facilities.

3-year Goal: To provide winterized housing for adult groups.

Camp C — The purpose of this camp is to help each individual camper gain skills that help him or her achieve a strong self-concept, a sense of self-responsibility, and an ability to get along with his or her peers.

Outcomes and Goals for Years 1–5

Outcome 1: Improvement in skill level.

Goal 1: To provide progression in activities and expert instruction to assist campers in gaining specific skills.

Outcome 2: Increased social skills.

Goal 2: To provide new opportunities within the program for the development of interpersonal relationships and social skills.

Outcome 3: Increased self-reliance.

Goal 3: To design the living group and camp activities that help to develop self-reliance in each camper.

Camp D — The (name of organization)'s mission is to provide quality developmental programs to help disadvantaged youth become productive adults and citizens.

Outcome 1: Demonstrated progression in knowledge and personal skills.

Outcome 2: Increased interpersonal skills.

Outcome 3: Increased sense of belonging.

Outcomes and Goals for Years 1–5

Goal 1: To provide a tutoring program in certain knowledge areas.

Goal 2: To organize program activities in small groups with emphasis on interpersonal relationships.

Goal 3: To organize evening activities so each living group can develop its own name, song, and/or cheer.

Note that each statement of goals further defines the stated purpose and directions for a given period of time but leaves room to define the specifics in measurable statements later. It is certainly possible to be more specific in the purpose. For example, in the purpose for Camp C, the skills to be gained could be specified if the camp specializes in one or two areas. As you review the outcomes, you will note that:

- Identifying a goal and pre- and posttargets makes the outcome measurable.
- The focus is on the change that will occur or benefit to the participants regardless of the program or service.
- Each outcome relates to the overall mission and philosophy of the camp and to the time-sensitive goals. Some goals help accomplish more than one outcome.

Though all outcomes will remain vague or idealized, they require measurable targets/ indicators with identified methods or action plans and evaluation tools for staff to be able to evaluate success.

Evaluation / Indicators

After detailing the mission, outcome, and goals statements of a camp, there must be some process for evaluating or determining the indicators of their success. Based on the evaluation of successful achievements, the camp can make adjustments to its operation and set new targets. A variety of methods are useful in measuring the successful achievement of targets, all of which should include camper, staff, and parent written or verbal evaluations in some form. *Illustration 3.1* shows a model often used to plan and evaluate participant outcomes.

Illustration 3.1

Mission: The purpose of this camp is to help each individual camper gain skills that help him or her achieve a strong self-concept, sense of responsibility, and an ability to get along with his or her peers.

Outcomes	Resources or Inputs	Methods or Action	Indicators and/or Targets	Evaluation Method(s)
Improvement in skill level. 3-year goal: To provide progression in activities and instruction to assist campers in gaining specific skills.	Program equipment appropriate to age and skill. Staff trained in helping campers to improve skills.	Provide activities where campers have time to progress and gain competency in specific skills. Design a system for recognizing camper's progress.	**85%** of the campers progress at least one skill level in two of the three activities during the session.	Pre and post skill tests. Parent evaluations.
Increase social skills. 3-year goal: To provide new opportunities within the program for the development of interpersonal relationships and social skills.	Staff trained in group development and conflict resolution. Equipment for four different team sports.	Design a team sports program where campers can participate on two or more different teams. Assign members to teams rather than use cabin groupings.	**80%** of the campers demonstrate an increase in respect for others. **75%** have friends outside their cabin group by end of session.	Staff observation. Camper evaluation.

In terms of training and measuring the progress of staff, it is helpful to align specific target experiences with methods to accomplish the outcome. When all staff members understand the desired youth development outcomes and the changes they should be able to see, they can be much more intentional in their work with the campers and are more likely to be successful.

A checklist for each activity can be developed as an evaluation tool that can be marked for each individual both at the beginning and the end of the camp session. This can provide a checkpoint both for any report to parents and for evaluating the achievement of the camp's goals and specific targets for participant outcomes at the end of the season.

At that point, the director and staff can then use the degree of success to determine adjustments or alterations, if necessary, to the outcomes, goals, and targets for the future. After the process is in place, making adjustments in the targets and methods from year to year becomes relatively easy.

The American Camping Association's Web site (*www.ACAcamps.org/research/*) has additional information on both past and current research, including youth development outcome research.

Other methods for evaluation are presented in chapter 16. Some of these methods measure aspects other than the developmental outcomes of a successful camp and include such operational outcomes (sometimes called outputs) as participants served, budget met, and facility vacancies.

Checkpoints

1. Do you have a written statement of the camp's mission?

2. Have you developed written outcome statements and goals specific to your camp?

3. Have you tested the purpose, outcomes, and goals with the operator (supervisor or committee or board)?

Related Standards, Guidelines, and Regulations

Accreditation Standards for Camp Programs and Services: PD-2, 6, 7, 9;
   "Additional Professional Practices": 32–38

Guidelines for Conference and Retreat Centers: II-1

Regulations: Only those that may apply to the 50I(c)(3) status with the
Internal Revenue Service (tax-exempt status)

[1] Alice Van Krevelen. 1979. "Camp as a Fresh Start." *Camping Magazine*, Vol. 51, No. 3, February. p. 9.

[2] *Webster's Third New International Dictionary of the English Language 1986*. Springfield, MA: G & C Merriam Company.

[3] Camp Fire USA. *All About Us Mission* (online), Kansas City, MO (cited 8 October 2003); available from: *www.campfire.org/all_about_us/mission.asp*

[4] YMCA of the USA About the YMCA. Chicago, IL (cited 8 October 2003); available from: www.ymca.net/index.jsp

[5] Peter F. Drucker. 1990. *Managing the Nonprofit Organization: Practices and Principles*. New York: Harper Collins Publishers. p. 4.

Crane Lake Camp, New York, New York/Edwin Ulanoff

The Participant

The center of the camp is the camper. He is the only reason for operating the . . . camp. As the center about which all life revolves, we need to give our immediate attention to knowing him, to helping him learn to do things for himself, and to helping him learn to do things with others. The staff is in camp for that . . . purpose.[1]

Exchange the word camper for the broader participant and Ott's words from fifty years ago still underline the essence of what camp is about.

Lofty statements of purpose, desired outcomes, and definitive goals alone do not ensure that the camp will endure or succeed in accomplishing those statements. No matter how elaborate the program designed to support those outcomes and goals, success is unlikely unless the people to be served are matched with that program.

From the very beginning, the focus of the director and owner must include defining the participant or target population, the needs of that population generally and individually, and finally, the program design that will meet those needs and accomplish the outcomes and goals of the camp. As you will see in chapter 5, "program" is everything that happens in camp, from activities to group living to the design of the food service.

Determining Your Target Population

Initially, it is helpful to describe the market areas for the participants you wish to serve. This information may relate to the camp's mission, outcomes, and goals. Some camps by their sponsorship will draw campers primarily from the sponsor's sources (Girl Scout membership, a church or synagogue, a neighborhood, a specific disability) and that sponsor's mission will have given direction to the purpose, outcome, and goal statements. Other camps may choose to look nationally and internationally for campers but may target families at a specific income level or age group.

Throughout the year, it is not unusual for camps to serve a range of populations, often resulting from alternating the timing of sessions: summer for children and youth, weekends for family groups, and weekdays for school groups or senior adult groups or adult conferences. In these instances, camps will need to identify target populations for each different program.

Make no assumptions about the selected population. For example, there may not be sufficient population in the targeted geographic area, or there may be more groups trying to serve a given population than is economically feasible. This is particularly true for day camps, where daily transportation is an issue. So the analysis begins.

I. Camp Market

Once the camp's market area is clearly defined (a county, a state, several states), a demographic analysis is essential. Gather demographic information about the selected population or area(s); include age, gender, geographic area, and economic and ethnic characteristics. If the camp's market is the membership of a sponsoring organization, it is important to secure the demographic breakdown of that membership. Whether the camp serves a specific membership or the entire country and international markets, it may be helpful to compare the actual composition of the camp's existing participants with the broader demographics of the country. Some indications of the limitations of the potential market can be gained from this comparison, especially for long-range planning.

Analysis of the camp's potential market should include answers to the following questions. What is the population by ages, gender, socioeconomic groups, and ethnic groups broken down by geographic areas (zip codes, communities, counties) within the target market area? What have been the trends over the past five years? What is the projection for the next five years? Where is the largest concentration of prospective campers or groups? What are the economic ranges of the population in given areas? The U.S. Census Bureau's Web site (*www.census.gov*) provides regularly updated projections to its ten-year enumeration of the country's population giving age, gender, and ethnicity information by census tracts. The federal government also offers more statistics at an interagency Web site for The Forum on Child and Family Statistics. If the participant population is narrowed to include only people with certain physical or mental disabilities, additional information may have to be secured through public or private organizations that provide services to those groups. The combined data provide a way to examine the various components of potential participants in the chosen geographic area.

Even if the market is limited to the membership of the camp's sponsoring organization, a breakdown of the membership by age, gender, geographic, economic, and ethnic characteristics should be secured. That breakdown should be compared to the similar population statistics of the geographical area covered by the membership and the organization's plans for membership expansion. Some indications of the limitations of the potential market can be gained from this comparison, especially for long-range planning.

2. Camp Enrollment

Review the statistics from the camp's enrollment over the past five years; break out the statistics by geographic areas, age groups, socioeconomic groups, and ethnic groups for which you have secured demographic information. Has the camp's previous enrollment followed the trends in the general population for the same period? How does the camp's enrollment match the demographics of the geographic areas it serves or wishes to serve? How does it match the demographics projected for the next five years?

It may be beneficial for the staff to reflect the diversity of the camper population. Review the composition of the staff over that five-year period. Overlay that with the camper composition and study how the two differ.

3. Camp Diversity

If diversity of the participant population was not considered in the initial development of the mission statement, it is important and appropriate to consider that now. How diverse a population does the camp wish to serve? How diverse is the population of the market area? What are the projected changes over the next five years? Do the outcome and goal statements illustrate a need to diversify the makeup of the participant population?

Areas of diversity are shown in *illustration 4.1*. Each basic area of diversity should be considered first, followed by secondary ones. Basic areas are difficult to change and are most visible to others. Secondary areas are generally chosen or learned and can often be changed.

"Camps ought to be outdoor environments where differences and diversity are not merely tolerated, but appreciated and celebrated. Not all camps will address diversity issues in the same way, but the goal of all camp programs can be to strive toward developing multicultural organization where social oppression does not exist,"[2] states Dr. Karla Henderson.

In today's society, a camp that ignores the issue of diversity in its target market is also ignoring the growing diversity of the country's population and the importance of individuals learning to recognize and consciously deal with prejudice and stereotyping.

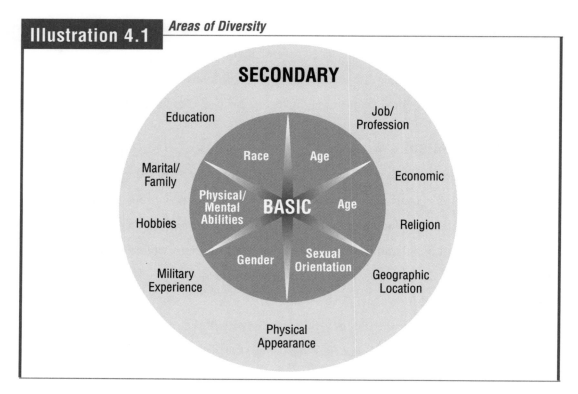

Illustration 4.1 *Areas of Diversity*

Diagram labels:
SECONDARY
Education
Job/Profession
Marital/Family
Economic
Hobbies
Religion
Military Experience
Geographic Location
Physical Appearance
Race
Age
Physical/Mental Abilities
BASIC
Age
Gender
Sexual Orientation

4. Camp Competition

Identify the camp's competition and whom they are serving. Competition may come from other types of programs, other camps, schools, sports, and other types of activities that involve the entire family or segments of it.

At this point, the goal should be to see if more programs with similar goals are serving the same population. Is the target population saturated with existing programs?

5. Data Analysis

After the director has compiled and thoroughly analyzed all this data, he or she should compare the analysis with the population the camp wishes to serve. Where is there overlap? Where are there groups not being served by the camp or other programs? Where is there diversity?

6. Information Assessment

The information should then be shared with others. Key staff members who have extensive experience with the camp may have insights that will help. If the camp operates with a board or committee, that group should be presented with the information and given an opportunity to react to it. Another camp director or mentor may be able to offer some observations. Often, outside consultants from the camping field can provide a clearer analysis of these data from a broader perspective and guide the director, board, and committee in developing an overall market analysis and marketing plan.

7. Reevaluation

At this point the camp should reevaluate and consider narrowing or broadening its targeted population.

Understanding the Participants: Growth and Development

Determining a target population is not enough. It is equally important that the director and staff be cognizant of the basic concepts of human growth and development and any special needs of the age groups being served.

Bob Ditter, a speaker and child and family therapist specializing in child and adolescent treatment, states in his book *In the Trenches*, "Today, as never before, camping is in a position to be a pivotal player in the growth and development of children. To realize this potential, camping professionals must become more aware of the social and emotional needs of both children and parents. We must be clear, articulate, and specific about exactly how the camp experience makes a positive impact on children and then practice the profession in a more conscious, consistent, and deliberate way."[3]

Parents have high expectations of camp, and it is important for directors to create a partnership with parents in the development of their child. This strategy helps the camp deal with both the developmental needs and the problems of a specific child. It also reduces the exposure to risk when taking on the responsibility of children with behavioral problems or medical, physical, or psychological conditions.

Additionally, it would be ideal if the director and full-time program staff had completed courses in human growth and development during their college curriculum. However, this cannot always be the case, and it is not likely that many of the seasonal staff will have had exposure to such courses. A careful review of current literature in the field should be made after the target population is determined, and an overview of developmental needs should probably be included in staff training. The American Camping Association offers an on-line course for counselors covering youth development in the camp setting.[4]

Developmental Needs

It is difficult to plan an effective developmentally appropriate program or even hospitality services unless one has an understanding of the particular characteristics and needs of the age group being served. Because, ideally, camp outcomes and goals are based upon meeting certain developmental needs, this is a starting point for a program.

An overview of varying age groups is shown in *illustration 4.2* as a stimulant to learning more about the applicable groups. This material was originally developed by Jean E. Folkerth for the Project REACH Camp Staff Training Series and has been updated with information from the University of Connecticut.[5]

Illustration 4.2 — *Areas of Diversity*

FIVE TO SEVEN YEAR OLDS

Physical
- mastering physical skills (physical activities)
- better control of large muscles than small muscles
- high activity level (restless and fidgety)
- working on eye-hand coordination

Social
- learning to be friends and have "best" friends
- becoming more aware of peers and their opinions
- beginning to experience empathy for others
- still family oriented (beginning to relate to non-family adults)
- becoming aware of sexual differences
- want to structure their environment as home is structured
- want assurance of an adult's presence

Emotional
- see fairness as being nice to others so they will be nice in return
- seek parent and adult approval
- behave in ways to avoid punishment
- developing modesty
- expressing feelings and emotions, upsets are usually short-term

Intellectual
- increasing attention span (activities best limited to fifteen to thirty minutes)
- more interested in process than product
- learning to sort things into categories and arrange in a series
- learning concepts of right and wrong, cause and effect
- handle well only one mental operation at a time
- can distinguish between reality and fantasy, but may be afraid of scary figures

Activities and Special Considerations
Provide opportunities for:
- experimentation using bodies, ideas, and material in different ways
- active, boisterous games, climbing and balance, rhythmic activities
- practicing skills in eye-hand coordination such as cutting, pasting, drawing, etc.
- practice in group cooperation, sharing, and good work habits
- freedom to do things for themselves (no longer babies) and use and develop their own abilities
- use of senses requiring use of ears, eyes, nose, mouth, and skin
- reenacting routines and events of their known world
- developing friendship skills of sharing, helping, taking turns, and working with others
- finding appropriate ways of channeling emotions and behaviors

EIGHT TO TEN YEAR OLDS

Physical
- experience steady increases in large muscle development
- increased strength, balance, and coordination
- active with boundless energy, often restless and fidgety
- boys and girls maturing at differing rates (boys are slower to mature)
- increasing in manual dexterity, eye-hand, and small muscle coordination

Social
- sees adults as authority
- follows rules out of respect for authority
- can be noisy and argumentative
- feels loyalty to friendship group, often with "secret" words
- identifies with same sex group
- expanded use of reasoning skills to solve problems, negotiate, and compromise

Emotional
- view right behavior as "obeying" rules set by those in power
- accepts parent/family beliefs

EIGHT TO TEN YEAR OLDS

- admires and imitates older boys and girls
- developing decision making skills
- beginning to take responsibility for their own actions
- needs acceptance from peer groups
- emphasizes similarities between self and friends
- looks to adults for guidance and approval
- needs involvement with caring adult
- comparisons with the success of others difficult and eroding of self-confidence
- self-conscious, afraid to fail, sensitive to criticism
- feel they can do no wrong and are quick to correct others
- name-calling and teasing are methods for responding to being upset
- feel too "cool" for emotions

Intellectual

- quick, eager, and enthusiastic
- vary greatly in academic abilities, interests, and reasoning skills
- increased attention span, but interests change rapidly
- beginning to think logically and symbolically
- learning to use good judgement
- beginning to learn about moral judgments, applying principles of right and wrong
- wants to know how to, what, and why of things
- see things as "black and white" and "yes and no" and have difficulty with opinions different than theirs

Activities and Special Considerations

Provide opportunities for:

- using large and small muscles in activities
- organized team games and sports where everyone can be successful
- to work in groups in cooperative activities
- to use skills to explore and investigate the world
- assuming responsibility
- discuss other people's viewpoints
- to explore interests in collections and hobbies
- express feelings and imagination through creative writing or acting
- discussing reasonable explanations for rules and decisions
- interested in making and doing "real" things and using "real" tools, equipment, and materials

ELEVEN TO THIRTEEN YEAR OLDS

Physical

- exhibit a wide range of sexual maturity and growth patterns between genders and within gender groups (girls are about two years ahead of boys)
- rapid change in physical appearance
- growth of hands and feet, nose and ears my be faster than arms and legs and face causing concern for appearance
- may try experimental behavior to enhance sensory stimulation, e.g., drug and alcohol use

Social

- shifting from emphasis on same sex to opposite sex — girls develop interest in boys earlier than boys in girls
- looking more toward peers than parents, seek peer recognition
- seek acceptance and trust
- tend to regard sex in a depersonalized way
- search for adult role models and often identify with admired adult hairdos, dress, and mannerisms of popular sports and music stars
- question authority
- question family values
- willing to submerge self for benefit of group
- discipline can be a problem because of spirit of group
- friendship groups or cliques are often small but intense
- more realistic understanding of who they are and what they can do

The Participant **41**

Illustration 4.2 *Areas of Diversity,* continued

ELEVEN TO THIRTEEN YEAR OLDS

- more interested in social activities

Emotional
- compare themselves to others
- concerned about development and emerging sexually
- see themselves as always on center stage
- conscious about bodily changes
- concerned about being liked by friends, social graces, grooming
- strive for independence, yet want and need parent help
- seek privacy from parents/adults
- want to be a part of something important
- aware of degrees of emotion and seek to find the right words to describe their feelings
- exaggeration and sarcasm are frequently used to describe subtle meanings

Intellectual
- need information for making decisions
- find justice and equality to be important issues
- think abstractly and hypothetically
- can solve problems that have more than one variable
- can imagine consequences
- ready for in-depth, long-term experiences
- have moved from fantasy to realistic focus on their life's goals

Activities and Special Considerations
Provide opportunities for:
- more structured and adult-like activities
- explore other cultures, foods, languages, and customs
- completing projects (emphasis on precision and perfecting)
- discuss issues and opposite sex with friends
- opportunities to making decisions
- fun, learning experiences
- interested in activities involving the opposite sex and learning to deal with opposite sex

FOURTEEN TO SEVENTEEN YEAR OLDS

Physical
- sexual maturity, with accompanying physical and emotional changes
- concerned about body image, may have complexion problems
- smaller range in size and maturity among peers
- tend to have realistic view of limits to which body can be tested
- desire to do things that give an adrenaline rush, or the extraordinary
- boys have enormous appetites; girls tend to watch weight

Social
- achieving independence from family
- tend to romanticize sexually, but moving toward more realistic understanding
- search for intimacy
- prefer to set their own goals rather than accept those set by others
- more accepting of differences
- makes and keeps commitments
- see adults as fallible
- renegotiate relationships
- want adult leadership roles

Emotional
- strong identification with admired adult
- desire respect
- beginning to accept and enjoy their own individuality, but still seek status and approval of peer group
- take on multiple roles
- are introspective

- can see self from the viewpoint of others
- can initiate and carry out their own tasks without supervision of others
- desire a role in determining what happens in their world

Intellectual
- beginning of occupational choice
- want their point of view heard
- enjoy demonstrating acquired knowledge
- develop theories to explain how things happen
- will lose patience with meaningless activity
- good problem solvers but are frustrated when not consulted
- can better understand moral principles
- idealistic view of adult life
- beginning to think of leaving home for college, employment, marriage

Activities and Special Considerations
Provide opportunities to:
- be a part of the decision making process
- be empowered to make a difference in what's happening
- show and value their individual differences
- take on responsibility for others
- be a part of coeducational activities
- apply leadership skills
- demonstrate self-expression
- discuss issues and values

Young Adult Characteristics (18-26)
- becoming independent and making it on their own
- focusing on developing marketable skills and knowledge to earn a living
- rather idealistic view of adult life
- formulating values and developing a philosophy of life
- beginning to focus on choosing a mate
- interested in expanding base of experiences — travel, vocational experiences, etc.

Adult Characteristics
- achieving satisfaction in one's vocation
- assuming social and civic responsibilities
- developing skills that are family-centered
- becoming parents and raising children to become responsible and well adjusted
- learning to relate to (or care for) parents and older adults
- testing and refining values
- learning to cope with anxiety and frustration
- more financial pressures
- increased family and work-related stress
- expect housing that will provide some privacy and comfort

Senior Citizens' Characteristics
- adjusting to declining energy and physical changes of aging, i.e., decreased flexibility, balance, auditory and visual problems, less strength and endurance, slower reaction time
- building new relationships with grown children and grandchildren
- learning to relate again to one's spouse
- coming to terms with one's life goals and aspirations
- principled moral reasoning
- may have less financial pressure
- may have a more conservative outlook on life than younger adults
- expect housing that will provide privacy and accessibility

In examining the developmental characteristics in *illustration 4.2*, the staff should be conscious of the varying conditions that could alter certain of those characteristics:

- Cultural differences

- Economic situations

- Environmental conditions (home, school, peers, etc.)

- Physical conditions (diet, disabilities, genetics)

- Current societal trends or issues that put children at risk (violence, drug use, sexual activity, technological changes, etc.)

These conditions may slow or accelerate certain elements of physical growth or behavior.

No matter how narrow the age range served by a camp may be, the director and staff need a general understanding of all age groups because they may have ongoing relationships with other staff, parents of participants, board/committee members, and so on, who may go beyond the age range of participants.

In examining the characteristics and developmental needs of various age groups, the staff should also understand the basic competencies needed by a given age group. All these attributes should be clearly addressed in the previously developed stated outcomes and goals. In *illustration 4.3*, several youth development experts have identified these competencies for children and youth. Although the terminology may be different, there is general agreement among these experts about what competencies or attributes are essential to the health development of young people.[6]

In these examples, each relates to the way in which outcomes and goals are developed for children and youth in a camp setting. Second, these competencies materially affect the way in which program tools are used to accomplish outcomes and goals. As one examines the basic concepts of human growth and development for a specific target population, one also needs to examine the viability of the stated outcomes and goals for that population.

Persons with Disabilities — Physical, Mental, Emotional

When participants have physical, mental, or emotional disabilities, an understanding of those specific disabilities is critical in helping participants gain the identified competencies. In some situations, a special camp or session is held for participants with a given disability or similar disabilities. This may provide some common starting points for these participants, but it does not eliminate the varying developmental needs of individuals. Disabilities should be considered one of the physical/mental abilities of people, as identified in the basic areas of diversity.

Camp directors need to consider the implications in the Americans With Disabilities Act of 1990 (ADA) for making programs available to all people, regardless of disability. ADA requires that all camps, except those operated by religious groups and private clubs, make

Illustration 4.3 | *Child and Youth Development*

Competencies or Attributes Essential
to the Healthy Development of Young People

Center for Early Adolescence — Peter Scales, 1991
- positive social interactions with adults and peers
- competence and achievement
- structure and clear limits
- creative expression
- meaningful participation in families, school, and communities
- physical activity
- self-definition

Character Counts — Michael Josephson, 1996–98
- trustworthiness
- respect
- responsibility
- fairness
- citizenship
- caring

Reweaving the Tattered Web — Basil Whiting for Kauffman Foundation, 1993
- interpersonal and social skills
- basic academic skills and knowledge
- cognitive, creative, and mental skills
- emotional and psychological maturity and stability
- commitment to higher values
- vocational skills

40 Developmental Assets (in these seven categories) — Peter Benson, Search Institute, 1997
- social competencies
- commitment to learning
- boundaries and expectations
- constructive use of time
- empowerment
- positive values
- support
- positive identity

Desirable Youth Outcomes — Karen Pitman, International Youth Foundation, 1996
- social competence
- intellectual competence
- character (responsibility, spirituality)
- connection (safety, structure)
- membership and belonging
- civic competence
- physical and emotional health
- confidence (self-worth, mastery)
- cultural competence
- employability

A Matter of Time — Carnegie Council on Adolescent Development, 1992
- social
- cognitive or intellectual
- emotional
- cultural
- civic
- physical
- vocational

their programs and facilities accessible to individuals with disabilities. Religious groups and private clubs are exempted only when serving their own members and then only if they are not receiving any federal funding or food or milk commodities from the U.S. Department of Agriculture. Further details on these implications are discussed in chapter 12.

Where integrating a camper with a disability into a living group, it should be clear that the goal is to provide a camp experience as close as possible to that provided to other campers. Helping the members of a living group to appreciate and understand each other is one goal of every camp living group, with or without members who have a disability. Counselors and activity specialists should be given as much information as possible about the disability of a camper who is being placed in a living group or program activity, including limitations, danger signals, medications, previous camp or outdoor experiences, and parental expectations. The more education and information the staff is given, the better able each staff member will be to work toward achieving the outcomes and goals of the camp.

Behavior Management and Discipline

I n camp, behavior management is a tone, an atmosphere in which a desired behavior is achieved without damaging relationships or hurting people. It is the director's responsibility to outline appropriate and inappropriate camper behavior, as well as appropriate and inappropriate consequences and staff responses to such behavior. These should be clearly outlined during staff training.

There are a number of positive ways in which camp leadership can encourage good behavior. One is to establish a caring relationship with campers by opening lines of communication and encouraging campers to come to staff members if there is a problem. Praise is another effective way to encourage positive behavior. When counselors praise positive acts and ignore negative ones, the message is sent that campers must behave in a positive way to gain attention. Another way of encouraging good behavior is to create an atmosphere at camp that is full of cooperation and fun. Children are prone to imitate the behavior of those who are important to them, without judging whether the behavior is positive or negative. Staff members need to be sure that their individual behavior is worth being copied.

When dealing with a large number of youth from a variety of backgrounds and family patterns in a setting where they can try new and different behaviors, there will be instances when those behaviors will be unacceptable and require discipline. "In every . . . camp, one of the major demands placed on directors and counselors is discipline. The key to handling this issue well is being prepared, which starts with having a plan and understanding different techniques that work."[7] The camp that enumerates a lengthy list of rules immediately upon arrival at camp invites the violation of those rules. Yet, some rules are necessary in any community, and the method of educating youth about those rules and gaining their participation in setting and agreeing to those rules is critical to the educational purposes of the organized camp.

Staff training is a time to set guidelines for discipline and to prepare counselors for dealing with problem behaviors. The camp's policy on, methods of, and circumstances requiring discipline should be clearly outlined during this training. Time should be devoted to conflict resolution techniques, modeling behavior by staff, and the use of praise, I-messages, time-outs, and other behavior-shaping methods. Role playing a set of situations that require disciplinary action or group analysis may help the staff gain a better understanding of the variable situations as well as appropriate disciplinary measures.

Discipline is sometimes regarded as an old-fashioned word; it is also a principle that helps subordinate selfish interests to the welfare of the whole group. Before discipline becomes an issue, there are some considerations that need to be understood and accepted by anyone dealing with children:

- A child has the occasional need to test the limits.
- A child cannot always manage self-control.

- A child has a strong tendency to accept the values of his or her peer group.
- A child has the right to make mistakes.
- A child has a right to be respected as an individual, regardless of unattractive attributes.

When discipline is required, there are some guidelines that can be of help. Discipline should always be used sparingly to be effective — if a camp director chooses to discipline constantly, it becomes the accepted norm. Discipline should never be used vindictively or emotionally — those in charge should never let a problem being dealt with put them off balance. Punishment, if any, should follow the deed as quickly as is possible. Using work as a punishment usually creates a poor attitude toward work; the exception might be when the punishable deed created work for others. Physical punishment is not acceptable, nor is verbal abuse, which can be as destructive as physical force. (Note that physical punishment or verbal abuse of a camper by a counselor or any other staff member may be symptoms of stress on the part of the individual.)

If initial attempts to control or change an unacceptable behavior have failed, these processes may help:
- Maintain the initiative and try to persuade the camper that it is better to conform.
- Avoid specific threats by using a broad warning of a possible course of action. Rather than saying, "If you do that again, you will be sent home," try saying, "There are consequences for breaking camp rules or for not cooperating." A child may imagine far more fearsome punishments than you can suggest. A specific threat commits you to carry it out or back down and may even dare the child to try you out, whereas a general warning reinforces the idea that compliance will be better than defiance.
- Involve other campers in the process. An indication that peers may not like the behavior brings in a different aspect. (For example, in a situation where an older group of boys were bullying a younger group, the camp director got the two groups together and, by asking questions, forced the older boys to face up to their actions. There were no threats or punishment, but the behavior changed.)
- Check age characteristics to assess the level of comprehension or the motivation for obeying authority.
- Review any punishment before setting it. Does it fit the offense? (For example, if one camper has peppered another's dessert, is it fair that the culprit goes without his or her dessert?) Is punishment necessary to deter a repetition of the behavior? Any persistently antisocial behavior should not be allowed to pass without some appropriate action. Some children respond better to negative consequences, while others respond better to rewards or positive reinforcement.
- Look for causes. Avoiding difficult situations is much better than having to deal with them once they arise. Campers with too much energy can get into trouble; overtired campers are prone to react badly to provocation. If there is a camper more prone to negative behavior, try to start each day in a manner that will encourage proper behavior. Try to identify campers who might cause problems and have strategies in mind to deal with them; having a plan will keep the problems from seeming overwhelming.

Medical or Psychological Conditions and Inappropriate Behaviors

No matter how well the camp director understands human growth and development, special types of problems and situations require some advance planning by the camp director. In an informal survey of camp directors conducted by Bob Ditter, the four major concerns most often mentioned were eating disorders, ADHD, increased aggressiveness and conflict among campers, and a surge in rudeness toward adults. The staff should be prepared to deal with these and other problems or conditions based upon training and information, rather than intuition. In addition to being trained on general behavior management, the staff should be given practical guidance in dealing with special behavior concerns such as those listed here.

Abuse. Camp is often a place where abusive behavior (i.e., physical, sexual, psychological) that has occurred in the home environment comes to the surface, as youngsters find adults they trust and admire. Abuse by staff or other campers may also occur in the camp setting. (See chapter 6 for information on references and background checks.) Counselors can pick up signs of abuse in the living situation if they have been given appropriate training. For example, a counselor who observes unusual bruises or scars on a camper should discuss the potential of physical abuse with the camp nurse and director.

Symptoms of psychological abuse may be obvious but dismissed as other types of behavior: depression or withdrawal, lack of self-esteem, endless approval seeking, hostility, rigidity, an inordinate attention to details, or constant denigration of him- or herself.

Symptoms of sexual abuse may also be dismissed or may be difficult to confirm. Some symptoms include abuse of animals, persistent or inappropriate sex play with toys or peers, and inappropriate understanding of sex for the child's age. Other symptoms have been identified by the National Center for Missing or Exploited Children:

- "Changes in behavior, extreme mood swings, withdrawal, fearfulness, and excessive crying
- Bed-wetting, nightmares, fear of going to bed, or wearing lots of clothes to bed
- Acting out inappropriate sexual activity or showing unusual interest in sexual matters
- Regression to infantile behavior
- A sudden acting out of feelings or aggressive or rebellious behavior
- A fear of certain places, people or activities, especially of being alone with certain people
- Pain, itching, bleeding, fluid, or rawness in the private areas"[8]

Staff should be given a clear understanding of the steps to be taken should there be any suspicion of abuse before or during camp. In most states, the camp staff has a legal obligation to report child abuse to the authorities.

Some of the sexual behavior identified as a normal aspect of human growth and development may become abuse when a camper exhibits that behavior with a younger camper or by force on a peer. Camper-to-camper abuse has been a growing concern at camp, and what, in the past, may have been considered a prank or hazing is today considered abuse.

ADD/ADHD. Attention Deficit Disorder/Attention Deficit Hyperactive Disorder is a combination of symptoms that include inattention, distractibility, impulsiveness, and other difficulties associated with attention. Three to five percent of children in the United States have ADD/ADHD. Affected boys outnumber girls three to one.

Though most youngsters can be overactive at times, a child with ADD/ADHD may act impulsive and inattentive, race ahead, take chances, and will seldom persist in any activity or goal. Such behavior requires considerable supervision. The role of the counselor is to protect the child from his or her own actions and to try to get the child to participate in the normal activities. Some children will be on medication such as Ritalin for this condition; some parents take their children off the medication for the time away from home. In such cases, it is important that the health care manager and related counselor be alerted.

Aggression and Violence. Incidents in schools and elsewhere of violence, weapons possession, and threats against others have brought a heightened concern about these problems in camp. (See chapter 10 for a plan for prevention.) It is important that staff be trained to recognize warning signs that may precede acts of violence both in themselves and in others. Although there is no foolproof system for identifying potentially dangerous youngsters, the National School Safety Center identified some behaviors that could indicate a youth's potential for harming him- or herself or others, such as engaging in tantrums and serious disciplinary problems; having uncontrollable angry outbursts; name-calling; cursing, using abusive language, and making violent threats; having few or no close friends; being preoccupied with weapons; being bullied by or bullying peers or younger children; preferring movies and reading materials dealing with violent themes or rituals; participating in a gang or an antisocial group on the fringe of peer acceptance; demonstrating significant mood swings; and threatening suicide.

AIDS. Autoimmune Deficiency Syndrome is not a behavior, but if some of the campers are aware that another youth has been diagnosed with AIDS, identifiable behavior patterns can result. People with AIDS should be treated as normally as possible. Counselors should be prepared to deal with situations that might cause bleeding or where bleeding might occur (i.e., they should have rubber gloves available in the living quarters — or in first aid kits when out of camp — and be trained in universal precautions). People with AIDS ordinarily will understand the dangers to others. If the issue arises in the living group, counselors should be prepared to educate the group to the ways in which AIDS can and cannot be spread to alleviate the fears that some campers may have.

Eating Disorders. Anorexia nervosa, bulimia, and binge eating disorder (BED) are the three eating disorders that are most familiar to the general public. These conditions tend to be more of a problem for girls and are closely associated with depression, low self-esteem, and stress. Adolescent girls who are concerned about weight gain often limit their food intake to a degree that can be problematic, or they may go on eating binges, followed by induced vomiting to rid themselves of the food. These are not problems that can be solved at camp unless there is a staff person with understanding of and training in treating these maladies. Of all the behavioral difficulties a child might have, this is one that parents are extremely likely to deny, even if confronted with the facts. Because of this parent denial and the secretive aspect of these disorders, children often arrive at camp without the director being informed of the condition.

However, any counselor should be aware of what to do if he or she believes a camper is suffering with an eating disorder. The camper may react with embarrassment or become defensive or angry. Counselors should assure the camper that they will not discuss the problem with other campers or counselors, but because they really care about the camper and want the camper to be happy, they will report their concern to the director or camp health care manager. The camper should be able to sense acceptance from the counselor, not shock or disappointment. The counselor should encourage the camper to share feelings at any time he or she is disturbed or upset. (Directors should also be prepared to address a staff member who is suffering from an eating disorder.)

Encopresis. It is not unusual for younger campers to "soil" themselves in the process of play or excitement. The key to the situation is to avoid embarrassing or humiliating the child. The counselor may also help the situation by encouraging a regular time for a bowel movement or reminding the youngster about going to the toilet.

Enuresis. Neither is it unusual for younger campers to be faced with the embarrassing situation of bed-wetting in the resident camp setting. Bed-wetting is not a behavioral problem. No child wants to wake up in a wet bed. Camp is not the place to try to remedy the problem. The role of the counselor is to avoid embarrassing or humiliating the camper before his or her peers. A procedure for handling the clothes and bedding should be developed so that counselors can deal with this quietly and sensitively without punishing the camper. Counselors can also help children by encouraging them to limit fluid intake after dinner and by reminding all campers to go to the bathroom before going to bed. Counselors can also wake children in the night and walk them to the bathroom.

Homesickness. Nearly ninety-five percent of campers have some feeling of homesickness. Homesickness is defined as the distress or impairment caused by an actual or anticipated separation from home. It is characterized by acute longing and preoccupying thoughts of home and attachments to objects. One of the best preventive measures is to raise the campers' comfort levels right from the start. Make sure they feel welcome and know what will be happening on the first day. Many youngsters miss parents, friends, home, or pets and become despondent and tearful. Though involving the youngster in activity that helps one gain friends and forget home is one solution, many times it is not as easy as it sounds. Counselors need guidance during staff training about how to deal with this problem, how it may affect the living group, and when it would become necessary to consult with the supervisor or director.

Sexual Behavior. Young people often find camp an opportunity to explore or "act out" sexual behavior, given that they are in regular contact with peers and out of their home environment. This behavior may be aggressively heterosexual or homosexual in nature and may be somewhat open in the group or secretive in nature. It is important to deal with sex honestly and openly without great moralizing so help youth understand the normality of sex but also to appreciate accepted behavior patterns and the respect of others' rights.

Sleeping Problems. Sleepwalking or nightmares may occur, and if any campers have a history of either, the counselor will need to be particularly watchful of them.

Stealing. Recovering stolen items may be best handled by discussing it with the group and exerting some peer pressure. When it is discovered that a youngster has stolen something, he or she should be confronted and faced with the responsibility of returning the item and apologizing. Some discussion with the affected group is important, but ostracizing the individual should be avoided.

Stress. Though stress is a causal factor rather than a behavior, there is enough stress imposed upon youth in today's society that it is important to emphasize its significance in staff training and supervision. Dr. David Elkind has probably been the most articulate voice about the stress on children in the article from his book *The Hurried Child*. He states: "Children and teenagers are being hurried today as never before. Clock hurrying, [or] being asked to do or achieve too much in too little time, stresses children directly and gives rise to many stress symptoms such as eating, sleeping, and learning disturbances. Calendar hurrying, [or] being asked to do the wrong things at the wrong time, stresses young people indirectly by lowering self-esteem and thus rendering them more vulnerable to stress. The result is a dramatic rise in stress related behaviors in all age groups."[9]

The role of camp should be to relieve the stress of children rather than to create it. Helping staff understand their role in this endeavor is another step toward preventing problems or acting-out behaviors.

Substance Abuse. Camp is not isolated from alcohol, tobacco, or nonprescription substance use, consumption, or sharing among campers or staff. Certainly there is a high consciousness of substance abuse, and ample materials are available for the education of the director and staff. The staff and director, as well as campers, must understand that there are legal implications. Most importantly, the camp director must emphasize that it can happen at camp and provide adequate training before campers arrive. There should be clear statements in the literature distributed to campers and staff concerning the camp's position in this area, the consequences if violated, and the camp's policy on searching a camper's belongings.

Suicidal Behavior. Society has become much more aware of the seriousness of suicide among youth. Suicide is the third leading cause of death for young people fifteen to twenty-four years of age. Counselors need to understand the signs of depression and the types of symptoms that often precede suicidal behavior.

The warning signs that might present at camp include a camper (or staff member) who

- Has sudden changes in behavior

- Gives away prized possessions

- Threatens suicide or talks about previous suicide attempts or suicide methods

- Exhibits extreme or extended boredom

- Demonstrates reckless behavior, carelessness, or self-destructive acts

- Withdraws from friends and family and loses interest in activities

- Is unusually sad, discouraged, and lonely and then suddenly calm and happy

- Expresses feelings of hopelessness and/or worthlessness

- Is preoccupied with death (perhaps evident in written expressions or artwork)

- Makes statements about not being missed if he or she were gone

- Has family or relationship disruptions, divorce trauma, ending of a romance

- Demonstrates an unusually long grief reaction from death of a friend, loved one, or even a pet

- Shows physical symptoms such as eating disturbances, sleeplessness, or excessive sleeping

- Has chronic headaches or stomachaches, menstrual irregularities, apathetic appearance

Any such behavior needs to be considered serious, not only by the counselor but by administrative staff as well. Make it clear that talking about thoughts and feelings is okay, express concern, listen attentively, be empathetic and not judgmental, don't promise confidentiality, stress that suicide is a permanent solution to a temporary problem, and remind them that there is help and that things will get better. Most importantly, don't assume you can help them by yourself; know where you can get professional help in your area (i.e., mental health professional, crisis hot line, intervention team, minister, peer counselors). A number of organizations offer Web sites that carry information about suicide statistics and prevention, such as: The Youth Online Club's *www.soonet.ca/starla/suicide*; the American Academy of Pediatrics' *www.aap/advoacy/childhealthmonth/prevteensuicide.htm*; the American Academy of Child and Adolescent Psychiatry's *suicide.mentalhelp.net*; and the Center for Disease Control's *cdc.gov/ncipc/dvp/suifacts.htm*.

Vandalism. When personal or camp property is vandalized by campers, it may be a symptom of deeper problems. However, vandals should be dealt with directly and in a fashion that not only helps them gain an understanding of the seriousness of this behavior but also requires them to have a role in restoring or replacing the vandalized property.

Preparation of Participants

Individuals

Determining and understanding a camper or group population are only the first steps in building a positive growth experience that meets your camp objectives. Participants should be made aware of the camp's philosophy and expectations. Thorough preparation can eliminate or, at least, lessen some of the concerns identified earlier.

A camp director who begins or concludes enrollment of a camper with a personal interview will already have begun this preparatory process. In addition, after an interview, the camp director will have a better idea of who that camper is and how he or she will fit into the camp setting.

Many camps have found increasing numbers of international campers enrolling. Since expectations vary from culture to culture, a special effort should be made to help such campers and their parents understand not only the mission of the camp but also the specific activities and foods that are available. It is better to have dealt with differences in expectations before the youth arrives at camp and to have planned to make adjustments to meet the needs of certain international participants.

Many camp directors are not able to interview every new camper; consequently, it is most important to carefully prepare a plan for the orientation of campers. The first step is to mail confirmation of enrollment and receipt of the deposit with a welcome letter, indicating pleasure that the camper is coming to camp and when he or she might expect further information.

An information packet is usually sent to the camper and his or her parents at least two months before the camper arrives at camp. First and foremost is a clear interpretation of the type of program the camper and the camper's parents may expect at camp, with very specific references to out-of-camp trips, unusual activities, and the like. Charles R. "Reb" Gregg states that "a participant in your program deserves, fairly, to know what to expect. Perhaps more significantly, a person or family affected by an event or condition cannot be assumed to have consented to participation in that situation if they don't know of it beforehand. . . . Failure to disclose the prospect of a remote field trip, or the absence of radios, for example, may allow a family to make a claim that would not otherwise be available to it."[10]

Second, a number of items should be included in this packet.

- A sample clothing list should indicate the type and amounts of clothing needed. If special equipment, such as boots, riding gear, or a sleeping bag, is needed, specifications or details should be given about the type needed and potential sources for purchase. Information should be given about the appropriate marking of all possessions with the camper's name to assist in lost-and-found problems. Any restrictions regarding personal items such as radios, CD players, cell phones, knives, pets, or guns should be spelled out.

- Information about laundry should include whether the camp will arrange for service, whether the camper washes his or her own clothes, or whether the quantities of apparel suggested are usually ample for the length of the camp session.

- Health examination information, including a form requesting information the parent needs to provide for a health history, should be included. If an examination is required, the form should specify the information the physician needs to furnish, the maximum length of time allowed between examination and camp opening, the inoculations required, and the health care available at camp. See illustrations 11.2 and 11.3 for samples of health forms. The health examination form should be mailed early enough for parents to arrange for an appointment with the physician. The form should be explicit about the information needed in addition to the health examination, such as

  - Health history information — allergies, operations, previous illnesses, inoculations, disabilities.

  - Medications that the camper is taking currently or was taking immediately prior to coming to camp along with written instructions from the doctor.

  - A release signed by parents or guardians enabling the camp to provide a minor with routine health care and prescribed medications and to seek emergency medical treatment. Some hospitals now require notarized signatures.

  - Health insurance information (if the parent's insurance is expected to cover any incidents at camp).

  - Emergency addresses and phone numbers of parents or guardians.

  - Any limitations on activity participation or living situation and any necessary medical attention.

- Information regarding transportation to camp. Will parents be expected to transport camper to camp? If group transportation is provided, list the times, fares, and other pertinent information. If arriving campers can be met at air, train, or bus terminals, explain the procedure and any charges. For day camps, a schedule and times of the pickup and drop points for campers should be provided, along with a plan for emergency arrangements.

- Visiting days or times, if any.

- Information on the camp's mailing address; the use of fax, e-mail, or telephone for making or receiving communications; and the handling of mail and packages containing food items for campers.

- Information concerning religious services at camp and the availability of services out of camp, especially if the family wishes child to attend special services.

- In day camps, an explanation of the plan for daily lunch, including what is to be brought by the camper and what is to be furnished by the camp.

- In day camps, if there is to be an overnight offered during the period, the plan and preparation for it.

When the majority of campers come from the same population center, a camp may have an orientation session or open house during April or May to answer any questions from campers and parents and to prepare new campers for their first year at camp. This session may include introduction of staff, slides or movies, and comments on what to bring to camp. It will also provide a chance for campers of the same age groups to get acquainted and for parents to gain a better understanding of the camp organization and policies.

Groups

Preparation of individuals who are coming as part of rental or program groups is no less important, but it does not require the same direct contact with the individuals since the group leader or organization has that responsibility. Because the information goes through that second party, it is even more important that the information be thoroughly and clearly written and mailed early with the confirmation of the reservation. Such an information packet could include the following items:

- A map of the camp property, as well as directions on how to get there

- A description of the sleeping accommodations and what bedding is furnished

- Rules and regulations that affect the activities and behavior of the group (e.g., alcohol, radios, firearms, drugs, skateboards)

- What health care, if any, will be available

- The camp telephone number for emergency purposes

- If the camp is responsible for any specialized programs, information about clothing or equipment that participants are expected to bring

- If the group is responsible for providing people with certain certifications (lifeguard, nurse, etc.)

- Who the on-site contact will be

- Expectations for clean-up and check-out.

When preparing these materials, the director should assume that the people reading it will know nothing about camp. The words and information should be checked for clarity. Every opportunity should be taken in the material to emphasize the potential fun, excitement, and value of the experience.

Checkpoints

1. Identify your camp's participant population and describe efforts made to provide diversity in that population.

2. Review the developmental characteristics of the age group(s) served by your camp and devise a method of sharing these with the camp staff during precamp training.

3. In the precamp training schedule, outline how and where appropriate growth and development, as well as problematic behaviors, of campers is covered.

4. Examine the camp program and schedule in light of preventing unnecessary stress in the lives of campers.

5. Identify everything a new camper needs to know about camp before his or her arrival.

6. Organize, in chronological order, the steps parents of campers need to take before camp.

7. Identify what you would need to know and do as a leader of a group that is being brought to your camp for the first time.

8. Check your written materials to make sure they reflect the information in checkpoints 5, 6, and 7.

Related Standards and Guidelines

Accreditation Standards for Camp Programs and Services: OM-11E, 12, 19, 20, 21; PD-5, 8; SF-31–32; HW-6, 7, 8; "Additional Professional Practices": Items 9, 16, 17, 23, 27

Guidelines for Conference and Retreat Centers: II-1, II-6–4, II-19, II-20, III-21, 22, 23, 25

[1] Elmer Ott. 1949. *So You Want To Be a Camp Counselor*. New York: Association Press (YMCA of the USA). p. 21.

[2] Karla A. Henderson. 1994. "Unlearning the Isms." *Camping Magazine* Vol. 67, No.1, September/October. p. 19.

[3] Robert Ditter. 1997. *In the Trenches*. Martinsville, IN: American Camping Association.

[4] Connie Coutellier and Kathy Henchey, *1999 Camp is for the Camper: Counselor Guide to Youth Development*, Martinsville, IN: American Camping Association.

[5] Connecticut Department of Human Resources and the University of Connecticut Cooperative Extension System. "Beyond Opening Day: Building Excellence in School-age Child Care Programs"; and Jean E. Folkerth. 1981. "Developmental Characteristics." *Perspectives on Camp Administration*. Dr. Elizabeth Farley, ed. Martinsville, IN: American Camping Association. pp. 26–28.

[6] Peter C. Scales. 1991. "The Developmental Needs of Young Adolescents Today and Tomorrow." *Proceedings of a Symposium on Year-Round School*. Martinsville, IN: American Camping Association; and Basil J. Whiting. 1993. *Reweaving the Tattered Web, Socializing and Enculturating Our Children*. Kansas City, MO: Ewing Kauffman Foundation.

[7] Donnie Jackson. 1997. "Disciplining Campers." *Camping Magazine*, Vol. 70, No. 4, July/August.

[8] National Center for Missing and Exploited Children. 1988. *Camp Director's Guide: Preventing Sexual Exploitation of Children*. Washington, DC: Office of Juvenile Justice and Delinquency Programs, U.S. Department of Justice. Rhulen Agency in cooperation with the American Camping Association. p. 19.

[9] David Elkind. 1985. "The Hurried Child." *Camping Magazine* Vol. 58, No. 1, September/October. pp. 25–26.

[10] Charles R. "Reb" Gregg, 2002. "Staying in Camp and Out of the Courthouse," *The CampLine*, Vol. X, No. 3, February. Martinsville, IN: American Camping Association.

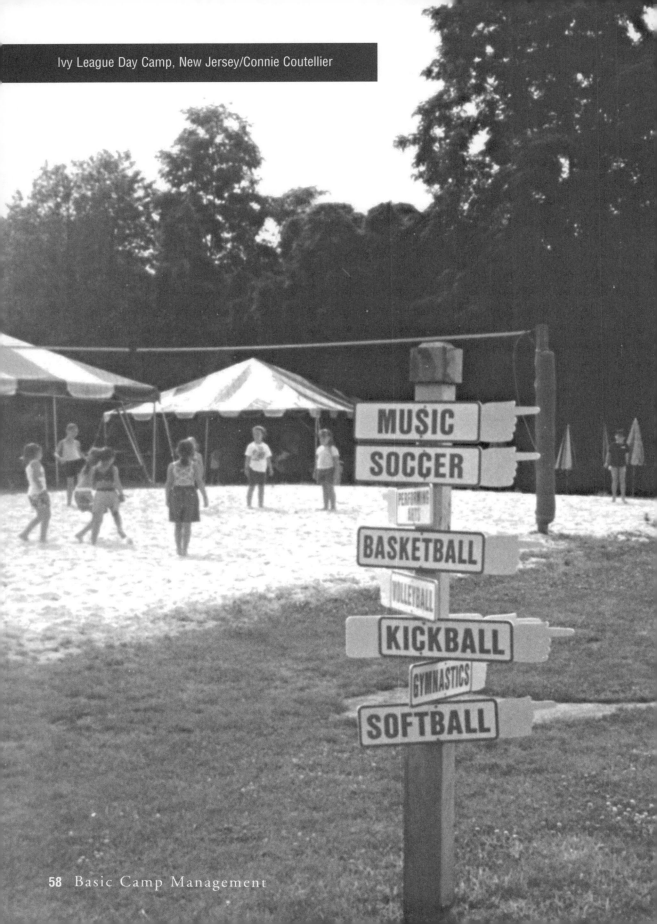

MUSIC
SOCCER
PERFORMING ARTS
BASKETBALL
VOLLEYBALL
KICKBALL
GYMNASTICS
SOFTBALL

Designing the Program

And at each day's end a child should surely have experience with a small fire—sit close to it, tend it, feel its warmth and the warmth and security of her or his close-knit small family group gathered round; and in the wonder and magic of firelight be able to talk, in the semidarkness, of the problems that bother—begin to form attitudes, think out values, grapple for the ends for which he or she might live—begin to put together the fragmented pieces of learning toward becoming a whole person.[1]

Program is, as we have already suggested, only a tool that grows out of the camp's philosophy, mission/purpose, and desired outcomes and goals. To develop program activities without youth development outcomes and goals in mind is simply to provide a potpourri of activities, many of which may be just as easily available in the camper's home setting. Program is not just the activities; it is "all activities, conditions, and relationships that affect the camper: the planned activities as well as the unplanned; the subtle conditions that surround him as well as the more obvious conditions; the relationships that he has with other campers and with counselors; the counselor's attitudes toward him as well as the methods the counselor uses."[2]

If program is everything that happens in camp, it cannot be covered in this one chapter. But it is touched upon in many aspects of the living experience that are discussed from chapter to chapter: eating, sleeping, health care, staff, transportation, the camp setting, and, of course, activities. In *Community Programs to Promote Youth Development*,[3] a publication from the National Research Council and Institute of Medicine, eight features of positive developmental settings are identified. This research identified the program features that help create the kind of positive environment where youth development opportunities flourish.

They are those that provide
1. Physical and psychological safety and security
2. Structure that is developmentally appropriate
3. Supportive relationships
4. Opportunity to belong
5. Positive social norms
6. Support for efficacy and mattering
7. Opportunities for skill building
8. Integration of family, school, and community efforts

In smaller camps, the director may give immediate supervision to the coordination of program activities, but, as the number of campers and the complexities of camp operations grow, the director will have to secure assistance or delegate this primary responsibility to a program director or coordinator. It is important that this ongoing responsibility be assumed by one individual so that the evaluation of the entire program rests with a single individual. That person needs a clear understanding of the camp's desired outcomes and goals, of the background of the target population, and of the age groups in camp, as well as the ability to maintain a working relationship with the staff. Regardless of the size of the camp, the director can never completely delegate supervision of the program.

The camp director and the program director must share a cohesive and collaborative approach to all the elements of camp life to make the experience fruitful and to monitor the camp's progress toward meeting its desired outcomes and goals.

With the expansion of a summer youth camp into a year-round operation, the program may be different depending on the purpose of the expansion and any new target population. Therefore, this chapter has been subdivided to discuss not only the summer-camp approach but also some of the other types of programs and groups that may use a site in other seasons.

Steps in Program Development

There is a temptation to begin program development simply by determining the activities you want to offer. However, there are twelve steps in program development as shown in *illustration 5.1*. The first step in the development of program is to *evaluate the camp's philosophy*, mission/purpose, outcomes and goals, and identity to determine one or more target populations or customer groups. Only with these clearly in mind is it safe to proceed in the planning process. Information gained in the program planning process may lead to the revision of the camp's philosophy or mission statement. When this happens, it will be a conscious revision or change in direction and may influence the actual identity of the camp.

The second step is to *assess your customers' interests and developmental needs*. This is a multifaceted assessment since, even if the camp serves solely youth, the parent and the camper

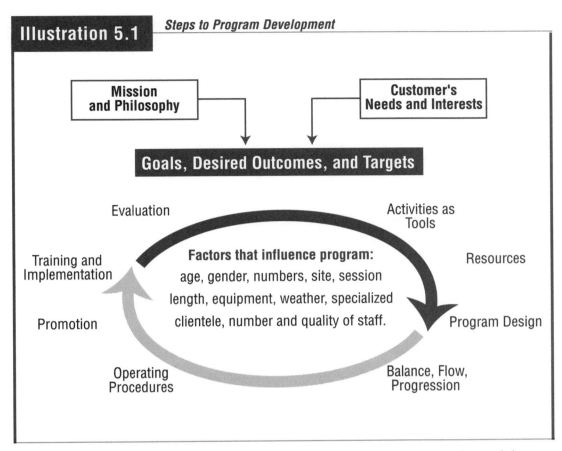

Illustration 5.1

Steps to Program Development

Mission and Philosophy

Customer's Needs and Interests

Goals, Desired Outcomes, and Targets

Evaluation

Activities as Tools

Training and Implementation

Factors that influence program: age, gender, numbers, site, session length, equipment, weather, specialized clientele, number and quality of staff.

Resources

Promotion

Program Design

Operating Procedures

Balance, Flow, Progression

are both customers, often with differing viewpoints. Many camps serve not only youth but also adults, rental groups, and schools, as well as special populations within age groups, further necessitating an examination of each group's expectations and needs. Such assessments may take the form of questionnaires, individual interviews, or focus group interviews. Questions should be formulated carefully to avoid bias on the part of the author or interviewer, as well as to provide the type of information desired.

The third step, once the assessments are compiled, is to *review the camp's desired outcomes and goals* to see if these are compatible with the needs and interests of the customers. In other words, can you really develop a program that will meet the interests and needs of your potential customers and also meet the camp's outcomes and goals? If not, this necessitates a reassessment of either the audience served or the camp's mission, outcomes, and goals. These factors must align if the camp is to be financially viable and have community support. The fourth step is to *consider the factors that influence the program* including age, gender, numbers, session length, equipment, weather, specialized clientele, number and quality of staff.

The fifth step is to *identify potential program activities* that will attract your customers, pique their interest, contribute to their developmental needs, and help accomplish the desired outcomes and goals.

The sixth step is to *appraise the camp's resources*, including the environment in which the program is to take place. A careful look, not only at facilities but also at the natural environment, will be useful in appraising whether the type of program planned will fit in the environment. Will the program be inappropriate or counterproductive in the natural environment? Does the program take advantage of the natural resources at hand? What about staff? Can people with the expertise and leadership skills required for this particular program be found? What about fiscal resources to initiate the program? What are the start-up costs? What is the cost effectiveness of the program?

The seventh step relates to *program design* and includes how the total camp experience is organized to fit together and communicate the camp's identity. See the following section for the overall program design.

After the resources are appraised and the activities identified, the director and key staff should begin the eighth step, to *refine the specific program, outcomes and goals, and activities*. An effort should be made to create a balance between small-group and total-group activities, active and quiet times, and structured and informal times. In addition, the program should be age appropriate and provide progression during the session and from year to year. Progression will add to a camper's opportunity for challenge and success.

The ninth step is to *determine operating procedures* for each program activity in the ninth step. Further emphasis is given to this process later in this chapter. Such procedures include eligibility requirements for participants, staff-to-camper ratios, appropriate equipment, safety regulations, emergency procedures, and the qualification of the staff supervising the activity.

Only when the program is clearly defined and outlined consistent with the camp's mission and identity, and fiscal resources are committed to its accomplishment, are you ready to begin the tenth step, to *promote it to prospective customers*. A dry run with a small group of prospective customers is a good idea prior to broadly promoting the program. This information not only excites the potential participant but also informs parents and/or organizations of the nature of the anticipated activities.

Having secured the customers and determined the staff needed, the next step is to *train the staff* in the delivery of the program to accomplish the desired outcomes and goals. The next step is to *implement the program*. Generally, participant training is integrated into the program design and implementation.

Both during and at the conclusion of the program, the final step is to evaluate the program. This process will lead to setting new desired outcomes, goals, and targets to improve the program before it is conducted another time. Evaluation is discussed in chapter 16. As each step is being designed, keep in mind the program features that maximize youth development.

Program Design

After completing the first six steps, the director must begin designing the program to meet predetermined outcomes and goals. The first part of this process is to make decisions about how program activities will be planned by individuals, by living groups, by staff, or by the central administration and whether the living group will carry out the activities or individuals will move into other groups for activities.

Historically, two different philosophies, *centralized* and *decentralized*, have evolved in camp programs. Under a *centralized* program philosophy, activities are carried out so that each individual camper may participate in activities with a variety of campers. These activities may be scheduled by one or more staff members or by staff in collaboration with a camper council. By taking part in activity selection and scheduling, a camper learns to take responsibility for his or her decisions. The living group is usually a focus only for special events, sleeping, and sometimes eating. The emphasis in this type of camp tends to be on developing individual skills, as well as participating in occasional all-camp activities or unit activities.

When registering for or arriving at a camp with a centralized program, individual campers (or their parents) may sign up for specialized instruction sessions. Depending on the length of the sessions, it may be possible to change to other activities at various points in the camp session. Campers generally move from one level of instruction to another as the camper gains skills.

On the other hand, under a *decentralized* program philosophy, campers participate in activities with their living group, using a group work process. The group work process is a social work method that places its emphasis on "helping individuals to enhance their social functioning through purposeful group experiences and to cope more effectively with their personal, group or community problems."[4] The group work process began in the early part of the twentieth century as the basis of program in clubs, troops, and settlement houses throughout the United States and found a natural home in many camps.

The group performs the planning function for their program. The group joins the larger camp community only for special events, common meals, and/or primary services such as health or acquisition of supplies. The emphasis here tends to be on the group relationships and on developing independence from the larger camp community, even to the preparation of certain meals. In this design, most scheduling is done within the living group. The central program personnel are consulted particularly as scheduling affects the use of central facilities or staff or as the plan of one living group impinges on another.

In the original format as developed by Dr. L. B. Sharpe of Life Camp in New Jersey, a decentralized experience would consist of a living group that constructs its own campsite complete with cooking and toilet areas and shelters. The group would plan its own daily activities and prepare its own meals.

In reality, most camps do not operate a purely centralized or decentralized program. Naturally, it is possible to combine the two philosophies. In many camps, the camper's day is a combination of centralized and decentralized activities. This pattern can move along a continuum between centralized and decentralized. The position along this continuum, where a camp's program design fits, should grow out of an analysis of the first six steps of program development: (1) the philosophy and goals of the camp, (2) interests of campers, (3) desired outcomes and goals, (4) factors that influence the program, (5) program activities, and (6) facilities and staff of the camp. *Illustration 5.2* identifies a variety of organizations' designs ranging from the pure centralized to the pure decentralized.

Finding the camp's position along this philosophical continuum takes thought and

Illustration 5.2 — *Organizational Designs*

ORGANIZATIONAL DESIGN	CENTRALIZED	CENTRALIZED	COMBINATION	DECENTRALIZED	DECENTRALIZED
Camper/Staff Organization	as a whole camp	as a whole camp	half day as a whole camp and half day by unit or living groups	as units or cabin groups	as units or cabin groups
Program	designed and scheduled for individuals	individual choice by age or skill level	half day by individual choice and half day by living groups	planned and scheduled by staff for groups	planned and scheduled by small groups
Activities	specialized, standardized, familiar, skill development	specialized, individual skill development and options	specialized skill development half day and group activities half day	specialized, standardized, skill development as small groups	general guidelines, creative, group interaction
Motivation	individual competition, awards and rewards	competition is individual's choice, awards and rewards	individual skill improvement and group decision making and involvement	group competition or teambuilding, awards and rewards	group decision making, involvement, awards and rewards
Leadership	primarily specialists with counselors assisting	primarily specialists with counselors assisting	half day with specialists and half day with generalists	primarily generalists with some certified specialists	primarily generalists with some certified specialists
Evaluation	individual skill progress measured	individual popularity and quality of program areas measured	individual skill progress and quality of group interaction	quality of group interaction, some skill progress measured	quality of group interaction, some skill progress measured

experience. The place to begin is with the camp's stated outcomes and goals, the camp director's leadership style, the facility, and the type of staff the camp has. In looking at these elements together, it is possible to examine several different ways of using the philosophies and to see which one can possibly meet the goals in the most effective manner. With experimentation from summer to summer, one can soon reach the philosophy that seems to be most effective in that particular camp.

The program philosophy will naturally affect staff recruitment, organization, and design. Consider the following:

- Program specialists are most often the primary focus of the day's activities in a centralized program, while counselors are the primary focus in a decentralized program.

- Authority for program scheduling and supervision lies with program and administrative staff in a more centralized philosophy, whereas it resides with the living-group counselor and unit leader in a decentralized approach.

- Program specialists are more likely to determine program content and the schedule in a centralized design. Campers are often assigned program activity times by age or skill level, or program counselors may assist campers in selecting their activities and determining their individual schedule.

- When the living group is used as the basis of programming, program specialists need to be prepared to have campers with a variety of skill levels and ages participating at the same time.

Therefore, the more a camp program leans toward a centralized structure, the more important it is to employ people with competence in specific skill areas and with good instructional abilities. Obviously, each instructor must know how to teach children and should have enough child psychology training to understand the tasks suitable for various developmental stages of children. Having experience and skill in a program does not necessarily guarantee the ability to teach that skill or apply it at the readiness level of different ages of children.

In a centralized program, program specialists often live in a camper living unit as a secondary counselor but usually do not assume the chief responsibilities of a counselor. On the other hand, the counselor in a living unit usually also assumes responsibility for assisting in a specific program area, since only a few hours of the day are spent in direct living-group activities.

A decentralized program requires counselors to have more general skills in a variety of program areas, since the primary authority for daily planning and scheduling lies within their group. Depending upon the degree of decentralization, counselors will need greater maturity and experience since they will be supervising campers nearly twenty-four hours a day. Under a decentralized program, there are usually fewer program specialists, and those are usually required to hold certifications. They may be available to lead activities for individual living groups at a group's request.

The location of living areas and physical facilities will influence a camp's ability to operate fully on either a centralized or decentralized basis. Though it is possible to make certain adjustments, the physical layout of the camp must be considered early in program planning. For example, a dormitory arrangement that has several camper groups occupying the same building makes operating a truly decentralized program somewhat difficult.

Elements of Program Organization

Program organization is essential whether the camp is decentralized, centralized, or some combination thereof. The schedule is one means of organizing the program, and it enables the camp to use a variety of elements in its development. Scheduling and organization relate directly to the camp's program design. Many new directors and staff are more comfortable with a more structured centralized program. They know the schedule and where everyone is at all times. The same comfort level can be achieved with an unstructured decentralized program. In the process of developing the schedule, the director should look at many elements. The sample schedule in *illustration 5.3* shows these different program schedules.

Illustration 5.3 — Sample Schedule of Centralized/Decentralized/Combination Programs

CENTRALIZED	DECENTRALIZED	COMBINATION
7:30 am Arise	8:00 am Breakfast	7:30 am Arise
8:00 am Flag raising		8:00 am Breakfast
8:15 am Breakfast	Activities that have been planned by	Cabin cleanup
Cabin cleanup	living groups, which may include	9:00 am Individual choice
9:30 am Activity Period 1	cabin cleanup, some program	of activities for
10:45 am Activity Period 2	activity and lunch as a group or in	one-hour period
12:30 pm Lunch	central dining hall; some restful	10:00 am Same as above
Rest period	activity and time	11:00 am Same as above
2:15 pm Activity Period 3		12:30 pm Lunch
3:30 pm Activity Period 4	12:30 pm Lunch	Rest period
4:45 pm Open swim	Rest period	2:15 pm Activities planned
Other activities		by living groups
6:00 pm Dinner	Activities planned by living groups	6:00 pm Dinner
7:00 pm Free time		7:00 pm Free time
8:00 pm Evening program	6:00 pm Dinner	8:00 pm All-camp planned
9:30 pm Taps		evening program or
	Activities in living groups or units;	living group activity
	occasional all-camp activity	9:30 pm Taps

Many new directors and staff are more comfortable with a structured program. They know the schedule and where everyone is at all times. The same comfort level can be achieved with an unstructured program. Campers, as individuals (centralized) or groups (decentralized), may sign up for activities at the beginning of a session, week or day and then a schedule is made so staff and campers know what activities they are participating in and how many will be there for that period.

The Living Group

I n a decentralized program, the living group is the principal structure for the accomplishment of program. The only interaction with the total camp may be during meals and special activities or all-camp events. Even the all-camp events can be designed for participation by living groups.

In decentralized design, a living group and its counselor may tour camp and discuss program possibilities and then plan a schedule for the group. This schedule can be negotiated with other staff so that the things that require a specialist or a given number of campers at a time can be scheduled. A master schedule is created for coordination purposes. In some camps, groups may change their schedule based on "being considerate of others." For example, if they have told the cook they are cooking out on Tuesday night, it would be hard for the cook to count on having enough food if they changed their mind at the last minute. If they decide to work quietly on a craft in their cabin during their rest hour, it probably won't affect another group, unless they are using all the scissors. A unit or living group may have a basic supply of tools and supplies so that they are able to be more self-sufficient.

If the group doesn't plan their program until the morning or afternoon they expect to participate, they may then take their chances on getting a space. For example, only two groups can be at archery at a time because there are only twenty bows. A good comparison of this is a family on vacation; they may reserve a space at a popular tourist attraction before they leave home to make sure that they have the space they wish.

In a centralized program, there is a place for the living group to have time to do things together, whether it is simply meals, cabin cleanup, bedtime chats, or specific activity period designated daily. Some camps use the living group in competitions with other living groups, whether in sports or other contests. However, too much competition at this level can be counterproductive to the real outcomes and goals of group living.

The Individual

I n centralized camps, the individual is given a choice of activities in set periods both morning and afternoon, and the program is tailored to that person's interests, skill level, and expressed needs. Choices are usually limited by eligibility requirements for certain activities, including a requirement that the camper stick with the activity for a minimum number of days. The camper is assigned a set of activities and given a schedule. In most cases, these are very skill-oriented camps, and there is an expectation of some degree of mastery in the skill or subject (e.g., some sports camps, science camps, performing arts camps, weight loss camps, or scuba camps).

Even in a camp where the camper has chosen specific activities in which to participate, there is an anticipation of improvement in the skill(s). In some less-structured situations, older campers may be allowed to decide what they want to do in each time period and just show up. These campers may be limited by other factors. For example, if all the horses are taken for the ten o'clock trail ride for beginners, these campers will need to go to another activity and come back at another time.

In any program design, there should be opportunities for individuals to have some free time and to be able to do some things on their own. Care should be given that a variety of appropriate activities are available when free time is scheduled. A camper may wish to spend time on a specific craft project or fish off the bank of the lake or simply lie on the hillside and watch the clouds or visit with friends. It is just as valuable for free time to be used for reflection or relaxation as for an activity.

Free time is, however, the time when the greatest number of accidents or incidents occurs and should not mean unsupervised time. Campers should know where they can and cannot go. Staff should be stationed in program areas to assist and to be available where campers gather in case of a problem. Such a period should be followed by a meal or enrolled activity so that counselors can check their groups for the wanderer or lost child.

Interest Groups

There are advantages in having several living groups join together in a common interest for a given period. In some camps, participation in a joint activity is based upon skill as well as interest; for example, campers who have achieved a given skill level in canoeing can choose to go on a canoe trip. In other situations, it may be interest in a given project, such as an archaeology dig or the building of a footbridge across a small creek, that draws groups together. In another example, a camper council with representatives from various age or living groups may be formed for planning an evening program, recommending changes in the camp, or evaluating a project. The camp's ability to be flexible and provide staff support where needed can make interest groups an exciting dimension of camp life. This may also be an opportunity to combine centralized and decentralized structures for a period of the day, the length of a project, or a special trip.

Some camps organize sessions by interest groups or by special theme; for example, the third session may be a "Western" theme and feature more activities and instruction time within the riding program. The camp may have an "international week" where activities or all-camp programs feature cultural experiences from the countries represented by their international staff. Session themes are promoted in camp brochures so that campers who are really interested in a theme may choose to attend a particular session.

Instruction

It is very common for camps to offer skill classes and for campers to move in and out of those classes as they achieve a certain level. For instance, swimming instruction is typically organized in this fashion. In a decentralized program, individuals from a living group may all attend swimming at one time but, once at the site, divide up by skill levels. In this design, the plan and convenience of the group is more important to meeting the outcomes and goals than having the schedule revolve around the activity specialists. In a centralized program, campers are normally assigned or sign up by the level of skill revealed in a test or an evaluation of their previous experience (e.g., a swimming test).

The Unit or Section

Several living groups usually form a unit or section in a camp. Often, evening programs are planned by the unit for all the living groups included, or one meal is cooked out daily within the unit. This works best where the living groups in a unit consist of campers of the same age range and maturity level.

All-Camp Activities

The enthusiasm generated by a well-planned all-camp event is not easily matched by any other type activity. This type of event can be more spectacular or exciting than a small-group activity and often gives campers an opportunity to perform before others, as with a drama group presentation or a carnival where each living group designs a booth and takes turns leading the activity in their booth. All-camp activities often involve decorations or dressing up for the event.

Some long-term camps operate two or three days of all-camp activities around a theme near the end of the season. Some events may involve individual participation, while others involve living groups or units.

The wealth of program ideas usually generated by staff and campers may well replace a manual of operation. However, the perusal by staff members of various program resource books during staff training and throughout the summer can often provide the stimulus needed for staff and campers to generate variations or new ideas.

Bus Program

In day camps, campers are often transported daily by bus or van to the camp location. Resident camps, trip camps, and special field trips often involve transportation by bus, van, train, or boat. The time on the bus should be used as part of the program structure. Staff, other than the driver, should be aboard to give leadership and supervision. This is a period when new campers' anxiety can build or boisterousness can get out of hand. Some activities may be individual in nature, while others may be grouped by sections of the bus. Singing can provide an outlet as can a group spirit-building exercise. The balance of maintaining enthusiasm and variety without distracting the driver will prove a challenge.

Pacing/Flow

The pacing of the day's activities is as important as the activities and structure. There should be plenty of physical activity to meet the energy and exertion needs of most children. On the other hand, there should also be time for quiet, relaxation, rest, and individual initiative. A midday break should be planned during which participants and staff can catch their breath by lying down, sitting on their bunks or under a tree, reading, or writing letters. The camper's age will dictate the logical approach for this break and its supervision. Younger children may need more regimentation or routine to get them to bed for rest; but once there, their bodies generally take over if the morning has been an active one. Teenagers will benefit from a more flexible approach, and of course, adults need this sort of flextime, too.

Varying the scheduled activities with those in which the camper has some choice, as well as varying living-group activities with instructional activities, provides more interest for the camper.

In a resident camp, evening also affords an opportunity for activities paced differently from those during the day. Evening activities are often broadened to include the unit or other portions of camp, if the day's activities have been in small groups. In camps where daily activities take place outside the living group, a more specialized evening can provide an opportunity for living-unit activities. Such activities should be paced so that the more physical or boisterous activity takes place earlier in the evening; a general slowdown in activity and noise level close to bedtime will help the counselor to quiet the living group for sleep in the resident camp.

Program Emphases in the Summer Camp

A growing trend has been for some camps to focus their entire program or certain sessions on a narrow range of activities, which is then used as a marketing tool. This emphasis has ranged from overall sports to specific sports, such as basketball, golf, tennis, and gymnastics, and from foreign languages to music, scuba, and canoeing. The appeal has often been to the consumer's interests as stimulated by schools or commercial sports and/or the customer's concern for his or her development of certain skills.

On the other hand, the majority of camps continue to offer a general program with a variety of program activities as well as a number of all-camp or all-unit activities. Many general program camps do provide more expertise and experience in certain activities than in others (e.g., providing a general program for younger campers and specialties for older campers). The geographic setting of the camp often lends itself to certain specialties (e.g., mountain climbing, sea kayaking, lake sailing, and river canoeing). To argue that specialized or general programs are better or worse is a doubtful exercise because the value of any camp experience is far more dependent upon the camp leadership and upon the rationale for the program design than it is on the specific activities.

Staff in the specialized camp or unit should be careful not to overemphasize skills in one sport or area at too early an age or the child's experience will be too narrow. Even in a camp specializing in one area, there should be opportunities for other activities and experiences. More general program camps must recognize that, to attract older campers, a greater challenge in skill development and/or adventurous activity is needed. Similarly, in specialized programs, a staff member striving for greater experience and expertise should not be allowed to overshadow his or her overall counseling role. Although every staff member need not be a living-unit counselor in every camp, every staff member should have concern for the camper and be willing to deal with the needs and welfare of each individual.

Progression in Programming

In any camp program, the campers in the age groupings served need to be tested to determine their human development and readiness level for certain experiences. The same program design and activities may not meet the needs of both an eight-year-old and a seventeen-year-old. If there is not age-appropriate program design, there may be few returning campers at one end of the age spectrum or the other.

There has been a growth in the number of camps, especially day camps, that serve younger and younger campers. Almost simultaneously, as a marketing tool, camps have tended to expand their variety of program activity offerings. Unless there is careful program planning, this expansion can lead to campers perceiving by age eleven or twelve that they have experienced everything that camp has to offer.

Developing outcome statements for different age ranges based upon developmental needs and readiness can provide a youth with a different experience at camp each year of his or her life right on through high school. This process requires enough study of human development to understand the social and coordination readiness of each age group. The camp manual should include a plan outlining developmental characteristics and needs for each age group. Identified for each age group should be each program activity and the emphasis corresponding with those age characteristics and needs (i.e., what five-year-olds do in swimming instruction should be very different from what fifteen-year-olds do, even if neither knows how to swim). Not recognizing the age-appropriate program could mean the challenge and excitement of participating could turn to embarrassment and an unwillingness to try. Staff training should emphasize those differences and the philosophy of age-appropriate program progression.

Group Living

The day-to-day living experience should be as carefully considered as the scheduled activities. The interactions among campers, as well as between camper and staff in the living setting, are influenced directly by age-specific developmental characteristics and needs, as is participation in activity skills. Especially in the resident camp setting, more actual hours of the day will be spent in living activities, such as eating, sleeping, and congregating in the living area, than in planned activities. In the day camp, certainly a significant part of the day is spent being transported to and from camp, moving from activity to activity, and gathering during lunch and rest periods.

It is critical that the leadership assigned to supervision of the living group during these times be as sensitive and mature as the leadership in charge of activity periods. Day-to-day activities present some of the most important teachable moments — when the right words, tone of voice, intervention or nonintervention, a smile, or an arm around the shoulder can make all the difference to an individual or group. These moments cannot be programmed, but staff can be educated and sensitized in the process of staff training and supervision to watch for and take advantage of them.

Mealtimes should be designed to reinforce desired outcomes and goals and to offer a learning and social experience. Providing this opportunity requires thought concerning the shape and size of dining tables, how table groups are formed, the way food is served, the role staff should play at the table, whether everyone comes and goes from the dining hall at the same time, and the agenda before and after meal service. Mealtimes, even breakfast, can easily become the high points of the day to campers and staff alike. Many camps use them as a time for singing, with program staff or counselors alternating as song leader. During this time, tables and food can be cleared before campers are excused. This activity offers a wonderful opportunity to promote camp spirit with the singing of current and traditional camp songs.

Mealtime programming is as important in a day camp setting with sack lunches as it is in the largest resident camp with multiple dining rooms. The principles and opportunities are the same. To a large degree, this is also as true for the youngest child and the oldest adult participant.

For children, the use of the toilet/bath facility may be one of their first exposures to group use of such facilities. In any case, this is another area in which the living-group leader provides not only supervision, but also leadership in attitudes, language, sensitivity, and privacy. Responsibility for one's surroundings is taught in the care of facilities such as the toilet/bathhouse and the sleeping areas in a resident camp.

Program Design Beyond Summer

More and more camps are offering year-round or short-term program events beyond the summer. Such short-term events for youth, by the nature of the school week, tend to be on weekends or during holiday periods. Being short term in nature does not lessen the attention that needs to be given to programming, planning, and staffing. In some ways, they are more important because the camp has less time to reach its outcomes and goals. The same steps in program development need to be applied in the planning process.

Certainly, the basic outcomes and goals for a short-term experience need to be within reach for the time allotted. Therefore, outcomes and goals need to be succinct, as well as clearly communicated to participants and staff. The experience provided by peer relationships, mealtimes, and nonscheduled activity is as important here as it is in the longer term experience in the summer.

During the week, a camp might work with one or more school systems to provide outdoor education opportunities for students. Before offering this type program, a camp director should gain an understanding of the school's desired outcomes and goals for bringing a classroom to the camp setting. A school operates under certain state-mandated standards and curricula and must align outdoor education experiences with attaining certain elements of a curriculum. Jim O'Donnell points out in a *Camping Magazine* article that "camps talk about activities, while schools speak of curriculum . . . teachers often look on 'activities' as something less than what they themselves offer. Similarly, camps may tend to talk about 'fun' experiences and building self-esteem, while schools are more concerned with developing academic skills and outcomes."[5]

Providing outdoor or environmental education programs for schools allows the camp to share responsibilities with the classroom teachers involved. The development of the program will require teamwork and cooperative planning; however, most development work should use those staff members and the resources of the camp that will provide the best program. Many camps have personnel with education and experience in environmental education beyond that of classroom teachers. Working to make those personnel available to classroom groups is an opportunity to expand the camp's services and to have an impact on more children.

In this conjunction, many camps have developed adventure and challenge courses that have added an exciting new educational dimension to the camp setting. However, these courses require careful construction after consultation with outside experts, and also need carefully trained leaders who can demonstrate both the skills and the safety awareness needed. There should be no assumption that a low ropes course will need any less capable leadership and safety precautions than a high ropes course or a rappelling program. In a number of camps, these courses have opened the door to serving at-risk and adjudicated youth. This exciting expansion provides service to a population that can greatly benefit from the camp experience. However, careful planning is essential as are a mature and experienced staff if the program is to be effective. In some locales, year-round school schedules have caused camps to offer regular camp sessions at various times throughout the year. School vacations in some places are no longer "summer" vacations.

Non-summer events for adults vary from weekend programs to weeklong programs. The care and attention given to adult programming should be no less than that given to youth. Though it may require fewer staff members, it requires no less development of outcomes and goals, and no less planning based upon the needs, interests, and human development characteristics of the particular age group being served. In fact, because many camp directors and their staffs are more experienced in working with children, more time may be required for the initial preparation and planning.

Many camps provide facilities and/or program activities for rental groups as their principal clientele in the non-summer weeks. These camps are designed to be used by an organization's local group(s) year-round, or by other groups during the non-summer months. They may include conference and retreat. If this use is one of the camp's principal goals, then its desired outcomes should be developed accordingly, following the program development steps. In this process, the camp becomes an enabling device to help others accomplish their goals. This requires a service-oriented staff and program philosophy; it should not be viewed as simply another source of income.

In this type of program, facilities become the primary focus and should be developed to meet the needs of the user groups. The assessment process is critical before expending considerable sums in facility improvement or development. The ACA *Guidelines for Conference and Retreat Centers* is an excellent resource and reflects this service orientation.

Specialized Clientele

M any camps have been designed specifically to meet the needs of special populations, while other camps use only part of their season to serve a special population or, possibly, mainstream special populations into regular program groups. Such clientele often have special physical or programmatic needs, and grouping with others who have similar special needs may provide a more comfortable environment for their first camp experience. Such groups include senior adults and at-risk youth, as well as people with similar physical conditions or disabilities (e.g., asthma, diabetes, cancer) or people who have restricted mobility (e.g., use wheelchairs or do not have sight). Some camps work in partnership with a hospital or organization that serves a particular special population and is willing to send medical personnel to camp with their clients.

For some years, many camps have been trying to mainstream people from certain special populations into the rest of the camp community wherever the particular difference does not prevent participation in the camp's activities or where facilities or specially trained staff members are not necessary. The passage of the Americans with Disabilities Act in 1990 underlines the greater obligation on the part of camps to accommodate individuals with disabilities. It dictates that any camp, except a religious camp that serves religious groups, may not exclude such individuals from camp program on the basis of a disability alone. Note: Religious camps that serve the public (e.g., public schools, scouts, or other organizations) are not exempt from the ADA.

The entire camp community can gain greater sensitivity and learning from such integration, if there is a readiness on the part of all participants and careful planning. As Bedini, Bialeschki, and Henderson state in a *Camping Magazine* article: "People with disabilities often are overprotected by society, separated from others and given few participation options. Camp is a place where they could become fully functioning members of a community. . . . By integrating camp programs, camps will gain the opportunity to celebrate diversity and show how each individual, regardless of ability or disability, has something to contribute to the group's outdoor living experience."[6] To include the camper with a disability does not demand the elimination of any overall set of camp activities; this principle has been demonstrated again and again by creative and determined individuals who have adapted almost all possible activities in the camp setting.

The critical element in serving a special population is that the camp administration has researched any special needs and characteristics before agreeing to serve that special population. To quote the *Camp Director's Primer to the Americans With Disabilities Act of 1990*: "In a resident or day camp, the issue of program accessibility is of equal or greater importance as the issue of site accessibility. For a camper with a disability to be successful in an integrated program, careful planning is critical to every aspect of the camp operation."[7]

Staff will need additional training and understanding of any particular special population served. There may need to be additional medical staff, special menu considerations, or facility modification. The director of a camp seeking to serve a special population must be careful not to assume that certain things cannot be done but rather must approach the program with an enabling attitude and seek possible alternatives when the traditional approach does not work.

The Camp Director's Primer suggests that, in planning for the participation of the camper with a disability in the camp program, several guidelines should be followed. (1) Adapt only on an individual basis. The program goal is to keep the camper's experience as realistic as possible; it is best not to assume automatically that a particular condition means problems with an activity. Consultation with the camper or his or her parents will highlight specific difficulties that need to be overcome in order to get him or her involved. (2) Adapt only as much as is necessary. If unnecessary changes in the activity are made to accommodate the camper with a disability, he or she will stand out from his or her peers.

In considering what form these adjustments or accommodations should take, three specific areas should be considered:

1. Materials or equipment adaptation. Some campers with disabilities may need special devices to function fully in a particular activity, and temporary modifications may be necessary. A camper with little upper body strength may have difficulty with swinging a bat in a softball game (a good substitute is a whiffle ball and bat). Or, a boy with paralysis in the lower body may want to wear socks in the pool to prevent abrading his feet on the rough surface of the bottom.

2. Procedural and rule adaptations. By making minor changes in rules for the individual with a disability, the staff can guarantee successful participation for all. For instance, if the general rule in archery is that each participant retrieves his or her own arrows, a fellow camper may be asked to pick up the arrows for a friend who uses a wheelchair.

3. Skill sequence adaptations. If a particular skill is being taught, the staff may find it easier to adapt the process by breaking the skill down into smaller stages and working on each individual part.

Many of the adjustments to be made are minor and easily accomplished with understanding and a little ingenuity. Since, in the camp community, the accepted goal is to meet the individual needs of each camper, stretching to meet the needs of special children adds to the challenge.[8] Because each child and each situation may be unique, it is wise to consult available resources with expertise in the Americans With Disabilities Act of 1990.[9]

Specific Program Activities

Camps continue to broaden the variety of activities that can be used in the camp setting. There is virtually no limit to that variety, except in the camp's program philosophy and consideration of what can be done in the camp setting that cannot be done easily in the camper's normal environment. Obviously, the fact that most camps are located in a setting with natural environmental resources would indicate that using those resources wherever possible and building on them as the core of the program emphasis is advantageous.

It is not practical to deal with individual activities in detail in this book, and a wide variety of resources for those activities is available in the resource list in appendix C. However, here are the general areas of activities that occur most often in camps.

Land Sports and Games

Team sports: baseball, basketball, football, soccer, softball, lacrosse, volleyball

Individual sports: archery, badminton, horseback riding, horseshoes, riflery, snowboarding, table tennis, tennis

Informal games: tetherball, all sorts of chase-and-hunt games that have developed in various camps

Water Sports and Games

Swimming activities: competitive, instructional, recreational, synchronized, water ballet

Water activities: fishing, water polo, water slides

Watercraft activities: canoeing, kayaking, rowing, sailing, sailboarding, waterskiing

Arts

Performing arts: creative writing, dance, drama, music

Arts and crafts: ceramics, jewelry, leatherwork, metalcraft, nature crafts, painting, photography, weaving, woodwork

Outdoor-Oriented Activities

Outdoor living skills: overnights, fire building, knot tying, orienteering, outdoor cooking, shelter building, tent pitching (see appendix I for more information on *ACA's Outdoor Living Skills Program*)

Physical skills: backpacking, climbing, canoe tripping, cross-country skiing, hiking, mountaineering, ropes courses, snowshoeing, snow skiing

Nature-oriented activities: animal lore or care, astronomy, bird watching, butterfly catching and releasing, conservation activities, gardening, marine life study, nature hikes, rock collecting and painting, weather predicting

Vehicular activities: biking, go-carting, flying, driving miniature racecars

Special Events

All-camp events that use a theme are common in camp settings: Christmas in July, Regatta, Paul Bunyan Days, Circus or Carnival Days, Olympics of all sorts, and Pageants. In general, these sorts of events involve campers and staff in planning, preparation, costumes, and performance. Sometimes, the event is tied into a presentation on a Visitors' Day or a Parents' Weekend or a Fourth of July celebration. Preplanned short skits that use staff in amusing ways often contribute to the sense of fun and provide opportunities for sharing.

International counselors and campers can often be encouraged to do presentations about their home countries, adding a wider dimension to the world of camp. Many camps have an international night that includes displays, traditional dress, music, and information from the home country of the international staff. (If you communicate such requests to international staff prior to their arrival, they can come prepared with a program, as well as with items representative of their countries.)

Social Recreation

Social recreation events range from quiet games in the living area to all-camp cookouts or banquets. Games such as charades and skits that require no equipment are a staple of campfires and evening social programs. Singing is an important ingredient of many of these events and is often a part of campfires and evening programs. Some camps have dances and other coeducational events.

Spiritually Oriented Activities

Spiritually oriented activities range from nonsectarian vespers, chapel services, or bedtime chats to camps where the religious emphasis is a major focus in the program. In the latter, daily study groups and religious services occur, and religious philosophy in all aspects of the living-group experience is emphasized. Almost all camps develop certain devices that are used to assist participants in building character and recognizing the spiritual aspect of life and its integration into the physical, mental, emotional, and social elements. Clarice M. Bowman said it well: "Spiritual values are not just another group of desired outcomes; rather they comprise the core of the constellation of all other values, the pulsating heart of the camping program. Very little may be said about spiritual values in words, but they will be communicated if they are present in the spirit of the leaders, in their motives for being at camp, in their vision of the outcomes and goals, and in their sensitivity for helping campers have worthy goals of their own that may be achieved by engaging in delightful activities."[10]

Operating Procedures for Program

Whatever the activity or program event, some specific standards should be applied in preparation for that event. Part of these standards relate to the concern for risk management (see chapter 11), and all of them grow out of the camp's concern for quality in its operation. The camp's operating procedure for each activity should include the following information:

1. Supervisor and activity leaders' qualifications and skill verification procedures
2. Means for controlled access
3. Appropriate equipment availability
4. Eligibility requirements for participation
5. Staff-to-camper supervision ratios
6. Identification of appropriate protective equipment
7. Safety regulations
8. Emergency procedures
9. Equipment maintenance procedures
10. Identification of safety concerns related to the use area

Leadership

L eadership is the key to any program activity, and the availability and qualifications of staff for an activity are the first considerations. What skills are essential to making this a quality experience for campers? Is the activity such that it requires some type of documented training (e.g., Red Cross certification) or completion of a given course? If the activity involves teaching a skill, does the person have the ability to teach? (There is considerable difference between being skilled at an activity and being able to teach that skill to others.) What is the staff-to-camper ratio?

A staff-to-camper supervision ratio should be established for each activity since the degree of supervision needed and the risk involved will vary for each activity. In addition to the skills related to the activity, the staff member who is to lead the activity must be trained in the safety regulations established by the camp for the activity. He or she should have the maturity to be able to identify hazards that may be present in the environment of the activity or any other situation that might arise. The safety procedures that should be observed in the conduct of the activity should be clear to the staff person as should the emergencies that could occur and the procedures that should be in place to deal with them. The staff member leading the activity (or another who is present) should be trained in first aid or related situations that might arise from an accident or health situation during the activity.

Appropriate Equipment

A ppropriate equipment, including protective equipment, for the activity, stocked in adequate numbers, is essential so that there are no lengthy waiting periods or safety hazards created for campers. Appropriate indicates that, in some cases, the equipment needs to be sized for the age and size of the camper. To use an adult-sized PFD (personal flotation device) for a nine-year-old during a boating activity is dangerous and inappropriate. In some cases, such as for riflery and archery, the equipment will need to be stored in such a manner that it is not accessible except when the leader is present. In all cases, such equipment must be checked regularly and be well maintained.

Appropriate Level of Activity

T he age and skill level of the participants dictates the level at which an activity is to be conducted. The eligibility requirements for age and skill should be established from the outset. If the number of people competent to supervise and instruct the activity is limited, the number of campers who can participate should also be limited. Consequently, established staff-to-camper ratios will ensure quality time with safety for each camper.

In many cases, the resource materials and certification programs developed by various national organizations will provide guidance and an outline of skill levels and appropriate age for participation at those levels. However, many activities have no national certification programs. There is resource material on most activities that the camp director or program director can study, and various experts can assist in the development of a written curriculum for instruction and supervision identifying appropriate age and skill levels.

Safety and Emergency Procedures

Obviously, when one reviews the variety of program activities available, there are differing levels of risks and skill involved. These factors should be considered for each and every program and become part of the risk management program of the camp as outlined in chapter 11.

Safety regulations for each program area need to be established. A more detailed approach would obviously be required for rappelling than for an all-camp campfire. Safety concerns about a given program area should be reviewed at the same time. These regulations and concerns should be put into writing, addressed during staff training, and posted where appropriate.

Emergency procedures relating to certain program areas (such as the waterfront) need to be clearly defined in writing, and training needs to be given to staff and in many cases reviewed with campers.

Checkpoints

1. List all the program activities utilized in your camp last summer.

2. Test the program development guidelines against those activities and see if other program directions arise.

3. Using the modified list of program activities, test each activity against each of the following elements:
   - Outcomes and goals
   - Experienced and qualified staff
   - Adequate and appropriate equipment
   - Safety and emergency procedures
   - Eligibility and numbers of participants

4. Review the flow of a typical day at camp; consider when there are times for:
   - Strenuous physical activity
   - Quiet, reflective, relaxed time
   - Choosing an activity
   - Learning new skills
   - Meeting campers from other living groups

5. What special populations does your camp serve? What are their special needs?

Related Standards and Guidelines

Accreditation Standards for Camp Programs and Services: PD-1–24, PA-1–35, PC-1–16, PH-1–13, PT-1–20; "Additional Professional Practices": Items 30–39

Guidelines for Conference and Retreat Centers: III-1, 8–31

[1] Lois Goodrich. 1979. "A Time for Discovery." *Camping Magazine*, Vol. 52, No.1, September. p. 16.

[2] Hedley S. Dimock. 1948. *Administration of the Modern Camp*. New York: Association Press (YMCA of the USA). p. 123.

[3] National Research Council and Institute of Medicine. 2002. *Community Programs to Promote Youth Development*. Committee on Community-Level Programs for Youth. Jacquelynne Eccles and Jennifer A.Gootman, eds. Board on Children, Youth, and Families, Division of Behavioral and Social Sciences and Education. Washington, DC: National Academy Press. p.

[4] Gisela Konopka. 1963. *Social Group Work: A Helping Process*. Englewood Cliffs, NJ: Prentice-Hall. p. 20.

[5] Jim O'Donnell. 2002. "The Changing Role of Camps." *Camping Magazine*, Vol.75, No. 1, January–February.p. .

[6] Leandra A. Bedini, M. Deborah Bialeschki, and Karla A. Henderson. 1992. "The Americans With Disabilities Act: Implications for Camp Programming." *Camping Magazine*, Vol. 60, No. 4, March/April. p. 53.

[7] National Camp Executives Group. 1992. *Camp Director's Primer to the Americans With Disabilities Act of 1990*. Glen Allen, VA: Markel Insurance Company. p. 17.

[8] Ibid., pp. 17–20.

[9] The Americans With Disabilities Act of 1990, Washington, DC: U.S. Department of Justice *www.usdoj.gov/crt/ada*; 800-514-0381

[10] Clarice M. Bowman. 1954. *Spiritual Values in Camping*. New York: Association Press (YMCA of the USA). pp. 39–40.

Personnel
Organization

The tern "organization" is given to the process of bringing individual elements in a situation into such relationship with each other that they will function as a whole in achieving the central purpose of the enterprise. Since there are many parts in every camp, the necessity of organization is immediately apparent if the camp as a whole is to function effectively in the achievement of its purposes.[1]

Over fifty years later, that statement stands. The accomplishment of a camp's mission and its outcomes and goals largely depends upon the staff members who work directly with the participant in that camp.

How qualified, committed, and effective those staff members are is largely dependent upon the camp director and his or her ability to recruit and train that staff. Each and every staff member is important to the accomplishment of the camp's mission and its outcomes and goals. One staff member who does not understand and follow the camp's policies and procedures could be more than an impediment; he or she might commit some negligence that could trigger a lawsuit.

It is important that every prospective staff member be given a clear picture of both the type of situation and the staff and camper community in which he or she will work. The ability or willingness of the staff person to be flexible will be as vital to a good experience as the flexibility of the camper and staff community.

The background of a prospective staff member is another factor to consider in hiring. If a person comes from a cultural or ethnic background different from the majority of the staff, he or she can add an exciting dimension to the experience of both campers and staff. These staff members, like all other staff members, should be made aware of the diversity or composition of the camper and staff population.

Elements of Organization

I t is important to design a staff organization that parallels the camp's mission, its desired outcomes and goals and the resulting program, and that matches the camp's philosophy. The camp director now needs to outline the following elements:

1. Specific job responsibilities that will be required by the program design

2. Ratio or the number of each position required to the number of campers

3. Line of supervision of each position

4. Job descriptions for each position

Job Responsibilities

S tarting with broad general areas of the camp operation such as food service, health and wellness, facility maintenance, and program, the director needs to identify both the overall responsibility and the specific responsibilities each staff member has. For example, the food service overall responsibility may be to provide healthy meals for campers and staff. The specific responsibilities would be kitchen staff supervision, meal preparation, cleanup, and so on. Only one person performs this job. On the other hand, some positions, such as the living-group counselor, will be performed by more than one staff member.

Ratios

S taff-to-camper ratios are critical in terms of accomplishing desired outcomes and goals as well as maintaining the health and safety of each camper. Some industry ratios are clearer than others. For example, the American Camping Association Standards identify minimum ratios of staff on duty with campers in living groups and activities (see *illustration 6.1*).

Illustration 6.1

Camper Age	Number of Number of Staff	Number of Residential Campers	Day Campers
4–5 years	1	5	6
6–8 years	1	6	8
9–14 years	1	8	10
15–18 years	1	10	12

Despite the recommendations enumerated in illustration 6.1, the type of program, environment, or presence of campers with special physical, medical, or behavioral needs may require a higher ratio of staff to campers. There are no standard guidelines concerning the ratio of administrative staff to camper population. However, some general guidelines for ratios can be projected as follows:

- **Food Service** — one cook and one dish and pan washer for every fifty to sixty campers.

- **Health Service** — one nurse for the first 125 to 150 campers and one additional nurse for each 100 campers over 175.

- Each program activity will require analysis of a variety of factors including age group served to determine the ratio of leadership to campers. For example, the ACA Standards ask the camp director to determine the number of lifeguards or lookouts needed for supervision of a given number of campers in a swimming situation. There are many varying factors that help the director determine that ratio: type of swimming area (pool, river, or lake); size of the swimming area; size of the group that will be swimming at one time; design of the swimming area, and so on. Each activity needs to be evaluated separately, and ratios should be put in writing after they are determined and then reviewed each year.

- Maintenance ratios are almost impossible to generalize because of the variation from camp to camp in the number and complexity of facilities such as running water, electricity, living facilities (buildings versus tents), laundry, and sewer. The employment of a year-round, full-time caretaker or ranger may lessen, to some degree, the number of seasonal employees needed.

- The establishment of year-round usage will also affect the number of employees needed in several areas.

Supervisory Lines

At this point, consideration should be given to which position will supervise other positions. Except in the smallest camp, it will become apparent that the camp director cannot supervise everyone. The amount of emphasis placed on various positions will depend on the degree of centralization and structure desired, and the size of the camp will determine the number, experience, and complexity of staff. A generally good rule for supervisory ratios is that one person cannot adequately supervise more than seven people.

The camp's program philosophy will also affect the number of supervisory personnel needed. A centralized program will most often require a number of program department heads such as waterfront, crafts, sports (which can be broken down by individual sports), as well as a unit leader or head counselor who supervises a certain number of living units and their counselors. In a more structured centralized camp, program scheduling and a camper's individual schedules are a function of the director or program director in conjunction with the unit leaders or head counselors and department heads. Counselors usually carry cabin responsibility and assist in a program area.

A decentralized program will normally require fewer department heads in specific program areas and more unit leaders or head counselors. Counselors will normally concentrate on the living group and either develop the program or help campers plan their program as part of the ongoing group living process. A program director in a decentralized program serves more as a program resource, supervisor, and coordinator of unit leaders and program areas in which a certified specialist is needed for safety or as a resource. An overall or basic camp schedule may or may not be done depending on whether meals or other all-camp activities are done together. Some decentralized camps require the counselor or, at least, the counselors in a unit to carry the program certifications.

Most people find that, in determining supervision patterns, a diagram begins to take form. Endless time can be spent on the best type of diagram. Though symbolism of any design is important, the ability of the diagram to show clearly the relationship of one position to another is the most important element. The diagram will be primarily used for the director and supervisory staff, but all staff should know the reporting and accountability structures. A general ground rule of organization is that a person should not be supervised by more than one person. If it is essential to split supervision, careful consideration should be given as to how that supervision will be coordinated. Solid lines in an organization chart indicate supervision, enabling a person to follow the solid line to the next box identifying the supervisor. Dotted lines indicate advisory or consultative relationships. An arrow in the direction of supervision is helpful if a nontraditional diagram is developed; for example, see *illustration 6.2*. Several sample organization charts for camp staff are shown in *illustrations 6.3* and *6.4*. The size of the camper population will determine, to a large degree, the size of various program or support departments.

However, it must be emphasized that it would be unwise to adopt any one of these organizational patterns until the camp has established clear desired outcomes and goals. Staff organizational patterns grow naturally out of these, and the examples shown are meant to be illustrative and can be adapted for specific uses. The overall design, whether narrative or diagrammatic, should be outlined and analyzed carefully.

Illustration 6.2 — *Organization Chart - Nontraditional*

DIRECTOR EVALUATION FORM

Director's name _____ Date _____

Scale
5 = superior performance; consistently goes beyond expectations; demonstrates appreciable growth
4 = consistently meets expectations; shows personal initiative; shows progress in personal growth and competency
3 = meets minimal expectations most of time; little personal initiative or personal growth; performs to level of abilities
2 = achieves at a level lower than abilities; occasionally meets minimal expectations; shows no growth
1 = fails to meet expectations; performs below level of ability; no discernible growth; performance unacceptable
0 = no knowledge

	0	1	2	3	4	5
1. Demonstrates vision regarding camp's objectives and long-range plans						
2. Sets high standards for the committee, staff, and campers						

Illustration 6.3   *Camp Staff Organization Charts*

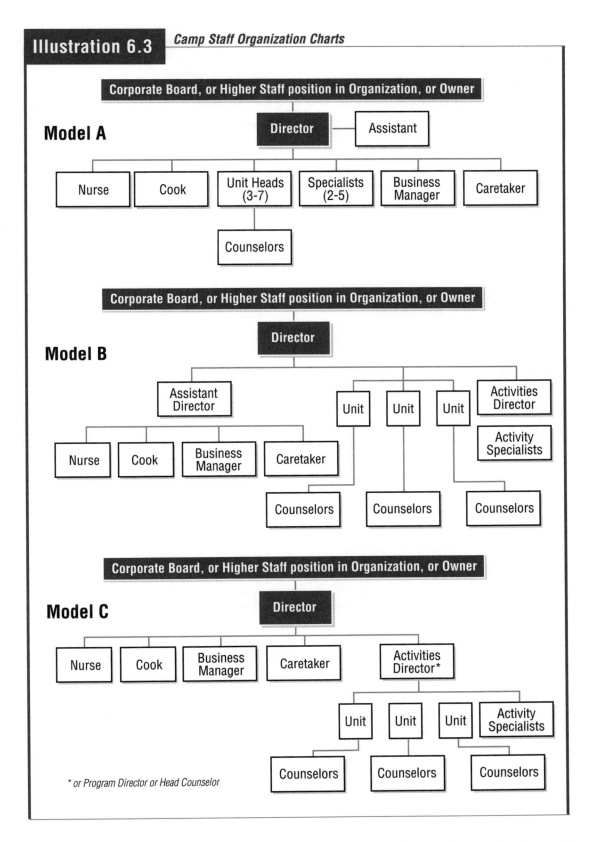

Model A

Corporate Board, or Higher Staff position in Organization, or Owner

Director — Assistant

Nurse | Cook | Unit Heads (3-7) | Specialists (2-5) | Business Manager | Caretaker

Counselors

Model B

Corporate Board, or Higher Staff position in Organization, or Owner

Director

Assistant Director | Unit | Unit | Unit | Activities Director

Nurse | Cook | Business Manager | Caretaker | Activity Specialists

Counselors | Counselors | Counselors

Model C

Corporate Board, or Higher Staff position in Organization, or Owner

Director

Nurse | Cook | Business Manager | Caretaker | Activities Director*

Unit | Unit | Unit | Activity Specialists

Counselors | Counselors | Counselors

* or Program Director or Head Counselor

Illustration 6.4 — *More Staff Organization Charts*

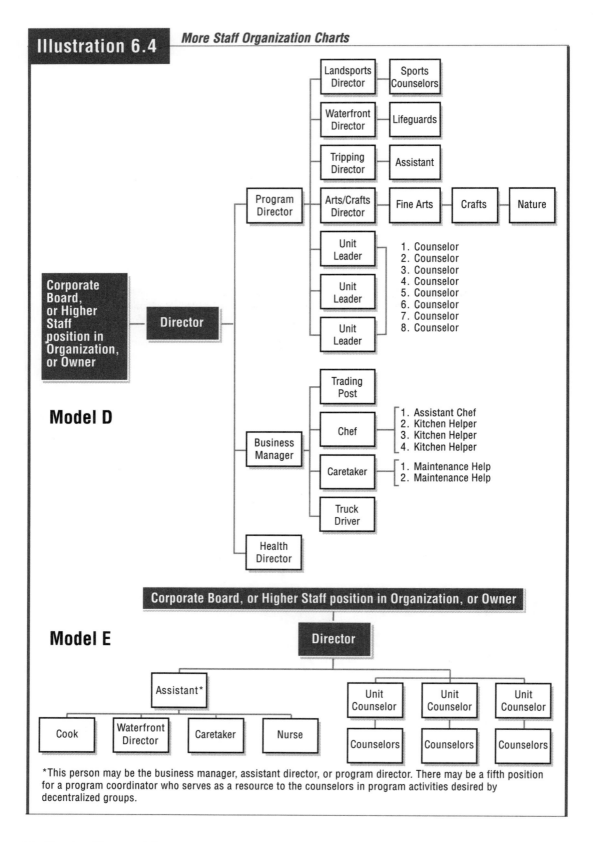

Model D

Corporate Board, or Higher Staff position in Organization, or Owner — Director

Program Director:
- Landsports Director — Sports Counselors
- Waterfront Director — Lifeguards
- Tripping Director — Assistant
- Arts/Crafts Director — Fine Arts — Crafts — Nature
- Unit Leader
- Unit Leader
- Unit Leader
  1. Counselor
  2. Counselor
  3. Counselor
  4. Counselor
  5. Counselor
  6. Counselor
  7. Counselor
  8. Counselor

Business Manager:
- Trading Post
- Chef
  1. Assistant Chef
  2. Kitchen Helper
  3. Kitchen Helper
  4. Kitchen Helper
- Caretaker
  1. Maintenance Help
  2. Maintenance Help
- Truck Driver

Health Director

Model E

Corporate Board, or Higher Staff position in Organization, or Owner — Director

- Assistant*
  - Cook
  - Waterfront Director
  - Caretaker
  - Nurse
- Unit Counselor — Counselors
- Unit Counselor — Counselors
- Unit Counselor — Counselors

*This person may be the business manager, assistant director, or program director. There may be a fifth position for a program coordinator who serves as a resource to the counselors in program activities desired by decentralized groups.

Job Descriptions

After jobs have been identified and lines of supervision developed, the camp director must develop job descriptions for each position. These are essential in helping each staff member understand the specific elements of the job for which he or she is responsible, as well as abilities and skills needed in the performance of that position. A good job description shows how one particular job correlates with others in the staff organization and provides the basis for performance appraisals.

By definition, a job description is a written statement of the minimum qualifications, general responsibilities, specific responsibilities, and essential functions pertinent to a particular position. It also identifies the supervisor by title. Each job description should also be assigned a position title that clearly identifies to other staff, campers, and the public what the staff member does.

A general outline for a job description includes the following six areas:

1. Position title

2. Title of the supervisor to whom the person in the position is responsible

3. General responsibility — a simple descriptive statement

4. Qualifications

5. Specific responsibilities — the specifics relating to the general responsibility

6. Essential functions

The *position title* should be as clear as possible and relate directly to the responsibilities. It also may be helpful to identify in a job description that the person in that position is the next responsible person (e.g., Assistant).

Clarity as *to whom the person in the position is responsible* is critical. Noting the title of the supervisor to whom one reports implies authority as well as the source of counsel and performance appraisal.

The *general responsibility* of a position was identified in the early stages of outlining staff organization. Refining the language into a basic descriptive statement should be relatively simple.

The *qualifications* for the position grow not only out of the general responsibility identified but also out of the related governmental regulations and accreditation and organizational standards. For instance, the requirement that the person must be an adult depends on the legal age of adulthood in the governing state. Qualifications describe the minimum age, education, experience, and characteristics necessary for an applicant to be considered for the position.

Age is a primary employment factor that must be considered carefully. Often industry standards, certification criteria, or government regulations will specify minimum ages for certain functions such as drivers of vehicles or waterfront personnel. These need to be researched carefully, even though the director may choose to require an older age or higher skill level if specific responsibilities are beyond the ordinary. For example, the group may be a considerable distance from the central camp support or public assistance, or the individuals in the group may have special characteristics. In both cases, higher skill and more maturity are required from the responsible staff.

In the industry, the accepted age for camp counselors is eighteen or above. Certainly, age is no guarantee of maturity, but experience has shown that, generally, individuals over eighteen tend to be more mature than younger people. There are also federal labor regulations prohibiting individuals under eighteen years of age from being employed to operate or clean kitchen slicers or mixers or to operate vehicles in excess of 6,000 pounds.

It is essential to have a person of legal adult age in certain positions such as supervising the waterfront, supervising camper groups taken off-site for extended tripping or travel, and driving passenger vehicles. Supervisors should generally be at least two or more years older than the staff they supervise.

Gender appears to be less of a factor in camp employment, except where counselors are assigned to live in the same quarters as campers of the same sex. Some camps with very young campers may not find this a factor. Of course, neither sex nor age can legally be used to discriminate in employment. The fact that a certain age base or sex is a requirement of a particular position should be carefully documented in the job description.

That a position demands a certain level of education should be spelled out, along with any particular training necessary. Personal qualifications such as flexibility or ability to work with others may be included if they are essential. However, according to equal employment regulations, all qualifications must be *directly* related to the job. In every job description, it is wise to have a statement that identifies that the position has responsibility for the health and welfare of campers.

Experience is a plus in any position, but for certain staff positions it is essential to hire staff with previous experience. Obviously, the value of a potential staff member's experience depends upon the situation in which it was acquired. A camp director can best determine the value of such experience from references, though an interview may assist greatly in that evaluation. Both of these methods are discussed in detail in chapter 7.

The camp director must consider skill as well as experience when hiring staff. In all camps, some areas of responsibility require that individuals have specific outside certification, ranging from Registered Nurse to a Commercial Driver's License.

For staff expected to drive vehicles carrying passengers, a current driver's license for the state in which the camp is located is required. If drivers are expected to operate vehicles designed to transport sixteen or more people or vehicles in excess of 26,000 pounds, a commercial driver's license is required. In either case, it would be wise to run a background check of previous driving history through the state police.

Various kinds of skill certifications are available in such areas as aquatics, riflery, campcraft, and horsemanship. In other areas, where certification is not available, documented evidence of experience and expertise, as well as instructional skills in that specific program, needs to be provided. The director must go beyond the applicant's statement of experience and skill to talk to or correspond with people who have actually supervised the applicant in the specific area or who have observed the person in action. If the person is to be an instructor in a skill area, then questions about teaching ability are as important as the person's own technical skills.

Though adventure or challenge programs such as ropes courses, rappelling, initiative courses, and climbing have multiplied in recent years, there is no nationally recognized certification of instructors at this time. Authorities in the field believe that accreditation of a site-specific program is more appropriate than certification of individuals in these activities. However, several reputable organizations and regional resources provide training in these skills; twenty hours of such instruction and experience should be the minimum expectation of an applicant to supervise such programs. (See appendix C.)

Certification is available in the skills of waterfront, archery, boating, riflery, waterskiing, and horsemanship. Equestrian programs offer an area of potential danger unless properly staffed and administered. Safety factors and the importance of animal care require people with experience and instructional skills. Horsemanship training is available at various universities, riding academies, and the U.S. Army, and certification is available through the Camp Horsemanship Association and the Horsemanship Safety Association.

No area of camp program has consistently contributed to as many deaths in camps nationwide as water-related injuries. Therefore, extreme care needs to be taken in the selection of the person responsible for overseeing the aquatic program, staff, and facilities. That person should be at least twenty-one years of age with previous experience in the supervision of an aquatic area for at least one season. In addition, the person should hold certification from a nationally recognized certifying body such as the American Red Cross or Boy Scouts of America. The director of aquatics needs to be a person with the maturity of judgment to train and supervise other members of the aquatic staff, as well as to recognize any potentially dangerous situations in the specific aquatic environment. Specialized training from the American Red Cross is available for head lifeguards and from the YMCA for the waterfront director. A list of ACA-approved certifying bodies is listed in the appendix of the *Accreditation Standards for Camp Programs and Services*. See appendix C for additional organizational resources.

Where recreational swimming is conducted, the lifeguards should hold certification from a nationally recognized certifying body (such as American Red Cross Lifeguard Training, YMCA Lifeguard, Lifeguard Boy Scouts of America, or Royal Lifesaving Society National

Pool Lifeguard). Similarly, swimming instructors should hold a certification from a similar body (YMCA Youth and Adult Instructor I and II, BSA Aquatics Instructor, or Red Cross Water Safety Instructor).

If there is aquatic activity other than swimming, the person supervising each specific activity should have skills specific to that activity. This person should be certified through a nationally recognized certifying organization and have documented experience in the knowledge and skills required to teach and supervise the program, as well as in rescue and emergency procedures specific to the aquatic area and activities. In addition, any staff dealing with boats should be conversant with U.S. Coast Guard Boating Safety Standards and the proper registration labels for recreational boats. Instructor certification programs are available through the American Canoe Association, U.S. SAILING, the American Water Ski Association, and from some chapters of the American Red Cross. Additional training in powerboat operation is available through the U.S. Coast Guard Auxiliary, the U.S. Power Squadrons, and the state boating agencies. Many states have mandatory education requirements for individuals who operate any motor-powered vessel. Courses from these organizations will fulfill those requirements. See appendix C for contact information.

At each location of aquatic activity, one staff member should be certified in American Red Cross Standard First Aid or its equivalent and must be certified in cardiopulmonary resuscitation (CPR) for the age level served. CPR training that also includes training in the use of breathing devices is highly recommended and is available through the American Red Cross, American Heart Association, and National Safety Council. It is not possible to identify a ratio of lifeguards to swimmers that applies to every situation. Therefore, the camp director, along with the aquatic supervisor, needs to study carefully the various aquatic locations, activities, and participant skill levels and then establish an overall aquatic policy that includes reasonable ratios of lifeguards to swimmers. This policy will determine the number of certified people the director needs to employ.

Note: The Occupational Safety and Health Administration (OSHA) has defined a lifeguard as someone who has a legal "duty to act" or is a professional rescuer. Where an employee by designation is required to perform a task, it is implied that the employer must provide the appropriate tools for the job. For example, rescues that include mouth-to-mouth resuscitation or treatment of wounds require equipment to protect the rescuer from communicable diseases and blood-borne pathogens. In this case, required tools include protective breathing devices and latex gloves.

To determine essential functions, the camp director must return to the general and specific responsibilities to identify the physical, cognitive, visual, auditory, and other abilities essential for an individual to fulfill these responsibilities, with or without reasonable accommodations. See *illustration 6.5.* For instance, does the position require physical ability to lift a certain weight, walk or climb a certain distance, or swim? Reasonable

Illustration 6.5 *Sample Job Requirements*

Position Title: Counselor
  Responsible To: Unit Director
General Responsibility: To live with and guide eight campers throughout their camp experience
Qualifications:
  * At least eighteen years of age
  * High school diploma or GED required; one or more years of college preferred
  * Experience as a camper or working with children as a leader or assistant leader
  * Ability to relate to one's peers as well as to children
  * Good character
  * Flexibility with ability to accept supervision
Specific Responsibilities:
  * Live in a cabin with eight campers
  * Assume responsibility for leadership and guidance of those campers in daily living, with special attention to: personal hygiene and safety, camper participation in all-camp activities, camp participation in planning cabin activities, meal-time behavior and habits
  * Assume responsibility as assistant activity specialist in an assigned activity area
  * Assume responsibility for interpreting the rules, policies, and traditions of the camp to the camper
  * Serve as a good example in personal language, appearance, and health habits
  * Assume responsibility for health and welfare of campers entrusted to his or her charge
Essential Functions:
  * Be physically able to accompany the campers to any of the camp activities
  * Be able to communicate verbally with campers and provide instructions
  * Have visual ability to recognize hazards in the camp setting as well as physical symptoms of camper injury or illness
  * Have auditory ability to respond appropriately to hazards and any camper concerns
  * Be able to observe camper behavior in daily camp life, to respond verbally to health and safety concerns, and to deal appropriately with any improper behavior

accommodations include making existing facilities readily accessible to and usable by people with disabilities, restructuring the job, or making accommodations in order that a person with a disability can perform the job (e.g., modifications of equipment, providing devices, and interpreters).

Since the Americans With Disabilities Act was passed in 1990, it has brought employers to a renewed awareness of their responsibility to avoid unlawful discrimination against a qualified individual with a disability because of that disability. "The term 'qualified individual with a disability' refers to a person with a disability who, with or without reasonable accommodations, can perform the essential functions of the job. All employers must therefore identify the essential functions, as opposed to the marginal functions, of each job."[2]

Many camp directors also find it prudent to include in every job description a statement that additional tasks may be assigned at the discretion of the director or supervisor.

After identifying the specific responsibilities and essential functions of a position, the camp director would be wise to review the qualifications identified earlier for the position. This review will enable the director to adjust or add to those qualifications.

In starting the process of writing new or revising existing job descriptions, the director can gain insights by asking supervisors and staff to organize a checklist of tasks related to their individual positions. This may also identify some misconceptions regarding the actual responsibilities of the position. "Job descriptions require systematic thought and continual revision. They cannot be written in a vacuum; careful consideration of how the camp operates is an integral part of the job description."[3] Changes may need to be made in initial descriptions after people are employed and the summer staff is in residence, but these adjustments should be done with the full participation of the staff members concerned. A sample job description format is given in appendix A.

Directors who are writing job descriptions for the first time will find that the most cogent information on the process is available in Edie Klein's book, *It's My Job*. For those who are rewriting some job descriptions and wish to increase the effectiveness of the descriptions and, at the same time, avoid discrimination as defined by the Americans With Disabilities Act, the same book provides efficient guidelines and sample descriptions for more than thirty camp jobs.

Salary and Benefits

In advance of staff recruitment, the camp director should carefully consider the camp policy of compensation and benefits for staff. Obviously, the philosophy of the organization will dictate the plan, to some degree. For example, Girl Scout day camps or local church camps may be staffed by volunteers. However, even camps with a predominantly volunteer staff need a policy.

In addition to wages, benefits can include meals, lodging, transportation, laundry, baby-sitting, insurance, or a camp experience for children of staff members. Each benefit costs the camp money and saves money for or provides the staff member with something of value; such benefits should be clearly identified in a statement of personnel policy. In addition to salary, the camp director should also consider what portion of the benefit has FICA or income tax associated with it. Each situation will be different, so guidelines should be developed before staff recruitment begins. Each benefit has special considerations.

Meals. Most camps that serve meals automatically provide meals to staff members, for the convenience of the camp, at no additional charge. However, meals for the staff member's dependents are a negotiable matter. Some camps charge cost and deduct it from salary; some include meals as a benefit. Others require families to prepare their own meals in separate living quarters, while the camp takes responsibility for the staff member's meals only when he or she eats with the staff and campers.

Lodging. Resident camps generally provide lodging for staff members, most often in multiple-living units. Counselors are usually required to live with campers, although a privacy division or room in the same building may be provided. Lodging for dependents of staff members is sometimes charged against salary or, in other cases, given as a benefit of employment. Many camps provide housing for families in order to secure older or returning staff.

Transportation. Day camps generally require some staff members to ride on camper buses and usually provide space for any staff member at no charge. Resident camps often meet staff at central locations. Some camps provide a transportation allowance, particularly for staff members who travel more than a minimum number of miles to get to camp.

Baby-sitting. Day camps utilizing volunteers often provide a central baby-sitting service for children of staff members or reimburse volunteers for the cost of home baby-sitting.

Insurance. Worker's compensation, automobile, and liability insurance are covered later in chapter 11. Many camps provide a health and accident insurance policy to staff members as a benefit of employment or offer it as an option, which the staff member may purchase.

Camp Experience. Where a single parent or both parents come as staff members to camp and have camper-age children, it is not unusual for those children to be enrolled as campers in their proper age group, as a credit against wages. Even for volunteers, the value of this benefit may be considered income and be subject to taxes.

Salary. If any amount is agreed upon and paid to a staff member in advance (whether it is called an honorarium, a stipend, a scholarship, or a gift), that remuneration is considered salary. Initially, the director should secure information on the state's minimum-wage laws as well as the applicability of federal minimum-wage laws. It may also be helpful for him or her to visit with camp directors of comparable camps in the area to learn what salaries are being paid in similar circumstances.

International Staff. Camps that have international staff often need to provide additional benefits including bedding and transportation to town on time-off. Often international staff members go home with American staff; however, if this is not the case, they must have the opportunity to get to stores to purchase incidentals or to enjoy the area around camp. ACA has a list of best practices for working with international staff on its Web site.

If minimum wage is applicable, rooms or other facilities provided by the employer may generally be a part of the minimum-wage calculation. (The rule of thumb for determining the value of these services is to document the average cost of the meals including overhead, labor, and raw food. For lodging, the documentation should include the value of the lodging provided based upon the local community market, with consideration given to whether the lodging is private, semiprivate, or dormitory style.) It is best to check with a human resources expert or lawyer because federal and state wage-hour laws change frequently.

Increments in salary levels are decided in a variety of ways:
- By number of years on the staff
- By age and experience
- By certain qualifications (cook, nurse, waterfront certification, outdoor living skills certification)
- By position in the organization chart

- By need (i.e., the camp finds that the only way to secure staffers from the inner city is to pay considerably more than the going rate because of economic circumstances)

The camp director should give careful thought to salary scales, to any increases built into those scales, and to their fairness to staff members. Though most people do not work in camps solely for the monetary benefit, there is sensitivity in such a close community to differences or unfairness in wages that can interfere with the more important parts of camp life. It is essential that it not be implied that counselors are the lowest point on the scale because there is, potentially, no more important person in terms of the health and safety of campers or camper relationships than the counselor. The program philosophy as well as the outcomes and goals will emphasize that responsibility more in some camps than in others, but, in every case, it is vital that the nature of the counselor's responsibility be fairly recognized.

Personnel Policies

Although the camp director may be covered by the personnel policies of his or her employer, seasonal staff may not be. It is generally the camp director's responsibility to develop personnel policies that define the guidelines and expectations for seasonal staff. Each staff member should be given a copy of the personnel policies. See illustration 6.6 for a sample of some personnel policies. For further information, see appendix R in the Accreditation Standards for Camp Programs and Services. Ideally, they should be attached to the employment agreement and reviewed by the staff member before a contract is signed.

Personnel policies generally cover the following issues:
- Pay periods: dates, deductions, method of payment
- Overall benefits
- Termination: length of notice necessary, termination pay, causes
- Time-off: amount to be expected, method of determination, scheduling, sick leave days
- Work rules: use of tobacco, alcohol, and controlled substances; a specific sexual harassment policy; and so on
- Other regulations: use of personal automobiles or equipment in conjunction with camp program and so on
- Equal employment opportunity statement
- Performance appraisal system: discipline, grievance procedures, and so on
- The camp's policy statement concerning the welfare of children and the action to be taken in case of child or sexual abuse
- A statement that because camps serve as the first line of defense for medical treatment for camp staff, it is important that the health staff have the critical medical information to determine whether a doctor or additional professional medical care is required and that, without the appropriate information, camp health staff cannot make an informed decision.[4]

Illustration 6.6 | *Sample Personnel Policies*

SAMPLE PERSONNEL POLICIES FOR SEASONAL STAFF

The camp wishes to make your employment period with us as enjoyable and beneficial as possible. Camp is a community and the actions of each member of that community affects the other members. Certain policies help clarify the expectations of the employee and the employer, and minimize any difficulties within the community.

It should be recognized that employment at camp is "at will." Either party can terminate the relationship at any time, for any or no reason, with or without notice, under the state's "at will" doctrine.

1. Camper Welfare

The first responsibility of each and every staff member is the health and welfare of the campers. Each staff member is expected to take every care to protect the privacy and person of each camper. Physical punishment or any sexual contact between staff and campers is inappropriate, and will be grounds for dismissal. Staff members should never touch campers in any area covered by a bathing suit or show outward signs of affection that could be misinterpreted as sexual abuse.

2. Insurance

Worker's compensation and health insurance is carried by the camp on each employee for work related injuries or illnesses. This insurance does not cover nonwork related injuries or illnesses.

Liability insurance is carried by the camp which covers each employee when carrying out assigned camp responsibilities, as long as the employee is not negligent in carrying out those responsibilities, is following the policies and procedures of the camp, and acting within the authority of their job.

3. Pay Periods

For the convenience of the camp office, the wage agreement is based on a weekly rate. It is impossible to clock the actual work hours in the camp setting for counselors, program personnel, and program supervisors. However, the kitchen and maintenance employees must furnish a daily record of the hours worked on the cards provided. The camp will issue pay checks on the first and fifteenth of each month during contracted time.

4. Time Off

Time-off periods will be scheduled as regularly as possible, but necessarily at the convenience of the camp program. Each week staff can normally expect one twenty-four-hour period free of duties, agreed upon with the employee's supervisor a week ahead. In some cases, days off may be accumulated for a two-week period to provide two successive days off. Days off cannot be accumulated without advance permission.

At least two hours daily will be freed up for persons related to living groups. A plan for coverage of the living group should be worked out with the staff member's supervisor.

5. Sick Leave

If a staff member is sick, a camp director, supervisor, or health director may request that he or she see a doctor or go home to recuperate from an illness or injury without pay.

6. Alcohol/Tobacco/Controlled Substances

Alcohol and controlled substances are not allowed on the camp property. Employees are expected to follow this policy. In addition, employees are not to return to the camp grounds under the influence of alcohol or controlled substances. Breaking this policy is grounds for immediate dismissal.

Smoking and chewing tobacco is discouraged, but is permitted in the staff lounge or the living quarters of staff not living with campers. All employees are asked to refrain from smoking in any areas of camp frequented by campers, as well as in the kitchen.

Staff are asked to be sensitive to the people in the communities near the camp. Each staff member represents the camp in his or her dealings with members of the local communities, as well as in behavior off the camp grounds.

8. Tips/Gratuities

Staff members are asked not to accept any tips or gratuities from the parents or relatives of campers.

Illustration 6.6   *Sample Personnel Policies* continued

9. Health Services

A registered nurse is on duty at camp and staff members have access to his or her services as needed. The cost of prescriptions and doctor or hospital visits must be covered under one's personal insurance or that purchased through the camp unless the injury or illness is work related (See 2.)

10. Grievances

Should there be a disagreement over the interpretation of camp policies or a grievance related to one's duties or relationships with fellow staff members, it should be reported to one's supervisor promptly. Should the supervisor be the source of the grievance, the staff member may report the grievance to the supervisor of his or her supervisor or to the camp director.

11. Performance Appraisal

In an effort to help each staff member perform his or her duties at an optimum level, each staff member is evaluated on a regular basis. The employee's supervisor will indicate the frequency of the supervisory conferences, and, at the conclusion of each conference, will share a written evaluation with the employee. The employee and supervisor will both sign the agreed upon evaluation and it will be filed in the staff member's personnel file.

A staff member does not have to wait for a scheduled supervisory conference to seek advice or counsel from his or her supervisor. The primary responsibility of a supervisor is to be available to deal with the day-to-day problems of his or her supervisees.

Because of the current litigious climate, the camp director may do well to include in the personnel policies a statement indicating that the policies are designed to clarify, generally, the employer/employee relationship and should not be considered as a contract or as a guarantee of employment. It should also be indicated that the employer/employee relationship is an at-will relationship that may be terminated with appropriate notice by either party at any time. At-will relationships are discussed in more detail in chapter 7.

Termination is a matter that directors seldom consider until they are faced with a staff member who is not fulfilling his or her responsibilities. Discussion, prior to the season, with other camp directors concerning their termination practices can be helpful. It is important to recognize that, despite one's concern for the employee as a person, termination of that person may be the most beneficial action for the total camp community. Because of the twenty-four-hour living situation in a residential camp and the short season of many camps, termination becomes necessary where, in other settings, more time could be given to coaching or waiting and seeing whether the problems could be solved. For these same reasons, it may also be better to pay the terminated employee for the notice period and have him or her leave camp immediately rather than to have a disgruntled employee in the living situation for that period.

The camp director should also pay careful attention to a plan and pattern for time-off for resident camp staff. The living situation at a resident camp demands twenty-four-hour responsibilities from most personnel; however, because of that continuing day-to-day situation, it is vital that time-off be arranged for each staff member. In addition, some free time to pursue personal needs should also be available each day. That time will occur naturally for many staff members who work given hours, but program and counseling personnel, in particular, need a plan. For safety reasons, those plans should be coordinated carefully, and counselors should always know how their camper-group responsibilities will be supervised in their absence. A minimum of two free hours a day, apart from sleep time or eating with campers, is the accepted norm.

In addition to daily free time, every staff member needs a minimum of twelve consecutive hours free each week (or twenty-four hours every two weeks) so that there is time to get away from the camp community or to find uninterrupted time for personal needs in camp. Obviously, such time has to be scheduled and, in most jobs, personnel replacements arranged. Adequate flexibility in job descriptions and numbers of staff is needed so that other staff can substitute for those who are off duty and still maintain an appropriate staff-to-camper ratio. Provision for time-off is an obligation of the camp as an employer but scheduling may be at the employer's convenience. It is important that the camp director also take a day off, for his or her own good as well as for the benefit of staff.

If the new director begins after staff recruitment has been completed, he or she should make a careful review of the program to determine how it is affected by the individual abilities and skills of the staff. Program plans should then be adjusted accordingly. Of course, it is desirable that the new director has the opportunity to develop an ideal organizational plan for his or her staff before beginning recruitment.

Checkpoints

1. List the positions that your program design necessitates and to whom each staff member reports.

2. Review present job descriptions for each position. Check them, if possible, with people who have filled the positions previously.

3. Outline the general responsibilities and specific functions, of each position.

4. Outline the qualifications necessary to accomplish the functions as well as those imposed by position or regulations (i.e., age, certificates, degrees).

5. Test the number of counselors against the number of campers at one given time to find your camper/counselor ratio.

6. List all of the various sorts of remuneration you will be giving staff and develop the actual cost for each one. Compare this with line items in the budget.

Related Standards and Guidelines

Accreditation Standards for Camp Programs and Services: HR-2, 6, 8–10, 21; "Additional Professional Practices": Items 25–29.

Guidelines for Conference and Retreat Centers: II-26, 31–33, 35, 36, 40-41.

[1] Harvie J. Boorman, "Organization of Camp." *Administration of the Modern Camp*, Hedley S. Dimock, ed. 1948, New York: Association Press.

[2] Edie Klein. 1992. *It's My Job*. Martinsville, IN: American Camping Association. p. 3.

[3] Karla A. Henderson. 1990. "Job Descriptions Help Measure Staff Performance." *Camping Magazine*, Vol. 62, No. 4, February. p. 24–25.

[4] "Interviewing and the Americans With Disabilities Act." *The CampLine*. February 2003.

Personnel Recruitment

The quality of the camp staff is of the greatest importance in the successful operation of a camp program. Comparisons of the relative success that different camps have with their programs show that the physical factors, such as size, layout, buildings, and equipment, are also important. But camps with similar or comparable facilities vary considerably in the quality of their programs. The differences are largely explainable by the variations in the ability of the personnel who make up the camp staff.[1]

After developing a clear organizational design and job descriptions, the director can effectively begin the recruitment process. A director cannot approach this task lightly, for finding qualified staff is a challenge and takes much time and effort.

The director should organize his or her recruitment materials and examine them for clarity, attractiveness, and appeal. These should include a camp brochure, a job description, an application form, and a description of the job benefits and unique aspects of the camp. The materials must compete with those from many other seasonal jobs and camps trying to recruit the same personnel.

Sources

Where does one find staff? Here are a variety of different possibilities.

Through Former and Present Staff. Because former and present staff members have a clear understanding of the camp's philosophy, working conditions, and the type of personality that will be most effective in the camp's setting, their recommendations may be beneficial. Beware, however, of staffing primarily with friends; cliques may be formed, and newcomers may be left out. Some camps provide a bonus to previous staff members who recruit someone who is hired and stays for the entire summer.

Colleges and Universities. A contact person in the university setting can be a former or present staff member or someone in the summer placement office or in the recreation, physical education, or education department. Resident hall assistants often have experiences that prepare them for camp supervision. Explore internships as a possibility for students to gain credits. Make sure brochures, applications, and job descriptions are given to your contact. Arrange for a day of interviews on campus.

Job Fairs. The camp director can take advantage of college and university campus job fairs or plan a tour of fairs in schools in the same state. *Camping Magazine* carries a regular calendar of locations, dates, and contacts for job fairs. Fairs often have so many participating camps and summer employers that it is difficult to attract the attention of students unless you develop an unusual display or graphic and include video or pictures of the camp. Most directors soon find that some college and university profiles better match their camp program, location, and staffing "personality" and concentrate on those fairs.

Directories of Summer Employment. These directories provide the opportunity to draw staff from broader geographical areas. The American Camping Association publishes an annual *Summer Camp Employment* Booklet.

Former Campers. Former campers and particularly past participants in counselor-in-training or leader-in-training programs are already familiar with your camp. Many directors believe that this source is best for recruiting staff.

Faculties. Educators and administrators from elementary, middle, and high schools, colleges, universities, and private schools have valuable experience with young participants.

Membership of the Sponsoring Organization. The sponsoring organization is the first source of volunteer staff. The local Volunteer Bureau may also be helpful in the search for volunteers.

Placement Services. These services offer an opportunity for the director to file a list of positions along with job requirements. They include departments of manpower or employment services in many states, as well as some American Camping Association section offices.

International Staff-Placement Organizations. Several excellent agencies screen potential staff applicants at different overseas locations and provide applications and interview information to the camp director. Individuals from other countries can broaden and stimulate the camp experience for campers and staff alike. Addresses of such organizations (BUNAC, Camp America, Camp Counselors USA, International Camp Counselor Exchange Program, International Camp Counselor Program) are in appendix D. In addition, the International Camping Fellowship publishes an annual *Resource Directory*, which lists individual members who are looking for an international camp experience.

Community Groups. Neighborhood or community centers, block clubs, churches, and youth boards are good sources for staff, especially minority staff.

The Internet. A camp Web site with photos, program descriptions, location, and a list of jobs available will attract the attention of students and others. An application form can even be included on the camp's site.

There are also job directory services on the Internet. For example, the American Camping Association has an on-line service and a printed booklet *Summer Jobs in Camps*. If your camp is accredited by the American Camping Association, its listing in ACA's *Find a Camp* searchable database can be linked to your camp's Web page.

Advertise. Advertising is most effective, if it can be done in a publication specific to the skill or type of position needed.

Parents. A parent may be quite willing to take a camp position if his or her child can attend camp at a reduced rate.

Seniors. An alternative source of staff, which many camps have found productive, is senior adults. Seniors have discovered the joys of being with children in a beautiful setting and of being able to continue to use skills and abilities gained from previous jobs. Camp administrators have discovered among seniors a wealth of practical work experience unmatched by younger staff. "Camps that employ seniors can enrich the camper's experience and provide a great summer for senior adults. This attractive staffing alternative is gaining momentum."[2]

Although these sources may provide most of the program and counseling staff, the camp director will probably need to turn to more specialized sources for cooks and nurses. The state employment agency, schools with cafeterias, and fraternity and sorority houses are good sources for cooks. Similarly, the state nursing association, state employment agency, nursing schools, and school systems can provide leads for camp nurse candidates.

As Christy L. Phillips writes, in the recruitment process it is important to "remember that there are good people who are just waiting to work in your camp. Now, all you have to do is find them. Make a staff recruitment calendar and work with camp associations and other camp professionals. With some persistence, your staff recruitment efforts will be successful."[3]

International Staff

I n recent years, the number of staff members from outside the United States has increased steadily just as the national population in the traditional camp-staff age group (eighteen to twenty-five) has decreased. There are great advantages to having international staff members, if those people are well prepared for the particular camp setting, possess the skills for the position for which they are employed, and are used to stimulate international education through the camp program. There are two kinds of international staff programs — one that provides counselors or program staff and another one that is for support staff. Designated sponsors or international exchange organizations as regulated by the U.S. Department of State Visitor Exchange Program operate these programs. Support staff includes kitchen, maintenance, laundry, and other nonprogram positions. The regulations for these J-1 cultural exchange visas in the two programs differ and are very specific. Because the application and screening process takes time, camp directors wanting to participate in the program should contact one of the international exchange organizations early in the year.

Some international exchange organizations, such as the International Camp Counselor Program, are able to sponsor visas for year-round international interns or other training positions. Environmental education programs and conference centers may find this helpful in maintaining an international presence and program during the fall, winter, and spring seasons.

"Campers and staff from the United States gain valuable insights into other cultures — their language, history, ways of thinking and looking at the world, customs, food, and dress. Learning from staff with whom they interact on a daily basis can be a . . . powerful learning experience. . . . International staff members have allowed us to view our program and staff training through fresh eyes,"[4] states Nancy Halliday of Hofstra University.

However, to simply employ such staff because it is the easiest way to fill difficult positions is unfair to the camp and to the international applicant. It is critical that information be shared with all applicants so that they understand not only the scope of duties but also the type of living accommodations, working conditions, and proximity (or lack thereof) to cities. If a personal interview is not available, it is essential that the camp director take extra steps to communicate with the applicant and a former employer, even at the cost of international phone calls. This is particularly true of applicants who would be working directly with campers on a day-to-day basis, where the ability to work with children and the applicant's fluency in the language spoken in camp are both important. Faxes and e-mail have speeded up communication with potential international staff.

The American Camping Association has developed an outline of *Best Practices for International Staff* that details exemplary as well as expected practices of camp directors and is shown in appendix G. Directors would do well to study this document before ever beginning to search out international staff. Delegating responsibility for recruitment of a staff member does not absolve the employer from careful and responsible actions in the employment process.

Negligent Hiring

A lawsuit for negligent hiring is based on the theory that the employer is liable for the actions of an employee who was unfit or who created an unreasonable risk of harm.[5] To translate this process to camp vernacular, negligent hiring is an action wherein a parent sues a camp for injuries sustained by a camper that were caused by the careless actions of a staff member or of an unqualified staff member. Camps have been sued for negligent hiring of staff who had previously been convicted of sexually abusing children. Generally, the expectation of the parent is that the director should discover this fact before hiring the person.

Many of the steps described in this chapter are designed to provide protection against such suits: clear job descriptions, complete application forms, references, a thorough screening process, interviews, and documentation of each step. All these steps are equally important for the camp that has a volunteer staff. Though some steps may be more difficult in such a camp where staff often changes from week to week, it is critical that a modified plan that covers the same basic steps be developed.

To help you be consistent in your hiring practices, you may want to log all the steps you take for each person. A sample hiring log is shown in appendix H.

Applications

Beyond the data ordinarily required for employment, a camp staff application form should emphasize the skills and experience required in the job description. A director should be aware of the importance of eliciting only that information needed for a decision about the job and, on the other hand, of requiring all information needed to determine if an applicant meets all personnel selection qualifications. For example, it is permissible to ask the applicant's sex or whether the person is at least a certain age only if the job requirements demand a certain sex or minimum age. Asking for that information when the job does not require it may open the camp director to charges of discrimination. *Illustration 7.1* shows an application developed by the American Camping Association.

It is also wise to provide enough space on the application form so that every previous job may be listed, enabling the director to check for gaps in employment. Such gaps give the interviewer an opportunity to ask questions about that period in the event that such incidents as convictions of a felony or crime related to abuse were the cause of the lapses of time.

Where a license or certain level of experience is required, a copy of the license or, in the case of experience, outside documentation should be required.

The steps taken after an application is received are critical in the selection of competent and conscientious staff. The type of references desired, the format of the interview, and the delineation of the camp's philosophy and policies should be carefully planned before implementing these steps. Training and supervision cannot cure the employment of an incompetent and potentially negligent person in a staff position.

Specific questions should be asked about previous convictions for child abuse; however, one should clear those questions with the camp's attorney. For instance, the application might ask: "Have you been previously convicted of a felony or misdemeanor? If the answer is yes, please indicate on a separate sheet of paper the convictions, dates, and circumstances," or "Have you been previously charged with any crime related to the abuse, mistreatment, or molestation of children?"

Illustration 7.1 *Camp Staff Application*

Camp Staff Application Form FM 10N

Developed by *American Camping Association*®

Return to:

(Please type or print)

Date of Application _____

Name _____ Social Security Number _____

Permanent Address _____
Street & Number   City   State   Zip

Phone _____ Fax _____ E-mail _____
Area & Number   Area & Number

School or Business Address _____
Street & Number   City   State   Zip

Phone _____ Fax _____ E-mail _____
Area & Number   Area & Number

Dates available From _____ To _____

What type of position do you want at camp? _____ Salary desired? _____

Do you meet or exceed any minimum age requirements for that position? ☐ Don't know minimum age ☐ Yes ☐ No

Can you perform the essential functions of the job for which you have applied, with or without reasonable accommodation? ☐ Yes ☐ No

If you are hired would you desire or need housing for any person(s) other than yourself at the camp? ☐ Yes ☐ No

Past Work History Provide a full record of all employment — paid and volunteer — and explain any gaps in employment. Include any positions on camp staff. Use a separate sheet, if necessary.

Dates	Employer/Supervisor	Address & Phone	Nature of Work	Reason for Leaving

Indicate any employer you **do not** wish us to contact, and the reason _____
_____
_____

This form has been drafted to comply with federal employment laws; however, ACA assumes no responsibility or liability for the use of this form.

Copyright 1979 by American Camping Association, Inc. Revised 1990, 1991, 1992, 1994, 1996, 1998, 1999.

References Give names and addresses of three persons [not relatives] having knowledge of your character, experience, work habits, and ability.

Name	Address & City	Phone

Camp Experience

Dates	Camp & Director	Location	Camper or Staff?

Education High School and Beyond

Years	School	Major Subjects	Degree Granted

Write a brief biographical sketch, including specialized training in camping, and experience or training in other fields which might have a bearing on the position(s) for which you are applying. Attach a separate sheet if necessary.

_____

_____

_____

_____

_____

_____

_____

_____

_____

Illustration 7.1   *Camp Staff Application, continued*

Camp Program Skills   In the following list, put a "T" *before* those activities you can organize and teach as an expert, and an "A" for those activities in which you can assist. Put a "C" *after* those in which you have *current* certification and attach a copy of your certification.

Adventure/Challenge
_____ challenge/ropes course
_____ climbing/rappelling
_____ spelunking/caving
_____ _____

Arts/Crafts
_____ ceramics/pottery
_____ drawing/painting
_____ leather craft
_____ metal work
_____ photography
_____ woodworking
_____ _____
_____ _____

Campcraft/Pioneering
_____ backpacking
_____ campcraft
_____ hiking
_____ orienteering
_____ outdoor cooking
_____ outdoor living skills
_____ overnights
_____ wilderness trips
_____ _____

Dance (list)
_____ _____
_____ _____
_____ _____

Drama
_____ clowning
_____ theater
_____ _____
_____ _____

Music
_____ singing
_____ instrument (list)
_____ _____
_____ _____
_____ _____

Nature
_____ animals/animal care
_____ astronomy
_____ birds
_____ environmental studies
_____ flowers
_____ forestry
_____ insects
_____ rocks/minerals
_____ weather

Sports/Fitness
_____ aerobics/exercise
_____ archery
_____ baseball/softball
_____ basketball
_____ bicycling/biking
_____ boxing
_____ fencing
_____ fishing
_____ football
_____ golf
_____ gymnastics
_____ hockey (ice/in-line)
_____ horseback riding (English)
_____ horseback riding (Western)
_____ informal games
_____ martial arts
_____ riflery
_____ skating (ice, roller, in-line)
_____ soccer
_____ snow sports (list)
_____ _____
_____ tennis
_____ track/field
_____ volleyball
_____ wrestling

Waterfront Activities
_____ board sailing/wind surfing
_____ canoeing
_____ diving
_____ kayaking
_____ rafting
_____ rowing
_____ sailing
_____ SCUBA
_____ swimming
_____ synchronized swimming
_____ water skiing
_____ _____

Miscellaneous
_____ academics
_____ aviation
_____ community service
_____ farming/ranching/gardening
_____ foreign language
_____ leadership development/CIT
_____ radio/TV/video
_____ storytelling
_____ team building
_____ worship services/religious studies
_____ _____

Certifications and Camp Support Staff Skills   In the following list, please check those items in which you have experience and skills. Mark with a "C" those for which you hold current certification and attach a copy of your certification.

Business/Administration
_____ bookkeeping/accounting
_____ computer/technical
_____ computer/software (list)
_____ _____
_____ _____

Health/Safety
_____ CPR
_____ first aid
_____ lifeguard
_____ nursing

Maintenance
_____ auto mechanics
_____ carpentry
_____ electrical
_____ plumbing
_____ _____
_____ _____

Food Service
_____ cooking/meal preparation
_____ Food Handler's Permit/Certification
_____ menu planning
_____ purchasing
_____ sanitation
_____ _____

Answer these questions *only* if applying for a position requiring driving

Do you have a valid driver's license?   ☐ Yes ☐ No   State _____

Do you have current chauffeur's-type license?   ☐ Yes ☐ No

Do you have a commercial driver's license?   ☐ Yes ☐ No

What contributions do you think you can make at camp? _____

_____

_____

_____

_____

_____

_____

What contributions do you think a well-run camp can make to children? _____

_____

_____

_____

_____

_____

_____

Harassment The camp's policy is to prohibit all forms of harassment by our employees. This includes sexual, racial, religious, and other forms of harassment. Have you ever been accused of harassment of any person including, but not limited to, workplace harassment? (Note: a prior accusation or conviction is not an automatic bar to employment. The type of conviction or accusation and when it occurred will be evaluated by the camp before any decision is made.)

☐ Yes ☐ No

Explain _____

_____

_____

Criminal Record Have you ever been convicted of a crime, other than a minor traffic offense? If yes, please describe. (Note: a prior conviction is not an automatic bar to employment. The type of conviction and when it occurred will be evaluated by the camp before any decision is made.)

☐ Yes ☐ No

Explain _____

_____

_____

I authorize investigation of all statements herein, including any checks of criminal records, and release the camp and all others from liability in connection with same. I understand that , if employed, I will be an at-will employee unless there is an agreement or law which alters that status. Furthermore, I understand that any agreement must be in writing and signed by the designated camp official. I also understand that untrue, misleading, or omitted information herein or in other documents completed by the applicant may result in dismissal, regardless of the time of discovery by the camp.

Signature _____ Date _____

All statements become part of any future employee personnel files.

References and Background Checks

In the development of the application form, a camp director will need to decide the number of references required and how they will be utilized. Generally, of course, applicants request references from people they know will give favorable recommendations; and it is unusual for individuals who write references to make negative comments. This tendency does not necessarily mean that references are useless, but rather that care should be exercised in requesting them.

If job performance is the primary concern, the director should ask for the names of an applicant's supervisors in the last three jobs rather than for general references. Here, it is important to ask specific questions about performance as an employee, any dismissal, and if so, the reason for it. If the basic concern is the applicant's ability to relate to children, then the director should ask for the names of people who have had the opportunity to observe the applicant in a position where he or she taught or led children of specified ages. Here, questions about judgment and disciplinary methods should be included. If performance in a certain skill area is more of a concern, then the director should ask for the names of people who have observed the applicant as a teacher of that skill or as a member of a team practicing that skill. Simple character references should not be from relatives. Additionally, if written references are requested, it is only courteous to include a stamped return envelope. A sample reference questionnaire is shown in *illustration 7.2*.

Even though it is often difficult to get former employers to be frank about an applicant, it is unwise to employ a person without some check of references. ACA has developed "a legal document the applicant would sign releasing former employers from any liability while providing information about the skills and work habits of former employees."[6] The use of such a release may encourage the person giving references to relate adverse information that one should know about an applicant.

A telephone check of references may be the most effective approach to references because some people are more willing to make negative observations verbally than in writing. However, if you use telephone references, you should develop a system for recording notes on the conversation that can be filed with the job application. The recorded note should be dated and signed by the person making the call. If you have questions about an applicant after you have received written references, you should make a final telephone check.

References are more important than ever with the new awareness of the potential of employing child abuse offenders. Questions should be asked to determine whether the applicant may have any proclivity toward child or sexual abuse. See the last question in *illustration 7.2*.

In addition to references, the director must consider the question of background checks. The American Camping Association Standards require either a criminal background check or

Illustration 7.2   *Reference Questionnaire*

REFERENCE QUESTIONNAIRE	Confidential

_____ has applied to work on the staff at Camp _____ for this summer. This person has given your name as a reference who could evaluate his or her past performance as well as potential for the above position. Please give careful consideration to the ratings below.

Objective Rating

Under each general heading, check the phrase which most accurately describes the applicant's HABITUAL behavior with regard to that specific trait. Please remember that it will be the truly exceptional person who ranks high in all categories.

1. How well is the applicant able to direct and influence others along definite lines of action?
- ❏ Poor leader; incapable of directing others
- ❏ Usually follows the lead of others
- ❏ Normally successful in directing and controlling others
- ❏ Very successful in leading others
- ❏ Exceptional leader: inspires others along desirable lines of action

2. How well does individual work with associates and others for the good of the group?
- ❏ Cooperates grudgingly: makes trouble — obstructionist
- ❏ Gives limited cooperation: neglects common good for own interests
- ❏ Cooperates with others toward accomplishment of common cause
- ❏ Cooperates willingly and actively regardless of self-benefit: makes things go smoothly
- ❏ Exceptionally successful in working with others and inspiring confidence

3. How does this person react to suggestions or criticisms by others?
- ❏ Takes criticism as a personal insult
- ❏ Resents suggestions
- ❏ Listens to suggestions but may act without considering them
- ❏ Follows suggestions willingly
- ❏ Asks for criticisms and suggestions

4. How responsible is applicant? Able to competently get things done on own?
- ❏ Irresponsible even under supervision
- ❏ With constant supervision will do satisfactory work
- ❏ Usually needs detailed instructions with regular checks of work
- ❏ Carries out routine activity on own responsibility
- ❏ Exceptionally able to accomplish work without close supervision

5. How well does individual put his or her principles and convictions into action?
- ❏ Fails to carry out convictions under adverse circumstances
- ❏ Acts according to convictions under normal circumstances
- ❏ Carries out principles and convictions constantly and boldly even in fact of obstacles

6. How well does this person apply energy and persistence in following a job through?
- ❏ Needs much prodding to complete work
- ❏ Rather indifferent; does not finish job
- ❏ Completes assigned tasks of own accord
- ❏ Industrious, energetic; dependable at all time
- ❏ Unusual perseverance; does more than expected

7. How well does applicant control emotions?
- ❏ Easily depressed, irritated, or elated
- ❏ Tends to be over-emotional
- ❏ Unresponsive; apathetic
- ❏ Tends to be unresponsive
- ❏ Usually well-balanced
- ❏ Well-balanced
- ❏ Unusual balance between responsiveness and control

Illustration 7.2 | *Reference Questionnaire, continued*

Narrative Report

Please briefly state specific instances in which you have observed the applicant's behavior as it applies to any of these items. If you have no knowledge, please say so.

1. Impression of suitability as a camp counselor. Would you be willing to have your children under individual's supervision for a period of weeks in a camp situation? If not, why not?

2. Maturity of judgment. How does this person react in situations of stress, i.e., make decisions?

3. Ability to lead campers toward spiritual objectives of the camp. Ability to lead devotionals, worship? Influence of life?

4. Nature of associates. Describe the types of people with whom individual habitually associates.

5. Dependability. Can be relied upon? Does person weaken in absence of authority?

6. How long have you known the applicant? _____ How have you observed applicant?

7. Have you seen him or her in a leadership role with youngsters? _____ What role?

8. To what extent does the individual use drugs or alcohol?

9. To your knowledge, does the applicant have any proclivity toward child or sexual abuse?

Please return promptly to:

Name _____

Address _____

City _____ State _____ Zip _____

Position _____

Employed by _____

---

voluntary disclosure statement for each employee. Many states now require criminal background checks on all people who work with children in child-care situations. The application form can include a statement to give permission for the camp to conduct a criminal background check and/or fingerprint check and require a signature. A voluntary disclosure statement outlines similar questions as well as requiring residences for the previous five years. See *illustration 7.3* for a sample voluntary disclosure statement.

Where such a check is not required by the state, the camp can require the applicant to obtain a check on him- or herself as a requirement of employment. Commercial companies will perform background checks for a fee. These companies are subject to the Federal Credit Reporting Act (FCRA), which places an obligation on the camp as the employer to obtain permission from the applicant to secure the check, preferably with a copy of the applicant's rights under FCRA. Should negative information that causes one not to employ the applicant result from the check, the applicant must be notified of your decision and given a copy of the report, the address of the agency providing the report, and another copy of the rights under FCRA.

Illustration 7.3 *Sample ACA Voluntary Disclosure Statement FM 16*

Voluntary Disclosure Statement
All Camp Staff _____ **FM 16**

Developed and approved by the
American Camping Association®

Mail this form to the address below by _____ (date)

Name _____ Birth date _____
        Last   *First*   *Middle*

Home address _____
        Street Address   *City*   *State*   *Zip*

Social Security # _____ Other names by which known (e.g., maiden name) _____

Home phone _____ Business phone (if applicable) _____

School or College _____

Address _____
        Street Address   *City*   *State*   *Zip*

Driver's License # _____ State _____ Expiration Date _____

1. Previous residence(s) for last 5 years (include college and home residences):

   City _____ State _____ Years _____

   City _____ State _____ Years _____

   City _____ State _____ Years _____

   City _____ State _____ Years _____

   (Continue on separate sheet if necessary.)

2. Have you ever been convicted of any crime relating in any manner to children and/or your
   conduct with them?   ☐ Yes ☐ No

   If yes, please explain: (Use a separate sheet if necessary.)

   _____

   _____

   _____

   _____

3. Have you ever been convicted of any crime including, but not limited to, those listed below
   and/or any crime similar in any manner to those listed below?   ☐ Yes ☐ No

   • Indecent assault and battery on a child under fourteen
   • Indecent assault and battery on a mentally retarded person
   • Indecent assault and battery on a person who has obtained the age of fourteen
   • Rape
   • Rape of a child under sixteen with force
   • Assault with intent to commit rape
   • Kidnapping of a child under sixteen with intent to commit rape
   • Distribution and trafficking of narcotics or other controlled substances
   • Intent to commit any of the above crimes

   If yes, please explain: (Use a separate sheet if necessary.)

   _____

   _____

   _____

   _____

   _____

   (over)

Illustration 7.3 *Sample Voluntary Disclosure Statement, continued*

4. Have you ever been adjudged liable for civil penalties or damages involving sexual or physical abuse of children? ☐ Yes ☐ No

   If yes, please explain: (Use a separate sheet if necessary.)

   _____

   _____

   _____

   _____

   _____

5. Are you now or have you ever been subject to any court order involving sexual or physical abuse of a minor, including, but not limited to a domestic order or protection? ☐ Yes ☐ No

   If yes, please explain: (Use a separate sheet if necessary.)

   _____

   _____

   _____

   _____

   _____

6. Have your parental rights ever been terminated for reasons involving sexual or physical abuse of children? ☐ Yes ☐ No

   If yes, please explain:

   _____

   _____

   _____

   _____

   _____

I understand that:

a. The camp may deny employment to any person who answers "yes" to any one of questions 2-6. If hired and the employer later discovers circumstances that would indicate a "yes" answer to any of the above questions, employment may be terminated immediately.

b. The information provided on this form is subject to verification, which may include a criminal history check and request from any Central Registry of child abusers.

c. The camp may terminate employment or volunteer service of any person if that person is found, regardless of when discovered, to:

   1) have a history of complaints of abuse of a minor;
   2) have resigned, been terminated or been asked to resign from a position whether paid or unpaid, due to complaint(s) of sexual abuse of a minor; and/or
   3) have falsified or omitted information in this disclosure statement.

d. This disclosure statement must be updated yearly.

Signature _____ Date _____

Signature of Minor's Parent or Guardian _____ Date _____

Such checks are generally not available for minors and international counselors. ACA's Voluntary Disclosure Statement form, is also useful in this regard.

Criminal background checks generally require the applicant to request such a report to be forwarded from the state police or to provide written permission from the applicant if the camp requests it. However, the director needs to check in advance on the promptness with which the individual state responds to the request, to make sure it is timely enough to be useful. The average cost of $15 to $35 per applicant legally should be borne by the camp as a condition of employment. There is a serious question about the usefulness of such checks in the seasonal camp employment situation if most of the staff members are of college age because they may be only one or two years beyond the age where such a record could be documented.

On the other hand, for individuals who are over twenty-one or are employed year-round, such a check can be a valuable precaution. It is also wise to secure an FBI fingerprint check on such employees, if your state has passed legislation enabling access to the Criminal History Records Repository. The most practical approach is to contact your state law enforcement agency regarding the process and fees. Despite the lack of uniformity of reporting to the national system and the fact that some states do not require such checks be made of volunteers and employees, questions of liability can arise if an alleged incident occurs and a camp has not made such checks. It is, therefore, important for a camp to make a policy determination about whether such checks and/or voluntary disclosure statements will be required.

Employment Process and Child Abuse

The camp director should take steps in the employment process to minimize the risk of child abuse. The director should examine job descriptions, application forms, interview checklists, reference forms, contract forms, and staff-training outlines to make sure that all opportunities to uncover clues as to past abuse history or the proclivity toward such abuse exist.

This means checking references, doing a background check, investigating for a criminal record, asking questions in the interview about the applicant's experience, and checking gaps in employment history. Even though many states recognize claims for negligent hiring, most courts protect employers who can document a reasonable job of checking prior to employment.

The application form offers an opportunity to document the applicant's own statement as to previous convictions, as well as to alert him or her that abuse is a concern of the camp. Specific questions are noted later in this chapter.

Wherever statements are made about the position and the requirements (i.e., on job descriptions, in the interview, and in the staff manual), there should be clear statements that abuse will not be tolerated and that the welfare of the camper is a primary job responsibility of every staff member.

During the interview, the director should pose questions that delve into areas that may give clues or danger signals. Bob Ditter, a licensed social worker specializing in adolescent treatment, suggests several such questions to be asked twenty minutes or so into the interview.

"Do you have a best friend? Tell me about them — how long have you known them? What's one thing they've taught or done for you?

"Would you say you are most comfortable with people your own age, older or younger? (Explore this.)

"How were you punished as a child? What did you think of it then? Now? What do you think works best with children?" [7]

In her book, *For Their Sake*, Becca Cowan Johnson, Ph.D., points out that, while there is no way to determine whether or not a person is a molester from traits alone, there are traits and characteristics that can be used as guidelines for identifying potential abusers. She states that, generally, the abuser will have a negative attitude and a hot temper and will blame others — either the child or a circumstance. Continuing further, Ms. Johnson provides listings of the traits common to potential physical, emotional, and sexual offenders. [8]

The Job Interview

The employment interview is probably the most traditional and widely used method of selecting individuals to fill job openings. It can generally be defined as a purposeful exchange of ideas through the asking and answering of questions. Studies by various management associations have shown that training in interviewing guidelines can effectively increase the ability of the interviewer to select the candidate with the best potential for the job, and that experience in conducting interviews over a period of time increases the accuracy of selection.

A 1995 study conducted by the American Bar Association revealed that personal interviews were perceived as the most effective screening practice by youth development organizations. The second most effective tool was previous-employer reference checks.

Preinterview

A number of things should be done prior to an interview so that the time available can be used to the best advantage. Ideally, some information should be in the hands of the applicant prior to the interview time.

A Job Description. Applicants should have a copy of the job description as outlined earlier in this chapter, plus an outline of salary, benefits, starting and closing dates of the position, number of hours of work expected, and the amount of time-off allowed. If food and housing costs are to be deducted from salary, specific amounts should be noted. In addition, if food and housing are provided as part of a salary, their relative worth should also be noted.

Job descriptions are helpful in the interviewing process because they will help to give the applicant a more comprehensive understanding of the position for which he or she may be applying.

Information about the Camp. Applicants should also have copies of brochures, material describing the general focus, the general outcomes and goals, objectives, and pertinent information about the age of campers served, fees, length of sessions, type of program, and copies of recent newsletters.

An Organization Chart. Applicants should have some indication of where in the staff line-up the position in question falls, the immediate supervising position, and the relation of that position to others on the staff.

Ideally the interviewer can review all the facts available on the candidate through pertinent correspondence, the completed application form, written references received, or the notes from telephone calls made to individuals given as references. These materials will help the interviewer plan for the areas in which he or she wishes more information and will serve to pinpoint trouble or blank spots that need further inquiry. To avoid possible charges of discrimination, the questions need to be confined to job-related material. In states where marital status is a protected category, you may not ask if the person is married, single, divorced, who resides with the applicant, or what title (Mrs., Miss, etc.) they would prefer to be called. You may not ask race, color, religion, national origin, age, or the year they graduated from high school or college. You may, however, ask how many years of high school or college the applicant completed and which degrees they have been awarded. Other questions such as what clubs they belong to, what they do in their spare time, political affiliations, or personal financial matters are also not considered job related.

Under the Americans With Disabilities Act of 1990, it can be viewed as discriminatory if you ask questions about an individual and his or her abilities that are not directly related to abilities necessary to perform job-related functions. Therefore, it is inappropriate to ask whether the applicant has any disability. You may, however, ask a question that takes the focus away from the disability and places it on the completion of essential job functions. For instance, "Are there any reasons you would have difficulty performing any of the essential elements of the job?"[9]

It is well to review some of the questions you may and may not ask in this area:

You May Ask	You May Not Ask
Can you perform the essential functions of this job?	Do you have a disability?
Describe or demonstrate how you would perform this job or function.	Do you need reasonable accommodations to perform functions?
Can you meet attendance requirements?	What number of days were you absent on your last job?
	Were you ever addicted to drugs or treated for drug addiction or abuse?
Are you currently using illegal drugs?	
Have you had prior illegal drug use?	Do you take legal drugs?
What are your drinking habits?	What is your worker s' compensation history?

At the time a director decides to offer a position to a person with a disability, it is possible to ask additional questions or pose additional requirements before the person starts work. At this point, the candidate may be asked about his or her workers' compensation history, illnesses/disease/impairments, and prior sick leave history and require that the person with the disability take the same physical examination required of other entering employees.[10]

The Interview Setting

The setting of the interview provides an important background that may help or hinder the director's efforts. The time set aside should be free from distractions, telephone calls, or interruptions from other people. The room where the interview takes place should have adequate lighting and ventilation and comfortable chairs. Avoid placing the desk between the interviewer and the interviewee to reduce the interviewer's dominant role and to help break the ice. Sit side by side in comfortable chairs for a more relaxing and less threatening environment. Privacy is an important factor; the interview should not be held in an area where other people can pass through or look on, or where the conversation can be overheard.

The Interview Plan

After the available information has been organized, the interviewer should develop a specific plan for the interview. It is helpful to prepare a list of questions to ask all candidates for a particular job, as well as specific questions that relate to the information provided by the applicant. Generally, the director needs to explore five basic factors with applicants.

Intellectual Skills and Aptitudes. During the interview, the interviewer needs to assess the applicant's intellectual capacity (or the ability to solve problems) and his or her skill application or effectiveness (how well the applicant applies and uses intellectual capacity). This information can be obtained from a general survey of a scholastic record, together with pertinent questions on work experience and performance.

Motivational Characteristics. Primarily, these characteristics may be evaluated by discovering what a person likes to do or finds satisfaction in doing: interests, activities, best subjects in school. These may well come to light in discussing his or her long-term goals and aspirations and reasons for applying for the position in question.

Personality Strengths and Limitations. Behavior, traits, characteristics, and temperament all reveal how a person interacts with work environments and with people. Questions regarding relationships with people with whom the applicant has worked on prior jobs may open this area for more information. Interpersonal relationships indicate what a person is like: shy, confident, aggressive, withdrawn, forceful, arrogant, open, outgoing, passive, or dependent. Occasionally, the interviewer may begin to get vague, negative feelings in this area, along with subtle and nonverbal clues. These should be heeded; if the interviewer reacts negatively to the person, it is possible that others will also.

Knowledge and Experience. From his or her past record, which of the job experiences will be most helpful to him or her in the job that is open? Will any of the applicant's experiences hinder him or her in the current job?

Degree of Comfort with the Philosophy and Approach of the Camp. Rather than seeking acquiescence to the camp's philosophy, questions that reveal whether the person's individual approach is consistent with the camp's approach should be asked. Dr. Richard M. Strean suggests that the director "take advantage of the hiring process as the first, often overlooked step in counselor management, an opportunity to hire people who share the camp's philosophy and understand directors' expectations. . . . Such a candidate is far more likely to do what the director would want done when supervisors are not watching for the simple reason that the candidate would tend to do it anyway."[11]

In the light of these five areas, another look at the application and reference material will aid in blocking out areas where additional conversation is needed. A list of these questions in logical order will serve as a reminder during the interview and also provide documentation of specific questions used in interviewing candidates.

The General Approach

Note Taking. During the interview, the taking of notes provides an organized way of recording data that may be overlooked and of ensuring that a significant response or reaction is not forgotten. It is difficult, however, to take notes and give attention to what is being said at the same time, and the note taking may distract the person being interviewed. To best facilitate note taking, the pad should be placed as unobtrusively as possible, preferably in a position where the interviewee cannot read what is being written. In this way, the process becomes an integral part of the situation and can be more readily accepted by the applicant.

Establishing a Good Climate. Applicants are often ill at ease and apprehensive as well as threatened in the face of authority. If the interviewer can show a friendly and interested acceptance at the beginning, the applicant may be willing to respond in a frank and open manner. If the applicant seems reluctant to talk, a genuine compliment or sincere praise on some past experience or achievement noted in the application may put the person at ease. If an open, frank, and relatively nonthreatening climate can be established, the interviewee will generally respond as desired.

Leading Questions. Questions phrased in such a way as to indicate the response desired should be avoided. The question, "Did you take part in extracurricular activities in college?" indicates to the applicant that this is important. The applicant will then begin to search his or her experience for a suitable reply. A more general approach might be, "Tell me about your college experience; what did you find particularly helpful?"

Open-Ended Questions. It is good to open each topic area with a broad, open-ended question, for instance, "Would you tell me something about your high school days?" The interviewer will then be free to take notes and observe mannerisms and behavior patterns while the applicant determines how much or how little to tell. Questions can be used to guide the direction of the interview, to open areas for discussion, and to encourage participation.

General to Specific Questions. Questions should move gradually from the general to the more specific. From "Would you tell me about your work with the YMCA?" (general question) to "What did you like least and most about that job?" (specific question).

Self-Appraisal Questions. Questions should be directed to motivating self-appraisal. "Do you believe that you effectively accomplished that particular job?" "If you could repeat that experience, what would you do differently?"

Controlling the Flow. Although the interviewer should be in control of the interview at all times, it is to his or her advantage to listen and to try not to interrupt. Natural pauses can be used to check the sequence of points on the interview plan, to see that facts in each area are adequate, and to keep the communication moving along. While the applicant provides the factual answers, the interviewer can determine the answers to some other intangible questions: How does the applicant communicate ideas? Can he or she conceptualize effectively? Is he or she shallow or superficial in his or her thinking? Is he or she perceptive to the social situation?

Conducting the Interview

An interviewer should remain impartial, neither condemning nor condoning what he or she hears. To provide a positive setting, the person conducting the interview should not react negatively to new ideas or unfamiliar subjects. Opinions should be disassociated from facts; time should not be wasted in disagreeing with an opinion. Time should not be taken up with facts contained on the application, but the emphasis should be on moving in the direction the interview needs to go. Although first impressions are important, it is essential that the interviewer try not to form conclusions too quickly.

If it is necessary to secure information that may not be comfortable for the applicant to reveal (e.g., why a particular job was held for a short period or details on a problem with a particular supervisor), the interviewer should indicate that such discomfort is understandable. Essential questions may be asked more than once in different ways to find out from the reaction how strongly the applicant may feel about a particular topic.

Concluding the Interview

An effective technique for ending the appointment is to summarize the interview. At this point, the applicant may be more relaxed and relay additional information. If it is determined during the interview that the person is not qualified for the position, he or she should be told so at this time. If additional information is needed, the interviewer must be sure that the interviewee understands specifically what is required, and a time should be set for receipt of the information. The applicant should also be told the time at which he or she may expect to hear the decision regarding the position.

Documentation

As soon as the applicant has departed, the interviewer should make any additional notes. If a number of applicants are being interviewed in close sequence, making notes immediately after each interview will help to crystallize facts and impressions and help distinguish one applicant from another. Answers to critical questions such as those about abuse and discipline are important to record. The notes from the interview should be dated and signed by the interviewer and placed in the personnel file; this provides further documentation in the endless task of showing that every precaution was taken in employing an individual in case there is allegation of a child abuse incident and subsequent litigation or unfounded litigation. Some interviewers find it useful to review by making a list of positive and negative facts ascertained during the interview and to rate job qualifications against a predetermined list.

Evaluation of the Interview

One effective way of developing and refining skills essential to good interviewing is to make a personal evaluation of the performance immediately after the session. One approach is to look at the original interview plan and compare it to the actual interview. Did I follow the general plan? Did I miss any important category? Did I succeed in putting the applicant at ease? Did my questions get the responses needed? Did the interview move smoothly and stay on track or was it sporadic and difficult to control?

Another means of evaluating an interview is to work from the personal angle. Did I talk too much? Did my personal prejudices and attitudes come through to the applicant, or did I maintain objectivity? Did I conduct the interview from the point of view of the applicant? Did I respond negatively in any instance? If I could redo the interview, what would I add or delete? What approach would I change? When considering impressions from the interview, it is important to remember that the overall picture is the most important. If you are undecided, you may wish to review your notes and information with a colleague.

These few minutes spent in considering interview performance will pay off in terms of increased perceptiveness and flexibility in handling the next interview and in operating more effectively in the selection process. In the final analysis, of course, the acid test of the interview is whether the result is a successful selection of a staff member who performs well on the job.

As part of an interview evaluation, Robert Ditter suggests some warning signs that he terms "red flags" which possibly characterize a personality prone to abuse children.

"Who ran the interview, you or the candidate? If you found that you were answering a lot of questions or being distracted by tangential conversation consistently throughout the interview, raise a red flag. Such behavior should make you wonder what a person might be avoiding. (Such behavior could indicate a 'controlling' or 'insecure' personality.)

"How much of a peer support system does this person have? Is he or she a drifter? Currently, are there significant other adults in his or her life? Are there strong connections to others, besides children, to give a sense of balance and support? If there are a lot of negative answers, raise a red flag.

"Does this person spend too much time with children? Does he or she seem to plan time-off activities which sound too much like work (typical of a physical abuser) or involve more time spent with children? If he or she also has weak peer relationships, this is a serious cause for a red flag alert."[12]

Becca Cowan Johnson, author of *For Their Sake*, would add: "How does this person describe how he or she was disciplined while growing up? Was it strict, appropriate, abusive? That is, does a person report an abusive past? Was the abuse emotional, physical, and/or sexual? Studies indicate a strong tendency toward repetition of experiences."[13]

Employment Agreement

It is accepted practice to provide each staff member with an employment agreement at the time of hire. The formality of the written agreement will vary from situation to situation, but in any event, the staff member and the director should each have a copy of the document that they have both signed. A signed agreement between a director and a volunteer can also be healthy since it clarifies obligations on both sides and shows the responsibilities assumed by the volunteer.

In many states, employees are regarded to be at-will employees unless there is a written agreement specifying an employment period. The advantage of at-will status is that the employer can release the person earlier than had been anticipated if enrollment is slow or conditions warrant. An employment agreement may specify the dates of expected employment and indicate that the employment is at-will. Of course, an employment agreement does not force the employee to remain should he or she decide to terminate. Using the word *contract* instead of *employment agreement* may imply an independent contract or relationship. It is wise to have the format and wording of such an agreement reviewed by the camp's legal counsel because there are legal implications that may be binding.

A sample employment agreement is shown in illustration 7.4. Such a letter usually contains the following items:

- Dates of employment or time commitment, with expected termination date

- Title of the position and reference to job description

- Remuneration

- Statement that employment is at-will and may be terminated by either party

- Policy for termination by the staff member or the camp

- Statement of agreement by the staff member that he or she will abide by the personnel policies that are attached or the specific policies included in the agreement

- Dates of signing

- Signatures of staff member and director (where the staff member is under the state legal adult age, the director may wish to have the letter cosigned by one parent)

Personnel Files

Personnel files that include the application, references, contract, and eventual performance appraisal reports are normally kept for each staff member. These are confidential files and should be kept out of reach of all but supervisory personnel. Medical records on staff members should be kept separate from personnel files. Note that an employee may request to see his or her file. All of these files should be kept for a lengthy period of time, at least until the youngest camper at the time of that person's employment has reached six to eighteen months beyond the age of majority in the state of operation. Again, this is a matter to be reviewed with legal counsel.

Rehiring

Returning staff are important in the entire recruitment process. A director counts on retaining a significant number of staff from the previous season in order to maintain quality, continuity, and tradition. However, rehiring previous staff must not be done blindly. It must be recognized that often nine months or more has transpired since the last experience with the person. Much can happen during that period to change a person's attitude, experience level, and relationships.

Some directors go as far as to require returning staff to go through the entire employment process again: application, references, background checks, and so on. Other directors use a form to ask the person to update the earlier application, perhaps by attaching a photocopy of the face sheet of the previous application and asking once again about driving record or criminal convictions. At the same time, the applicant can share additional experiences relative to the camp setting that would enable him or her to expand his or her duties. Where a state requires a criminal background check, such a check would need to be done annually. In any

Illustration 7.4

Staff Employment Agreement

Dear _____:

Camp _____ is happy to offer you a position as a _____ (insert position) on our staff. The position of _____ is described in detail in the attached job description, but do keep in mind that from time to time the administration may assign other duties deemed appropriate.

Your employment will begin on _____, 200___, and we expect that it will terminate on _____, 200___. Your salary will be based on the gross rate of $_____ per week. Deductions from your gross salary will include:

- federal and state withholding tax
- health insurance of $_____
- resulting in a net weekly rate of $_____

It should be noted that all of our employees are employed on an at-will basis.

Attached is a copy of the camp's personnel policies, outlining time off, behavioral expectations, and related matters. Your signature to a copy of this letter indicates your acceptance of the terms of employment and agreement to these personnel policies. Please return no later than _____ (date).

The camp community provides a unique opportunity for team work, leadership, and service to our participants. We trust you will join us in our endeavor to make this a successful season for our campers, and for you.

Sincerely,

Camp Director

I accept this position as outlined.

Signature _____Date _____

case, the director has a responsibility for developing a specific plan for ensuring his or her confidence in the background, suitability, and fitness of every individual on the staff, including individuals returning to the camp staff, however tremendous they may have been the previous year.

Appendix B provides a checklist for risk management in the recruitment and screening of employees.

Checkpoints

1. Identify the different steps taken during the staff screening and employment process to prevent employing people with a proclivity toward child or sexual abuse. Identify the steps taken to protect the camp in case of an incident.

2. Write out a series of questions you would ask in a job interview. Read them aloud to see how they sound. After revision, try them in an interview. Keep adapting them as necessary.

3. Outline the process your camp will use to screen returning staff members.

Related Standards and Guidelines

Accreditation Standards for Camp Programs and Services: HR-1, 3-5;

Guidelines for Conference and Retreat Centers: II-34

[1] Reuel A. Benson and Jacob A. Goldberg. 1951. *The Camp Counselor*. New York: McGraw-Hill. p. 41.

[2] William A. Becker and Dawn Shelar. 1991. "Employing Seniors at Camp." *Camping Magazine*, Vol. 63, No. 4, February. p. 49.

[3] Christy L. Phillips. 1996. "Find the Staff You Need." *Camping Magazine*, Vol. 69, No. 2, November/December. p. 4.

[4] Nancy Halliday. 1998. "International Flavor — The Value of Including Internationals on Your Staff This Summer." *Christian Camp and Conference Journal* by CCI/USA, Vol. 2, No. 1, January/February. p.12. Reprinted with permission.

[5] Marge Scanlin. 1993. "Getting References — The Task of Finding Good Staff." *CampLine*, Vol. 2, No. 2, October. p. 1.

[6] Ibid. p. 2.

[7] Robert Ditter. 1986. "Protecting Our Campers: How to Recognize Various Forms of Child Abuse." *Camping Magazine*, Vol. 58, No. 3, January. p. 23.

[8] Becca Cowan Johnson. 1992. *For Their Sake*. Martinsville, IN: American Camping Association. pp. 103–113.

[9] National Camp Executives Group. 1992. *Camp Director's Primer to the Americans With Disabilities Act of 1990*. Glen Allen, VA: Markel Insurance Company. p. 17.

[10] *Interviewing and the Americans With Disabilities Act of 1990*. Glen Allen, VA: Markel Insurance Company. p. 17.

[11] Richard M. Strean. 1996. "Invisible Counselors — Managing What You Don't See." *Camping Magazine* Vol. 69, No.1, September/October. p. 34.

[12] Ditter. 1986. p. 23.

[13] Johnson. 1992. p. 116.

Staff Orientation & Training

To the camp director falls the task of taking a number of individuals and helping them to achieve this peak of know-how-on-the-job, at the same time welding the total staff into a smoothly functioning team. It is no simple job, but one to which the camp director must turn much of his energy and planning.[1]

taff training is probably one of the most difficult but potentially productive functions for a camp director who seeks to create a favorable climate and to set the tone for the summer season. The training of staff falls into three general categories:

Orientation — the period from the signing of the employment agreement to the staff member's arrival at camp.

Precamp training — the intensive period at camp set aside before the arrival of campers.

In-service training (during the camp season) — ongoing supervisory conferences, day-to-day problem solving, and staff meetings which include in-service training.

Orientation

The preparation of the staff member for his or her job begins with the materials that are presented with the application for employment and the subsequent interview. It is essential that the prospective staff member understands the philosophy and desired outcomes and goals of the camp, as well as the unique makeup of a camp community, because the interplay within that community has much to do with the accomplishment of the camp's desired outcomes and goals. The information given a staff member in the interview and in correspondence must cover not only the job functions but also the living conditions, transportation arrangements, philosophy of operation, and patterns of staff relationships.

During staff recruitment and interviews, the interviewee's concern for securing the job and the director's concern for hiring a staff member often push concerns about the details of camp living into the background. The director cannot, therefore, depend on the description given at the interview or in prospective employee materials to familiarize the employee thoroughly with the setting and responsibilities. The time between recruitment and reporting to camp is longer than it is for many other jobs and provides candidates a long time for second thoughts and opportunities for other jobs. This timing issue, added to the potential for a last-minute vacancy, makes it even more important to use the time between a staff member's hiring and reporting to camp for additional orientation.

If staffers come from within a hundred-mile radius, a number of orientation approaches that cannot normally be used by a camp whose staff comes from across the country can be used. In the former case, two or three meetings can be planned at a central location over the spring — giving new staff an opportunity to meet each other and former staff the chance to begin developing relationships and to secure informal orientation. Local authorities or resource people who would ordinarily be unable to travel a longer distance or to come for a more extended period to precamp training can often be recruited for presentations at such meetings.

A winter sport weekend, spring work weekend, or a day at the camp can provide orientation to the facilities and property, as well as give further opportunity for new employees to get acquainted with returning staff and to experience the camp living situation. These events also give the director a firsthand look at the new staff members and a chance to determine what approaches or content should be included in staff training.

A spring meeting of the local section of the American Camping Association or Christian Camping International usually provides a number of workshops and opportunities for additional certifications that are of interest to newly hired camp staff. In addition to workshops, these section meetings provide the opportunity for staff from all the camps in the area to interact. Such interaction provides a broader insight into the camp profession and, often, as the staff member gets involved, can lead to a commitment beyond the current summer. Many camp directors encourage membership in one or both organizations and may financially contribute in order for staff to attend workshops or join organizations.

In the case of camps with geographically scattered staff, orientation will most often depend upon a visit with the director, Internet communication, or printed materials. Frequent newsletters help stimulate interest and familiarize staff members with other staff, place names, and other features of camp. In addition, a staff manual can be a valuable orientation and training device as well as a helpful administrative tool for outlining policy and procedures. It takes a great deal of time, the cooperative assistance from key staff, and constant revision to prepare and maintain the most useful staff manual. "Current employment law emphasizes . . . that a carefully written employee handbook is essential."[2] A staff manual should include the following items. Those items with an asterisk (*) and other items of similar nature may be added to the manual during precamp training as the matters are discussed.

- A brief history of the camp

- The camp's purpose and desired outcomes and goals

- A map of the property

- An organization chart of staff, clearly delineating supervisory lines

- A job description for each position

- The personnel policies, including a statement concerning compliance with local, state, and federal nondiscrimination laws

- Other policies and operational procedures:
  - Rules with specific disciplinary actions
  - A description of compensation policies including a statement that all raises, other than uniform or automatic wage increases, are at the discretion of the employer
  - Any laws affecting the duty of the employee

- A description of the operating body (agency, church, corporation)

- A list of items staff members will need to bring to camp

- A bibliography of helpful materials

- General counseling tips*

- Emergency procedures (e.g., for lost campers and natural disasters)*

- A statement that the staff manual/employee handbook does not constitute a contract of employment and that the camp reserves the right to terminate employment at any time

Some directors use a rotating library of three or four books or articles that best describe the camp's program and counseling philosophy for staff orientation. Some materials can be transferred to the camp's Web page giving staff the ability to access information there. The assignment of certain articles or portions of the books for discussion by individual staff during staff training may motivate further reading and focus interest.

Whatever information is sent to new staff before camp, it is vital that it be condensed as much as possible and its importance or value highlighted. If the staff member is a teacher or student, classes will occupy much of his or her attention, and only a limited amount of preparation or reading can logically be expected. Therefore, the director should choose material carefully and plan to get it to staff well in advance. ACA has a youth development/behavior management online course, *Camp is for the Camper*, for camp directors to use with their staff prior to precamp. The course gives staff a chance to interact with each other and to discuss camper development and behavior prior to camp. The camp director serves as the instructor, and directors have found this especially helpful for international staff. Information on the course can be found on the ACA Web site.

Orientation is equally as important in day camp as in resident camp. Because day camp staff members tend to be from the same community and many times hold full-time jobs, staff sessions on Saturdays or Sundays may provide the orientation and training time needed prior to staff training immediately before camp.

It is important that the camp director plan ahead to ensure that staff members receive needed camp information as early as possible. Students can often use school health service personnel for their physicals if they receive the form early enough. Providing a list of clothing and equipment needed at camp soon after employment will enable the staff member to shop carefully. Other information sent to staff should include: the date and time they are expected at camp, the transportation available, the phone number and address of camp, and the directions to camp.

However experienced in camp life a new staff member may be, he or she will always feel a degree of concern about a new site, a new camp community, and a new employer. Every step the director takes to relieve this concern and to help the new employee adjust and feel more confident will better his or her chances of success upon arrival at camp.

Precamp Training

A precamp staff training program is one of the most effective forms of staff development and of assuring the camp will fulfill its mission. Basically, the purpose is to bring staff together to develop personal skills and competency for the job and to mold individuals into a functional team for accomplishing the camp's desired outcomes and goals. Precamp sessions also seek to provide opportunities for personal evaluation and growth.

In order to plan the most productive type of staff training, the camp director should begin early in the year to pull together possible topics and activities and to see what suggestions can be found in evaluations of the preceding year's training. If at all possible, the planning should include members of the program and administrative staff for the coming season; it is often good to add one or two experienced counselors to the group. As the planning begins, the camp director needs to consider a number of factors.

Staff Come from Varied Backgrounds. Many will have had experience in other types of camps and will be prone to making comparisons, while others may not have been exposed to the demands of camp living. Some may come from other countries or sections of this country remote to the camp location and will have no knowledge of or familiarity with the natural environment or other resources of the new area.

New Staff and Experienced Staff Will Be Trained Together. There are usually some difficulties in planning the training with returning staff and new or inexperienced staff in the same group. Variation in the format and schedule of the training from year to year and the use of experienced staff to share their abilities with the new group can help to alleviate some of the problems. Working in small groups, when possible, gives new staff a chance to integrate more easily into the larger staff.

All Staff Need to Participate in the Training Process. This does not mean that every staff member needs to participate in every session of training, but certain sessions apply to all staff (i.e., administrative, support, counseling, returning, and new staff). For example, it is very important that kitchen staff or maintenance staff understand the philosophy of the camp and the importance and goals of the program operation, but they may not need the additional sessions related to camper behavior, conflict resolution, and the like. All staff members need to review personnel policies and practices as well as camp rules so that there can be no misunderstanding.

Training Usually Centers On Counselors and Staff Who Work Directly with Campers. Because they make up the largest portion of the staff and are primarily responsible for helping the camp achieve the desired youth development outcomes and goals, the training usually centers on counseling staff. The difficulty is that this group is probably composed primarily of individuals whose age and lack of experience may mean that they are at a loss about how to translate the mission or desired outcomes and goals into everyday activities. The director's task is complicated by the need to clarify for them the connection between the camp's desired outcomes and goals and its procedures and policies of operation. Such understanding will, it is hoped, be gained in precamp training.

Experiential Training

Some directors find it helpful to organize the training period, to some degree, after the pattern in which counselors will work with campers. The counselors, in this plan, are divided into small living groups under the supervision of an administrative staff member or experienced counselor acting as counselor or facilitator. Within these groups, they can function as their camper groups will later in the season. They will move through the usual opening schedule: check in at the office, report to the health center with their health examination forms, tour the campsite, eat a meal in the dining hall, clean their cabins, and so on. This plan has the potential of orienting the counselor more swiftly and provides a small living group to whom new counselors can more easily relate. This pattern can be continued daily throughout the training time and related to the camper experience in as detailed a manner as is desirable.

In any case, the training needs to be experientially based. Bob Ditter suggests that activities used in staff training "either provide a shared experience for counselors or tap into the counselors' own experience to make them more sensitive to children." He further quotes Ray Diamond of Camp Kokanda as suggesting, "If my Group Heads and Head Counselors have seen it first and have had a chance to practice it, they are less worried that some activity they might do with staff will be a flop."[3]

During the initial training period, habits will be formed, patterns established, attitudes developed, and relationships with peers and supervisors begun. Regardless of the necessarily high concentration of time on the factors that create a good experience for the campers, the staff member's greatest gain should be in his or her own growth, maturity, and development of potential. The advantage, of course, is that such personal development among staff members results in increased benefit to the campers with whom staffers will live and work.

On the practical side, some basic outcomes and goals need to be reached during staff training:

- Infusing staff with the basic philosophy and the desired outcomes and goals of the camp and defining their implication for procedures and operations

- Fostering a sense of pride in the camp job and developing a harmonious working relationship among staff

- Teaching and providing practice of necessary program skills

- Developing an understanding of the characteristics of various age groups being served and providing an insight into working with them

- Providing the opportunity for staff to understand working policies and procedures as they relate to individual staff responsibilities and the camp as a whole

- Teaching individual and group skills in working with people

On a more individual and personal level, there are other desired outcomes and goals for the staff. There should be opportunities during the training for personal interaction so individuals find it easy to establish personal relationships with peers, immediate supervisors, and administrative staff. The use of experiential training activities can help guide a staff member to an increased self-knowledge and understanding of him- or herself.

Scheduling

To deal successfully with all these factors and to accomplish the desired results in the time allotted demands careful planning. The time set aside for training never seems to be sufficient to cover all the priorities; even an experienced director who has worked at staff training over a period of years may not be pleased with the results.

The time allotted to precamp training varies from a minimum of twenty-four hours for day camp staff and six days for resident and trip or travel staff to as long as two or more weeks depending upon the program and size of staff. A period of six to ten days will usually suffice. Shorter time periods seldom allow sufficient time for building the spirit of camaraderie so important in a camp community. Generally, staff are contracted to arrive for and are paid for this training period.

Before beginning to fill in a time schedule or consider topics, a director may find it helpful to review training schedules and postcamp evaluations from previous years.

Discussions with staff who were present for some of those periods may provide insights into the character and effectiveness of the methods used. The evaluations at the end of the previous training sessions and the summer season can add additional data.

After a block of time is set aside, a director is ready to decide what he or she expects to accomplish during the training period. Setting these intentions and desired outcomes and goals will do much to help choose and prioritize subjects and activities.

As the schedule is developed, the progression of the activities and sessions during the week should be considered. Early get-acquainted activities in the larger group will help put new and old staff at ease and give opportunity for new relationships. From this point, it is easier to move toward team-building activities in smaller groups. As staff members experience various program elements, the flow of camp will become more real. At this point, the group will be more open to child-centered training, and various techniques and approaches can be tied into the camp's program design and desired outcomes and goals. The smaller the living or working group (up to five or six people), the greater the personal involvement and commitment will be.

Child Abuse

One of the topics that should be dealt with during training is child abuse. The topic should be presented in such a way as to reinforce the alliance between the director, staff members, and parents, rather than to create an atmosphere of mistrust or fear. Placing comments about child abuse in the context of the stress or wear and tear that camp life can have on everyone provides an opportunity to talk about the possibility of impatience or unintentional meanness of counselors toward campers. This is one of the chief symptoms of burnout. Including this topic in staff training will send a clear, specific message that you, as a director, are concerned and are moving to ensure the quality of care for all campers.

The discussion should include a clear and frank detailing of the basic definitions, tips for helping staff monitor their own level of fatigue, and guidelines for handling a situation that may have the potential for child abuse or child abuse accusations. Legal ramifications should be clearly pointed out, both for the director, who is required by law to report allegations of possible abuse, and for the staff member who may be involved. Ground rules concerning the continued employment of a staff member alleged to have abused a child should be concisely stated. The camp administration has a responsibility to report such alleged abuse if observed at camp. Legal responsibility for reporting suspected child abuse differs from state to state, but every state has a reporting requirement today. Make certain that you and your staff are aware of laws and reporting methods in your state. (Some states, such as California, require every staff member in contact with children to sign a form acknowledging their awareness of state laws that mandate them to report any suspected or known incidents of child abuse.)

Practical examples of behavior management should be discussed. Role-playing can be helpful as different behavior problems are illustrated and methods of management discussed.

In addition, staff should be alerted to watch for signs of physical or sexual abuse that may have occurred to the child prior to his or her arrival at camp. Symptoms outlined in chapter 4 should be discussed with counselors, and policy concerning notification of the appropriate camp administrators should be outlined.

In her book, *For Their Sake*, Becca Cowan Johnson suggests two different formats that can be used to cover this topic for staff training. Other chapters in the book provide a wealth of reference material and current information that can form an excellent basis for staff discussion.[4]

Varying Training Sessions

Actual training sessions should be planned for variety and balance. For instance, sessions requiring physical activity should be alternated with sessions requiring sitting and listening. A variety of teaching techniques should be employed to ensure maximum attention and comprehension: guest speakers, demonstrations, films, charts, discussions, panels, and human relations games and activities. Variation in numbers can stimulate participation; group sessions where all participate may be alternated with small group gatherings.

In any case, the training needs to provide participation, demonstration, and interaction around the learning. Since many staff people are college students, they will have been exposed to all types of academic techniques and may have some resistance to being bombarded with facts and theories beyond the end of the school year. They may well expect to be far removed from the formal presentation of knowledge and anxious to have physical exercise.

Work sessions, with specific tasks assigned to small groups, can get necessary work done before camp opening and provide an opportunity for small groups of staff to work together. However, the director should avoid the temptation to spend fifty percent or more of the staff training time on the physical tasks required to open camp. The painting, cleanup, and repairs should be completed by a work crew well in advance of staff arrival so that the time set aside for training can be devoted primarily to the desired outcomes and goals.

In searching for ways to make the training successful, the director must assess the needs and feelings of individual staff members. An open-ended discussion early in the period can reveal needs felt by a number of staff. Some directors also use a written needs assessment to identify needs that a staff member may be hesitant to mention early in the camp relationship. The size and experience of the staff will, in part, determine the method the director uses to gain an understanding of staff members' individual needs and objectives. Assigning sessions or topics to individual staff with expertise in a specific area can increase staff participation.

Outside resource people from universities, county health departments, the U.S. Forest Service, or state natural resources departments can often provide additional expertise for specific presentations. The involvement of such people will also build relationships in the local area. However, the selection and spacing of such presenters should be carefully scheduled so that they do not interfere with the development of group spirit and the overall thrust of the training.

Several other processes should be included in the training period. Specialty program directors or department heads should have an opportunity to confer with staff who will be under their immediate supervision. Procedures and responsibilities of each staff member can then be defined before actual operations begin. A tour of the campsite should also be included, along with an orientation about the region in which the camp is located. Health and safety procedures need to be covered in detail, as do rules and procedures regarding the dining room, waterfront, and camp store. There should also be some opportunities for relaxation and fun — and simply for talking together. Appendix G offers a list of training topics suggested to meet ACA standards.

An overnight camping trip (or one slightly longer) can be a productive part of staff training. Such a trip would allow time for practice of camping or outdoor living skills and latitude for working and relaxing together in a more informal setting. This type of overnight or trip is even more important in a day camp where training may be day-only sessions that do not allow the time needed for socialization.

When setting the time schedule for training week, the director should plan a day off for staff between the close of training and the arrival of campers. The intensity of the training period can often be exhausting, and the staff needs the relaxation and perspective of time away from camp as well as an opportunity to purchase any items they did not know to bring with them.

Training for Supervisory Staff

The supervisory staff will need some training that will not be of general interest or profit to other staff. However, supervision skills must be addressed because the supervisors are responsible for the staff who must seek to achieve the camp's desired outcomes and goals directly with the campers. A good supervisor with the framework of a well-executed supervisory program can effect changes in staff performance and skills resulting in better experiences for campers and more personal development and a higher return rate among staff.

As a result of a study of 100 camps and how they train supervisors, Becker and Shepard state: "In many cases, however, new supervisors are often thrown to the wolves with little or no supervisory training. Camp administrators almost never start a summer without extensive, comprehensive precamp training. So, then, why do many camps skimp on training and orientation for head counselors?"[5]

The 7.5-hour training resource, *So You Want to Be a Supervisor*, available through the American Camping Association, outlines the roles supervisors play, a process for analyzing skills and handling appropriate and inappropriate behaviors, as well as an individual supervision plan for each staff member. The curriculum also covers many of the following responsibilities that should be covered in supervisory training:

- **How to oversee staff.** What are the specific functions and roles the director expects supervisors to carry out?

- **How to treat staff members as individuals.** It is important that a supervisor learn early in his or her experience the importance of treating staff as individuals and respecting that individuality. In the beginning, the supervisor ought to learn all the details about his or her staff: likes and dislikes, talents, skills, motivations, and how they react to different situations and to their supervisor.

- **How to praise staff.** Recognition of work well done has long been known as an important factor in motivating staff. This recognition can be on a personal basis, at staff meetings, or part of a supervisory conference. Public recognition or recognition before one's peers is even more effective as a motivator.

- **How to challenge staff.** A supervisor who believes in the potential of individuals he or she supervises can inspire them to accomplish a task simply because he or she believes that an individual has the ability to do the job. It is essential that a supervisor always remember to look beyond current job performance to the capacity a person has for achieving.

- **How to deal with inappropriate behavior.** This is an important function of a supervisor, especially in a camp setting, since staff problems may very quickly exert a negative impact on other staff and campers. The biggest hurdle is to get the staff member to see the problem; if this is accomplished, methods of solving the problem can then be dealt with. An important part of the supervisor's effectiveness with problems is to address the behavior and to be supportive but not to condemn the person.

- **How to conduct supervisory conferences.** These conferences may be difficult for new supervisors, particularly if there are negative points to be discussed. It is essential that he or she learn how to conduct such conferences with the proper balance of support, praise, and constructive criticism. A supervisor needs to comprehend how to make negative feedback a more positive experience by suggesting ways in which the staff member can improve his or her performance. Most importantly, the supervisor needs to convey that his or her regard for the staff member has not changed because of the problems.

- **How to provide on-the-spot supervision.** Not all supervisory comments can wait until a supervisory conference. On the other hand, pointing out an improper method or a violation of a procedure in front of other staff or campers at the time of occurrence will likely be embarrassing and difficult and is not appropriate unless the issue is one of immediate health and safety. Supervisors need help in learning the best way to share tips and observations with staff soon after such behavior is observed.

- **How to work with the camp director.** Supervisors should be able to solve routine camper and staff problems in a consistent manner without consulting with the director. But some problems should be discussed in full; the dilemma is to identify which is which. The director needs to be kept in the picture because he or she is usually one step removed from the day-to-day operation, but he or she does not need to be consulted about every detail.

- **How to handle framework.** A clear understanding of the underlying philosophy and desired outcomes and goals should be discussed so that supervisors know how their responsibilities and the responsibilities of their subordinates fit into the total framework; this knowledge allows them to work from a secure base of full understanding of the whys and wherefores.

- **How to handle the supervisor's role.** It is often difficult for a new supervisor to understand how much his or her role has changed as he or she moves into supervising other staff. To be adequately prepared for this role, he or she must recognize that with such leadership comes a difference in the way he or she is viewed by subordinate staff. As the person ultimately responsible for performance of staff, he or she may become the motivating force behind outcomes and goals that other staff members may not share.

- **How to deal with the alleged abuser.** The general rules for reporting an alleged abuse situation and the protection of the abused child are covered earlier in this chapter; however, in most camps, there is a policy about what the process is when an accusation is made. The staff member is usually suspended with or without pay. The director should give advanced thought to any role the supervisor might play with the alleged abuser (e.g., reporting to director, being with the accused until he or she leaves camp). John Durall suggests that "the abusing staff person may feel anxious or depressed. He may be preoccupied with immediate issues, such as being arrested and going to jail. He may be embarrassed to face co-workers and the director. He also may be worried about going to court, being sentenced to jail, handling the effects the incident may have on his future, and facing family and friends. On a deeper level, he may feel shame, guilt, and self-devaluation, as well as hopeless and desperate."[6]

The supervisory and appraisal process is discussed in detail in chapter 9.

Documentation

A schedule of the entire precamp training week with annotations about content and presenters should be kept in the permanent file. It is also wise to have an attendance sheet for each session for staff to sign as they enter the training area. They should be helped to understand that this is a protection for them in the sense that it documents that they have had training in the identified areas, in case their qualifications are challenged after an alleged incident at camp; the director should also document how staff that are new or miss precamp training receive instruction. Again, all of this documentation is part of the risk management plan and a protection package that the camp director develops and preserves in case of a lawsuit or alleged abuse incident.

In-Service Training

When precamp training concludes and campers arrive, the training of staff does not end. With seasonal staff, training must be continued throughout the season: first, in an effort to ensure at all times a quality experience for the participant and, second, to address issues that come up during camp. Also, many of the staff will return another season and the training will bear further dividends. After precamp training and during supervision, supervisors often have the best handle on what topics need to be covered in such training and can help develop the format. Common problems or voids in performance will appear in a number of staff members as the season goes along. This can occasion a meeting or staff-training module designed to fill that void or deal with a specific problem. Because time is precious and staff is under pressure, such training periods should be planned carefully and developed for a succinct and practical presentation.

A meeting devoted solely to a training problem or concept focuses staff attention on the training without the time competition and attention pressures of a regular staff meeting. However, topics for the special training sessions are often derived from the regular staff meeting, supervisory observation, or conference.

In-service training sessions may also be an extension of topics begun during precamp training, where time or readiness of staff members did not allow more advanced discussion. In fact, many training topics become more meaningful after the staff members have had experience in their program areas or with participants. Because of the experience gained at this point, it is vital that some time in the training module be allowed for discussion and sharing among group members.

The use of outside resource people is most effective in these in-service training sessions when the topic requires a certain expertise or authority. For example, if abuse is the topic, a psychologist or social worker with experience in the field can add a certain authority to the issue, answering questions from experience. Similarly, a naturalist with knowledge of local flora and fauna can bring expertise to a nature walk or presentation that may not have been possible during precamp.

It is critical that the topics chosen for in-service training events be timely and of practical use by the staff at that point of the season. Staff will be under considerable pressure from the ongoing program and relationships and will exhibit impatience and inattention if they do not find the session pertinent to their current day-to-day experiences.

Also, one of the realities of a camp staff group is that there are always some individuals who arrive in the middle of or after staff training. The termination of an employee necessitates a replacement early or midseason. A returning staff member cannot leave university classes until midway through staff training. A weak link is created each time a director assumes that a returning staff member understands all of the assigned responsibilities or that a new employee can "pick up" the information he or she needs as he or she goes along. Therefore, it is important to have a plan to make sure that the training topics such a staff member missed are covered before the person assumes assigned duties.

Staff Meetings

I n-service training modules are different from administrative staff meetings or all-staff meetings held on a regular basis throughout the season. The purpose of regular administrative staff meetings is the coordination of program events, operational details, personnel, and personal concerns. An opportunity should be given for all staff members to share concerns, to clear up details, or to explain decisions. It is important that matters announced or discussed at all-staff meetings be distributed in some fashion to those not present who may be on duty with campers or in other operations. Some immediate behavioral problems may be resolved at such meetings or identified for future in-service training. Staff may learn by leadership behavior modeled by the director or other administrators. These staff meetings can be considered training only in a limited sense.

Checkpoints

1. Have the dates for precamp training been clearly identified to staff at the time of the contract?

2. What are the specific desired outcomes and goals to be accomplished during the precamp training period?

3. Have staff applications and interview records been reviewed to determine areas in which particular help or instruction will be needed by individuals?

4. Which staff members with particular expertise can be used during staff training as group leaders, presenters, or instructors?

5. Are there outside resource people within fifty miles of camp who can be helpful?

6. Are you, as a director, going to assume the leadership role in staff training, or are you collaborating with other key staff or delegating the training to others entirely? How are those roles to differ?

7. Have you involved staff in designing a needs assessment to try to uncover the type of training that individual staff believe they need?

Related Standards and Guidelines

Accreditation Standards for Camp Programs and Services: HR-11–17, 19; "Additional Professional Practices": Items 26, 27

Guidelines for Conference and Retreat Centers: II-38–40

[1] Catherine T. Hammett. n.d. *A Camp Director Trains His Own Staff*. Martinsville, IN: American Camping Association. p. 7.

[2] "Written Employment Policies." 1996. *Trendlines*, Vol. VIII, No. 3, January/February.

[3] Bob Ditter. 1995. "New Direction in Staff Training and Development." *Camping Magazine*, Vol. 67, No. 3, January/February. p. 38.

[4] Becca Cowan Johnson. 1992. *For Their Sake*. Martinsville, IN: American Camping Association.pp. 121–128.

[5] W. A. Becker and Tony Shepard.1989. "Study Suggestions to Improve Camp Supervisory Training." *Camping Magazine*, Vol. 61, No. 1, January. pp. 32–35.

[6] John J. Durall. 1997. "Encountering Child Abuse at Camp." *Camping Magazine*, Vol. 70, No. 6, November/December.

Staff Supervision and Performance Appraisal

Chapter 9

Supervision is seen to be—first, last, and all the time—a relationship of persons; as such, it calls for deep qualities of heart and mind and spirit, and for acceptance of whatever disciplines and plain hard work are necessary to develop the needed abilities and skills.[1]

Possibly one of the most overlooked and underestimated procedures in general camp administration is a regular system of supervision and performance appraisal for staff. Under the pressures of the summer season, it is difficult to allot sufficient time for supervisory functions unless a plan is developed prior to camp. A regular program of supervisory conferences provides countless opportunities for stimulating individual growth, for deepening supervisor and staff relationships, and, ultimately, for upgrading job performance.

This supervisory process, if carried out in a relationship of mutual trust and respect, can be a major factor in the retention of staff. As staff members become conscious of their own personal growth through the supervisory procedure, the usual result is on-the-job satisfaction and a desire to repeat the experience. There are few jobs available to young people today that provide such a climate of interested and productive supervision.

The director has no more valuable asset for ensuring good job performance than his or her personal knowledge and relationship with the supervisory staff members who assess the job performances of their charges. This interplay of relationships provides an opportunity for the director to share in the lives of individuals with a people-oriented commitment to the camp and its programs.

Functions of a Supervisor

A supervisor has been defined as a person who holds the following responsibilities:

- The conduct of others in the achievement of a particular task

- The maintenance of quality standards

- The protection and care of materials and people under his or her control

- The rendering of services to those under his or her control

There are numerous ways to categorize functions of supervisors. Writers and trainers generally identify the following functions of supervision.

1. **Teaching Staff Their Job**

   - Understanding all the tasks required in the job being supervised

   - Teaching skills in a progressive manner (i.e., what has to be learned first, second, etc.)

   - Assessing whether and how well the skill has been learned

2. **Delegating Responsibility**

   - Assigning staff

   - Delegating tasks (e.g., ordering supplies, planning an event, supervising the wash house)

   - Determining time off and coverage for staff responsibilities (e.g., days off, rovers)

3. **Evaluating Performance and Accountability**

   - Observing performance

   - Writing reviews of staff performance

   - Holding supervisory conferences

   - Providing verbal feedback on a regular basis, both praise and constructive criticism

4. **Improving Performance**

   - Observing behavior

   - Analyzing skill performance

   - Determining what has to be improved and how to improve it

   - Establishing and maintaining a positive relationship with staff so that they accept instruction

   - Communicating what needs to be changed

5. **Dealing with Problems**

   - Listening and observing

   - Handling conflict

   - Confronting problems rather than letting them fester

   - Recognizing the difference between a complaint and a real problem

Guidelines in Supervision

Some further guidelines concerning relationships may be helpful to a supervisor who has had little experience directing others.

Trust. This factor is basic to establishing a meaningful relationship, both for job performance and for personal interaction. Each staff member needs to know that the supervisor can be trusted to deal objectively and unemotionally with problems and discussions that arise. He or she must also know that the supervisor can deal with matters involving other individuals, seeing several sides of his or her personal problems and concerns. The staff member also must know that his or her job performance and discussions with the supervisor will remain confidential (unless the disclosure must be shared with the camp director, and then the staff member should be informed of the intent to do so). To maintain this trust relationship with staff, the supervisor must show staff that he or she values and respects them regardless of job performance. It may be difficult, at times, for the supervisor to maintain this attitude, but it should grow out of his or her innate respect for the worth of every individual, a respect that can transcend differences or personality conflicts.

Rapport. The ability of a supervisor to establish communication and a relaxed interaction quickly with staff members who may be unaccustomed to and wary of the supervisory framework is paramount. Along with the belief in individual worth, a genuine liking for all sorts of people and skills in human relations will help create the desired climate.

Sharing. The supervisor should cultivate the habit of sharing with employees, individually and collectively, his or her appreciation of the job being done. Regular commendation of a job well done will also help to prepare the staff member to accept criticism when it is necessary. It is also helpful if the supervisor has a plan to observe regularly the people he or she supervises—while with campers "on the job," while teaching, while interacting at meals, and so on. If the staff members find that this is done in a benevolent spirit, they will gradually become less self-conscious about observation. A supervisor's support and appreciation may very well not be perceived by others unless it is expressed verbally and backed up by his or her benevolent treatment.

The details of the staff supervision process should be shared with the group during staff training. It is helpful, also, to give an idea of general expectations and the criteria to be used in performance appraisals. If written notes from supervisory conferences and observations are to be added to personnel folders, the staff should be told this.

How Does One Begin?

As preparation for beginning a staff supervision program, time can well be spent in reviewing personnel information folders of returning staff and the application and interview papers of new staff. Acquaintance with staff backgrounds and facts is an asset when meeting the individuals because it helps to establish them in memory. Before the opening of the camp season, the supervisor might well seek opportunities to chat and get personally acquainted with local staff members who are new and with returning staff members who he or she may not know well. With out-of-town staff, beginning a relationship is more difficult and perhaps limited to letters and e-mail; nevertheless, it is important.

With the opening of camp and the beginning of staff training, personal contact can be broadened through discussion sessions, small group activities, human relations training, unstructured social occasions, group work projects, and staff overnights or trips. Any personal interplay that strengthens a relationship between supervisor and staff is a major plus in beginning a supervisory relationship.

Legal Negligence and the Supervisory Process

In court cases where a camp is being sued for negligence in failing to protect a camper against accident or abuse, one of the lines of defense is to show that a plan or process for supervision is in practice consistently for all staff. To be adequate, this plan or process for supervision should include the following points:

1. Each employee must be given information as to who will be his or her immediate supervisor.

2. There should be a definite plan for supervision including observations, formal conferences, informal conferences, written reprimands signed by supervisor, and a performance appraisal system.

3. Supervisors should have a clear understanding of their authority and the options available to them when staff behavior does not match expectations.

4. There must be a specific plan for dealing with an alleged abuser.

5. There must be a system for dealing with alleged harassment, camper to camper, staff to camper, or staff to staff.

6. Special training must be provided for supervisors and should deal with a uniform performance appraisal system, observation and recording methods, appropriate and inappropriate staff behavior, and conference formats, recording, and techniques.

7. There must be a formal plan that includes authority for terminating an employee, documented evidence of events leading to firing, and a plan for the final interview.

Techniques for Supervising Others

The following is a range of possible supervisory techniques that help define the supervisory relationship and the behaviors, attitudes, knowledge, or situations supervisors may encounter. Supervisors need to be able to access quickly factors that are motivating behavior and select a course of action.

1. Teaching. Teaching assumes that the person being supervised lacks knowledge. This may be because information has yet to be presented on the topic, or because the staff member has forgotten the presentation or is unable to apply the knowledge to a different set of facts. The role of the teacher includes

- Directing
- Providing instruction

2. Coaching. Coaching assumes that the person being supervised lacks experience or confidence in performing appropriately or with high skill. The individual may not have connected the intellectual knowledge he or she has with its application in a given situation. The role of the coach includes

- Reminding about key principles
- Encouraging where necessary
- Instructing in parts of the skill where necessary
- Indicating confidence that the staff member will get it right
- Helping the staff member "walk through" the potential experience and rehearsing the skills

3. Modeling. Modeling assumes that the supervisor is always being watched and should be constantly demonstrating the skills and attitudes he or she expects of staff members. Staff members will notice if the supervisor says to be consistent in enforcing policies with campers but is not consistent in enforcing policies with staff. They will be aware of the supervisor who is not responsive to their problems but expects them to be responsive to any problems campers might have. The role of the model includes

- Always demonstrating positive attitudes
- Always demonstrating compliance with camp rules and philosophy
- Always taking problems to the source or to his or her own supervisor and never gossiping or talking behind people's backs
- Working hard and showing initiative
- Acting in the best interests of the camp and the campers, not in his or her own best interest

4. Reinforcing. Reinforcing assumes that the supervisor is observing staff members frequently enough to find them doing things right! It further assumes that the supervisor provides positive feedback when he or she sees appropriate behavior, recognizes positive changes the staff member has made, or notes a positive attitude in difficult circumstances. Reinforcing good behavior prepares the staff members to hear constructive criticism. They know that the supervisor is not just looking for the bad but is willingly praising the good. The role of the reinforcer includes

- Being a frequent observer of each staff member
- Complimenting and praising each staff member frequently
- Finding things staff members are doing well

5. Correcting. Correcting assumes that the supervisor is observing behaviors that have not changed in spite of teaching, coaching, modeling, and reinforcing. Except in cases where safety requires immediate intervention to correct a behavior, supervisors should generally use one of the first four techniques in dealing with staff behavior prior to correcting or disciplining. Correcting should be done in private and in a manner that focuses on the behavior rather than the person. More specific training will be provided on this topic later in this chapter. The role of the corrector includes

- Maintaining the self-esteem of the person being corrected
- Focusing on the behavior, not the person
- Teaching, coaching, reinforcing, and modeling prior to correcting except when safety demands immediate correction

Appendix B provides a checklist for risk management in the recruitment, screening, training, and supervision of employees to help administrators in the area of negligence. The American Camping Association has a training packet for camp supervisors that may be helpful to the camp director.[2]

The Supervisory Process: Counselors

Because counselors are the majority of staff members, a supervisory plan for counselors and the people supervising them (whether a unit director, head counselor, or the camp director) will be outlined here. However, this program can easily be broadened and adapted to other staff and departments.

In the case of each of the supervisory conferences, the supervisor needs to keep written records, along with pertinent reports and appraisals, filed in the individual's personnel folder. This provides a permanent, ongoing performance record while the person is employed by the camp; it also becomes a valuable resource during rehiring decisions and when references are requested by future employers. The overall goal is to help all staff members perform their jobs as expected and to feel success and appreciation for their work. Waiting until midseason or the end of camp to let people know how they are doing will not help job performance improve quickly and may be interpreted by staff as satisfaction with their job performance on the part of the supervisor. During precamp training, supervisors will want to assess their staff's attitudes and participation to determine if some staff will need additional training in certain areas and to see if they understood the training content.

Post-Staff-Training Interview

It is often effective for the supervisor to schedule twenty- or thirty-minute conferences with each counselor at the end of staff training and before the arrival of campers. There are some specific questions that can help the supervisor increase his or her knowledge of the staff member. Other questions can help get feedback on the training period and, at the same time, assist the staff member in solidifying and expressing his or her own personal reactions. Questions in the appraisal may include the following:

- What areas of the job, as you see it now, do you feel confident in handling?

- Are there any areas about which you feel apprehensive?

- Are there still areas where you feel less than competent? (If teaching skills, is there an area where you have difficulty with organizing and teaching material?)

- If age groups have not been assigned, is there a particular age group of campers you would prefer and why?

- How do you feel about your relationship with other staff? (Although the counselor's answer here is important, your observations may be necessary to complete the picture.)

- With which areas of staff training did you feel most comfortable?

- Were there sessions of training that were of little or no interest to you?

- What are your goals for the summer? (These goals should be measurable, attainable goals that can be evaluated in an objective manner later. There should be job-related goals as well as personal-growth goals.)

One very positive factor in avoiding a climate that may be favorable to child abuse is to stimulate staff to set personal goals. Another is to encourage staff, at this point, to plan ahead to spend some time each day refreshing and recharging themselves, without neglecting responsibilities, to keep from getting overly drained.

Observation

A planned program of informal observation provides a supervisor with an occasion to observe the counselor in various activities that are a part of his or her performance — in the living situation, in skills teaching, and while participating in program activities with campers and other staff. These observations, which should be carried out informally and on a regular basis, will provide information about the counselor's ability and potential. Concerted efforts should also be made to talk with campers in informal situations because these contacts may give further indication as to the job the counselor is doing. The frequent presence of the supervisor in daily activities will also provide latitude for interchanges that may not happen otherwise. Although these drop-in practices may cause some anxiety in the beginning, staff and campers will usually come to accept them as part of the routine.

Gwynn M. Powell suggests that "the periodic occurrence of brief conversations and observations, as opposed to setting up blocks of time, were viewed as both more helpful and easier to accomplish during busy days. Setting a goal of a certain number of contacts per week allows for mentoring to become an integral part of patterns within camp routines instead of viewing the mentoring time as an interruption."[3]

The best feedback to the counselor on his or her performance is that given immediately after the observation. But since the feedback should not be given when others are present, the opportunity may not present itself. In any case, notes should be made of each observation as quickly as possible after leaving the observation area. Such notes can be tucked into the counselor's personnel folder and used at the time of the next supervisory meeting. It is important that these notes include positive feedback as well as criticism, and they should show the date, place, and conditions of the observation (e.g., counselor teaching group canoeing). These notes also provide another link in the protective chain for the counselor and the camp if there should be alleged child abuse or negligence. It may be possible to develop a checklist that can be used in observation of all personnel in similar positions.

In his *Camping Magazine* column, "In the Trenches," Bob Ditter notes that being a good observer includes watching carefully, waiting to draw conclusions, checking assumptions and appearances, and observing one's own biases. He also suggests that using an observation guide will help keep the observer on track. The guide could include such things as eye contact, appropriate touch, one-on-one communications, pitching in, and working well with co-counselors.[4]

Periodic Conferences

Depending upon the length of the camp's sessions, another supervisory conference should be scheduled with each counselor after a primary period of working with campers. The conference should come at a logical program point within the first two weeks. This gives an opportunity for mistakes to be corrected or habits changed before the lapse of too much time. This conference should deal with a number of topics including the following:

- The counselor's comments on each camper in his or her group and the relation of each to the group as a whole. The discussion on this topic has a dual purpose. First, the supervisor receives information helpful in dealing with the individual campers. Second, the supervisor has a chance to check on the counselor's ability to relate to and observe campers, articulate understanding both of individuals and the group living process and of the achievement of desired outcomes and goals.

- Any problems or conflicts that arose or currently exist and whether they have been worked out. This probably will arise naturally out of the first topic; if not, it is good to include it as an indicator of how the counselor interacts and makes decisions concerning campers.

- The counselor's conclusions about what things he or she might handle differently if the time could be redone.

- The counselor's evaluation of his or her personal job performance, including frustrations and high points, if any.

- The counselor's assessment of the accomplishment of any personal goals and establishment of new or modified goals for the next period.

- A brief review of the supervisor's observations of the counselor in action. Good points should be given first, followed by any problems or suggestions for a more effective performance. It may be a good idea to introduce this area by asking the counselor to evaluate the weaker and stronger points of his or her own performance during the period. This often opens the topic on a more positive note and sometimes brings up the very areas the supervisor wishes to discuss.

A sociogram (*see illustration 9.1*) is often used in this type of conference, particularly if the camp's program is focused on small group living and camper relationships. Such a diagram serves as a visual reminder of questions that should be covered during this and subsequent discussions.

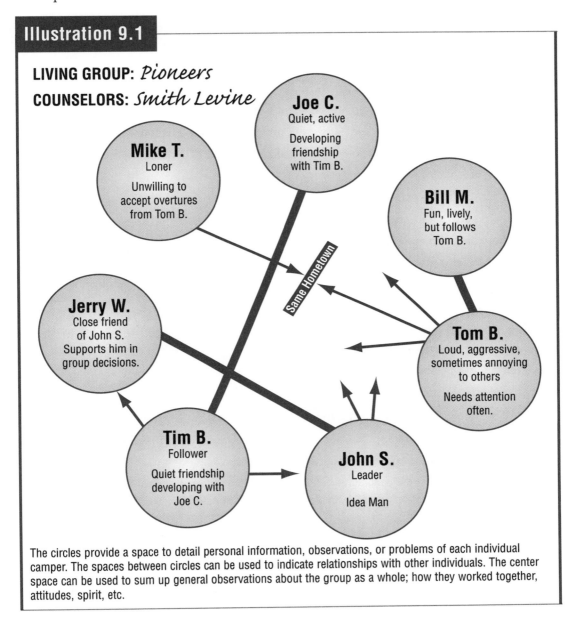

Illustration 9.1

LIVING GROUP: *Pioneers*
COUNSELORS: *Smith Levine*

Mike T.
Loner
Unwilling to accept overtures from Tom B.

Joe C.
Quiet, active
Developing friendship with Tim B.

Bill M.
Fun, lively, but follows Tom B.

Same Hometown

Jerry W.
Close friend of John S. Supports him in group decisions.

Tom B.
Loud, aggressive, sometimes annoying to others
Needs attention often.

Tim B.
Follower
Quiet friendship developing with Joe C.

John S.
Leader
Idea Man

The circles provide a space to detail personal information, observations, or problems of each individual camper. The spaces between circles can be used to indicate relationships with other individuals. The center space can be used to sum up general observations about the group as a whole; how they worked together, attitudes, spirit, etc.

This type of conference can well be repeated at the end of each camp session where there is a change in camper assignments, or on a regular basis if the camper group remains longer. The topics can be adjusted to deal more specifically with problem areas and with progress since the previous conference.

End-of-Season Performance Appraisal

The goal of any good supervisor is to enable the staff member to come to the point of effective self-appraisal followed by appropriate responsive behavior. However, certainly as one nears the end of a summer season or a three- to four-month period with a year-round employee, the performance appraisal, emerges as a responsibility of the supervisor. Any performance appraisal should relate to the employee's job description and especially the essential functions the employee is expected to perform. There may be other areas of evaluation tied to performance that are related to stated job functions, of course.

So far, only the evaluation from the viewpoint of the counselor and his or her immediate supervisor has been pinpointed. This, however, provides only a partial view of the counselor's job performance. In addition, some system should be devised for evaluating the counselor by supervisory personnel in other departments or areas of camp with whom he or she has had some contact during the summer. Some of these, depending upon the basic staff organization, may be the nurse, the program or unit directors, the assistant director, the business manager, the trip director, the food service director, and the waterfront director. It is helpful if these evaluations can be devised in such a manner that they can be added together to get a numerical average in various areas of concern that can be readily communicated to the counselor. See *illustration 9.2* for a sample staff appraisal form. Note that the evaluation form is tied to the sample job description shown in *illustration 9.3*. The performance appraisal refers to specific responsibilities in the job description.

There should be few surprises for the counselor when he or she comes to the end-of-season performance appraisal. Any major performance concern or problems will have been dealt with as the occasion arose during the summer. The final conference of the season should begin with an end-of-period appraisal for the last camper session of the summer. This conference also offers other opportunities to the supervisor:

- To share his or her evaluation of the counselor's performance over the summer, along with any comments and evaluations from other staff gained through the evaluations mentioned previously

- To hear the counselor's feelings about camp, the experience, and his or her own performance

- To hear the counselor's assessment of his or her accomplishment of job-related and personal goals for the summer

Through this closing conference, the supervisor should seek to guide the counselor in understanding the importance of self-evaluation as a necessary part of growth and development. It is also an occasion for the supervisor to share his or her support of the counselor along with an expression of appreciation for the job carried out.

The Supervisory Process: Noncounseling Staff

Asupervisory process similar to that designed for counselors is applicable to noncounseling positions and administrative staff. The supervisor can follow similar principles and steps:

1. Establish initial ground rules and understandings of responsibilities and performance goals with the staff member in a conference at the close of the training period.

2. Observe the staff member at work and make notes of these observations.

3. Establish a scheduled time for periodic conferences to discuss the staff member's concerns, job performance, personal goals, and accuracy of the job description.

4. Hold an end-of-season performance appraisal in which some feedback is given, pointing out improvements over the season and evaluating together the staff member's accomplishment of personal goals. Again, this appraisal of performance should be related to the specific responsibilities and essential functions from the job description and should not be a surprise to the subordinate. This discussion should open the way for any feedback from the staff member and for his or her self-evaluation of job performance.

Illustration 9.2 — *Sample Staff Performance Appraisal Form*

Explanation:

1. Person doing rating studies each square in horizontal row and circles one number (1-10) indicating appropriate level of skill. High numbers indicate a high rating; low numbers indicate less satisfactory performance or areas that need work. Particularly appropriate phrases can be circled and inappropriate phrases can be crossed through.

2. Various persons' ratings are recorded on a central form and a line is drawn through the form connecting the ratings for each row (see bold, vertical line).

3. Employee being evaluated is invited to mark a form on him or herself, with supervisor pointing out the importance of self-evaluation as a growth tool.

4. The employee's evaluation line is marked in a different color on the central form (see dotted line), and the comparison of the two lines is used as a basis of the supervisory conference. Again, emphasis is placed on self-perception in the evaluation process.

(Continued on next page)

Illustration 9.2 | *Sample Staff Performance Appraisal Form, continued*

PERFORMANCE APPRAISAL FORM

Confidential Appraisal of _____

Please circle a number in each row which best approximates your position of staff member or skill area noted in the first

Understanding of and Relationship with Campers *Relates to specific responsibility #2.*	• limited understanding of groups/individuals • communication on basic level only • no close relationships with campers **1** **2**	• beginning comprehension of groups/individuals • begins to communicate • occasionally develops close relationships with campers **3** **4**
Manner/Responsiveness *Relates to specific responsibility #2 / 3.*	• timid • overbearing • withdrawn • cocky • dominates conversations • curses, vulgarity **1** **2**	• quick tempered • irritating • indifferent • does not volunteer information • evasive • inappropriate language **3** **4**
Motivation *Relates to specific responsibility #6.*	• just wanted a job • not interested **1** **2**	• primarily interested in camp life, not campers • self-centered **3** **4**
Appearance *Relates to specific responsibility #5.*	• untidy • sloppy • often dirty • disheveled **1** **2**	• careless in dress/cleanliness **3** **4**
Attitudes Toward Camp Operation *Relates to specific responsibility #2/3/4.*	• avoids participating in certain camp activities • complains about assignments • sees only small part of total operation of camp as important **1** **2**	• participates but avoids active leader-ship in activities • attitude discourages participation of campers • ill at ease before a group – timid, hesitant • lacks confidence to secure group's attention **3** **4**
Teaching of Specific Skill *Relates to specific responsibility #3.*	• disorganized • wordy • unsure of self • limited ability in skill area **1** **2**	• ill at ease • knows basic skills • lacks organization/confidence in teaching **3** **4**

Notable strengths _____

Notable weaknesses _____

If you were director, would you employ this person another year? ❑ *Yes*   ❑ *No*

by _____

column. Mark through words or phrases that do not apply.

• basic understanding of group dynamics/personal growth • good communication but limited depth • develops friendships with campers • participates with campers	• good understanding of group – establishes rapport quickly • limited awareness of potential of individuals • some close relationships	• reveals excellent understanding of group/individuals • shows real involvement with and respect for campers • good communication skills • recognizes / develops individual/group potential • many close relationships
5 6	7 8	9 10
• well balanced • good listener • responds well • mature/balanced • appropriate language	• very confident/alert • self-assured • tactful • spontaneous • stable • appropriate language	• enthusiastic, warm • perceptive • imaginative • exceptionally self-possessed
5 6	7 8	9 10
• willing to work • interested in campers • considerate	• genuine interest in/love for campers • very industrious	• primary concern is to work with campers • always thoughtful/considerate of others
5 6	7 8	9 10
• good appearance • generally clean/tidy	• very neat • careful in dress/cleanliness	• gives evidence of concern/care in cleanliness at all times
5 6	7 8	9 10
• leads some activities • works in most any assignment without complaint • lends support to programs through attitude/participation	• relaxed/confident in leadership • gains enthusiastic response from audience • well prepared/organized • brings fun to any activity supervised	• participates in and enjoys activities/group • inspires enthusiastic response • can handle any situation when leading group
5 6	7 8	9 10
• comfortable • communicates skills well to individuals • adept at skill	• well organized • very much at ease • varies pace, involves group • involves individuals in trying skills	• exceptional command of organization • speaks camper language • involves individuals easily • expert at skill
5 6	7 8	9 10

Illustration 9.3   *Sample Job Description*

SAMPLE JOB DESCRIPTION

POSITION TITLE: COUNSELOR
Responsible To: Unit Director
Qualifications:

- At least eighteen years of age
- High school diploma or GED required; one or more years of college preferred
- Experience as a camper or working with children as a leader or assistant leader
- Ability to relate to one's peers as well as to children
- Good character
- Flexibility, with ability to accept supervision

General Responsibility: To live with and guide eight campers throughout their camp experience.

Specific Responsibilities:

1. Live in a cabin with eight campers
2. Assume responsibility for leadership and guidance of those campers in daily living, with special attention to:
   - personal hygiene and safety
   - camp participation in planning cabin activities
   - camper participation in all-camp activities
   - meal-time behavior and habits
3. Assume responsibility as assistant activity specialist in an assigned activity area
4. Assume responsibility for interpreting the rules, policies, and traditions of the camp to the camper
5. Serve as a good example in personal language, appearance, and health habits
6. Assume responsibility for health and welfare of campers entrusted to his or her charge

Essential Functions:

- Be physically able to accompany the campers to any of the camp activities
- Be able to communicate verbally with campers, and provide instructions
- Have visual ability to recognize hazards in the camp setting as well as physical symptoms of camper injury or illness
- Have auditory ability to respond appropriately to hazards and any camper concerns
- Be able to observe camper behavior in daily camp life, to respond verbally to health and safety concerns, and to deal appropriately with any improper behavior

For administrative staff, there should also be a plan for securing evaluations from counselors and other staff who work with and for them. A summary of these should be shared at the final performance appraisal at the end of the summer. The form shown in *illustration 9.4* is one example of a form for administrative staff evaluation.

If the camp director does not supervise certain staff directly, he or she can benefit from the supervisor's notes on each appraisal conference that are placed with the employee's personnel record. The director can also learn from administrative staff meetings and written records of the overall individual needs and performance of staff whom he or she may not be able to observe directly.

The supervisory program for full-time, year-round staff can operate under the same framework as that for summer adminis-trative staff. The timing of supervisory appraisals could parallel that of summer administrative staff and then be adjusted to long appraisal periods for the remainder of the year. A yearly performance appraisal should be scheduled according to the organization's personnel policies (e.g., end of year, end of fiscal year, anniversary date). Or, if the job description of the full-time staff member does not essentially

Illustration 9.4 *Evaluation of Administrative Staff by Counselors*

Evaluation of Administrative Staff by Counselors

- ❏ Boys' program director
- ❏ Girls' program director
- ❏ Office secretary
- ❏ Camp director
- ❏ Truck driver

- ❏ Naturalist
- ❏ Nurse
- ❏ Hostess
- ❏ Head cook
- ❏ Second cook

- ❏ Tripping counselor
- ❏ Waterfront director
- ❏ Arts/crafts counselor
- ❏ Unit director — seniors
- ❏ Unit director — juniors

It is helpful to have feedback from counseling staff on the above personnel. Please check the appropriate square as you complete the form. Positive and negative comments can be helpful.

Comment on:

1. Ability in assigned job (listed above):
2. Helpfulness to you in doing a better job as a counselor:
3. Congeniality:
4. Efficiency:
5. Attitude toward individuals (campers/counselors):
6. Interest in total camp program:
7. Any other comments or observations:

change during the summer season, evaluation might be more effective on a periodic basis apart from other members of the summer administrative staff.

Stress and Camp Staff

In any program of supervision at camp, the camp director and department supervisors need to be aware of the potential problems of stress. The intensity of living in the camp community provides its own proclivity to stressful situations. It is essential that the director and all supervisors have a somewhat technical understanding of stress, its symptoms and effects, and how to help alleviate those effects in themselves and the staff they supervise. Stress management in staff members has been previously named as one factor in risk management as well as in staff retention. Attention to the symptoms of stress has been shown to decrease the number of accidents/incidents greatly.

Definition of Stress

Stress is a physical, chemical, or emotional reaction that causes bodily or mental tension. Stress results from factors that tend to alter an existing equilibrium. These stressors are external demands or internal attitudes and thoughts that require us to adapt. Stress triggers a response from a complex part of our brains and bodies called the autonomic nervous system. This system creates the fight-or-flight response, which provides for bodily changes that enable humans to fight or flee from physical dangers to their survival. Stress may cause people to experience some of the following symptoms:

- Digestion slows so that blood may be directed to the muscles and brain — experienced as "butterflies in your stomach."
- Breathing gets faster to supply more oxygen for the needed muscles — experienced as being unable to catch your breath.
- The heart speeds up, and blood pressure soars, forcing blood to parts of your body that need it — experienced as a pounding heart.
- Perspiration increases to cool the body, allowing it to burn more energy — experienced as increased sweating.
- Muscles tense in preparation for important action — experienced as a stiff back or neck after a stressful day.
- Chemicals are released to make the blood clot more rapidly.
- Sugars and fats pour into the blood to provide fuel for quick energy — experienced as a surprising increase in strength and endurance during an emergency.

Response to Stress

Camp often triggers stress and its symptoms but provides few outlets for relief. Unlike other jobs where a person can go home and find outlets for relieving stress, the seasonal staff work long hours with little contact from their home or from others who might help them relax. Additionally, when human beings cannot run from anxieties or physically fight their fears, the result is emotional stress. Even if the chemicals produced by emotional stress could be safely burned off, the resulting psychological distress can interfere with productivity, learning, and interpersonal relationships. When stress reactions continue without relief, people become less and less able to handle even minor stress.

Short-Term Stress. In the short term (a period of hours), stress responses often manifest themselves by a jittery stomach, a lump in the throat, a tight feeling in the chest, a racing pulse and pounding heart, a pain in the neck and shoulders from tension, or a tendency to fly off the handle.

Long-Term Stress. In the long term (a period of weeks), stress responses become chronic and incessant and have much wider implications for the staff member. It is at this point that the supervisor may first become aware of the presence of stress because the staff member exhibits some of these symptoms. He or she

- Becomes less productive
- Never has enough time
- Becomes withdrawn and depressed

- Has increased smoking or drinking problems
- Experiences an increase in pain associated with chronic diseases (arthritis, headaches)
- May eat more and gain weight or eat less and lose weight
- Is subject to daydreaming and has difficulty concentrating
- Experiences sleeplessness or sleepiness
- Has feelings of worthlessness, inadequacy, and rejection
- Has difficulty dealing with campers and other staff

Stress Management

To help the stressed staff member cope with the situation, the supervisor needs a basic understanding of the biological systems related to stress factors. The major system, the autonomic nervous system, has two divisions. The first, called the sympathetic nervous system, is the one that triggers the fight-or-flight response to danger and is responsible for the changes in the physical body. The second system, the parasympathetic nervous system, influences the body in ways that are almost the exact opposite of those of the sympathetic nervous system. This second division is responsible for conservation and replenishment of energy and modification of the sympathetic nervous system response. There is some evidence to suggest that the parasympathetic nervous system can be activated through relaxation procedures, thus minimizing and negating the physical responses of the sympathetic nervous system.

A supervisor who observes the symptoms of stress can counsel the affected staff member to take practical steps toward managing the stress. Most stress can be divided under three main categories: stress from your situation, stress from your mind, and stress from your body. Within these categories, there are some immediate solutions or ways of handling stress that staff members can be taught to use.

Situational Stress

- Assert yourself; say "no" or ask for exactly what you need.
- Remove yourself or escape from the problem.
- Plan specific steps to avoid, reduce, or correct the problem in the future.
- Pace yourself and schedule time to relax.

Mental Stress

- Catch yourself when jumping to conclusions, taking things personally, or attaching much importance to a minor event.
- Mentally yell "stop!"
- Replace negative or anxious thoughts with positive thinking or your happiest memory.
- In your mind's eye, see yourself taking charge in a relaxed and confident way.

Physical Stress

- Breathe in deeply, counting slowly to five; as you exhale completely, count slowly back to one and relax all muscles.

- Imagine that you are loose and relaxed from head to toe.

- Avoid caffeine, nicotine, or any stress-causing chemicals; substitute a quick stretch or a brief walk.

These solutions are of a temporary, stopgap, or preventive nature. They may be effective in some cases of short-term stress and may help to alleviate some problems. But in some individual cases, medical or psychiatric assistance may be necessary if symptoms seem severe and if the person is unable to function normally under the day's demands.

Burnout

Some degree of stress is healthy and helps the individual be productive and competitive in the day-to-day situation. However, if stress is unrelieved or moves to long-term stress, burnout can result. Burnout is a condition of emotional and physical collapse brought on by the unchecked escalation of pressure or stress. Particularly in the resident camp situation, where staff members are often with campers twenty-four hours a day, day after day, a counselor can find him- or herself burnt out by the end of the fifth or sixth week of camp, even with time off. Time off may actually cause additional stress when pressured to be with friends, do laundry, drive distances, and the like. There are signals that can alert the supervisor to the potential burnout of a staff member.

People who are overenthusiastic are prone to burnout. They get so wrapped up in the job and situation that they feel everything is wonderful and do not hesitate to share that with one and all. Antagonism toward others sometimes arises at this point, and the individual often moves away from peers who are less enthusiastic or who tire of the individual's enthusiasm. Those who frequent the health center with colds, neck pain, back pain, rashes, and other similar conditions are often actually exhibiting the early signs of burnout.

The individual begins to sense that his or her commitment level is lessening or that something is wrong with the assignment. The person may believe that he or she needs something more challenging, indicating that he or she is not enjoying the present assignment as much as in the past. Or a request may be made for more time off to provide a new viewpoint. Days off may be spent in frenzied activity to relieve this feeling or tension. However, the relief of time off does not seem to last; within a day or two, the old symptoms begin to show.

At this point, the individual begins to find it difficult to function as efficiently as in the past and often tries to cover up inefficiencies or mistakes by making excuses or lying. Relationships seem to deteriorate, and it is difficult to find peers who are willing to help or support the individual. The person may appear nervous, forgetful, or distracted. From this point, burnout can progress to desperate efforts to combat the feeling of defeat, and it can resemble depression. Day-to-day tasks become more difficult, and the person uses lies or deception to cover up the problem.

A well-developed supervisory process lends itself to helping the potential burnout candidate recognize the problem and the symptoms and to develop a program to utilize his or her free time and days off for relaxation rather than for frenzied activities. The supervisor and other staff may try to provide support and nurturing concern for the individual; at the same time, the supervisor should help the individual recognize the importance of opening him- or herself to those who are supportive.

Careful attention to providing the adequate time off and days off for all staff is important to prevent burnout and relieve stress in all staff. Though some types of personalities are more prone to burnout than others, the pressure of the camp living situation can bring on burnout in people who otherwise would not succumb. Therefore, as the season progresses and staff tends to get more tired, relaxing events for groups of staff members and careful coaching for individuals can help prevent burnout.

The Supervisor and Termination

If a supervisor utilizes all the techniques of supervision and does everything possible to encourage a staff member to function as expected, but the employee still doesn't have the skill or does not cooperate, it may be time to fire him or her. Today's increased awareness of many employment issues such as sexual harassment means that employers must terminate employees as a result of such unacceptable behavior. Failure to do so puts the supervisor, as well as the camp, at risk. Training and supervision, however, are designed to minimize the possibility of having to dismiss staff because of inappropriate behavior or inadequate job performance. A copy of the staff manual (containing the rules for termination) in the hand of each staff member ensures that the "no one told me" excuse cannot be used. Although most supervisors do not have the authority to fire a staff member without discussing it with the director, it is important that the procedures and roles are clear. Often the supervisor and the director are both present when the actual dismissal takes place.

If a supervisor is having difficulty with an employee, the first action is to confront the employee regarding the problem and to take steps to correct the behavior. In an article in the *Journal of Christian Camping*, Rob Crawford recommends a three-step process.

1. Sit down with the employee and talk it over. And, what is more important, listen to the employee. Most employees want to do the right thing; it may be that they need more direction or training, which the supervisor needs to provide. Following the conversation, there should be a follow-up memo to the individual, stating the problem and the appropriate action decided upon. If step 1 has not resolved the problem, go to step 2.

2. The supervisor and the staff member, together, agree upon a more formal process, which is agreeable to both. The agreement must stipulate the objective, measurable behavior which is required. A time line is set, and the consequences clearly set out. The consequence might not be termination; other disciplinary measures might be chosen. Everything should be clearly defined, with a reasonable penalty for failure to comply.

3. Follow through with what was agreed upon in step 2.

If all else fails and termination is the only answer, do it quickly. After the supervisor realizes that it is beyond the point of no return, give the employee a final check with a fair severance pay and request that he or she leave the property as soon as possible. To protect against the potential charge of discrimination, the supervisor needs to see to it that all employment policies treat everyone equally. It is also essential that the supervisor refuse to discuss the circumstances of firing with other staff members.[5]

Oddly enough, there can be a positive side to firing a staff member. It will confirm to other staff members, who may have witnessed the continuing problem, that the ongoing disruptive behavior brought its own result. In addition, the termination may actually prove to be a new beginning and a more positive move for the employee.

Checkpoints

1. Outline who supervises whom.

2. What is the plan for supervision of staff that you, as director, supervise?
   - How have you chosen to use conferences?
   - How do you plan to use observation?
   - What role will group meetings play?

3. How does that plan relate to the overall plan of supervision?

4. Outline the performance appraisal tools to be used.

Related Standards and Guidelines

Accreditation Standards for Programs and Services: HR-8–9, 18, 19, 20, PD-12, 14; "Additional Professional Practices": Item 26

Guidelines for Conference and Retreat Centers: II-41

[1] Margaret Williamson. Supervision — *Principles and Methods*. New York: Women's Press. p. 4.

[2] *So You Want to Be a Supervisor?* Martinsvillle, IN: American Camping Association Bookstore.

[3] Gwynn M. Powell. "Leadership Directions: Where Are We Going This Summer?" *Camping Magazine*, Vol. 75, No. 3. pp. 58-59.

[4] Bob Ditter. 1996. "Skills for Staff Supervisors." *Camping Magazine*, Vol. 68, No. 5, May/June. pp. 15–16.

[5] Rob Crawford. 1995. "The Firing Line." *Journal of Christian Camping*, Vol. 27, No. 3, May/June. pp. 16–19. Reprinted by permission from CCI/USA.

Selection, Development, & Maintenance of the Site

To guide the orderly development of any camp site, a plan is needed. This will govern the total development that may take place over a period of years. . . . While it may seem a lot easier and much more fun to skip planning more or less completely, such a course . . . can only lead to headaches, trouble, and possibly disaster. Impatience to get the job done and over with and unwillingness to spend money for professional planning services are poor excuses for not using hard won . . . funds to produce the best possible result.[1]

Physical Facility as an Asset

The physical setting of the camp is an important element in the planning of program and, therefore, in meeting the camp's mission and desired outcomes and goals. If used to its greatest potential, the setting can make the best experience even better. On the other hand, the neglect of the physical property of a camp can make even the best program a disappointing one for participants and staff.

Whether a camper, a parent, or new staff member, the first impression a person has of a camp is its appearance. The camp director needs to go to the camp one day and try to see it as a first-time visitor would. What is striking: cleanliness and loving care or neglect and disarray?

The most valuable asset a camp owns is its physical site and the buildings on it. With less and less suitable land available for camping and with land values continuing to escalate, the camp director has a tremendous responsibility to protect that asset. Part of the camp director's responsibility is to help safeguard and preserve a physical site and property for future generations of campers, as a camp, conference center, and/or outdoor education facility. Today there are many pressures from outside developers and urban sprawl, and from within financially struggling parent organizations, to use camp properties for other purposes or to gain capital from their sale. The camp director becomes the guardian of this asset, not only by discouraging the sale of the property but also by making that sure the property is accomplishing its purpose so well that discussion of its sale can be effectively fended off.

Selection

Though most camp directors inherit a physical site, other camp directors rent facilities and therefore have the opportunity from time to time to select a site. The most fortunate of all camp directors are those who get to select a site and build a facility from the ground up, but this book is not designed to provide all the steps necessary in that process.

As a camp director reviews a variety of camp facilities in the process of selecting a site, especially in regard to rental, here are some guidelines that may be helpful:

- Check to see if the appropriate local and state permits and licenses are available for review. Have there been appropriate water tests? When were they taken? Is the sanitation system approved and in working order? Have the fire authorities inspected the property? States and localities vary in their permitting systems and regulations, and the absence of certain permitting processes or regulations means that the director must be more knowledgeable and more careful in his or her inspections and questions during the selection process.

- Review the camp site for health and safety factors. Are there apparent natural hazards? Are buildings well maintained, or does their condition provide hazards? Are those hazards easily corrected, or does the condition of a given building require major repair or replacement? What is the swimming facility like in terms of water quality, location, ease of control, and safety? Is the kitchen clean and rodent free? What is the condition of major equipment such as walk-ins, refrigerators, ranges, dishwashers, and so on? Is the camp accredited by the American Camping Association?

- Look at the layout of the property, the location of buildings, the natural environment of the camp, and the program facilities. Do they complement your program mission, outcomes and goals? How would you have to adapt your program in this setting?

- Check the location. Is it convenient enough for transportation to and from the areas from which you draw campers or from major transportation terminals?

- Determine the distance to the closest medical, fire, and other emergency services.

- Survey the camp's closest neighbors. Do the homes or activities surrounding the camp create potential problems currently? What is the zoning of surrounding properties? What potential development could occur that might affect the camp in the future? Is a major highway or thoroughfare planned?

- Look for security problems. Are there any obvious problems that might endanger campers or staff? How many access points are there into camp? How easy is it to control those access points?

When a site is rented for seasonal use, it should not be assumed that the owner is routinely taking care of maintenance problems. At the time the lease agreement is signed, a careful inspection of facilities and a list of expected repairs and maintenance should be made and incorporated into the lease agreement. An advance understanding between the director and renter about meeting state and local regulations, as well as any standards set by the organization, is vital. A clear understanding about cleaning and other advance preparations should save some frustration later. Be prepared upon leaving to fulfill your part of the agreement.

Before signing a lease agreement, the director should study it carefully to understand the responsibilities of both parties. It is advisable to have an attorney check the agreement. Similarly, closer to time of use of property, an informal inspection should be made and reminders given to the owner about items not yet completed.

Development of an Owned Site

Most camp properties are in perpetual change, and every camp director is faced with decisions about these changes at some time: building new structures, remodeling and repairing older structures, constructing roads or sewer lines, and the list goes on. This may not be the primary interest or strength of the camp director, and it may seem to be an interruption of the more important aspects of programming and service to people. However, the camp director must develop a plan to deal with those changes effectively, both in acquiring funding and in designating staff to supervise and/or accomplish the changes.

Long-Term Planning

The wise camp director understands that form follows function and will work to help develop a facility that serves and enhances the program functions of the camp. If there is not a master site plan resulting from a long-term look at the camp's mission or philosophy, market, program, finances, and facilities, then this should become the first priority of the director, owner, or volunteer board or committee. To make extensive changes in the property without an overall plan could be both costly and frustrating.

A master site plan requires a commitment to study the overall camp situation and its potential. In most cases, an outside consultant will be most valuable from the beginning of the process. Whether that person is paid or a volunteer, it is critical that he or she be objective, have an understanding of organized camping with some depth of knowledge of camps beyond your camp, and have basic planning skills. Eventually you may also need the expertise of an architect and perhaps a landscape architect. There are professional campsite planning firms, as well as individual consultants, who offer services in this field.

A comprehensive site plan will encompass a number of procedures:

- A review and evaluation of the camp's purpose and philosophy
- An analysis of the clientele now served and a review of what potential markets the camp may desire to serve in the future
- A careful cost analysis of existing services and programs, as well as a look at potential funding sources
- An inventory of present facilities and property
- An inventory of present uses of each facility and each portion of the property year-round
- Statements by the director, owner, and, in not-for-profit camps, the committee or board about the purpose, new or existing target markets, overall program of the camp, and desired year-round use
- Evaluation of the accessibility of the buildings and program facilities for staff or campers with disabilities and the difficulty with which modifications/adaptations can be made
- Development of a schematic site plan that would best use the existing buildings and the natural resources of the property, showing where new buildings or program areas might be constructed
- Development of a time line and plan to accomplish whatever site plan is agreed upon after input and discussion among the planner, the director, the owner, and any volunteer structure

Often the first thought after securing proposals for a master site plan is that the cost of such a plan could easily offset some of the direct expenses of the actual development. Many camp directors may be tempted to short-cut the process and simply do it in-house. Though this may save money initially, most often it will cost a great deal more in the long term owing to the lack of objectivity or expertise.

Dan Smith points out that "while there are basic principles of design, arriving at a well-designed solution is not a simple cookbook process. Even though computers have placed the means to draw floor plans within the reach of almost everyone with a keyboard, there is more to good design than a wide selection of fonts and a big assortment of furniture symbols. Good design includes both a knowledge of design principles and an understanding of the concepts behind these principles. Also needed is an 'eye for design.' It is this knowledge, understanding, and 'eye' that consultants in the field bring to the camp."[2]

Short-Term Planning

Though development of a master site plan is ideal, not every director will be able to wait on such a plan before instituting development. However, there are some steps that will assist in making immediate decisions about such development. They will also be invaluable when retaining a planner and starting a master site plan.

First, make sure that you have accurate maps of the property, topographical as well as schematic. If there is not a topographical map on file and you cannot afford to have one made, purchase the U.S. Geological Survey map for your area. An aerial map will also prove valuable. There should be a survey map of the property that was secured at the time the property was purchased; however, that is not always the case. A survey map should indicate property lines, highways or roads, and rights-of-way or easements. Major buildings and utility lines should have been added to this map as they were built. Surveying questionable property lines should be a first order of business.

Second, make sure that all utility and sanitation lines are correctly drawn on a property map so that water lines, electrical lines, and gas lines (with cutoff points and valves) are clearly identified. Blueprints of buildings should also be gathered in one location.

Third, secure as much information about the land, soil, vegetation, wildlife, and water resources as possible. State or county foresters, fish and wildlife personnel, and conservationists will often be willing to walk the property with you and provide suggestions on such conservation measures as reforestation, improvement of the wildlife habitat, and protection and improvement of the lakes and streams. All this information will give you clues to areas that should not be developed with buildings or program activity areas and to other areas where development will do less damage.

Fourth, secure copies of the state, county, and local regulations and building codes that specifically apply to camps. Obviously, these documents become the first priority in the development of the site, should the camp not already comply. New development may be required to meet higher standards and to come into compliance. Also, state, county, and local health and sanitation officials often can provide guidance regarding developmental concerns in their areas as well as to the adequacy of the waste disposal system, water system, and related sanitation concerns.

The director should give careful attention to the implications the Americans With Disabilities Act of 1990 has for providing accessible facilities.

Camps must consider needs of persons with physical disabilities in relation to the site, facilities, and program. A camp is not relieved of its legal responsibility to make "reasonable accommodations" simply because it is not currently serving any persons with disabilities. As public accommodations, all camps must adhere to applicable laws. For the purpose of the ADA, camps must also consider hearing and visual impairments, emotional disturbance, developmental delays, and so forth.

For specific guidance, refer to the "Americans With Disabilities Act Accessibility Guidelines for Buildings and Facilities" (ADAAG) which is available through the U.S. Access Board. [See appendix G for contact information.] ADAAG standards refer mainly to buildings, toilets, bathing facilities, and parking.

Full compliance with ADAAG is required only for new construction and alterations. Existing facilities can be made more accessible through some "readily achievable" changes in which barriers are removed.

States will vary on accessibility regulations. Camps must comply with the most stringent requirements (that which provides the greatest access for individuals with disabilities) of the local, state, and federal codes that apply.[3]

Fifth, uncover the inventories of the physical facilities and major equipment. If an updated inventory is not available, make one, noting the years that buildings were constructed and the acquisition dates and identification numbers for all equipment.

With this information in hand, intelligent planning can be set into play. Take a walk through the camp's property and examine each building and program area. Note where improvements are needed (e.g., areas with erosion problems or natural hazards, and buildings needing modifications to comply with the ADA) and where additional development may complement the program and appearance or provide new opportunities to serve new groups). Divide this list into (1) repairs or corrections that can be done quickly and easily or that need to be made immediately to alleviate risks and (2) those that may require more funding or assistance than is immediately available.

The list of repairs that can be made immediately should be at the top of the development plan. These items should be prioritized, with those that affect health or safety receiving earlier priority than those that are cosmetic or programmatic in nature. Each development project should be evaluated against the information secured in the earlier surveys to determine the project's effect on the natural environment, its fit in the overall aesthetics of the camp, its seasonal use, and, as far as possible, its carefree maintenance. With this background, detailed plans should be developed, involving a structural architect, landscape architect, or engineer where necessary. Only then will it be feasible to begin to develop a budget and time line for completion. This process becomes the camp's short-range plan until such time as an overall master site plan can be developed.

Maintenance

A Maintenance Plan

The first list of immediate repairs and corrections will fall under maintenance as opposed to development and should be resolved as part of an ongoing maintenance plan. This overall plan should be developed in collaboration with the year-round site manager, caretaker, or ranger who normally supervises camp maintenance. It should include

- A routine inspection of all facilities after their use by a group to assess any damages and identify cleaning needs

- A regular schedule of painting or application of protective finishes to exteriors and interiors of buildings

- A schedule of draining, unhooking, and connecting water lines if the camp is located in the freeze zone and lines are not winterized

- A plan for checking and correcting erosion throughout the camp grounds, including a plan for alternating activity areas or traffic patterns to restore a setting to a healthy state

- A routine inspection schedule of all water and sewage systems, including the swimming pool and its maintenance, and a regular testing schedule of drinking water, the swimming pool, and any natural bodies of water used for swimming

- A routine schedule for cleaning, lubricating, and checking each piece of machinery and equipment with moving parts, including tests of smoke detection equipment and replacement of filters

- A schedule for routine inspection, replacement, and repair of screens, windows, railings, steps, docks, and roofs

- An annual inspection of all electrical service and heating systems

When these various routines have been established for cleaning, repairs, and testing, a written record, giving scheduled and completion dates, person responsible, and specifics of what is done, is wise. Keeping a maintenance logbook will greatly assist other staff and preserve a record of all work done. Preventative maintenance will lengthen the life of buildings and equipment and make the facilities more attractive to guests. Samples of two forms that may be adapted for use in routine inspections are shown in *illustrations 10.1* and *10.2*.

A daily schedule of the prioritized tasks can then be prepared with specific assignments made to staff members who may be assisting. It is to be recognized that emergency repairs will come up on a day-to-day basis, sometimes pushing scheduled projects on to the next day.

As part of the maintenance plan, a strategy should be developed for the cleaning and upkeep of high-traffic areas in camp: bathrooms, dining hall, meeting areas, pathways, and so on. In most camps, the day-to-day cleaning of living areas such as cabins or dorm rooms is left to the camper groups that occupy the areas, through camper assignments or group projects. However, in other year-round programs or rental situations with certain types of adult groups, the cleaning of rooms may also need to be assigned to staff. Many camps depend on campers to clean the bathrooms, but supplemental cleaning and checks by staff will help. Campers and staff should use rubber gloves and follow procedures for handling blood-borne pathogens when cleaning the bathrooms.

Most camps have a large number of older buildings that require constant maintenance and upgrading to extend their lifespan.

Not enough can be said about the importance of regular annual maintenance of each and every building in camp. Camps in a budget squeeze often look first to see which repairs or improvements can be postponed. However, to postpone maintenance whether it is painting, replacing screens or water pipes, or reroofing is "penny-wise and pound-foolish." Delay only increases the wear and tear and the eventual cost, as well as often leaving the camp open for potential accidents or injuries.

Illustration 10.1 *General Maintenance Inspection Checklist*

General Maintenance Inspection Checklist

Camp name _____ Date_____

Check as okay, or indicate assigned job card number.

1. Utilities		3. Food Handling		Walks		Communication	
Water System		Arrangement		Pool walls		equipment	
Well casing		Stoves		Pool floor		Office furniture	
Well cover		Refrigeration		Gutters		Inspected by:	
Spring protection		Freezer		Drainage		Date:	
Intake screen		Mixer		Dressing rooms			
Pump(s)		Ovens		Showers		8. Program Areas	
Pump motor(s)		Dishwasher		Toilets		*Waterfront*	
Chlorinator		Sterilization		Filters		Piers	
Filter		Sinks		Chlorine equipment		Floats	
Control system		Tables/counters		Cleaning equipment		Boat dock	
Pipe lines		Dishes		Inspected by:		Guard tower	
Storage tank		Dish storage		Date:		Beach	
Valves		Utensils				Control fence	
Winter drains		Storage space		6. Land Management		Check board	
Sanitation		Ventilation		*Lakes/Ponds*		Boats	
Sewer lines		Lighting		Silt control		Oars	
Septic tanks		Garbage		Aquatic weeds		Canoes	
Seepage pits		Inspected by:		Dam		Paddles	
Disposal field		Date:		Spillway		Sailboats	
Garbage disposal				Control gate		Lifesaving equipment	
Grease trap		4. Maintenance		*Conservation*		PFDs	
Electrical		Trucks		Erosion control			
Power lines		Tractor		Wildlife management		*Tripping/OLS*	
Line clearance		Tractor equipment		Stream management		*Equipment*	
Telephone		Trailers		Forest management		Rope	
Telephone lines		Power tools		Landscaping		Axes	
Line supports		Hand tools		Foot trails		Saws	
Gas/Oil		Spare parts		Soil conservation		Compasses	
Gas lines		Standby equipment		Obnoxious plants		Cooking equipment	
Storage tanks		Fire equipment		Conservation		Shovels	
Regulating equipment		Fire extinguishers		equipment		Tents	
Inspected by:		Camp signs		*Public Areas*		Packs	
Date:		Flammable/		Picnic area			
		hazardous material		Boundary fence		*Other Program Areas*	
2. Roads/Parking		MSD sheets		Lawns		Archery range	
Surface		Basic records		Inspected by:		Archery equipment	
Ditches		Utility maps		Date:		Rifle range	
Drainage		Mechanical				Rifles/guns	
Bridges		equipment records		7. Office		Fishing gear	
Culverts		Vehicle records		Computers		Ropes course	
Service roads		Inspected by:		Printer		Ropes course	
Gates		Date:		Copy machines		equipment	
Barriers				Phone system		Inspected by:	
Inspected by:		5. Swimming Pool		Answering machine		Date:	
Date:		Fence		Fax machine			

Illustration 10.2 *Building Maintenance Inspection Checklist*

Building Maintenance Inspection Checklist

Camp name _____ Date _____

Person making inspections_____

Check as okay, or indicate assigned job card number.

NAME OF BUILDING OR STRUCTURE ⇨																							
Foundation																							
Sills																							
Floors																							
Outside walls																							
Inside walls																							
Doors																							
Windows																							
Screens																							
Roof																							
Steps/rails																							
Chimney																							
Fireplace																							
Wiring																							
Plumbing																							
Fire protection																							
Building																							
Gutters																							
Drainage around bldg.																							
Housekeeping																							

In the day-to-day maintenance of a facility with a large number of staff and campers, it is important to have a system for reporting needed repairs. Oral transmission of such requests through the camp director or directly to the maintenance supervisor is unfair because it relies on the memory of a busy person. A form should be available so that any staff member can report an item that needs repair or attention. See *illustration 10.3* for an example of such a form. Providing a tear-off or duplicate copy enables the director or supervisor to keep a copy while forwarding a copy to the person charged with the repair. That person returns the duplicate copy indicating the date of completion and circumstances of the repair. It is wise to maintain a file of such forms for risk management purposes.

Essential to any extensive maintenance program is a building that houses tools, equipment, and vehicles and provides dry and heated or cooled workshop space with sufficient electric power to conduct repairs and build replacement items as needed. Adequate storage space is needed for supplies, extra beds and mattresses, and other equipment. Scott King points out that "at many facilities, one of the first things a guest sees is the maintenance building and the assorted objects and vehicles around it. Screen this area and other undesirable elements from the guest's view. A pleasing entry to your facility sets the tone for what guests expect when they arrive."[4]

Where the camp director has a supervisor or a volunteer committee off-site, it is vital to share information concerning facility needs and problems with the appropriate party on a regular basis. In this situation, it becomes a shared responsibility because the camp director may not be in a position to free the funds needed to undertake certain projects or to make a final decision about location and construction. When supervisors and committees are kept well-informed and involved, they will be more likely to help in finding unbudgeted funds to solve problems or expand facilities.

Personnel

Careful selection of property management personnel is as important to a camp as the selection of camp counselors. The responsibility for year-round maintenance must be assigned to one individual. That person is most likely the site manager, ranger, or caretaker

---

Illustration 10.3   *Request for Maintenance*

Request for Maintenance

Director (copy)

Date _____

Check one: ❑ Building repair ❑ Equipment repair ❑ Grounds repair

What building or piece of equipment? _____

Nature of problem _____

_____

_____

                                            Signed _____

- -

For Maintenance Department Use Only

Action taken _____

Date completed _____ By whom _____

---

who may or may not live on the property. It is important that such a designation carry with it the appropriate job description, level of responsibility, and compensation plan. However, not just any person will possess the skills to do the job. On the other hand, some on-site managers get so accustomed to being in control for most of the year that they take on a feeling of ownership, and seasonal directors and guests feel as though they are intruding on private land.

As a maintenance plan is developed and scheduled, it should help identify the pressure points where additional part-time or full-time maintenance assistance is needed or where certain contract services will alleviate that necessity. It will also show downtime when maintenance personnel can take time off. Much will depend upon the skills the caretaker or ranger brings to the job, and there may be skills that need to be supplemented by additional help or training.

The director should give some thought to the potential involvement of volunteers in repairs. A work weekend at a resident campsite or a workday on a day camp site can accomplish quite a bit at very little cost, if adequate energy and time has gone into the planning. One of the most important elements is recruitment of skilled parents, organizations, members, staffers, and volunteers, as well as campers and less-skilled volunteers for general labor.

Thought should be given to who supervises the volunteers. Some property managers may have the skills to work with and supervise volunteers, whereas others may feel inadequate or uncomfortable in such a role. If the latter is the case, the camp director or another staff or committee member may need to team with the property manager to ease relationships, while the property manager supervises the projects and ensures that projects are completed properly.

Careful organization of the projects — including the assignment of teams, proper tools and materials, and clearly written instructions — are essential to the success of such volunteer experiences. Some projects are too lengthy or involved to be accomplished in a few days, and others require licensed personnel and should not be attempted during a volunteer weekend. The food service at such an event may be a volunteer effort where everyone brings a food item and the camp furnishes basic food and supplies, or the camp might provide total food service.

It is always a temptation to leave much of the cleaning and minor repairs for the week when staff arrives for precamp training. Except where certain work projects are used for a one- to three-hour period to build staff teamwork and ownership of the site, it is unwise to use this valuable training period for such routine cleaning and maintenance.

Written Records

Reference has been made to the importance of written plans, records, and reports. The importance of written records will be further commented on in chapter 11 on risk management. However, aside from alleviating liability concerns, if the property is truly the camp's most valuable asset, then written records to ensure its health and continuance are not too burdensome. These records should include:

- A surveyor's map of the property

- A topographical map of the property

- An aerial map of the property

- A schematic map of the property showing facilities and program areas

- A map of the property showing all utility lines, cutoffs, disconnects, and valves

- The property deed and any related easements or rights-of-way

- The blueprints or construction drawings of buildings

- A record of each structure, its construction date and subsequent repairs

- A master site plan

- Any written reports of land or resource conservation management

- An inventory of all mechanical equipment, including dates acquired, serial numbers, and repairs made

- All warranty information on equipment, along with instructional manuals and manufacturers' catalogs

- The ongoing maintenance schedule, with written checklist showing dates and work completed

- Inventories of supplies and minor equipment

A clear designation of which staff member is responsible for securing, storing, and maintaining these records should be made in job descriptions. A specific location should be identified where these records are maintained.

Winterization

Because camps have traditionally been summer-only operations, their buildings have often been built without protection of water lines from freezing temperatures and without insulation and heat. In the past three decades, camps have steadily moved to operating longer than the summer months. New camp buildings are almost universally being winterized for use in nonsummer months.

The modification of summer-only buildings into winterized facilities is often an expensive and unsatisfactory proposition. An analysis of the types of use that are desired and the nature of possible user groups should be made before any steps are taken toward winterization. A careful assessment should be made to see if the need for such facilities is being met in the area by other camps or conference/retreat centers or if a real interest is documented for a new program. A market analysis, as described in chapter 13, is a logical exercise at this point. After this analysis, a more informed decision can be made about the type of facilities that will attract these groups as customers, the feasiblity of modifying existing buildings, or whether the volume of business or service will justify the construction of new winterized facilities.

A camp should carefully consider the distance from the nearest metropolitan area, which is most often the source of extensive nonsummer use, as well as existing competition from other camps or conference/retreat centers in the area. Is there a demand for weekday as well as weekend use? There is no question that year-round operations can spread the cost of maintenance and staff over a larger number of users, allowing better cash flow; broader accomplishment of purpose, outcomes, and goals; and certain savings. However, without the appropriate market or facilities, the opposite may occur. Certain costs will increase with winter use. For example, buildings will need to be kept at a minimum temperature even when not in use, and additional cleaning and maintenance will be necessary, so energy and personnel costs will rise. There will be increased wear and tear as well. Careful study should precede a move toward a four-season facility to make sure that increased usage will more than cover the increased expenses.

Another critical factor in the decision to winterize or expand the summer program to other seasons of the year relates to the camp's overall purpose and philosophy. What is the overall mission and how will moving to year-round operation affect that mission? Will changes in the character or design of buildings have any effect on the summer program? Will expansion of program beyond the summer create different demands for the time and skills of the staff? Who will the primary audience be – youth or adults? Who will operate the program? Will continuous use of existing buildings or grounds over a year have any detrimental effects for their use during the summer?

Checkpoints

1. Do you have the appropriate maps of the property — topographical, survey, schematic?

2. Do you have a map showing all current buildings with utility lines, cutoffs, disconnects, and valves?

3. Do you have an inventory of all equipment?

4. Do you have a maintenance schedule for all mechanical equipment on the grounds? For all buildings (painting, caulking, repairs)?

5. Do you have a master site plan? If not, are you working toward securing such?

6. Have you inspected all buildings and program areas, listing needed repairs and corrections? Have you prioritized them and outlined a plan for their correction?

7. Have present buildings and program areas been evaluated to determine what modifications are needed to bring them into compliance with the Americans With Disabilities Act of 1990?

Related Standards and Guidelines

Accreditation Standards for Camp Programs and Services: SF-1–25, 28–30;
"Additional Professional Practices": Items 1–8, 14, 19, 22

Guidelines for Conference and Retreat Centers:
I-38, I-46–50, II-2, 5, 6, 9–17, 24, III-18–19, 30–31

[1] Julian Harris Salomon. 1959. *Camp Site Development*. New York: Girl Scouts of the United States of America. p. 29. Reprinted by permission.

[2] Dan Smith. 1995. "Design — Good or Bad — Influences Your Ministry." *Journal of Christian Camping*, Vol. 27, No. 5, September/October. p. 19. Reprinted with permission from CCI/USA.

[3] American Camping Association. 1998. *Accreditation Standards for Camp Programs and Services*. Martinsville, IN: American Camping Association. p. 197.

[4] Scott King 1988. "The ABC's of Facilities and Maintenance." *Journal of Christian Camping*, Vol. 20, No. 5, September/October. p. 9. Reprinted by permission from CCI/USA.

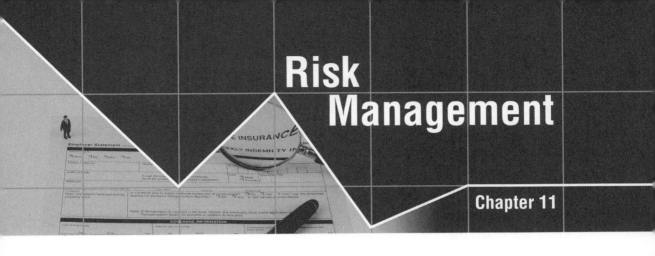

Risk Management

Risk management is one of the most important tasks of camp administration. . . . The board must establish risk management policies in conjunction with the director, and the director must work with the staff and campers in implementing the policies. . . . The quality of the camp experience deteriorates in direct proportion to the extent of unreasonable risks to which the camper is subjected. A camper must be able to participate with confidence that the experience will be a safe one in regard to instruction given, the nature of supervision, and in environmental conditions. A safe experience is a primary responsibility in the conduct of a camp. However, fear of legal liability . . . should never be the reason for not having adventurous, challenging activities. Such activities are needed in today's society.[1]

Definitions

R isk is an uncertainty or probability concerning the loss of resources. The loss of resources, depending on their importance and value, can endanger the very life of an organization. Through a poorly managed risk, camps can potentially suffer such losses as the reputation of the camp, the health and safety of staff, the loss of camp property or financial resources, and, ultimately, the loss of the camp as a resource for future generations. Some of those aspects are very tangible (e.g., money and property), while others are intangible (e.g., the camp's reputation and public attitudes).

Although camps have always been concerned about the health and safety of the campers, the litigious climate of the past four decades has caused camps to broaden their understanding of the risks involved in camp and conference center operations. In this process, risk management has become a critical facet of camp administration. The term risk management implies an overall integrated plan that seeks to manage the risks that might occur in any and every aspect of camp life.

A risk management plan is a system to identify a camp's physical, human, operational, and financial resources and to develop a plan to evaluate, reduce, or control the losses that might result from the operation. It is first an attitude, the attitude that risks can be managed and minimized even if they cannot be eliminated. It is impossible to remove all risk from camp life. Therefore, developing a system to identify and handle those risks in a variety of ways in advance of such losses is wise and necessary.

The areas in which camps are exposed to risk are generally categorized as physical assets, human resources (e.g., personnel or participants), operational financial resources, and standard of care or third-party liabilities. Physical or property assets can be lost through fire, floods, theft, vandalism, poor maintenance, and negligence. Risks affecting people, whether campers, staff, or the public, include death, injury, abuse (physical, mental, sexual, emotional, or verbal), and loss of their service or property. Operational financial risks involve fidelity and income risk. Fidelity risks involve the loss of financial resources through theft, nonperformance of duties, or mismanagement. Similarly, risks to income include events that close the camp or prevent continuance of a camper period, thus requiring refunds or the nonpayment of fees. Third-party liabilities are those imposed by law or assumed under contract (contractual or tort liability).

Incidents and accidents are often used interchangeably, but a delineation in meaning is helpful. Ed Schirick suggests that "An *incident* is generally considered to be an event specific as to date and time that could have resulted in injury to people, damage to property, or financial loss to the business. . . . An *accident* is an incident that results in unintended injury to people or damage to property that will cause a loss to the enterprise."[2]

Legal Aspects

In each of these areas, the camp may suffer direct loss and may become entangled in litigation. Of course, the goal of good risk management planning is to avoid either. When a suit is brought against a camp, both the corporate entity and an individual can be involved in the legal action.

Litigation has become a byword in today's society, and no camp is exempt from lawsuits. To avoid them, the camp needs good legal advice as well as advice concerning camp management and public relations. The camp also needs regular access to an attorney who has a good understanding of the camp program and operation. To achieve this goal, the camp director and attorney must meet for a period of orientation and education. A good risk management plan requires advice from the camp's attorney, among others, about avoiding legal entanglements without hampering the camp program. Regardless of how capable the camp's attorney is, the director will also need some basic understanding of both civil and criminal law. A discussion of some legal terms and principles of law follow.

Initially, the director needs to understand the *doctrine of respondent superior*, which states that a corporate entity is accountable for the actions of employees (including volunteers) if acting within the scope of their responsibility or authority. Understanding this concept gives the corporate chief employed officer and board reason to make sure that the responsibility and authority given employees is clearly identified in job descriptions and training. Similarly, helping an employee understand this concept encourages that employee to carry out his or her responsibilities carefully as outlined in the job description, follow camp policies and procedures, and use only the amount of authority so delegated.

Individuals in camps can be guilty of *criminal acts*, where the offender is punished for actions that might include child abuse, using drugs, harassment, or theft, among others. However, it is far more likely that camps will also get entangled in civil law, where an injured party seeks financial compensation for negligent hiring or actions of the camp or an individual at the camp. Such litigation is likely to be very costly, even if the camp has not been negligent.

Most litigation in camps involves either *contractual* or *tort liability*. The camp enters into contracts with various busi-nesses, individuals, campers, parents, groups, and employees; some are written, and some are verbal. Where there is a disagreement concerning the terms of that contract, whether it relates to the refund of a camper fee or the purchase of equipment or a service, litigation can develop. The development of language in implied contracts such as camper registrations, staff agreements, and rental agreements needs careful thought by the author and review by legal counsel. Verbal contracts are even more difficult, and clear policy statements should be developed about who can make alterations in written policy or commit the camp to financial or other obligations.

Tort liability involves wrongful acts against a person other than through contracts. Torts may be *intentional* or *unintentional*. Camps can avoid the intentional torts relatively easily because they include such actions as slander, physical attack, or invasion of privacy. However, camps are exposed to unintentional torts wherever there is an allegation of negligence. There must be some evidence of negligence, which involves proof that all four of the following occurred:

1. The person in charge had a legal duty to the individual injured.
2. The person in charge violated that duty to prevent an accident or incident that was foreseeable.
3. That breach of that duty was directly related to the incident.

4. There was actual loss or damage resulting from the incident that was caused by the breach (e.g., emotional, physical, mental).

The term *in loco parentis*, "in place of the parent," applies to camps/conference centers at any time the entity assumes the responsibility for a minor "in place of the parent." The entity, whether the corporation or a cabin counselor, has the responsibility of maintaining the same or better level of care of that minor than would be expected from the minor's parents.

Identification of Risk Exposures

The camp director should list all the assets he or she can identify that might be exposed to risk before methods of managing those risks can be chosen. Organizing those risks first by category (who or what is exposed) and then within those categories by types of exposure should help in this process. For example, risks can involve

1. Physical property or equipment (fire, theft, vandalism)

2. Personnel and participant (injury, death, loss of personal property)

3. Operational financial (cancellation or interruption of a camp session, embezzlement)

4. Standard of care or third-party liabilities (contractual, tort action)

Types of exposures within these four areas could be

- Program activities (swimming, tripping, rappelling)

- Business operations (contracts, tax status and documentation, trademark)

- Natural hazards (poisonous animals or insects, insects that transmit diseases, lightning, cliffs near trail, rushing rivers)

- Natural disaster (floods, hurricanes, tornadoes, earthquakes)

- Operation, maintenance, and supervision of facilities and equipment (loose steps, faulty PFDs, weapons on the property)

- Behavior of people (campers, staff, visitors, trespassers, abduction)

- Preexisting medical conditions (asthma, epilepsy, allergy to bee stings)

- National emergencies such as terrorism

- Environmental impairment risks (pollution, dangers from discarded substances)

- Privacy issues (copyright laws, health records, unauthorized access to electronic records)

A review of accident and insurance reports, health service records, and any history of lawsuits will reveal the frequency with which previous losses from these risks occur. Those that show up most frequently should be noted and analyzed. The analysis should include review of types of injury, locations of accident, times of day, days of week, ages of injured, types of activity, and amounts of supervision in place. Consideration should be given also to how severe various losses might be. For instance, even though the camp has had no record of a drowning or head injury from rappelling, either loss could be quite severe involving lawsuits, negative public relations, and long-term effects upon the participant. Those losses with greatest severity should also be noted and analyzed. Obviously risks that appear in both lists (frequency and severity) provide the areas of first concern.

Regulations

No risk management planning is complete without careful consideration of the laws and regulations governing the camp operation. These laws and regulations arise at the federal, state, county, and local level; and, except for the federal regulations, they vary considerably from state to state.

The first step is to secure a copy of those regulations. If no one in a camp knows about them, the director should make an effort to talk with other camp directors or the offices and staff of the local American Camping Association or Christian Camping International section. The department of health or social services and OSHA will often have regulations affecting camps, including specifics on how health records are maintained and what training is mandated for staff. Some states will require a permit or license to operate: some licenses will require an inspection by state or county personnel and some will not. Regulations also may be applicable to camps in other jurisdictions: fire, water, pollution, natural resources, building codes, and sanitation. Some states have integrated most regulations affecting camp into a single "Camp Safety Act." Most states, however, have regulations affecting camps in areas such as health, labor, child care, human services, agriculture, or even education.

If, after study of the regulations, the director finds some that are unclear or very difficult for the camp to comply with, he or she should call for an appointment with a person in the appropriate office. The role of the state or local official is to help the director know how to comply with regulations and to give some assistance in problem situations. It is wise to check on the pattern of inspections. Some departments require a preopening inspection as well as inspections during operation; others inspect annually or biannually.

Where a camp has its home office or its incorporated parent organization in one state and the camp's physical location in another, the regulations of both states must be examined. Although the governmental unit and state in which the camp is physically located may have jurisdiction over health, sanitation, vehicles, fire protection, and pollution control, the state of incorporation may have primary jurisdiction over payroll, employment practices, and tax laws.

Management of Risks

Four methods of managing risks have been identified. In general, risks can be avoided, transferred, retained, or reduced. Choices must be made as to which method or methods best fit the risk exposure.

Avoiding Risks

First, the director should review risks to see if the camp can simply avoid any unnecessary risks. For example, a potentially risky activity that is not essential to the accomplishment of camp outcomes and goals can be eliminated. A practice such as allowing anyone to ride in the back of an open-bed truck can (and should) be eliminated. An old dilapidated wooden shed that could easily catch fire and spread may be a risk that can be avoided by simply tearing down the shed.

Transfer of Risks

Many of the risks in a camp are transferred to another party through insurance or specific agreements or contracts.

Waivers

The camp attorney may develop "hold harmless" statements, which transfer responsibility for certain actions to the participant or sponsoring group. Leases are one method of transferring certain risks to the lessor. There is some debate in the legal community about "waivers," "hold harmless" statements, or "releases." A minor or even a minor's parents cannot waive the minor's rights. That is one reason a minor may file suit against a camp for a supposedly negligent act some months or years (depending on the state) after the minor reaches the age of his or her majority. However, properly worded permissions and releases can have the parent give informed consent rather than a general overall consent to participate. These waivers have been accepted in the courts of all fifty states as showing that the parent knew that the minor was participating in a given activity and that there was some risk involved. Releases can be effective tools in helping bar recovery by the parents or guardians when their child is injured.

On the other hand, a waiver by adult participants may be more binding or carry more weight in court. Janna S. Rankin states that "with regard to adult activities in a recreational setting, a release may be upheld if it is carefully worded, concerned with a risk normally associated with that activity, and the recreation service provider has not been clearly negligent."[3]

A general permission to participate and a release or a waiver should both be considered. A signed permission form is a consent by the parent or guardian to participate in some activity or activities of the camp generally. The camp enrollment process should provide a full description of the activities, including the nature of risks and potential dangers of any activities that are not commonly known to the average person. The camp should then seek a signed specific parental permission for that type of activity. In this way, the parent is giving informed consent, which is an essential ingredient of permission forms and waivers. In many cases, this requires two or more forms to be completed by the parents or guardian.

Many camps are now requiring releases in addition to permission forms. A signed release is an act whereby the participant, parent, or guardian gives up some claim, right, or interest to the people against whom the claim could be made. A parent may release his or her rights to sue the camp, but the parent may not waive or release the rights of the child. Beyond the permission form and release, some camps are now also using an *indemnity agreement*, which requests the parent or guardian to reimburse the camp for any expenses (e.g., legal, medical) incurred by the camp as a result of providing services to the camper.[4] Such permissions and releases need to be developed in consultation with the camp's attorney. An example of a permission form used by one camp can be found in *illustration 11.1.* Most camps include a photo release and the name of any person(s) that have permission to pick up the child, if the parents are not available.

Certainly an organization can assume responsibility for its own members or participants when renting a facility, if the contractual responsibilities of both parties are clearly drawn. However, requiring a certificate of insurance from the organization is often a safeguard to the written agreement.

Illustration 11.1 — *Permission Form*

Permission Form

I understand and certify that my child's participation in Camp _____ and its activities is completely voluntary and I have familiarized myself with the camp's program and activities in which my child will be participating.

I recognize that certain hazards and dangers are inherent in the Camp _____ events and programs and particularly, but not limited to, the activities of horseback riding, swimming, rock climbing, high ropes course, rappelling, and winter tubing, and I acknowledge that although Camp _____ has taken safety measures to minimize the risk of injury to camp participants, Camp _____ cannot insure nor guarantee that the participants, equipment, premises, and/or activities will be free of hazards, accidents, and/or injuries. I further recognize and have instructed my child in the importance of knowing and abiding by the camp's rules, regulations, and procedures for the safety of camp participants.

Insurance

A critical ingredient of any risk management planning is risk transfer. One risk transfer technique is buying insurance. Though some camps may be in a position to self-insure, buying insurance is the most common method camp directors use to transfer risk. The careful selection of an insurance agent or broker is the first step in securing insurance. If possible, an agent should be found who has some understanding of camps and does not cringe at each program activity that seems to pose a risk on the surface. If the agent has the designation CPCU (Chartered Property Casualty Underwriter) or CIC (Certified Insurance Counselor), that person has taken the time to seek the certification and has acquired a broad background in insurance. However, there are many qualified agents without either of these designations.

It is important also that the director be familiar with the various types of insurance that need to be considered. Here are seven general categories or types:

Property Insurance. Property insurance may be purchased for camp buildings and personal property. Coverage options are available for basic causes of loss, broad causes of loss, or special causes of loss. Basic causes of loss coverage, previously known as named perils insurance, covers damage from events such as fire, lightning, windstorm, and vandalism. Broad causes of loss insurance adds a few additional events to these causes of loss such as collapse due to weight of ice and snow. The most comprehensive coverage for camp property is offered by the special causes of loss form of insurance. The difference between the forms is that the basic and broad causes of loss forms cover only those events named in the form, whereas the special causes of loss covers all events, except those specifically excluded.

Some directors choose to insure the buildings and business personal property at their camp using replacement costs. Buying an appropriate amount of insurance is an important matter because of possible penalties for buying too little insurance compared to values at the time of the loss. Directors should obtain appraisals from real estate professionals or replacement cost estimates on buildings from local contractors as a basis for selecting the proper amount of insurance. Inventories of personal property and equipment should also be maintained and evaluated periodically to ensure that the amount of insurance purchased isn't too little, or too much. All property values should be adjusted annually to keep pace with inflation in subsequent years, even in years when inflation is relatively low. It has become very expensive to insure all camp buildings at replacement value, and an option to consider is insuring only the most valuable or essential buildings in this fashion. It is well to consider which buildings are the most valuable and without which it would be difficult to operate. In recent years, local, state, and federal laws regarding construction have been passed; these laws increase the cost of reconstructing a building after a loss. The additional cost of reconstruction is not automatically included under replacement cost insurance. Optional coverage for applying these building laws, including demolition and increased cost of construction, is available. Also factored into this equation should be any disaster, such as a flood or earthquake, that might destroy the entire camp.

A second option is to insure buildings and business personal property for their actual cash value (ACV), or depreciated value. Under these circumstances, if a building were damaged or destroyed, the camp would receive only the value at the time of the loss, and the camp would need to fund the difference between the depreciated value and the replacement cost. This option brings a reduction in rates in proportion to the reduction in value. Depreciation is a subject of negotiation. How much the camp property is depreciated depends on a variety of factors. Ed Schirick notes that "factors that reduce depreciation (and increase value) include proper maintenance, renovation, and repair practices. While there is some subjectivity in determining depreciation and actual cash value, detailed records of repair, maintenance and improvements help you negotiate successfully on this issue."[5]

Another option is to insure buildings and camp personal property on a functional replacement cost basis. This method is relatively new. It differs from the replacement cost valuation method. Instead of providing for replacement "with material of like kind and quality," in the event of total loss, functional replacement cost provides for the replacement of the building's useable square footage with less costly material than was in the original building. Partial losses requiring repairs would be paid for in the same architectural style, but with less costly materials. Directors should realize that some camp property is so unique that the materials to replace the building may no longer be available or may be so costly that the replacement cost is increased well beyond usual construction parameters. Unique camp personal property and memorabilia also present valuation challenges. If there are particularly valuable or unique items in some camp buildings, the director may wish to consider having them insured for their fine art or antique value. While functional replacement cost represents another option, directors should exercise caution and get proper advice about the use of "less costly materials." Appropriate planning is required in advance if this approach is to have any chance of working properly.

In any case, it is good risk management and business management practice to have a schedule of all buildings (insured or uninsured) and an inventory of their contents with their estimated replacement cost, actual cash value, functional replacement, fine art, or antique value noted. In this fashion, the difference between an item's value and amount of insurance is known. Accurate, up-to-date inventories, pictures or videotape of buildings and especially their valuable contents should be kept to document the loss should a fire or some other loss occur. These records should be stored at an off-site office or in a fireproof safe. Best practices require reevaluation and appraisal to ensure proper insurance to value given inflation or diminished value.

The amount of the deductible the camp assumes will also affect the premium. As premiums for insurance coverage have increased, camps have tended to partially retain the loss (self-insure) through higher deductibles (e.g., $1,000, $2,500, $5,000).

Commercial General Liability. A liability policy is designed to provide protection for the camp if lawsuits are brought as a result of alleged negligence. Such allegations may be brought as the result of property damage, bodily injury, advertising injury (e.g., infringement of copyright), or personal injury (e.g., emotional injury, loss of earnings). The insurance company generally evaluates all conditions that increase or decrease risk. For example, the number, experience, and training of horses for horseback riding; the number of motorboats for waterskiing; and the number of staff all affect the risk factors as viewed by the insurance company.

It is important that the camp director help the insurance agent understand the camp and its different risk exposures provided in the individual program and setting. It is at this point that the camp's risk management planning will help the agent understand the precautions and steps taken to minimize risks. The agent should also have exposure and understanding of the camp's American Camping Association Camp Accreditation or Conference/Retreat Center guidelines. Many insurance companies offer reduced rates to camps that hold ACA accreditation.

The camp director should be realistic in setting the limits of coverage to be purchased. In an increasingly litigious environment, camps need to be careful so that they have enough insurance to cover a major incident. Minimum limits to be expected today are $1 million in general liability and $1 million to $5 million in excess limits (generally called umbrella insurance) depending on the degree of risk.

The policy should be checked in detail to see if it provides malpractice insurance for improper medical treatment, product liability coverage for food service, and any type of coverage for independent contractors who may work at camp in construction or program. There also exists today a professional liability policy covering full-time employees that protects the individual against alleged negligence in the performance of professional duties. Having this type of coverage is prudent; however, it is also wise to check any policy carefully for exclusions. There have been many new exclusions and restrictions of general liability coverage in recent years, including terrorism, mold, bacteria, fungus, and communicable disease. Limitations may be placed on certain activities, such as amusement devices and the height of water slides in pools.

Given the increased awareness of inappropriate sexual behavior in recent years, camps should be sure that their policies provide coverage for sexual misconduct. One must not assume that coverage is provided when contracts are silent on this subject. It is advisable to have an affirmative statement that the policy provides this coverage through an endorsement to the general liability policy. Most insurance underwriters require a criminal background check program for all staff including volunteers as one of the methods for managing this risk.

Further, one should question whether this statement covers sexual harassment. An additional coverage, employment practice liability, may be necessary to cover sexual harassment, along with allegations such as discrimination and wrongful termination.

In addition, for camps with several year-round full-time staff who receive employee benefits, consideration should be given to the purchase of employee benefits liability coverage. This covers the camp against mistakes in the administration of their employee benefits plan.

Where there is a governing board, consideration should be given to coverage for directors and officers (D and O) insurance. This insurance provides protection to those people for their actions on behalf of the camp. In addition, if volunteers are used in any fashion in the camp operation, coverage should be checked to make sure they are included.

Economics and outside forces often alter the insurance marketplace. When a hard market for insurance develops, camps may have to look into secondary markets. Nonstandard insurance sometimes becomes an option in such a market. Examples include surplus lines placements, claims-made insurance policies, captive insurance companies, and risk purchasing group programs, none of which may provide the scope of coverage the camp has been accustomed to finding from camp insurance specialists. The director should be very careful in exploring these sorts of nonstandard insurance solutions because such approaches are confusing many times and may result in an incomplete risk transfer.

Workers' Compensation. Required by law, workers' compensation covers medical and hospitalization costs and loss-of-time (wages) compensation incurred for employees injured at work or suffering a work-related illness. The requirements for workers' compensation limits vary from state to state. Because the experience rating of a camp can affect the premium in certain situations, the control of staff accidents is an important part of risk management planning. In most states, international personnel are considered employees and as such are covered under workers' compensation insurance laws. Directors should be certain to show income paid to international staff members as part of their payroll records in this case.

Motor Vehicle Insurance. Vehicles, particularly where they carry passengers, are a major risk. It is vital that the vehicles owned or used by the camp be covered by insurance. Coverage should include liability, property damage, medical payments, and uninsured motorist coverage. Collision and comprehensive coverage is available but must be examined in light of the value of the vehicles and the additional premium. If the camp uses staff-owned vehicles for any purpose whatsoever, nonowner coverage should be secured. If the camp hires or leases vehicles, the lessor is normally expected to carry the insurance, but the director should require a certificate or letter of insurance before using a leased vehicle.

Concerns about the use of fifteen-passenger vans have grown in recent years. Some manufacturers are attempting to provide additional stabilizing mechanisms to reduce the risk of roll-over accidents. Directors considering the use of such vehicles should check safety records and insurance implications carefully.

Umbrella or Excess Liability Insurance. Umbrella insurance is aptly named because it is designed to sit over the top of primary liability insurance policies such as general liability, auto liability, and the employers liability coverage in workers' compensation insurance. This policy is also known as a catastrophe liability policy.

Over the years, coverage under most umbrella policies offered to camps has been scaled back to the point where the umbrella has become an excess policy. Excess policies usually provide higher limits than primary policies but provide no broader coverage than that provided by the primary policy itself. True umbrella policies provide broader coverage than the primary policies underneath and are subject to a self-insured retention (SIR) may fill in the gaps in some primary policies. Such policies have become very rare.

Buying umbrella or excess insurance is another area where the camp needs to be particularly careful in scrutinizing the detail because there is no standardization. In addition, for the past several years, one underwriter has been offering high limits of "umbrella" with sexual misconduct liability on claims-made basis.

Health and Accident Insurance. Health and accident insurance is designed to cover the costs of medical services and hospitalization for camper and staff accidents or illnesses occurring or contracted during the camp stay. Various kinds of coverage are available under such policies. Many camps automatically cover campers and offer coverage to staff as a benefit. Other camps offer campers and staff the option of taking the insurance or relying on their own family policy. If the policy covers staff, work-related injuries are still covered first under worker's compensation insurance. International staff members are usually covered under the contract with the sponsoring organization. Health and accident insurance that covers the cost of treatment may show the camp's concern for the well-being of all campers and staff, reduce costs to parents, and, thus, help minimize the likelihood of a lawsuit.

It is possible to secure a policy that covers the camper in coordination with the family's insurance. The policy pays the deductible on the family policy and anything in excess of the maximum paid by the family policy. Where no family insurance exists, then the policy becomes the primary insurance. This type of policy generally costs less than covering all campers directly.

Day camps typically buy accident-only insurance. Resident camps can also buy sickness medical expense insurance. Limits in these policies tend to be low, and there is usually an accidental death and dismemberment benefit. Some insurers provide a catastrophe medical benefit in the event a claimant is totally, or partially, paralyzed. Coverage can be primary or excess. Rates vary and are experience-rated. Coverage can be purchased with or without a deductible. Preexisting conditions are usually excluded. Because policies vary greatly, the director should examine a prospective policy carefully before purchasing it.

Business Interruption/Loss of Income Insurance. Business interruption or loss of income and extra expense insurance is designed to insure a camp for loss of business income and added expenses when the camp's normal operation is interrupted or suspended. It is not intended to cover the loss of the property that may have caused the cancellation of a session, as that normally would be covered under property and casualty. Such insurance normally requires a direct physical loss or damage to property that results in a loss of business income, but there is normally a clause that includes coverage for a limited time period when the loss is related to action by a civil authority.

Insurance Binders. The director should request and receive binders on each insurance policy on or before the date the policy takes effect, if the policy is not available on that date. A binder assures the director that the policy is in effect for a given time. It is wise to inquire of the agent as to the Best rating of the insurance companies issuing policies; the rating should be a B++ (Very Good) or higher, if at all possible.

Retention of Risk

Certain risks may be retained in instances where it is not possible to avoid or transfer the total risk. Insurance to cover all physical losses completely is too expensive for most camps, so some risk must be retained by the camp. Certain activities are so important to the mission, outcomes, and goals of the camp that one would not consider eliminating them. For example, though drowning may be a severe risk, a camp likely would not eliminate all aquatic activities. Some equipment or facilities would be less expensive to replace than to insure.

The retention of a risk should be a deliberate decision of the administration and the sponsoring organization, if there is one. Each risk should be identified and outlined with the potential consequences. The potential financial consequences of such risks should be estimated.

Where insurance is used to transfer part of the risk, there is normally a financial deductible or threshold that the camp must retain. The insurance company must pay the costs beyond the amount of the deductible. There should be a reserve or contingency fund set aside that can be tapped if such risks materialize.

Reducing Risks

When a camp retains a risk, then the management of that risk is examined to see how much of the risk can be reduced. After the camp has identified which risks are to be eliminated or avoided, the balance of risk management planning is developing the policies and practices that will reduce the remaining risks to an acceptable level. The plan for reducing risks examines what can be done before and during the operation of the risk. Much of the reduction of risks practices also reduce incidents that may increase insurance premiums or prove to be issues in public relations.

Staff other than the director should be involved in identifying risks, for there are others much closer to many risks. "All managers should be given the opportunity to brainstorm ways to reduce risk. They should constantly monitor their staff for behaviors that reduce . . . the opportunity for incidents to occur,"[6] states Chris Rollins.

For example, the camp's administration feels that providing a specific activity to every participant in a unit is important in attaining the desired outcomes and goals for the camp experience. In advance of the activity, several steps are taken to reduce the risk:

1. Leadership is selected on the basis of documented experience and maturity and on the demonstrated ability to work with types of campers being served.

2. Leaders' skills are tested and verified during precamp training.

3. Written operating procedures that include safety regulations and prerequisites for participation or eligibility are followed and used as the basis for all staff training.

4. Participants are given adequate training and are tested on the skills essential to their participation in the activity. Leaders are trained to watch for fatigue, overcompetitiveness, stress, and other signs that may bring a greater human risk factor to an otherwise safe situation.

5. Equipment that is appropriate and safe is provided for use in the activity.

6. The location where the activity is to take place is examined for potential hazards, such as natural hazards or outside interference from other activities and events.

7. A ratio of leaders to participants that ensures adequate supervision is established and carried out.

8. Leaders are trained to implement a clear action plan for emergencies that might arise from participation in the activity.

It is equally important that during the operation of the activity, the following steps be taken to reduce risk:

1. One or more of leaders must be present to supervise an activity at all times. Certain activities may require a minimum of two leaders at all times.

2. Participants must wear appropriate clothing and equipment during the activity.

3. An unsafe practice or violation of operational procedures is stopped immediately upon observation.

The foci of lawsuits in camps over the years have centered on supervision of the activity, the manner in which the activity is conducted, and the availability and condition of facilities or equipment related to the activity. With this knowledge, it is possible to examine program activities carefully, establishing clear policies by the camp administration and regular supervision to see that policies are continually implemented. Because the courts hold camp staff to the standard of care of a "reasonably prudent professional," the recruitment, training, and supervision of staff are critical to help prevent allegations of negligence. Not only is it important that such steps be taken, but there also needs to be documentation that appropriate recruitment, training, and supervision of staff occurred.

In addition, clear policies need to be put in writing and in the hands of all staff. A notebook or staff manual that organizes all such policies and procedures in an orderly fashion is perhaps the best method for preservation and annual review. Nothing is as helpful in litigation as producing written documentation that can be attested to as being available and used in an orientation or training process.

However, everything cannot be written. For instance, though there may be a written policy for the supervision of an activity, that policy does not ensure that the supervision did occur at a particular time and place. Where the risk in question is severe, it is wise to have at least two leaders present so that a second person can attest to the supervision given.

Handling Incidents

No matter how well a plan is put into practice to reduce risks, incidents will occur. Action taken at the time of the incident is as important as the preventive steps taken before the incident. As much as possible, the steps to be taken at the time of an incident should be identified in advance. Develop a crisis communication plan with a designated crisis response team when there is no crisis and there is time to outline carefully the critical steps and responsibilities. *The CampLine* suggests that the team be "interdisciplinary and include people from the camp administration, maintenance, health care, your owners/sponsors (of the camp), a mental health resource (counselor, social worker, community health services) and perhaps a clergy member."[7]

Key staff representing various areas of camp operation should analyze possible crises and their implications for camp operation. Linda Ebner Erceg suggests that completing a chart such as that shown in *Illustration 11.2* is a starting point in risk anaylsis.[8]

Staff members in leadership positions should be given training and directions in writing to cover such points as

- Providing immediate care of the individuals involved in the incident, both injured and uninjured.

- Notifying one's supervisor or designated person as soon as possible.

- Securing outside assistance, if necessary.

- Writing a report of the incident, documenting as many facts as possible (see OSHA requirements later in this chapter).

- If serious, reporting to appropriate individuals outside of the camp (e.g., government agencies, parents of the participant, camp's home office).

- Diverting or organizing the people not involved in the incident into other activities or other areas of the camp.

- Referring media and determining who speaks for the camp/organization. On this point, it should be recognized that media relations can be as critical an element in risk management as notifying parents. Adverse and incorrect publicity can account for long-term damages to the camp. As Dr. Bari S. Dworken points out, "In many cases, reporters and photographers often arrive at camp even before the emergency crew. This can create more than just the initial emergency to deal with."[9]

- Identifying the types of incidents that require special attention to the feelings of staff members and campers, as well as the individuals responsible for securing the expertise to help those people.

Illustration 11.2 *Accident/Incident Report Form*

Accident/Incident Report Form   **FM 01**
Developed by the *American Camping Association*®
(Fill out 1 on each incident or person)

Camp Name_____ Date_____

Address _____
            Street & Number   City   State   Zip

Name of person involved _____ Age _____ Sex _____ ☐ Camper ☐ Staff ☐ Visitor
                                      Last   First   Middle

Address _____ Phone_____
            Street & Number   City   State   Zip   Area/Number

Name of Parent/Guardian *(if minor)* _____

Address _____ Phone_____
            Street & Number   City   State   Zip   Area/Number

Name/Addresses of Witnesses *(You may wish to attach signed statements.)*

1. _____

2. _____

3. _____

Type of incident   ☐ Behavioral   ☐ Accident   ☐ Epidemic illness   ☐ Other (describe)

Date of Incident/Accident _____ Hour_____   ☐ a.m.   ☐ p.m.
                                      Day of Week   Month   Day   Year

Describe the sequence of activity in detail including what the (injured) person was doing at the time _____

_____

_____

_____

_____

_____

_____

Where occurred? *(Specify location, including location of injured and witnesses. Use diagram to locate persons/objects.)*

Was injured participating in an activity at time of injury?   ☐ Yes   ☐ No   If so, what activity? _____

Any equipment involved in accident?   ☐ Yes   ☐ No   If so, what kind? _____

What could the injured have done to prevent injury?_____

_____

Emergency procedures followed at time of incident/accident _____

_____

_____

By whom?_____

Submitted by_____ Position_____ Date_____

Phone number _____

Copyright 1983 by American Camping Association, Inc.   Revised 1990, 1992, 1999.
Printed with permission of and under license of American Camping Association, Inc.

Medical Report of Accident

Were parents notified? _____ ☐Yes ☐No   By ☐Writing ☐Phone ☐Other

By whom?_____ Title_____ When_____
                                                                                        Time   Date

Parent's Response_____
_____

Where was treatment given (check and complete all that apply)?

☐ At Accident Site: Where? _____By whom?_____
   Treatment given_____Date_____
☐ Camp Health Service: By whom? _____ Title_____
   Treatment given_____Date_____
   Released to ☐Camp Activities ☐Home ☐Other _____Date_____
☐ Doctor's Office: By whom? _____Title_____
   Treatment given_____Date_____
   Released to ☐Camp Activities ☐Camp Health Service ☐Home ☐Other _____
☐ Hospital: By whom? _____ Title_____
   Was injured retained overnight in hospital? ☐Yes ☐No If so, which?_____
   Where? _____Date_____ ☐Out-patient ☐In-patient
   Name of physician in attendance_____
   Date released from hospital_____
   Released to ☐Camp ☐Home ☐Other_____
Comments _____
_____
_____

Persons notified such as camp owner/sponsor, board of directors, etc.

Name	Position	Date
_____	_____	_____
_____	_____	_____
_____	_____	_____

Describe any contact made with/by the media regarding this situation _____
_____

Signed_____Position_____Date_____

Insurance Notification

                                                            Date

1. ☐ Parent's Insurance   By ☐Parent ☐Camp   _____

2. ☐ Camp Health Insurance   _____

3. ☐ Worker's Compensation   _____

4. ☐ Camp Liability Insurance   _____

In the same outline, the staff member who is accountable for certain responsibilities or actions at the time of the crisis should be clearly identified.

Some of the incidents will be emergencies and others will not be. It is equally important in nonemergencies to take the preceding steps where applicable. However, certain types of emergencies can be explored in advance, and procedures to cover them (e.g., drowning, fire, tornado, injury requiring medical assistance) can be developed. For each different type of emergency:

- Procedures should be put in writing, reviewed by various experts, and given to the staff.

- Procedures should be rehearsed during staff training, where practical.

- Emergency phone numbers and contact information should be posted in critical places, such as the swimming area, maintenance building, kitchen, and office.

- Staff trained in basic first aid/CPR should be assigned to pertinent areas where emergencies might occur.

Thought should be given not only to the first aid for physical injuries but also to how to deal with the stress brought on by the emergency. Stress in general should be discussed during staff training. Particularly where the participants are children, staff should be helped to understand the signs of mental and emotional stress, the areas where stress can increase the possibility of an accident, the behaviors in which stress can manifest itself once an incident is underway, and the appropriate responses.

For instance, where an alleged incident of abuse occurs, the first concern should be for the welfare of the camper(s). Therefore, the accused staff member should be relieved of his or her responsibilities, and a staff member with expertise and experience in dealing with children should be assigned to the camper group. One must not assume that the staff member is guilty just because an accusation has been made. That guideline should be made clear at the outset to the accused staff member and any other staff involved. However, to protect the campers, the staff member, and the camp, the staff member should be separated from any camper group.

Reporting allegations of abuse is mandated in all fifty states, though the procedures vary from state to state. Specifics on reporting should be determined before camp and be readily accessible during camp.[10] A clear understanding of the accusation and situation must be secured before making a report. It is important to get the facts but not interrogate the child involved and any other children who are witnesses. Any questions to the child must be kept very low key and witnessed by another staff member. Every effort to ease the child's emotional stress should be taken. Remember, it is not your responsibility to determine whether the abuse occurred; that is the responsibility of trained professionals. If there is an accusation or indication of some type of physical, emotional, or sexual abuse, the proper authorities should be notified.

From this point on, the role of the director should be related to controlling the impact of the incident by dealing with the parents of the child, the balance of the staff and campers, the owner of the camp or board of directors, the media, and perhaps the parents of other campers in the camp session at the time. Legal advice may be warranted in dealing with parents of other campers in the living group or total camp, as well as with the media. At this point, a written plan for such incidents made prior to camp is extremely valuable to help the director act and react carefully and logically.

Recent events including acts of terrorism have made camp directors more sensitive to the ways in which incidents outside of the camp itself can affect the feelings, attitudes, and behaviors of staff and campers. No matter how isolated the camp may be, today's communication systems make it impossible for camps to be isolated from knowledge of such incidents. The camp's crisis communication plan should recognize external forces and the type of measures the camp can use to assist campers and staff at such a time.

Recordkeeping

One of the functions for which the camp director must take responsibility is seeing that accurate records are kept of the entire camp operation. As Ed Schirick states, "Defining relationships and responsibilities, as well as terms of agreements with other parties, are examples of responsible risk management and represent good business practice."[11] Though the director will not be able to do this alone, it is important that he or she identify the types of records to be kept, who is to keep them, and where they are to be stored and for how long.

Records serve a number of purposes:

- To provide a paper trail that shows what, when, and why things were done

- To provide information about the current financial state of the organization

- To provide information to analyze operations and costs for efficiency, health, safety, and effectiveness

- To show that the operation is in compliance with local, state, and federal regulations and America Camping Association standards

- To protect against and be available as evidence in case of litigation

- To maintain a history of the camp

Certain records and information are needed so that those who follow the present personnel know what significant events and actions occurred over a period of years.

Health Records

The isolated setting of many camps means that the camp is the primary health care provider for campers and staff. To provide the best health care possible, a camp must collect information about each camper's and staff member's health (e.g., health history, medications, allergies) and inform the appropriate staff of any health considerations in their areas. For example, unit counselors and kitchen staff should be aware of food allergies, unit counselors should be aware of campers who need to receive medications at the health center, and program staff should be aware of campers with severe allergies or illnesses like asthma.

Collecting this information can be difficult because parents and staff don't always understand the significance of providing this information. While the forms may be separate from camper registration forms, the process for collecting this information should be part of registration and follow-up. Forms on which to collect this information should be mailed to parents and staff in advance, accompanied by an explanation of the importance of providing this information. See chapter 12 (*illustrations 12.2* and *12.3*) for an example of the health history and examination form developed by the American Camping Association.

It is important to recognize that information collected about a camper's or staff member's health history is to be used solely to provide accurate and helpful information to those providing health care to the individual and must not be used to refuse the individual a position as a camper or a staff member. In fact, regulations in the Americans With Disabilities Act of 1990 require that the health information on staff members be collected after a position has been offered and before camp begins.

It is also true that most of an individual's health history needs to be maintained confidentially and that some of that history need not be known by the camp. For example, knowing an individual's HIV status should not change the health care given at camp because all staff with health care functions should be trained in the use of universal precautions that would protect the staff member from transmission of such a blood-borne disease. Additionally, under the Americans With Disabilities Act of 1990, people who have tested positive for HIV may not be denied enrollment because of their HIV status.

Any health care provided to campers or staff members while they are in the camp's charge should be recorded. Various regulations affecting health records and a variety of methods for maintaining the health care are given at camp. American Camping Association standards and OSHA require that camper health care records and medical logs be kept separate from staff health care records. Other federal regulations require that health care information on staff be maintained apart from their personnel files.

Though the Health Insurance Portability and Accountability Act of 1996 places responsibilities on businesses and organizations alike in terms of health records, the rules come into effect only when the health care provider engages in electronic transmission of health records. Of course, if the camp bills a family's health insurance for health care services, this may well trigger application of the Act. A camp needs to examine its electronic communication in terms of health care, and double-check the applicability of the law. In any case, the camp should have a clear policy on the how health care information is handled.

Incident Reports

It is particularly vital that reports be made of all accidents or incidents and that uniform information be recorded each time an accident or incident occurs. The term incident is used deliberately, for there are occurrences in camp that are not accidents but are of such a significant nature that there should be a record in case questions arise at a later date. These questions tend to relate to emotional stress, inappropriate camper behavior, alleged abuse, and outside intruders breaching security, among others. No form will cover all potential types of incidents, so a narrative identifying witnesses and dates, precautions taken, actions taken, and any specific results will usually suffice.

The American Camping Association has designed an accident/incident report form that serves as a good model (see *illustration 11.2*). Such reports should be attached to insurance claims where applicable and filed along with all records of treatment of injuries and illnesses until the injured is at least one to four years beyond the age of majority (or for the period of statutory limits in the state where the camp is located, whichever is greater), along with the importance of completing appropriate workers' compensation and OSHA forms recording incidents involving employees. The appropriate recordkeeping of injuries and illnesses is also discussed in chapter 12.

Keeping the records of injuries and incidents is only the first step. One important use of these records is to assist the camp director and health manager in analyzing the frequency and severity of certain types of injuries and the location where those injuries occurred. Between the camper health record (see chapter 12), accident or incident reports, and insurance claims, the director has a clear source of data that requires tallying and analysis at the end of each season. A comparison of such data after several seasons will be most meaningful in risk management planning.

Record Retention

Recognizing that a minor may sue up to one to four years beyond the age of majority (statute of limitations), and therefore a child of the minimum age at the camp (e.g., seven years old) would have thirteen years to bring suit, it would be wise to maintain all records concerning campers involved in accidents or incidents for thirteen years (e.g., health records, accident reports, registration forms and permissions signed by the parent, insurance coverage records, witness). Further information on record retention is found in chapter 14 (*illustration 14.4*).

There are many different statutes of limitations with time periods that vary from law to law and state to state, especially in regard to taxes and unemployment and workers compensation records. Therefore, the director should give careful thought to record retention and should obtain legal advice. The policy of the organization or camp on recordkeeping and record retention should be developed on the basis of law, the rule of reason, and the risk involved. Such a policy should be in writing. In many cases, records may be microfilmed and serve as a legal record, but this needs to be checked with an attorney for the specific state ruling.

OSHA regulations require employers with eleven or more employees to maintain OSHA 200 forms, record all employee injuries, and post the summary of the form from February 1 to March 1 each year at a location where employees can read it. In addition, a supplementary record of each individual injury and illness must be kept on the OSHA 101 form and retained for five years. In some cases, a workers' compensation First Report of Injury form may serve both purposes if it covers all information required. An OSHA poster must also be posted in a location where it can be seen by all employees. Copies of the forms are available directly from the state OSHA office and, in some cases, the state labor department. See chapter 12 for other OSHA requirements.

Accreditation

Accreditation by an outside body has proven to be an invaluable step in all types of institutions across the country, from schools to hospitals. It gives validity to the concern of the camp, in this case, to meet professional standards and to stay abreast of the latest information concerning health and safety in the field. The fact that an outside body comes in to examine all aspects of the operation provides not only a checkpoint for the administrator but also a backup if litigation ever occurs.

The American Camping Association is currently the only national organization with an independent accreditation program for all types of camps and conference centers. Its long history of developing standards in the field as well as its research and constant updating of those standards has led courts and government bodies to hold these standards as industry standards. In other words, actions of a camp involved in a lawsuit will be measured against American Camping Association standards whether or not the camp is affiliated with or accredited by the association. Because ACA accreditation does not require a camp to meet every standard for accreditation, an ACA-accredited camp may find that in court questions are asked about standards the camp chose not to meet. Therefore, a camp needs to be prepared to provide rationale and documentation for standards not met.

Over ninety percent of the standards relate to risk management, and the paperwork related to those standards would meet many of the suggestions provided in this chapter. Local sections of the American Camping Association offer courses annually that explain the standards and the type of preparation that is needed for an accreditation visit. These courses are invaluable for directors, even if accreditation is not being sought.

The single most effective step a camp can take in risk management planning is to become accredited by the American Camping Association and to annually update all of the written procedures and policies. Of course, that step is effective only if the camp continues to follow the standards after the accreditation visit.

Checkpoints

1. Which state and local regulations apply to your camp?

2. Prepare a list of the risks that exist in your camp, starring those that appear to happen most frequently and those that carry the highest potential risk.

3. On that list, identify those risks that can be avoided or transferred to others.

4. Develop risk reduction steps for all risks to be kept or transferred.

5. Has your camp been accredited? If not, what is involved in the accreditation process?

6. What is your information collection and record retention plan?

7. Review the insurance of the camp and identify areas that need updating. Is the camp covered with fire and casualty, liability, workers' compensation, vehicle insurance?

Related Standards and Guidelines

Accreditation Standards for Camp Programs and Services: Nearly all the standards apply to risk management. However, Standards OM-1–21 are not referenced in other chapters and should be considered with the other standards. In fact, the preparation of *The Standards Organizer: Written Documentation Organizer for ACA Accreditation* published by ACA is probably the easiest way to develop risk management planning materials and to keep in one place most of the records necessary for such documentation. "Additional Professional Practices": Items 1–2, 4–5, 7–9, 10, 13–14, 16–23, 25, 30–31, 39

Guidelines for Conference and Retreat Centers: II-4–20, 30, III-3, 4–31

[1] Betty van der Smissen. 1993. "Foreword." *Management of Risks and Emergencies: A Workbook for Program Administrators*. Kansas City, MO: Camp Fire Boys and Girls, Inc. p. v.

[2] Ed Schirick. 2000. "Risk Analysis and Evaluations." *Camping Magazine*, Vol. 73, No. 4, July-August. pp. 12-13.

[3] Janna S. Rankin. 1986. "Waivers." *Camping Magazine*, Vol. 58, No. 3, January. p. 24.

[4] Marge Scanlin and Richard Smikle. 1994. "Reviewed Your Permission Form Lately?" *CampLine*, Vol. 5, No. 2, October. pp. 3–4.

[5] Ed Schirick. 1997. "Risk Management — Insuring Your Camp's Buildings and Contents." *Camping Magazine*, Vol. 70, No. 3, May/June. p..

[6] Chris Rollins. 1998. "Train Away Risk." *Camping Magazine*, Vol. 71, No. 5, September/October.

[7] "Crisis Response in a Troubled World." , *The Campline* Vol. XII, No. 1, Spring 2003.

[8] Linda Ebner Erceg. 2003. "Emergency & Disaster Planning: Responding to Camp Needs Using Updated Disaster Planning Paradigms." *ACN Compass Point*, Vol. 13, No.1, March.

[9] Bari S. Dworken. 1998. "10 Commandments of Risk Management." *Camping Magazine*, Vol. 71, No. 5, September/October. p.

[10] Becca Cowan Johnson. 1992. *For Their Sake*. Martinsville, IN: American Camping Association. p. 68.

[11] Ed Schirick. 1997. "Get It in Writing." *Camping Magazine*, Vol. 70, No. 4, July/August. p.12.

Operation & Supervision:
Central Administrative Services

An effective administration relieves program of all nonessential detail. . . . The tracks must be kept clear if program is to operate at its maximum degree of economy and effectiveness. Such matters as health, safety, and sanitation, although vitally important in program considerations are as much the concern of administration as feeding, housing, and transportation. In fact, it is hard to draw the line, when discussing responsibility, as to just what parts of the total camp life are administrative in contrast to those of program.[1]

Though every operation in camp is part of the overall program, certain services tend to be seen in a more supportive role to the direct program operation. The importance of these services in complementing direct program activities, as well as their role in the risk management plan, cannot be overemphasized.

Health Service

There are three broad functions of a camp health service:

1. To manage resources. The purpose of this function is to maintain an effort to promote a healthier, safer camp community and to make policy decisions in the area of camp health. Tasks include defining the scope of health care that the camp will provide, writing job descriptions for health service staff and supervising that group, determining budget, deciding what parents are told about camp health services and how that is communicated, arranging out-of-camp health service, signing medical protocols, and defining the chain-of-command of health service personnel. This comprises the function of camp health care administration and is most often fulfilled by the camp director in collaboration with the camp's supervising physician, but, in a very large camp or a camp serving a population with special medical needs duties, this function may be assigned to the physician in residence at the camp.

2. To provide care. The purpose of this function is to meet the individual health care needs of staff and campers and to manage the health of the total camp community. Tasks include medication management; screening practices, assessment, care, and evaluation of illness or injury situations; surveillance of the camp community health concerns; collaboration with out-of-camp providers to support recovery of ill or injured people; collaboration with other camp staff to provide a safe and well camp experience; collaboration with camp administration in an effort to improve camp health practices; and communication with external medical and health resources. This function is often performed by the camp nurse or camp physician, as the camp health care provider.

3. To respond to emergencies. The purpose of this function is to develop, implement, and evaluate the camp emergency response system. Tasks include plans to be followed by camp staff for site emergencies and coordinating with external providers. These tasks are usually identified by the camp director and completed by a group of camp staff, including the health care personnel. Staff members with CPR and certifications in aquatics and wilderness medicine often are involved in this process.[2]

Personnel

All camps need to identify clearly the positions of health care administrator and health care provider:

- A health care administrator is the person who develops the health care plan and coordinates all health care functions. This includes the basic medical oversight for the camp.

- A health care provider is the individual with day-to-day responsibility to implement the health care plan.

In some camps, both positions may be assumed by one individual who reports to the camp director. Within these positions, various other medical personnel may be involved: *illustration 12.1* provides a clearer picture of the variety of health care certifications that may come into play within the camp's health service.[3]   The term supervising physician is used to describe a physician who provides the medical oversight for the camp both in terms of helping to develop the health care plan and establishing the medical protocols to be followed. Such a person may or may not reside at or near the camp. If the supervising physician is not in residence at camp or in the nearby community, a camp physician should be secured in the nearby community. The term camp physician is used to designate the physician who is in residence at the camp or is available by telephone in the nearby locale to treat an injury and/or illness, delegate some medical authority to a nurse via standing orders for an individual, and provide liaison with the external medical and health resources in the local

Illustration 12.1 *Health Care Providers Comparison*

HEALTH CARE CERTIFICATIONS: A Comparison of Selected Characteristics

Note: Chart information is meant only as a guide; state regulations supersede chart information.

Title of Certifications	Conditions Impacting Ability to Practice	Primary Skill Based on Educational Preparation	Ability to Diagnose/ Prescribe Medication	Ability to Handle Emergencies	Skill with Individual/ Community Health Needs	Equipment Needed to Function in Role
Physician (MD)	Requires license to practice in the state. Works autonomously in medical role.	Diagnosis/treatment of injuries and illnesses.	Priority skill; related to diagnosis/treatment of injury and illness.	Varies with experience. ER ability usually stronger than field work; depends on specialty.	Well-skilled in individual injury or illness needs. Ability in psychosocial and community health domains varies.	Access to lab, x-ray, and routine items; strong physical assessment skill.
Physician's Assistant (PA)	Requires direct supervision of consenting physician. Limits of practice vary by state.	Assists MD with diagnosis and treatment of selected injuries and illness.	Limited to common injuries and illness per directives of supervising MD. Provides nursing diagnosis.	Varies with experience.	Works best with individual injury or illness needs. Community health ability varies.	Varies; some access to lab and x-ray. Physical assessment skill varies with experience.
Registered Nurse (RN)	Requires license to practice in the state. Works autonomously in nursing role.	Diagnosis/treatment of people's responses to health issues, actual or potential.	Does not prescribe meds; gives meds per MD; prescribes treatments.	Varies with experience.	Individual needs; also psychosocial. Community skills, if educated at BSN level.	Minimal/general needs. Physical assessment skill varies with experience and education.
Nurse Practitioner (NP or ARNP)	Varies. Some states don't recognize credential or limit practice (e.g., no prescriptive ability). Check state regs. Need RN license.	Diagnosis/treatment of injuries and illnesses; people's response to health issues; combines RN and PA abilities.	Varies; limited to common injuries and illnesses. State regulations vary; requires prescriptive authority.	Varies with experience.	Individual needs; also psychosocial. Community skills vary based on emphasis during practitioner education.	Varies; some access to lab and x-ray. Physical assessment skill varies with experience.
Licensed Practical Nurse (LPN or LVN)	Licensed to practice in the state. Requires supervision; who defines state regs?	Assists with care of ill or injured.	Limited; gives medication under RN/MD supervision; see state regs.	Limited; usually works under RN/MD direction.	Individual needs; limited psychosocial skills. No community health training.	Minimal/general needs. Minimal assessment skill.
Emergency Medical Tech (EMT)	Varies by state.	Responds to emergency situations.	Recognizes emergency situations; does not prescribe.	Emergency response is a primary skill. Wilderness training needed.	Focused on individual crisis needs. No community health training.	Uses equipment common to emergency work (e.g., ambulance supplies).
First Aider	Usually under Good Samaritan state statute.	Responds to critical situations.	Recognizes critical crisis; does not prescribe.	Limited to scope of training and experience.	Individual life-support needs; no community health training.	"Makes do" with items in the area.

community. It is critical that this person is comfortable with the camp's health care plan and protocols and has communicated with the camp's supervising physician. Of course, one person may serve in both of these capacities.

Careful attention to the early selection of a supervising physician and the camp health care administrator along with the development of comprehensive health care policies and procedures will save the camp director considerable time and worry later in the season. The director should be totally comfortable with the physician, whether supervising or camp, and that person's knowledge of camp and the age groups served. Although the camp director can seldom be an expert in medical areas, he or she should be very familiar with this particular part of camp life. Camps with boards or committees may have a health committee that includes a physician and/or nurse to help recommend such policies to the operating board or committee.

It would be ideal if a camp could have a physician and a nurse to provide most of the care of the camp population since both professions fulfill unique roles in the health care field. However, that is often impractical for the majority of camps to have both a physician and a nurse on their staff, except where the camp has a population with special medical needs or is a larger long-term camp. So most often a registered nurse is placed in the role of camp health provider.

A registered nurse treats people's reactions to injury, illness, and life events as well as operates under the medical authority delegated by a physician. In many camps, the nurse is the principal camp health provider. A separate scope of practice has been developed for the camp nursing practice,4 and the camp director should become familiar with that scope.

In selecting a nurse, a careful examination of the nurse's experience and approach is critical if it is to be a good experience for both the camp and the nurse. A nurse who has spent his or her entire nursing career in a hospital or doctor's office may be reluctant to take any step in a camp health center without direct immediate orders from a doctor. Experience in an emergency room, as a school nurse, or in pediatrics is more likely to provide the experience comparable to the camp health situation. The nurse also needs direct experience in first aid because so many of the minor ailments of camp life require that sort of attention rather than diagnosis or long-term treatment.

The role of the nurse in health education with both the camp staff and campers is not to be overlooked. Kris Miller Lishner points out that "the camp nurse is a health education resource person, collaborator, and consultant for the staff. . . . Everyone in camp is a health educator and has some responsibility for health teaching. Activity directors, kitchen managers, and administrative staff engage in health education when they point out safe ways to do activities, perform jobs and maintain environmental health and safety. In their daily routines with campers, counselors are their primary health teachers."5

Some camps use several physicians and nurses who are parents of campers or former campers or staff who rotate in for a couple of weeks each over the summer. Where there is such a turnover of personnel, the health care administrator needs to establish a system to ensure consistency in the day-to-day operation and practices.

American Camping Association standards recommend that, in a day camp, if a physician or registered nurse is not available, the camp should have a previous written arrangement with a physician or registered nurse to provide consultation and daily health care support. In resident camps where such personnel are not available, it is acceptable to make similar arrangements with a nurse or physician who comes to the camp site daily to consult. Of course, in camps that primarily serve people with special medical needs, it is crucial to have a resident physician or registered nurse. As noted before, the standards of the American Camping Association are minimum standards, and each camp needs to assess its own needs based upon program, location, and people served.

In addition to these requirements, it is essential to have at least one person present in camp at all times who has training in first aid and CPR. ACA acknowledges variations in the degree of training needed by the person depending on the proximity of the camp to an emergency medical system. If professional medical help is twenty minutes away or less, first aid and CPR are sufficient. Where the time for access is twenty to sixty minutes, a second-level first aid certification plus CPR is required. When the time for access is more than an hour, a person with certification from a nationally recognized provider of training in wilderness first aid and CPR is necessary. In all cases, previous arrangements with health care personnel and facilities away from the campsite should be made in writing.

Health Care Planning

The supervising physician, the director, and, if possible, the principal health care provider should develop a comprehensive camp health plan that defines the scope of health care the camp will provide, the various positions required, written job descriptions for health service positions, a supervision plan for staff and campers, what parents are told about camp health services and how that is communicated, the external camp health services required, and signed medical protocols.

Key policies and procedures should be addressed.

Policies. A set of written policies should address the following questions;

- What is the maximum time acceptable between physical examinations by a physician and arrival at camp for staff and campers?

- What is the maximum time between submission of a health history and arrival of the person at camp?

- What are the qualifications and authority of the health care administrator, providers, and assistant?

- What is the scope of health care, including emergency care, to be provided at the camp site as opposed to at external health facilities?

- What are the health care policies and procedures to be followed during the camp's operation?

- With what external health support resources does the camp need relationships (e.g., emergency room, hospital, dentist, mental health, pharmacy, crisis team, clinic/lab)?

- How is use of external health care resources to be determined, including a clear understanding about hospitalization and emergency provisions?

- What type of communication to parents about the camp's health service and treatments will be made? What is the line of responsibility and timing for that communication?

- How will the privacy of health information and records be handled? (See discussion in chapter 11.)

Procedures. A set of written procedures should address the following matters and may comprise a health care manual to serve as a practice guide by the health care provider:

- Name, qualifications, and location on site of all camp health providers, including where first aid and CPR certified personnel are required to be present.

- Supplies and equipment, including a plan for maintaining an inventory of stock medications, supplies, and medical equipment; ordering additional supplies; and storing existing supplies (e.g., in a locked cabinet or refrigerator for narcotics and prescription drugs).

- Method of health screening, in resident camps, of campers and staff upon arrival and return (if leaving on extended trips), including what records are kept. In day camps, the routine visual health check for observable evidence of illness, injury, or communicable disease is done on all campers on the first day and the plan for daily follow-up thereafter.

- Treatment procedures for routine health care emergencies in situations where health care personnel are not readily available (e.g., out-of-camp trips, camping and canoe trips).

- What information is to be sent with staff on out-of-camp trips and how it is protected from being seen by unauthorized individuals. (A list of campers with names, home addresses and phone numbers, birth dates, and emergency contact numbers for those individuals responsible for minors, along with all medical treatment permission forms).

- How campers and staff who have special medical needs are to be assessed for service.

- Management of stock medications kept by the camp and those brought by campers and staff to camp.

- Emergency medical care.
  - How life-threatening medical emergencies are to be handled when health care personnel are not readily available (e.g., out-of-camp trips, camping and canoe trips) as well as when they are available.
  - Emergency transportation, permission for use of private cars.

- Procedures for monitoring health and sanitation — identification of general routines to be followed for monitoring health and sanitation throughout camp and for specifying the roles of counselors, kitchen staff, and maintenance staff, including:
  - Sanitary procedures to be followed in dealing with medical wastes and bodily fluids
  - A plan for storage, pickup, and disposal of trash and garbage throughout the camp
  - Identification of staff member(s) to whom the health care provider expresses concerns about observations in area(s) outside his or her supervision
  - A plan for monitoring the health of staff members who handle food and areas used for food preparation
- Recordkeeping. Type of records to be kept by the camp health care administrator and/or providers including:
  - Health examination forms
  - Health screening records
  - A day-to-day bound health log with numbered pages for recording in ink (which cannot be altered or removed) all treatments of campers and staff
  - Injury/incident reports
  - OSHA forms
  - Any health care documentation required by a state licensing agency and/or the license held by the camp's health care provider, as well as any other supplementary records
  - Review of the previous years' injury/illness data for risk-reduction purposes
- Who has access to health records, and what privacy protection is provided under the standards resulting from the Health Insurance Portability and Accountability Act of 1996.

These health care policies and procedures and the health care provider's manual are a vital part of the camp's risk management plan and should be maintained with it as well as at the health center. The supervision of these health care policies and procedures is the responsibility of the health care administrator even though specific portions of it may be assigned by the camp director to non-health care personnel (e.g., maintenance or kitchen staff).

In advance of staff training, the camp health administrator and the director should sit down for a lengthy consultation with the camp health care provider and, if possible, the camp physician. The conference should include a review of the written camp health care plan, which includes policies and procedures describing the scope of health services provided by the camp, and an update of such items as

- Arrangements in writing with the hospital chosen by the physician and with providers of other emergency services, such as dental and mental health services
- Mealtime procedures for people admitted to the health center, including how to obtain meals from the kitchen, as well as arrangements for special menu requirements

- Laundering of health center linens and disposal of trash and medical waste, including sharps

- Biohazard materials

- Emergency transportation with names of drivers, location of vehicle keys, and gas

- Regular hours for the health center and how the health care provider(s) are to be reached at night or when not in the health center

- Daily procedures for living-group counselors to follow in the supervision of camper health, including procedures for regular check-ins at the health center or area

- A plan for regular inspection of the entire camp (e.g., who accompanies health care provider on inspection of living quarters?)

- A clear statement of insurance and billing procedures

This conference of the health administrator, the director, the health care provider, and the camp physician should also include a discussion of the medical protocols or treatment procedures under which the camp health provider will operate. Medical protocols are given by the physician so that an RN may carry out certain procedures for the camp population without further consultation, whereas standing orders are often provided in the treatment of an individual. Even if camp does not employ an RN, the camp's medical protocols should include procedures and responsibilities in first aid, emergency medical care, routine health care by staff other than the health manager, initial health screening, and professional therapy (if any). These should be discussed carefully, modified as needed, and signed by the doctor; a copy should be kept by the camp health care administrator, camp health care providers, camp director, and camp physician. Using the camp's previous year's protocols as a sample may make it easier for the physician to review and write them according to his or her viewpoint. Some physicians may be reluctant to sign protocols. If this type of hesitation is encountered, it is wise for the camp director and camp health manager to develop written health care procedures based upon conversations with the physician and then ask the physician to review and initial them with any corrections.

The camp director has an important role in orienting health care providers and providing the support that will make his or her time and work effective. Since a health care provider is often the only person in camp in that profession, opportunities should be sought to put the provider in touch with other camp health care providers by visits to other camps or workshops during the year. The Association of Camp Nurses has proven to be a rich resource for sharing experiences and knowledge among camp nurses across the country.

Louise Czupryna, a camp nurse, points out that "camp directors can play a vital role in welcoming a nurse to camp, especially newcomers to the field, and giving them the support they need to become a part of the 'camp team.' They often need to be 'helped along a bit.' One of camp nurses' biggest complaints, especially new ones, is the lack of deliberate effort to help them feel a part of the camp operation. Without the interaction and assistance of fellow health professionals that they receive in a hospital or clinic, new camp nurses are apt to feel lonely and disconnected in the rustic camp environment."[6] Camp directors, being in a people-oriented business, should understand the need for this personal attention to someone in a strange setting.

Staff Training

During the precamp training period for all staff, the camp health administrator and/or the camp health care provider should be assigned a period or periods to work with staff concerning their individual roles in the health care procedures. Everyone should be given a copy of emergency procedures and required to rehearse any drills. All staff should be given some training in basic first aid techniques. Training should include identification of the dangers of blood-borne pathogens and hepatitis B, precautions that should be taken to avoid exposure, and steps to be taken upon exposure. A clear definition of the types of things general staff can care for and what should be referred to the health center should be given to the staff members. They should be given the impression that the health center is not simply a place for the treatment of serious illness and injury, but rather a friendly, integrated part of camp life that ministers to many diverse needs in the camp community. Often, the health care provider will deal with homesickness and ailments growing out of stress or other emotional and psychological causes. The involvement of the health personnel in the fun activities of camp, whether as an occasional helper at the waterfront or in the craft shop or as a participant in skits or stunts at a campfire, can endear the person to the camp as an individual. With the proper attitude, health care personnel can become a listening ear for many of the problems faced by campers and staff that have little to do with medical treatment.

Living-group counselors need additional time with the health provider to better understand their day-to-day role in the health care of the campers entrusted to their care. They should understand how they are to be informed of special health problems of individual campers in their group, when they are to bring campers to the health center, and what symptoms or problems to watch for in their daily living routines (e.g., during dressing, personal hygiene routines, eating, and sleeping). The importance of cabin cleanup, daily inspections, and their relationship to the health of campers and staff should be stressed. Those daily inspections, the "walk around" along with regular visits to other parts of camp (e.g., the kitchen, maintenance shop, program activity areas, and staff living quarters), are a key part of health supervision. It is important that the health provider not be considered a spy by other departments or counselors. However, the health care administrator should be alert to possible health hazards; when one is spotted, it should be reported immediately to the department supervisor or to the director. Naturally, it is not wise for the health provider or administrator to approach the counselor, kitchen helper, or individual staffer on the spot unless it is an emergency. Rather, the problem should be called to the attention of the person's immediate supervisor.

Staff should also be trained in prevention as well as symptom recognition and first aid or treatment for any health problems specific to the geographic location. This is especially important when staff come from other areas of the country or the world. International staff should be given some orientation to the health standards, personal and group, of the country they are visiting. All staff should be aware of the signs and method for prevention of Lyme disease, a tick-borne infectious disease mostly in the northeast, and of West Nile Virus. West Nile Virus is thought to be maintained in a cycle involving infected birds and mosquitoes, which in turn pass the virus on to humans. Ellen Reynolds, M.S.N., C.P.N.P., and Holly Bauer, R.N., write, "The appearance of West Nile Virus in recent years is perhaps the most well-documented introduction of a new, vector-borne human pathogen into the U.S. in this century. Because of the spread of the virus via mosquitoes, the virus is of particular concern for camps located in rural, wooded, or wilderness areas. While the virus causes encephalitis and meningitis in serious cases, most cases are mild and require only symptomatic care. Education and prevention measures can help to place concerns about the disease in proper perspective."[7]

If the camp health care provider is to perform the role of overall health, sanitation, and wellness supervision of the camp, careful interpretation of that role must be given to the staff during training. In addition, a clarification of the manner in which the health care provider deals with problems he or she observes in areas outside of his or her direct supervision needs to be determined early on.

Staff training should also include information about disease transmittal and precautions to prevent transmission, including hand washing. As employers, camps are now mandated to give training on disease transmission, including blood-borne pathogens, and on universal precautions to prevent their transmission. Specific mention should also be made of AIDS and hepatitis as blood-borne pathogens. In light of having a staff that is conceivably old enough to be sexually active, it would be a serious omission not to also mention sexually transmitted diseases.

OSHA has a number of regulations regarding employee health and safety that staff should receive training on. Certain OSHA regulations require "providing personal protective equipment [for employees]. In the pool area, for example, OSHA requires a respirator, rubber gloves, and eye protection in the filter room. An eye wash station is also needed when chlorine is handled by employees. . . . In addition . . . employers are expected to examine workplace conditions to ensure they conform to applicable health and safety requirements," reports Ed Schirick.[8] Hazards are a key factor in OSHA regulations, which typically require that they be removed or guarded against. A written Hazard Communication Plan is required; it should include

1. A list of the hazardous chemicals on the site
2. How the staff is trained in the use of such substances
3. The requirements for labeling containers of such substances
4. How the requirement for Material Safety Data Sheets is met

Employers are required to distribute to employees information on any hazardous substances in work areas. Robert Bush states that "the OSHA definition of a 'hazardous chemical' is very broad" and identifies examples such as chemicals used in photography, pool cleaning, and arts and crafts, as well as industrial-strength cleaning materials and the like. These substances come with Material Safety Data Sheets (MSDS) that must be kept in a place accessible to employees.

In addition, a safety program should be developed with specific procedures to disable or to prevent starting machines or equipment inadvertently. These lockout/tagout requirements are designed to prevent the removal of guards or safety devices. The director must be able to show that the plan has been reviewed annually and that employees have been trained in the plan.[9]

Records

Written documentation is a vital ingredient of good health care and risk management. A variety of types of written records are important.

- Signed permissions for routine health care, for administering prescribed medications, and for seeking or providing emergency medical treatment for all campers and staff who are minors.

- Health examination forms on all resident camp participants, requiring the examination to have been performed within a minimum of two years (or twelve months in some states) prior to their arrival at camp and signed by a licensed physician who specified the date of the exam and any current medications, treatments, or medical conditions requiring restrictions on participation. A sample health examination form is shown in *illustration 12.2.*

- Health histories, with names, phone numbers, and addresses of those individuals to be contacted in case of a medical emergency. A sample health history is shown in *illustration 12.3.*

- Records of health screening, if resident camp, within twenty-four hours of arrival. A sample health screening record is shown in *illustration 12.4.*

- Health logs with records in ink of the date, time, and name of person ill or injured, general description of injury or illness, description of treatment (if any), administration of routine medications and treatments, and initials of person evaluating and treating patient. A camp director will find a bound health log with numbered and lined pages where records of all patients are recorded on successive lines in ink, the minimum requirement for a reassuring record in case of legal defense in a lawsuit. A sample health log sheet is shown in *illustration 12.5*. This practice does not eliminate or provide a substitute for recording the treatment of an individual camper or staff member in a method required by a state licensing agency and/or to the level required by the license held by the camp's health care provider. This separate record goes beyond legal defense to meet certain health care requirements.

The computer may serve as one source for health care records. However, legal defense depends on having records that can be demonstrated as having not been altered. Therefore, in most cases, computer records become backup or supplementary records to a written log. As the demand for computer records increases, careful attention must be given to the policies for access and use of the information. The use of passwords and such protections as well as the creation of a program that tracks any changes will make computer records more secure and accurate. In moving to computer records, the director should consult with not only the health care administrator but also a computer programmer and the camp's legal counsel.

In any case, the camp director has the ultimate responsibility for being familiar with how records are generated and making sure that there is the appropriate record for legal defense on behalf of the camp. Some of these records include

- Accident/incident reports completed on all injuries. A sample accident/incident report form is shown in *illustration 11.2*. A different form may be required by workers' compensation or OSHA and may substitute for the form used for campers.

- Inventories of medications and supplies at the beginning and end of the season.

- Records required by OSHA of all health information and training provided staff in the area of blood-borne pathogens, all treatments rendered to staff concerning blood-borne pathogens, and any incidents in which staff have had exposure to blood-borne pathogens. OSHA requires a written Exposure Control Plan that includes
  1. Identification of job classes or job tasks with occupational exposure to blood and other potentially infectious materials
  2. Procedures for evaluating the circumstances surrounding an exposure incident
  3. A schedule and method for implementing the various parts of the plan, including training of employees.[10]

All of these records should be placed together and, with the exception of the inventories, kept until one to four years after the youngest participant has reached the age of majority of the state of the camp's location and office (be sure to check the statutory limit in your state). They probably need to be immediately accessible during the twelve months following the close of the camp session and should be stored in a fireproof area thereafter.

Illustration 12.2   *ACA Health Examination Form FM 12*

For Office Use

Health Examination Form for Children, Youth and Adults Attending Camps FM 12

Suggested for resident camp use.

Developed and approved by the
American Camping Association®
with the American Academy of Pediatrics

Dates of Camp Attendance _____

Mail this form to the address below by _____ (date)

Year

The information on this form is not part of the camper or staff acceptance process, but is gathered to assist us in identifying appropriate care. Health exam must be completed by approved licensed medical personnel at least every two years.

Name _____ Birth date _____ Age at camp _____
    Last   *First*   *Middle*

Home address _____
        Street address   *City*   *State*   *Zip*

Social Security number of participant _____   Gender: ☐ Male ☐ Female

Custodial parent/guardian _____   Phone _____

Home address _____
(if different from above) *Street address*   *City*   *State*   *Zip*

Business address _____   Phone _____
        Street address   *City*   *State*   *Zip*

Second parent or guardian or emergency contact _____

Address _____   Phone _____
    Street address   *City*   *State*   *Zip*

Business address _____   Phone _____

If not available in an emergency, notify _____

Relationship _____   Phone _____

Address _____
    Street address   *City*   *State*   *Zip*

Cabin or Group

Health Care Recommendations by Licensed Medical Personnel

I examined the above camp participant on _____. (ACA accreditation requirements specify exams within 24 months of camp attendance. Individual camps may require annual exams. A new exam is not necessarily required for camp attendance.)

BP _____   Weight _____   Height _____

In my opinion, the above applicant ☐ is ☐ is not able to participate in an active camp program.

The applicant is under the care of a physician for the following conditions _____
_____

Recommendations and Restrictions at Camp

Treatment to be continued at camp _____
_____

Medications to be administered at camp (name, dosage, frequency) _____
_____

Any medically-prescribed meal plan or dietary restrictions _____
_____

Known allergies _____
_____

Description of any limitation or restriction on camp activities _____
_____

Additional information for health care staff at the camp _____
_____

Signature of Licensed Medical Personnel _____

Printed _____ Title _____

Address _____

Phone _____ Date _____

Name

Illustration 12.3 **ACA Health Examination Form FM 12**

For Office Use

Health History Form for Children, Youth and Adults Attending Camps FM 11

Suggested for resident camp use.

Developed and approved by
American Camping Association®
American Academy of Pediatrics

Dates of Camp Attendance_____

Mail this form to the address below by _____ (date)

The information on this form is not part of the camper or staff acceptance process, but is gathered to assist us in identifying appropriate care. Any changes to this form should be provided to camp health personnel

upon participant's arrival in camp. Provide complete information so that the camp can be aware of your needs.

Name _____ Birth date_____ Age at camp_____
     Last   First   Middle

Home address _____
          Street Address   City   State   Zip

Social security number of participant _____ Gender: ☐ Male ☐ Female

Custodial parent/guardian _____ Phone_____

Home address _____ Phone_____
(if different from above)   Street Address   City   State   Zip

Business address _____ Phone_____
          Street Address   City   State   Zip

Second parent or guardian or emergency contact _____

Address_____ Phone_____
     Street Address   City   State   Zip

Business address _____ Phone_____

If not available in an emergency, notify_____

Relationship_____ Phone_____

Address _____
     Street Address   City   State   Zip

Insurance Information
Is the participant covered by family medical/hospital insurance? ☐ Yes ☐ No

If so, indicate carrier or plan name _____ Group #_____

▶ **Photocopy of front and back of health insurance card must be attached to this form.**

Important — These boxes must be complete for attendance*

This health history is correct and complete as far as I know. The person herein named has permission to engage in all camp activities except as noted.

I hereby give permission to the camp to provide, seek, and consent to routine health care, administration of prescribed medications, and emergency treatment for me/my child, as may be necessary, including, but not limited to x-rays, routine tests and treatment, and/or hospitalization. I also give permission for the camp to arrange related transportation. I agree to the release of any records necessary for treatment, referral, billing, or insurance purposes.

It is my intention that the camp be treated as acting *in loco parentis* if the person herein named is a minor. Further, it is my intention that the appropriate representatives of the camp be treated as "personal representatives" for the purposes of disclosing protected health in-

formation pursuant to the privacy regulations promulgated pursuant to the Health Insurance Portability and Accountability Act of 1996. I hereby agree (pursuant to 45 CFR § 164.510(b)) to the disclosure to camp representatives of the protected health information of the person herein described, as necessary: for camp representatives to be involved in the person's health care or payment for car, including: (i) to provide relevant information to the camp representatives related to the person's ability to participate in camp activities; and (ii) in the case of minors, to provide relevant information to the camp representatives to keep me informed of my child's health status.

In the event I cannot be reached in an emergency, I hereby give permission to the physician selected by the camp to secure and administer treatment, including hospitalization, for the person named above. This completed form may be photocopied for trips out of camp.

Signature of parent or guardian or adult camper/staffer_____
Printed Name _____ Date_____

I also understand and agree to abide by any restrictions placed on my participation in camp activities.
Signature of minor or adult camper/staffer _____ Date_____

If for religious reasons you cannot sign this, contact the camp for a legal waiver which must be signed for attendance.

ALLERGIES List all known.   Describe reaction and management of the reaction.
Medication allergies (list)

_____   _____
_____   _____

Food allergies (list)

_____   _____
_____   _____

Other allergies (list) — include insect stings, hay fever, asthma, animal dander, etc.

_____   _____
_____   _____

MEDICATIONS BEING TAKEN

Please list ALL medications (including over-the-counter or nonprescription drugs) taken routinely. Bring enough medication to last the entire time at camp. Keep it in the original packaging/bottle that identifies the prescribing physician (if a prescription drug), the name of the medication, the dosage, and the frequency of administration.

☐ This person **takes NO medications** on a routine basis. OR ☐ This person **takes medications** as follows:

Med #1 _____ Dosage _____ Specific times taken each day _____

Reason for taking _____

Med #2 _____ Dosage _____ Specific times taken each day _____

Reason for taking _____

Attach additional pages for more medications.
Identify any medications taken during the school year that participant does/may not take during the summer: _____

RESTRICTIONS (The following restrictions apply to this individual.)

Does not eat: ☐ Red meat ☐ Pork ☐ Dairy products ☐ Poultry ☐ Seafood ☐ Eggs ☐ Other (describe) _____

Explain any restrictions to activity (e.g. what cannot be done, what adaptations or limitations are necessary) _____

GENERAL QUESTIONS (Explain "yes" answers below.)

Has/does the participant:

	Yes	No
1. Had any recent injury, illness or infectious disease?	☐	☐
2. Have a chronic or recurring illness/condition?	☐	☐
3. Ever been hospitalized?	☐	☐
4. Ever had surgery?	☐	☐
5. Have frequent headaches?	☐	☐
6. Ever had a head injury?	☐	☐
7. Ever been knocked unconscious?	☐	☐
8. Wear glasses, contacts or protective eye wear?	☐	☐
9. Ever had frequent ear infections?	☐	☐
10. Ever passed out during or after exercise?	☐	☐
11. Ever been dizzy during or after exercise?	☐	☐
12. Ever had seizures?	☐	☐
13. Ever had chest pain during or after exercise?	☐	☐
14. Ever had high blood pressure?	☐	☐
15. Ever been diagnosed with a heart murmur?	☐	☐

	Yes	No
16. Ever had back problems?	☐	☐
17. Ever had problems with joints (e.g., knees, ankles)?	☐	☐
18. Have an orthodontic appliance being brought to camp?	☐	☐
19. Have any skin problems (e.g., itching, rash, acne)?	☐	☐
20. Have diabetes?	☐	☐
21. Have asthma?	☐	☐
22. Had mononucleosis in the past 12 months?	☐	☐
23. Had problems with diarrhea/constipation?	☐	☐
24. Have problems with sleepwalking?	☐	☐
25. If female, have an abnormal menstrual history?	☐	☐
26. Have a history of bed-wetting?	☐	☐
27. Ever had an eating disorder?	☐	☐
28. Ever had emotional difficulties for which professional help was sought?	☐	☐

Please explain any "yes" answers, noting the number of the questions. _____

Which of the following has the participant had?

☐ Measles
☐ Chicken pox
☐ German measles
☐ Mumps
☐ Hepatitis A
☐ Hepatitis B
☐ Hepatitis C

TB Mantoux Test
Date of last test
Result: ☐ Positive ☐ Negative

Please give all dates of immunization for:

Vaccine:	Dates:	Mo/Yr	Mo/Yr	Mo/Yr	Mo/Yr	Mo/Yr	Mo/Yr
DTP		___	___	___	___	___	___
TD (tetanus/diphtheria)		___	___	___	___	___	___
Tetanus		___	___	___	___	___	___
Polio		___	___	___			
MMR		___	___				
or Measles		___	___				
or Mumps		___	___				
or Rubella		___	___				
Haemophilus influenza B		___	___	___			
Hepatitis B		___	___	___			
Varicella (chicken pox)		___					

Use this space to provide any additional information about the participant's behavior and physical, emotional, or mental health about which the camp should be aware. _____

Name of family physician _____ Phone _____
Address _____
Name of family dentist/orthodontist _____ Phone _____
Address _____

Illustration 12.4 — *Sample Health Screening Records*

Camp Health Record
Individual at Camp Form _____ FM 02

Developed and approved by the
American Camping Association®
with the American Academy of Pediatrics

Camp Name

Name _____ Age _____ Sex _____
Entrance Date _____ Departure Date _____

Examination Entrance by_____	Departure by_____	Important Observations to Follow While at Camp
Height		
Weight		
Temperature		
Eyes		
Nose		
Ears		
Throat		
Teeth		
Posture		
Skin		
Feet		

Meds Received_____

Dosage/Interval_____

(over)

Name
Last
First
Initial
Cabin or Group
Year

Health Record While at Camp (to include date, time, illness, treatment, initials of person treating)

Illustration 12.5 *Sample Page from Health Record Log*

Date_____

Camp Health Record Log   1

Time	Legal Name	Living Unit	Heath Problem or Concern	Health Care Provided	Treated By

SAMPLE

Food Service

Day Camps

M any day camps do not have the matter of institutional food service as a day-to-day concern. Most often in these camps, campers bring their own sack lunch except on cookout days. However, this does not preclude appropriate planning in the following areas:

- Care and refrigeration of lunches from campers' arrival at site until lunch

- Refrigeration and serving of the drink for the lunch meal (e.g., milk, juice, punch)

- Provision for drinking water throughout the camp day

- Disposal of paper and scraps from the lunch period

- Supplemental snacks for campers who bring inadequate lunches

- Provision of a relaxed community atmosphere during the lunch period to aid good digestion

- Sanitation procedures for food storage and handling for cookout meals, often done with the aid of campers

Some day camps do provide hot meal service for their campers and much of the information that follows is as applicable to such day camps as it is to resident camps.

The Food Service Supervisor

A resident camp travels on its stomach as much as an army does. Therefore, the director should turn his or her attention to the food service early in the planning for the camp season. The early recruitment of a capable food service supervisor is one key to dealing with this important area of camp life.

The qualifications set down for that food service supervisor will depend on the size of the camp and the type of food service desired. A small camp of 25 to 150 campers can seldom afford to employ a trained dietitian or nutritionist as food service supervisor. A cook with experience in a school lunch room or fraternity or sorority house can easily fill the bill, if the menus are carefully planned with a dietitian or nutritionist prior to camp. A camp of 150 or more will require a food service supervisor with more skills in meal planning and staff supervision than will a smaller camp. In fact, the larger camps need food service supervisors whose skills are best in the areas of purchasing, planning, and staff supervision rather than cooking. An experienced first or second cook can provide the cooking ability needed for tasty food. Recent surveys show that fifteen to twenty-five percent of a resident camp's budget is spent on food service, and twenty-five to thirty-one percent of that cost is labor.[11] Cutting corners on the salary or living conditions of the food service supervisor can lead to far greater costs than an increased salary might. Violation of state regulations and standard food service practices can lead to serious health and legal problems.

The development of menus is the first step in purchasing and summer planning. In order to give the food service supervisor (particularly if he or she is new) the best information for developing the summer's menus, the camp director should include the following items in the primary discussion:

1. The previous year's food budget in detail

2. The previous year's menus and any camper or staff feedback

3. A profile of the camp community

4. The style used for serving meals in previous years

5. Whether most preparation is from scratch or from packaged foods

6. The menu cycle, based on camp periods

7. The average daily meal count

The food service supervisor should then revise the proposed menus in light of any suggestions, the current prices of foods, the amount allocated in the camp budget for raw food, personal menu favorites, and the cycle of camp periods. If the camp qualifies for provision of food or financial subsidies from state or federal programs, the food service supervisor should be given appropriate information about these items and any menu requirements prior to preparation of menus and food orders.

Upon completion of the menus, the director should review them and raise questions or concerns he or she has about them. Unless the food service supervisor is a qualified dietitian or nutritionist, menus should be reviewed by such a person to ensure a balanced diet. Often, a specialist who will be willing to look over the menus for sound nutritional balance can be found in a district or city school office or in the home economics department of a nearby college or university. When the menus have been reviewed, the dietitian should be asked to sign the menus and explain his or her suggestions to the director or the food service supervisor. Ideally, this can be done early in the year so that adequate time is allowed for purchasing the food. A returning food service supervisor, or one who lives in the area of the camp, may know the best local sources for purchasing various foods. Otherwise, the director should research the best sources.

Food Purchasing

Normally, better prices can be secured on a large initial food order than on a week-by-week delivery. Therefore, there is an advantage in developing a list of the basic canned and dry foods needed for the summer and placing the bulk of that order for delivery at the beginning of the season. If food orders are placed early, companies will often guarantee quoted prices at the time of the order.

Mark J. Brostoff suggests seven factors to be taken into account in the selection of vendors:

- Price
- Quality
- Delivery of product
- Personal relations (with salesperson)
- Service
- Technical assistance
- Competitive position (discounts or rebates)[12]

Before placing an early order, the director should have a relatively stable count of the number of meals to be served during the period for which food is being ordered. To determine the maximum number of meals to be served on a seasonal basis, multiply the maximum number of people (campers and staff) that can be accommodated by three meals a day, and then multiply that result by the number of days feeding each period, including for staff training and days between periods, and add the totals. Dividing the total by the number of days in the particular season provides the average daily meal count.

If enrollment is slow or the camp has a variable record of enrollment, then the director should be cautious about the quantities ordered so that there is not a large inventory to carry over beyond the season. If the camp has enrolled only seventy-five percent of its capacity, it is foolish to order for a full camp until there is evidence that enrollment is climbing to that degree. The same principle follows with nonsummer groups. Where principal nonsummer usage is on the weekend, then food purchases of perishables must be carefully managed to avoid waste and thus higher food costs.

With appropriate food storage areas such as protected dry storage and freezer and refrigeration space, good prices on certain items can often be secured in advance of sudden price increases resulting from weather or shortage problems. For example, if the summer has been particularly dry and the fruit crop is short, it is wise to check on the availability of the previous summer's canned fruits early in the fall, for there is sure to be a price increase by the next year's season.

Securing bids on food orders can be helpful as a cost-saving device, but, for the director, this process may be an unnecessary burden unless a system of bidding has been established in prior years. On all bids, the grade and type of produce as well as the size container required must be specified or the prices received may not be comparable. In a bid process, the director should secure prices from several firms (if there are multiple delivery sources) on major food items such as milk, bread, meat, and certain canned fruits and vegetables that will be used in larger quantities.

One factor in food purchasing for not-for-profit camps in the United States is whether government aid is available in the form of food items or financial reimbursement for part of the cost of meals served to low-income campers. Availability and regulations continue to change in this area both at the federal and state levels. Appendix E gives the information available at the time of publication.

Food Service Staff

When considering the size of food service staff, there are some guidelines that can be used.

People per Meal	Staff Required
Up to 70	1 cook, 1 dishwasher
70 to 120	2 cooks, 1 dishwasher
140 +	3 cooks, 2 dishwashers

The employment of staff to assist the food service supervisor is a matter that should be clearly agreed upon between that supervisor and the director. The director and the food service supervisor should discuss expectations about housing arrangements, salaries, the type of skills needed for each position, and expectations for behavior or clothing. Any staff to be hired who will handle food will need to have or be able to secure before arrival at camp a food handler's permit as required by the state or county. It is always an advantage to everyone involved if the supervisor can meet or interview applicants before they are hired.

Though the degree to which food service staff is involved in camp life outside the kitchen varies from camp to camp, it is always an advantage if the food service staff feels a part of the total camp and participates in some of the all-camp program. Food service staff should be made aware that they are part of a much larger team and that their cooperation and teamwork are essential for a successful camp.

Housing away from the busy and noisy activities of the camp is important for kitchen staff because the schedule in most camps makes it necessary for food service employees to rise early and, therefore, to retire early in the evening. If camper facilities are rustic in nature, the director should give careful thought to the quarters for kitchen staff because they may expect and need some conveniences not provided for campers.

Meal Organization

The type of food service affects the number and type of staff required as well as the quantities to be cooked. Basically, there are two types of service: cafeteria and family style, though camps will often use a buffet for a special occasion or a salad bar in conjunction with one of the types of service. Both of these types of service have advantages and disadvantages. *See illustration 12.6.*

If the relationship between the counselor and campers is the most important concern and one desires a more intimate, homelike atmosphere, the family type meal will probably serve the camp better (see chapter 5). Other factors to be considered follow:

- Who will wait tables, clear tables, and clean tables and floor following the meal? Often, campers are used for any or all of these tasks, and their duties are rotated. Other camps employ waiters who set the tables and bring food and refills.

- Who will serve the plates? Food may be passed around the table, each taking the desired amount, or the counselor may serve the plates and pass them down the table. The latter method provides for a more careful check on what the camper does or doesn't eat; this is particularly important with younger campers. Serving the plates for younger campers also can prevent spills of foods and liquids.

- What foods must be apportioned, if any, and what foods may be refilled? This allocation depends on budget as well as nutritional desires. It is particularly important for milk, meats, and desserts, which are higher cost items.

- What plan is there for returning dishes and utensils to the kitchen for washing? Some camps have each table group wash its own dishes at the table; in this case, careful sterilization in compliance with state laws is essential. Dishes may be resterilized in the kitchen after table washing to ensure a 180°F rinse. If dishes are to be scraped, stacked, and returned to the kitchen, this procedure should be established and worked through during staff training.

- How much choice do you wish for campers to have? The camper may come from a school

Illustration 12.6 — *Food Service Comparison*

CAFETERIA STYLE	
ADVANTAGES	**DISADVANTAGES**
• Portions are more easily controlled. • Quantities served are more easily controlled, as are costs. • Table setting is not required prior to the meal. • If dining area is too small for the entire community, this style enables persons at the last of the line to fill tables vacated by persons in the first of the line.	• Some will be completing the meal while others are being served (unless the camp is very small). • It is difficult to have any all-camp activity (announcements, singing) at this type meal setting.
FAMILY STYLE	
ADVANTAGES	**DISADVANTAGES**
• The counselor can better observe how much and what each camper eats. • Family atmosphere and group spirit are better. • Everyone starts and finishes at the same time — this is helpful if singing and/or any announcements follow the meal and dishes can be cleared before campers leave the table. • Provides opportunities for camper groups to share in tasks around the meal service.	• Some will be completing the meal while others are being served (unless the camp is very small). • It is difficult to have any all-camp activity (announcements, singing) at this type meal setting.

or family situation in which choices of foods are always available. To what degree does the camp think that it is necessary to respond to this concern? Remember, some campers and staff may have food allergies, be vegetarian, or have religious beliefs about eating certain foods. How do you plan to address these issues so the participants aren't made to feel different or uncomfortable?

Cookout Meals

If a camp program calls for cookouts, overnights, or any sort of tripping program that removes campers from the dining room, the director should draw up a plan for notifying the kitchen of changes in meal counts early enough so that the proper amount of food is prepared for those meals. There must also be a plan for those groups cooking out to secure their cooked or raw food. Groups may be required to submit a food service requisition directly to the food service supervisor, or some other staff members working with the food service may be in charge of filling orders. If out-of-camp meals are few in number over the course of the summer, a system can be devised in which menus, established either by the group or the kitchen, can be picked up at the close of the last in-camp meal served to the group. However, as the number of out-of-camp meals increases, the importance of a carefully planned system will become more apparent. Here are some things to consider.

First, the type of experience that the camp wishes to give its campers will dictate the approach to planning menus for such meals. If the outcome is to have a camper group do planning and to understand the nutritional elements of menu planning or to have free choice, then it is more important that a food list be developed to assist campers and counselors in planning the menu and the quantities needed. Amounts available per person or per group should be standardized and made known. If the experience of cooking is a more important part of a trip experience, it may be simpler to have them choose between menus or accept predetermined menus.

A stock of food in sizes or types not normally used in institutional cooking should be gathered in one storage and checkout facility, and some staff member should be given responsibility for that area. There is a wide variety of dehydrated and freeze-dried food, which will make supply packs much lighter.

Foods to be secured from the kitchen (because of limited quantity or refrigeration needed) should be identified along with a method of securing them.

A checkout plan and the amount of advance notice must be clarified. The group may come with its food list at a specified time and check out the food across a counter so that the group may pack and check the food, or a staff member may accumulate the food from a list and pack it for a group in advance of departure. Careful attention should be given to procedures for keeping refrigerated foods cool and what foods (if any) can be returned to the kitchen.

Some camps operate the out-of-camp meals through a store, providing campers the opportunity not only of planning their menus but also of learning budgeting by purchasing the food items from that store with camp money. This type of learning experience takes preparation — pricing, order sheets, and orientation of staff. The director should also consider the impact of any such program on the food service supervisor, food purchasing, food costs, and nutritional standards before establishing the system.

Sanitation and Health

Camp kitchens range from rather rustic centers where campers take food to their units to cook over wood, charcoal, or gas fires to fully equipped commercial kitchens with all the appliances you would find in the finest restaurants. No matter how simple or elaborate, some basic health and sanitation standards need to be followed in food storage, preparation, and serving. The dangers of food-borne illness in a camp setting cannot be underestimated.

To prevent food-borne illness, a food service supervisor should give careful attention to Hazard Analysis Critical Control Points (HACCP), which is a food safety and self-inspection system that looks at the flow of potential hazardous foods through the camp's operation from receiving food to serving food. Hazard analysis encourages food service staff to ask where the food safety problems are most likely to occur. Critical control points suggests what steps are needed to take control of food safety problems and where or when to take them.

A good starting point is to find the sources of dangers of food-borne illness most frequently seen. The North Dakota Department of Public Health identified the following primary sources.[13]

Source	Percentage of Illnesses*
Inadequate refrigeration/cooling	63
Preparing food far in advance of service	29
Hot holding at bacterial incubating temperature	27
Infected individuals handling food	26
Inadequate reheating	25
Inadequate cleaning of equipment	9
Use of leftovers	7
Cross-contamination	6
Inadequate cooking	5
Storing acid food in toxic metal containers	4
Contaminated raw ingredients in uncooked foods	2
Intentional additives	2
Obtaining food from unsafe sources	1

*Many have more than one cause; percentages will not add to 100.

All food should be stored in areas protected from rodents or vermin. Perishable foods should be stored in *refrigerated areas* at 40°F or below. As a safety measure, a clipboard should be mounted beside each walk-in, freezer, or cooler, providing a form with a line for each day for the assigned individual to initial and indicate the temperature at the time of the check. This will ensure that, if the temperature begins to rise in a twenty-four hour period, corrective actions can be taken promptly. The walk-in will fluctuate some during mealtime when it is often opened, but it should quickly return to a safe temperature.

One of the greatest points of danger in food contamination falls in the period of thawing, or cooling after cooking, when pathogenic organisms can multiply more easily. It is best to thaw frozen items in refrigerated areas so that there is no chance the items will sit after thawing in temperatures higher than 40°F.

A minimum temperature of 140°F should be maintained in *keeping food warm* before a meal or for serving in a cafeteria operation, and it is wise to heat the food to 170°F before placing it in a serving container. The maximum periods in which perishable foods (e.g., meat, fish, eggs, milk, poultry, salads with dressings) should be allowed to sit in the 46 to 139°F range is two hours. Care should be taken that perishable foods be cooked in deep trays or large cooking pots that would take more than two hours to cool the center.

The food service supervisor and health care provider should sit down with all food service staff and discuss the *personal sanitary* and *hygiene practices* that should be followed, as well as the principles of careful food preparation and serving. Employees should be made aware that, should they have a contagious condition, they should immediately notify both the food service supervisor and the health care provider, so that they can be relieved of food service duties. A toilet for use by kitchen employees should be convenient to the kitchen area and display signs reminding employees about washing hands with soap after use of the toilet facilities. Other staff that may be handling foods on a cookout should be trained in handling food and sanitizing dishes, pots, and pans.

A definite system following state regulations for washing and sanitizing dishes, pots and pans, and utensils must be established. If there is a mechanical dishwasher, such regulations will require having wash water at least 100°F and rinse water at least 180°F, or using an approved chemical sanitizing solution. Some camps wash dishes and utensils by hand; however, the temperatures for washing and rinsing should be maintained at 100°F or above and a second rinse should use an approved chemical sanitizer. In both cases, dishes, utensils, and pots and pans should be air dried. As in refrigeration, it is wise to have a clipboard mounted near the dishwashing area where, at least once during the dishwashing process each day, the temperatures are checked, recorded, and initialed.

The cleanliness and sanitation of the kitchen work areas is very important. All work surfaces should be cleaned after use. Special attention should be paid to slicers and can openers, which are often overlooked in the daily cleaning. Surfaces on which food comes into contact should be identified to kitchen personnel, and the procedures for cleaning those surfaces before and after every food contact should be established.

Garbage and rubbish should be promptly removed from the kitchen into leakproof containers with tight-fitting lids. Removing and emptying those containers should be part of the daily maintenance schedule. Those containers should also be cleaned regularly, even when plastic bags are used inside the containers.

Contracted Services

Many camps have chosen to contract with food service companies to provide the entire food service operation, eliminating the employment and supervision of staff, the purchase of food, and the related bookkeeping chores. Though some control of menus related to what is served or what the camp can afford remains, most of the control and resulting problems become those of the contracted service. Many times the services that contract with colleges and universities find that camps are a natural customer and enable them to retain their staff between school seasons.

The applicability and affordability of such services vary from camp to camp. A careful analysis of the related costs for both types of service should be made. The director should interview current customers of the service and, if at all possible, observe the food service in operation before making a commitment.

Transportation

The transportation of campers and staff provides one of the key areas of potential liability to camps. Careful risk management, including a thorough review of insurance coverage and safety education practices, is essential. In camps, vehicles may include cars, vans, buses, boats, and planes. Transportation issues in a day camp are usually major factors in the program cost and schedule and most likely involve city driving.

The first step is to analyze what transportation is required.

- Do campers have to be transported to and from camp or will parents or the sponsoring group arrange that?
- Do campers have to be transported in groups out of camp for program activities or events?
- Does a camp vehicle haul supplies and equipment into camp?
- What vehicle will be needed within camp for maintenance personnel?
- What vehicle will be needed in an emergency to transport injured individuals to the doctor or hospital?
- Do campers or staff members need to be transported to and from transportation terminals?
- Will staff-owned vehicles be used for certain purposes?

The use of staff-owned vehicles should be considered carefully with a review of the camp's insurance coverage for non-camp-owned vehicles and its implications for rates. If a situation warrants the use of a staff-owned vehicle, then a clear agreement should be developed between the director and the staff member concerning insurance, reimbursement for mileage, and periods of use.

Recent lawsuits have brought into question the safety and reliability of certain types of vehicles. The safety of a vehicle for transporting groups of campers or staff is the first consideration to be made, and information on laws and reliability of available vehicles should be checked carefully.

Owning, Leasing, or Chartering

Initially, the question of whether the camp purchases and maintains its own vehicles must be answered. Because camp situations vary so greatly, there is no way to suggest that one method is best for every camp. There are some advantages and disadvantages of the three usual methods of securing camp vehicles. *See illustration 12.7.*

Some advantages can become disadvantages in certain circumstances, so consider carefully the cost, availability of qualified personnel, and the amount of use necessary. The number and type of vehicles required by the camp program will certainly affect the decision because the capital investment at one time for purchase may be more difficult than renting, leasing, or chartering annually.

Although some problems are removed by chartering vehicles, it does not relieve the camp of the responsibility of double-checking that the company carries the appropriate insurance, has a regular system of maintenance and vehicle upkeep, and checks on the safety record of its drivers. This should be part of the selection and contract process, and any signs of variance from stated practice should be immediately reported to the charter company.

Drivers

Selecting the drivers for such vehicles is the key to safety and public relations. The driver must regularly check that the maintenance of the vehicle is maintained; be friendly to campers, parents, or vendors; and yet maintain constant surveillance of safety factors. In a day camp, the daily nature of picking up, transporting, and dropping off campers adds an even greater element of responsibility in the areas of safety and public relations.

A careful check of each driver's driving record should be made each year (within four months prior to the camp season or annually for year-round drivers), either by the camp or by the camp's insurance company. The director should also analyze the type of driving experience and how it relates to the particular vehicles to be driven. Experience with the type of vehicle is very important; training should be provided if the person does not have previous experience with that particular type of vehicle.

State licensing laws vary. Some states require a different type of license for drivers of vehicles that carry a certain number of passengers or where children are transported by a hired

Illustration 12.7 — *Vehicle Chart*

	FACTORS	OWNING	LEASING/RENTING	CHARTERING
ADVANTAGES	Drivers	Camp selects drivers.	Camp selects drivers.	Company provides drivers.
	Cost	Cost may be less.	Some maintenance and repair costs may be covered. No capital investment.	Maintenance covered by company. No capital investment.
	Schedule	Camp controls schedule, employee, and vehicle.	Camp controls schedule, employee, and vehicle.	Contract specifies pickup and/or arrival time and transfers much of risk to company.
	Insurance			Company provides insurance and can add the camp to their policy as "additional insured."
	Other	Can advertise on side of vehicle.	Camp may have newer vehicles earlier than if owned.	
DISADVANTAGES	Drivers	Finding qualified drivers may be a problem.	Finding qualified drivers may be a problem.	No control over selection of drivers.
	Cost	Camp absorbs maintenance and repair costs. Purchase requires a large sum of cash.	Lease contracts vary and can contain much "fine print."	Cost is usually more. Multiple use increases cost.
	Schedule	Camp controls schedule. A careful maintenance schedule is required.	Camp controls schedule. A careful maintenance schedule is required.	No direct control of vehicle.
	Insurance	Insurance may be a problem.	Insurance may be a problem, requiring substantial deductible and offering only state-required minimum limits.	
	Other			

firm. State laws should be checked early so that the appropriate license for the vehicle to be driven can be part of the job requirements. Where a vehicle is designed to carry sixteen or more people or is in excess of 26,000 pounds, federal law requires a special Commercial Driver License issued at the state level. (Note: The design of the vehicle and not the number of actual passengers determines the license requirement.) A Commercial Driver License requires drug/alcohol testing.

Every vehicle carrying campers should have a staff member, which may be the driver, trained to carry out written accident procedures for providing or securing care for any injured, supervising the uninjured, specifying whom to notify in an emergency, and obtaining appropriate accident information at the scene. When a vehicle carries fifteen or more people, an additional staff member should be assigned to give attention to the campers to manage safety and group behavior. The number of staff members may need to be increased if the campers are younger than nine or if campers have mental, emotional, or physical disabilities.

Written procedures and policies should be provided to drivers, and specific training should be given during the precamp period. All drivers, even those who do not transport campers or staff, should have training in the following areas:

- Use of fire extinguishers and emergency reflectors stored in the vehicle.

- Safety inspection of all vehicles he or she is expected to drive.

- Inspection of the vehicle before use and procedures for reporting any needed repairs.

- Importance of not transporting campers in vehicles not designed for passengers (e.g., open-bed trucks or trailers).

- Procedures in case of an accident, including information cards for witnesses to complete and a camera for accident pictures (Disposable cameras in each vehicle is a good way to handle this.).

All drivers who transport campers or staff should have additional training in the following areas:

- Use of the first aid kit kept in vehicles

- Identification of appropriate behavior for passengers in loading, unloading, and traveling in vehicles

- Use of seatbelts or, in the case of smaller children (and some people with disabilities), restraints

- Maximum seating capacities of various vehicles

- Availability and location of medical information forms and permission-to-treat forms

- Procedures for backing up, loading and unloading passengers, dealing with vehicular breakdowns, refueling, and dealing with illnesses of passengers

- Procedures for rest stops and telephone use during long excursions (i.e., determining when they are needed, choosing locations, and checking to ensure that everyone is present at the conclusion of the stop)

- Procedures for determining when to unload campers or leave them in the vehicle

- Procedures for determining where campers are to be located during refueling of vehicle

- Division of responsibility among staff other than that of the driver

- Maintenance of an appropriate log of trips, including refueling and oil (*see illustration 12.8*)

One person on the staff should be responsible for checking out any staff before they are given permission to drive a camp vehicle. This is ordinarily done during the staff training period. In the frenzied pace of camp life, it is too easy to designate any staff member to take a vehicle and run an errand or transport campers. There should be designated drivers, in addition to the regularly assigned drivers, in order to deal with unscheduled trips as well as to allow for time off.

Maintenance of Vehicles

A regular maintenance plan for vehicles is the second key to good risk management in transportation. Even the best driver is dangerous in a poorly maintained vehicle. A specific staff member should be given the responsibility for maintaining all vehicles, and a system of regular checks should be established. The written maintenance plan should include

- Written records of all oil changes and repairs, with the mileage and date

- Regular checks to make sure that a fully stocked first aid kit, flares, fire extinguisher, and appropriate tools are kept in each vehicle at all times

- A regular schedule of safety checks of lights, tires, wipers, windshield, emergency warning systems, horn, brakes, and oil and coolant levels

- A quarterly mechanical evaluation of vehicles that carry passengers (or, in the case of a seasonal operation, within three months prior to use)

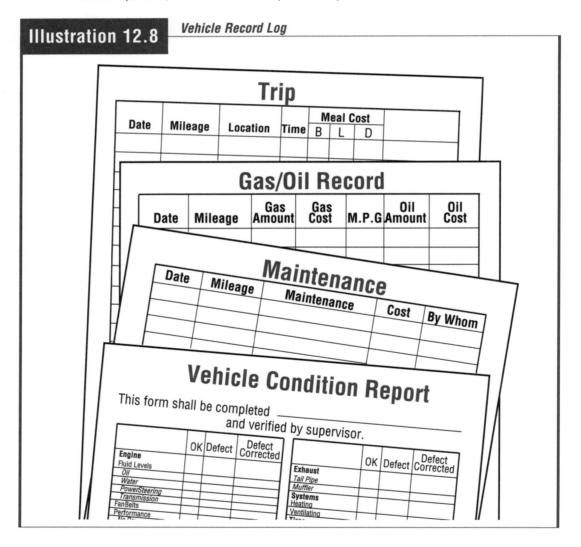

Illustration 12.8 — *Vehicle Record Log*

Camper Education

In addition to all these precautions, if campers are to be transported, they should be given instructions on appropriate behavior, safety regulations, use of cell phones, evacuation procedures, and use of seat belts.

Day Camps

Day camps that transport campers deal with these sorts of concerns on a daily basis and are generally very sensitive to the issues of safety and transport. Often multiple vehicles are involved in the transport of campers, and it is vital that a plan for the orderly arrival and departure of vehicles be developed. Areas for loading and unloading, parking, waiting, and moving traffic should be clearly delineated in writing, and staff should be made available to supervise arrival and departure periods.

A written schedule of camper pickup and drop-off times and locations, as well as safety rules and precautions, should be presented to parents along with a telephone number for contacting the central office handling transportation. Even in the well-organized transportation system, all sorts of things that can delay the arrival or departure of campers will occur. A system to notify parents of unusual delays in pickups or drop-offs will go a long way toward good public relations.

Checkpoint

Health Service

1. Are there protocols from the supervising physician for the health care provider?

2. Outline the health care plan for your camp.

3. Identify the types of health care certification or training that your staff will need.

4. What written records do you maintain in your health care service?

Food Service

1. Do you have on hand menus and inventories of food, supplies, and equipment?

2. Does the type of meal service used currently lend itself to the camp's program philosophy?

3. To what degree do you wish campers to assume responsibility in the dining room for preparation or cleanup?

4. To what degree do you wish campers to assume responsibility for their own meal planning and preparation during their camp experience?

5. Check your food service area sanitation practices against government regulations and American Camping Association standards.

Transportation

1. For what purposes do you need vehicles for camp? How many and what type?

2. Have you examined the options of renting, leasing, chartering, or owning vehicles?

3. In which vehicles are campers currently allowed to ride?

4. Is one person responsible for the upkeep of vehicles?

5. Is one person responsible for selecting and checking drivers?

6. If a day camp, is there a plan for picking up and dropping off campers and for notifying parents if plans change?

7. What is your provision for emergency vehicles?

Related Standards and Guidelines

Health Service

Accreditation Standards for Camp Programs and Services: HW-1–23;
   "Self-Assessment Document": Item 16
Guidelines for Conference and Retreat Centers: II-30, 42–46

Food Service

Accreditation Standards for Camp Programs and Services: SF-22–32;
   "Self-Assessment Document": Items 6–7, 9–13
Guidelines for Conference and Retreat Centers: I-24–35

Transportation

Accreditation Standards for Camp Programs and Services: TR-1–19
Guidelines for Conference and Retreat Centers: I-38–45

[1] Gerald P. Burns. 1954. *Program of the Modern Camp*. New York: Prentice Hall. p. 59.

[2] Linda Ebner Erceg, Association of Camp Nurses. Letter, January 1999, and e-mail, August 2003.

[3] Linda Ebner Erceg. 1994. "Who is Your Camp Healthcare Provider?" *The CampLine*, Vol. 3, No. 1, May.

[4] Association of Camp Nurses. 2002. *The Scope and Standards of Camp Nursing Practice*. Bemidji, MN: Association of Camp Nurses.

[5] Kris Miller Lishner and Margaret Auld Bruya. 1994. *Creating a Healthy Camp Community: A Nurse's Role*. Martinsville, IN: American Camping Association. p. 122.

[6] Louise Czupryna. 1989. "Partners on the Health and Safety Team." *Camping Magazine*, Vol. 61, No. 5, April. p. 30.

[7] Ellen Reynolds, M.S.N., C.P.N.P. and Holly Bauer, R.N. 2003. "Outdoor Hazards and Preventive Measures West Nile Virus: A Clinical Commentary for the Camp Health Care Community." *Camping Magazine*, Vol. 76, No. 2, March/April.

[8] Ed Schirick. 1998. "What is Your OSHA IQ?" *Camping Magazine*, Vol. 71, No. 2, March/April. p. 18.

[9] Robert B. Bush. 1994. "A Director's Primer on Selected OSHA Requirements." *The CampLine*, Vol. III, No. 2, October. p.

[10] Anon. 1992. "Camp Health, Bloodborne Pathogens, and OSHA." *The CampLine*, Vol. 1, No. 1, May.

[11] Armand Ball. 1990. "Food Service Cost Survey." *Trendlines*, May/June. p. 1.

[12] Mark J. Brostoff. 1989. "The Dynamics of Camp Food Purchasing." *Camping Magazine*, Vol. 61, No. 4, February. p. 28.

[13] *ACN Compass Point*. Bemidji, MN: Association of Camp Nurses.

Marketing

Ours is a field where the value is not experienced unless the participant is there. It becomes imperative that we become more aggressive in our advocacy of the camp experience. We cannot wait for the campers to come to us. For all directors this means earlier and more vigorous recruitment of campers. It means more talk about values, outcomes, and specifics in language that can be understood by parents, business people and organization boards.[1]

Camp Identity as the Key

The simple fact that campers are essential to the operation of a camp is often not considered early enough in camp planning, nor do camp administrators translate the word camper into customer often enough camps have much to learn from the business world about marketing and customer relations.

Marketing is an ongoing year-round process that involves not only the direct recruitment of campers and groups but also the constant interpretation of the generic values of the camp experience as well as a clear sense of what this camp is about. It is the foundation of all good financial development, public relations, and community relations. It is an attitude that should permeate each and every staff member and be heard in the voices that answer the telephone, seen on the faces of those who greet campers and parents, and sensed in the response to various and sundry complaints.

Dr. Dwight Jewson, marketing guru, underlines this in his statement: "Development of a state-of-the-art marketing begins with defining 'who we are' – the very identity of the camp, then:

1. Insuring that Camp identity is relevant to ('speaks to') its target audience.

2. Aligning everything the camp does with and around that identity.

"Marketing is the external voice of a carefully considered, clearly articulated sense of what camp is all about. It is the voice through which its target audience learns of the vision, purpose and mission – the very essence of the Camp.

"Insuring the Camp communicates its identity clearly and that everything the camp does is aligned around that identity is absolutely vital for service organizations where the experience people have is the product we provide. If the camp is not 'walking its talk,' literally 'practicing what it preaches' in everything no matter how 'nice sounding' its external message is, it will ring hollow to the marketplace it serves. In camps, the proof of this is crystal clear:

1. Returning campers are the primary source of enrollments

2. Word of mouth is the key and dominant 'media channel' for camps. Camp experience, not brochures or advertising, drives word of mouth." [2]

So, marketing involves everything that is done, both to attract customers and consumers and to keep them coming back. Marketing is not just a single promotional mailing, but the total package: staff, program, communication materials, food service, grounds and buildings, and so on. Communicating the essence or identity of the camp in each and every contact with the customer/consumer requires the careful analysis of philosophy and mission discussed earlier as well as ensuring that the total package speaks the same language throughout.

That language must "speak to" the targeted audience at their level of understanding and expectations. In camps for youth, it is usually the parent who must be convinced to pay the fee for the child to attend camp, with the caveat that children's opinions have quite a bit to do with the parents' decision. That parent becomes the primary customer. Similarly, in camps that serve schools or rent facilities, the school or organization that rents is the primary customer.

In this day, surveys show that children ages seven to seventeen influence their parents' decisions concerning leisure time activities in seventy-four percent of families. [3] Therefore, the camper is not only the consumer of the service in youth camps but also the secondary customer and must be considered in terms of customer concerns and marketing. The individual participant, group leader, or teacher in the rental situation becomes the secondary customer and consumer.

Because camps are no longer solely summer camps or children's camps, the marketing approach becomes more complex, requiring more market research and strategy if the camp is to attract a variety of potential clientele to fill its beds in all seasons. The customer in a camp may be an adult,; a child; a family; an organization; a school; a church, synagogue, or mosque; or a business; each type of customer requires a different method to interpret the identity of the camp. Ultimately the consumer is an individual, and it is that individual who must also sense the identity of the camp in his or her experience. Different segments of the camp operation may have different primary customers as well as consumers, thereby shaping the marketing tools differently for each segment.

As Edward L. Hayes states, "People form impressions about you and your camp the instant they see you advertised or mentioned in print. Even the way you handle correspondence conveys how you feel about your public. Unanswered inquiries and tardy, poorly typed letters speak worlds to your public."[4]

Early in marketing, the camp director must analyze the boundaries for marketing. They need to define the present market, target population, or customer base for the camp and determine what potential markets exist. Many camps are designed for a particular type of camper based on a specific geographical area, income level, or physical disability, which is usually reflected in the mission or purpose. This focus establishes the parameters of marketing efforts from the outset. In camps that serve broader geographical areas and appeal to campers with no particular physical disability, the potential market is much larger. The fee charged for the camp experience may limit the market to a more specific income level. A camp that operates a conference and retreat program during part of the year may, by mission, be limited to the members of an organization or to religious group of the same persuasion. Each of these requirements shapes the tools of marketing to be used. In other words, understanding the boundaries of the camp market enables the director to better design how the experience is packaged, how much money is spent on marketing, which markets are explored, and how the experience is promoted. Christian Camping International reports that the mean amount camps and conferences spent on marketing and promotion more than doubled between 1996 and 2000.[5] Such a budget impact requires careful consideration of the way in which that money is spent.

Market Analysis

A market analysis will be easier if the camp has kept good records previously and if a computer in which to record the data is available. The following eight steps need to be taken:

1. **Secure enrollment figures by sessions or type of program and use for the past five years.** Compare shifts in total enrollment, types of program and use, and sessions.

2. **Break down those enrollment figures for the same period of time, using various factors.** The factors will vary, based on the type of programs and the length of the season. Where individual enrollment is based on particular programs or sessions of different lengths,

break down the enrollment in each session by age, sex, zip code, religious affiliation, school affiliation, ethnic and racial groups, general family income, or any other specification that may affect the situation.

Where the enrollment is by groups, such as schools, churches, social clubs, or businesses, break down the enrollment by type of user groups, size groups, age groups, geographical origin, type of camp services used, and seasons attended.

Now, search for patterns or segments of the market where the heaviest and lightest enrollments occur to study further what creates the difference. For example, why do enrollments reflect large numbers from certain neighborhoods and fewer from others? Which types of groups seldom rent the camp facilities? Which are the primary segments currently being served?

Look back at the stated purpose and target market and compare them to the camp's existing demographics. Is the targeted audience being served?

3. Examine the return rate. What percentage of campers or user groups returns for a second year? A third year? Study evaluations from customers and consumers. Is there a reason for not returning?

4. Look at enrollment dates. When is the earliest registration? What are the dates when the largest number register? What seemingly prompted people to enroll more during a particular three-week period? Who enrolled earliest?

5. Compare enrollment with enrollment in other camps. The American Camping Association and Christian Camping International both run surveys from time to time to see what trends are occurring in camp enrollment. Talk with camps in the general area; if the camp is affiliated with an organization that has other camps in the region, seek comparative information. If the camp is facing a significant deviation from the pattern other camps are experiencing, look for clues to problems or unique features that need additional analysis before developing recruitment plans.

6. Gather some demographic information about the area served. What is the current population by age groups, socioeconomic groups, ethnic or racial groups? What has been the trend over the past five years? Is there a projection for the next five years? Where is the largest concentration of prospective campers or groups? Has the camp's enrollment followed the trends in the general population? The U.S. Census Bureau can provide a profile by state, county, or zip code.

7. Identify the competition. Competition comes in the form of other types of programs, other camps, schools, sports, and other types of activities that involve the entire family. Competition is not bad; in fact, it is indigenous to our democratic form of government. It is always wise to learn as much as possible about the competition, what they are offering, what fees they charge, and who they are serving.

Dr. Dwight Jewson, marketing consultant, states that "the camp competes with other products being marketed to youth. . . . The message or advertisement for the camp thus must be addressed to a specific market or markets. . . . That message exists in the context of many other messages or advertisements for alternatives for the summer, and thus must communicate directly with the needs and concerns of the market segment towards whom it is directed."[6]

8. Once a camp director has all this data in writing and has studied it thoroughly, it should be shared with others. Key staff members who have experience with the camp may have insights that will help. If the camp operates with a board or committee, that group should have a presentation of the information and an opportunity to react and discuss it. Another camp director or mentor may be able to offer some observations. Often, outside consultants from the camping field can provide a clearer analysis of this data and help give guidance to the director and board in developing a marketing plan.

Analysis of Current Market Strategies

Marketing efforts should be motivated by the desire to accomplish the purpose of the camp, meet customer and consumer needs, and provide a quality service that is superior to one's competition or unique in some way. Having already determined the purpose of the camp, time may need to be devoted to analyzing customer needs and the quality of services provided.

Doug Herron reminds camp directors that "headache sufferers don't need aspirin — they need relief from the headache." The benefit is the relief, not the aspirin. He goes on to state, "Benefits are the result customers and consumers derive from satisfactory use of the service. Features (the characteristics we most often talk about) are the distinguishing facts about the service that are true whether the service is ever used or not. Features are easily provable characteristics that are not debatable. They are the elements you can see, taste, touch, smell, and measure."[7]

"Staff members who base their selling strategy solely on a description of the program's features are hoping the prospective customer will bridge a conceptual gap and convert all the features into personal benefits. Professional salespeople and marketers know, however, that the typical prospect, no matter how well educated, has neither the time nor the inclination to convert all the features into benefits. At the same time, they realize that no sale starts without the prospect anticipating some benefits. You must persuade potential customers that use of your service will satisfy their needs and interests."[8]

In *Illustration 13.1* Herron depicts how the terms features, benefits, and derived benefits apply to the camp setting. The benefits and the derived benefits should be consistent with the camp's outcomes.

An analysis of the benefits offered by the camp to the potential customer and consumer needs to be made clear at the same time they generate excitement in the marketing

Illustration 13.1

Service	Features A feature is a fact about a service that is present in its design.	Benefits A benefit occurs when a feature of a service satisfies, or is understood to satisfy, a need of the user.	Derived Benefits
		Make friends more easily	Learn to work more effectively in group situations
	Good leaders	Learn skills	Gain greater self-confidence
Summer camp	Sleep in cabins	Protection from bad weather	Healthy
		Chance to take in a small group of peers	Practice leadership skills and conscious decision making
	1,000 acres of forest	Adventure	Safe risks rewarded
		Change in environment	Refreshing

Source: *Marketing Nonprofit Programs and Services*. Douglas B. Herron. San Francisco: Jossey-Bass Publishers, 1997.

information. In chapter 3, some of the benefits and/or outcomes of camp were outlined. Remember that the potential customer/consumer will compare the benefits outlined in materials describing a camp with those outlined by other camps.

In a 1990 study by the Maguire Associates, Inc., the five top camp characteristics rated by parents were caring counselors, enjoyment/fun camper has there, overall quality, safety, and personal attention given to each camper.[9] These were evidently the benefits perceived by the customers. Compare these with the benefits the camp purports as well as with the benefits campers perceive.

In analyzing customer-perceived benefits, an evaluation form that is used with present campers and parents or camper groups can provide some insights into which needs are being met (i.e., what makes them happy) and which are not being met (i.e., what both present and nonreturning campers disliked). The design of the evaluation form is critical, and some outside expertise or review will help hone the form to accomplish the desired ends. Remember that the questions asked of the primary customer (e.g., parent, organization that rents) may be different from the secondary customer or consumer (e.g., camper, participant). This different focus may necessitate more than one questionnaire.

The time when the person is given the form also can affect the outcome. For example, giving it to the leader of a rental group upon their arrival at camp or mailing an evaluation form to summer campers during the Christmas/Hanukkah season may not provide the return rate or information needed. Evaluation needs to be soon enough after the conclusion of the experience to be fresh but not in the moment of unpacking the suitcase. The matter of evaluation is covered more fully in chapter 16.

At this point, a camp director needs to examine current marketing materials and practices. Everything should be examined with care, from the brochures and videos to the schedule of mailings and promotional meetings, with an eye for its target populations, its accuracy, its attractiveness, and its effectiveness in identifying benefits and/or outcomes and goals. Make a list of all current marketing strategies and tools used by the camp.

To deal with a competitive marketplace, a camp must emphasize overall value and differentiate its identity and services from that of other camps. Simply offering more activities than the competition will not necessarily bring campers. Without a clear analysis of the identity the camp wishes to communicate, adding new program activities may actually negate or weaken that identity. Value does not necessarily mean having the fanciest buildings or equipment, rather it relates more directly to having clean and comfortable facilities with capable, mature, caring staff members.

The issue of quality is one that cannot be treated lightly. So much of a camp's reputation depends on word-of-mouth comments that a camp must ensure that it provides consistent and continuing service. News of a good camp travels fast, but today's parents are not overly loyal; consequently, when a camp does not produce what it promises, parents are quick to look for another camp.

A specific focus will often stimulate interest on the part of campers and parents. In marketing, this matching of a special focus with a particular group of customers is called "developing a niche." To emphasize a niche, a camp needs to understand the following:

- Establishing a camp identity that applies to the target audience is essential.

- Concentrate on what the camp does best. Emphasize quality and do not compromise in the area chosen.

- Make sure that the niche chosen is not too narrow, thereby limiting the audience too much.

- Be prepared to give up something else (e.g., a less appealing program, staff or equipment in another program area). It is difficult to finance, staff, and ensure quality in every program.

- Choose a name for the program or experience that communicates well. It must mean something to the camper. That may mean using contemporary or classic verbiage.

- Be patient. Success does not come in one summer.

- Provide what is promised. Deliver.

To market the site to user groups, the camp director still needs to determine the camp's competitive niche. Unless a program that is subsidized from some aspect of the sponsoring organization is being provided, one of the camp's goals is for revenue to exceed cost of service delivery. The competitive niche includes the qualities of the site and the quality and extent of services that are provided for the fee that is charged. For example, adults may be more interested in the indoors than the outdoors. That space should be physically and emotionally conducive to the program or to meeting goals of the user group. As with any good marketing strategy, the needs of the user group must be matched with the opportunities provided by the product. An outdoor education class or a troop camping experience will have different needs than a college class or an adult training group. The features of the site that are desirable for most adult groups include

- Quality meeting space

- Indoor bathrooms with privacy

- Comfortable beds and good mattresses

- Comfortable chairs and tables with good writing surfaces

- Good directions to the site and signs or maps of the site

- Hard-surfaced walkways

- Lounge furniture

In addition, the following amenities add to the desirability, comfort, and convenience for adult groups:

- Training aids, such as easels, markers, tape, and audiovisual equipment

- Telephones for individual use

- Copier

- Fax machine

- Privacy for meetings

- Flexible mealtimes

- Lounge and deck areas

- Recreation opportunities, including walking paths, game areas, and television

The hosting function is critical in working with user groups. The camp director's interest in meeting the consumer's needs from the first phone call to the checkout procedures should be carefully planned and be a part of your marketing strategies. The American Camping Association's *Guidelines for Conference and Retreat Centers* will help in analyzing any camp site against the standards of the field.

Developing a Marketing Plan

Having analyzed the present population served by the camp, examined the demographics of the service area, taken a look at competing services, and evaluated current marketing and services, the camp director should have the necessary information to develop a marketing plan for the coming year. This should be developed in conjunction with the staff and committee members who will carry out the plan.

First, reexamine what the message is and to whom it is to be communicated. Review the mission or statement of purpose, desired outcomes and goals, and what has been established as the camp's identity. Is it clear to others? Does it communicate the desired message? Is it concise?

Determining the camp's identity is the critical step in marketing. Though this certainly relates to the purpose of the camp, it also relates to the setting, staff, and strengths of the camp operation. Some camps find their identity as a camp that can provide a program that is general in nature with many different activities and programs. Another camp's identity may lead to finding a special niche in the marketplace.

This identity may need to be interpreted in a variety of ways if the camp is to serve multiple audiences. Most camps discover that they will need different tools for various audiences. In today's market, most camps have determined that they need more than the traditional camp brochure so they add different tools such as videos or Web sites. Whatever tools are selected, it is critical that they are consistent in communicating the mission, desired outcomes and goals, and identity of the camp.

Often camps are tempted to combine everything into one compartmentalized brochure in order to save dollars, but it is questionable whether such an approach can be effective in speaking to multiple audiences (i.e., summer campers, parents, schools, renters, weekend programs, and day and/or resident camps) on the same property. Trying to market messages to a variety of audiences can be confusing. So this step entails actually laying out on paper the audiences to be attracted and the message to be communicated to each of those audiences. If the camp's Web site is for different audiences, be sure that they can easily access their specific areas of interest (e.g., campers, parents, user groups, staff members).

Second, determine the promotional tools necessary to communicate the camp's message by reviewing those currently being used and then comparing them with tools used by other camps or similar types of operations (e.g., parks, recreation opportunities, conference centers). Most tools for communicating the camp's message will fall in four areas: personal interaction, promotional materials, advertising, and public relations. A mix of these tools will provide a balance of appeal.

Personal Interaction

Personal interaction as a tool deserves first consideration because camp is a very personal experience both for the camper and for the parents. In any discussion with camp directors around the country on the topic of marketing, all agree that the best way of securing campers is by word of mouth. As in the business world, referral by satisfied customers is the businessperson's best advertisement.

No matter how effective promotional or advertising materials are, the potential customer will be looking for identification with a person related to the camp. Confidence is instilled by some contact with a caring and informed individual. The following tools involve some person-to-person contact.

Returning Campers

Except in very unusual camp situations, the primary source of enrollment is returning campers. A national survey of all types of camps shows that the average percentage of campers returning to camps is fifty to sixty percent. From these percentages, many camps depend upon a much higher return rate. Obviously, the lower the return, the more difficult is the task confronting the director; recruitment of new campers requires considerably more effort, time, and money.

Therefore, the director's first concentration should be on approaching previous campers. An early mailing about the upcoming summer's sessions, dates, and special programs for returning campers is an important step. Follow-up Web site bulletins or newsletters can list the returning campers as they enroll. Many camps find that a regular bulletin or e-mail to campers and staff is a good means of maintaining contact, building spirit, and encouraging a return to camp. It need not be expensive, but it should be attractive and newsy with numerous names mentioned and pictures and memories from the previous summer included. Some camps have set up chat rooms for campers to stay in contact with each other between seasons.

Camper Reunions

A camper reunion often engenders enthusiasm among the previous year's campers and staff. A reunion each year provides an opportunity to share stories, pictures or videos, and fun. The involvement of staff and the showing of a visual presentation from the previous summer are natural elements of a reunion program. Camper reunions can stir memories of the previous summer's experiences and reunite campers who have not been in touch with one another. It is important to have next summer's registration material available at a reunion.

If the majority of campers come from a number of cities or states, then a decentralized plan of reunions or parties may be required. A larger, central reunion provides more excitement and greater contact among campers and staff, but a decentralized plan provides more personal contact between the director and campers, as well as a better opportunity to invite prospective campers and parents. Opportunities to share the names of prospective campers (or staffers) can be given for future follow-up. Some camps encourage attendees to bring a friend.

Fun Weekends at Camp

Where the camp property is close enough to a population center, the director can make the property available to groups for their use during the fall, winter, and spring. Day trips or overnight and weekend camping trips on the camp property offer an excellent opportunity for the group leader to describe summer camp experiences. If camp is rented by user groups, explaining other programs open to individuals is an excellent way to promote the summer experience. The director should see that displays, slide shows or videos, and photographs that show summer activities are available.

An "off-season" campsite with all the "in-season" amenities stored, such as canoes, horses, and waterfront and archery equipment, does not promote summer sales to visitors. Special care should be taken to have helpful staff, attractive audiovisuals, and a sampling of camp songs, games, and activities to give visitors a taste of the magic of the regular season.

Home Parties

A preplanned visit and presentation in a previous camper's home or neighborhood, where invitations have been issued to friends, is a tool that has often been used when the primary target is youngsters from upper middle income families and above. They are most effective when a parent or several parents invite prospective campers and their parents to a home for a private presentation by the camp director or a staff member. An invitation from a neighbor or friend stimulates more interest than a cold invitation received by mail or from someone the person does not know. It has become increasingly more difficult to persuade families to host such parties in a time-pressured climate where, often, both parents work. Where it is difficult to utilize a home, the same method may be used in a school, hotel, or church, with several parents of former campers inviting people.

Personal Calls

After a prospect's name and information has been secured and appropriate information about the camp shared by mail or in person, the camp director should make a follow-up call to answer questions and "close the sale." The personal interest shown, as well as the opportunity to answer even minor questions, can be a determining factor in enrollment. This is no less true of follow-up calls to previous campers who have not enrolled after the initial enrollment periods.

Individualized Responses to E-mail Requests

Though not as personal as the telephone or in-person visits, responses via e-mail to inquiries from the camp's Web page or e-mail address should be individualized. Many directors report that their Web page has become their most effective recruitment tool. With an e-mail response, a personal interest and concern can be expressed. With the permission of the parents of a returning camper, the camp director can suggest that the person contact given parents to secure their experience or endorsement.

Camp Representatives

Some camps recruit camper representatives, often mothers, in certain cities or neighborhoods to undertake referrals and recruitment. These persons are given training and recruitment tools. In a number of cases, these persons receive a commission from each new camper enrolled who actually attends camp.

Visits to the Camp

It is not unusual for parents to visit a camp the season before their child is anticipating attendance or for prospective renters to visit the conference/retreat center in advance. In both cases, this aspect of marketing should not be overlooked.

There should be a plan for welcoming visitors who wish to see the camp facility or program in operation. A positive approach is to invite such visits in brochures and newsletters. Signs at the entrance to the property should clearly indicate where visitors are to report upon arrival.

Similarly in recruiting rental or user groups or schools, it is good to invite leaders of prospective groups to visit camp while other groups are in operation. Having them see firsthand the type of facilities in use and the services offered can be an effective marketing tool.

It is important that the person assigned the responsibility of showing the visitors around the site be fully familiar with operation, program, and registration questions. This is not a chore to be done quickly in order to return to the business of the facility but rather an opportunity to interpret and sell. Similarly, when parents arrive with campers for a session or at the end of a session, it is important to provide the opportunity to meet the camper's counselor and to have any remaining questions answered.

Promotional Materials

All materials produced by the camp should be considered promotional materials, and their quality and content should be addressed with this in mind.

Prospective Campers and Groups

Abrochure, video, CD, or slide presentation, however good, is of little value unless there is a good, qualified prospect to whom it can be presented. Developing lists of qualified prospects requires a system, consistent follow-up, and good planning. With the help of the demographics of an earlier marketing analysis, an interested group can then brainstorm for sources of prospects. As indicated earlier, the best source is previous campers or groups and staff. The next best sources are personal referrals from previous campers and interested individuals. These are the prime prospects and should be cultivated with care. Therefore, a system of asking for names of friends or children of friends must be devised. A personal contact is most effective. Providing incentives for names and addresses is another approach. The development of a referral slip in each newsletter or mailing may be the first step.

Camps that are operated under the sponsorship of organizations or churches, synagogues, and mosques have a natural opportunity for getting referrals from other members as well as membership lists in specific age categories. Careful study needs to be given to how members of the organization can be reached for recruitment purposes in the most personal manner. Where members are recruited through troops, clubs, or other neighborhood groups, there is a natural opportunity for interpretation of camp through the troop, club, and group programs and activities; such interpretation of the camp should be part of the ongoing program and emphasis of each group. Many organizations try to get members of a troop, club, or group to come to camp together during the same session. Parents' meetings during the year also offer opportunities to interpret the value of camp for children. Few organizations today can rely solely on their membership for campers or groups, but certainly interpretation and promotion of camp to these organizations is much easier and more effective than it is to the public at large.

Many camps can cultivate schools or churches and synagogues for the opportunity of presenting a program to an assembly or a class group, or to distribute descriptive material. Though the willingness of a particular public or private body to permit this approach varies, it is worth exploration.

When following up on names received from other individuals, sending materials with a personalized note, indicating "you were recommended by _____," helps make the materials be more meaningful. Of course, individualized follow-ups by telephone or in person will strengthen the chance for enrollment.

A file should be maintained on each prospective camper or group including as much personal data as can be secured: name, address, phone number, name of person referring the prospect, and age (if an individual) or type (if a group). A file of index cards often suffices, though the more sophisticated operation may computerize the list and develop a system to transfer persons to the enrollment file as individuals or groups are signed up. All inquiries received by telephone or mail, or at events such as camper fairs or slide showings, should be entered into this file.

Brochures or Flyers

The most traditional method of telling people about the camp experience is the printed word. The size and quality of printed materials marketing the camp experience varies greatly. Many camps print a high-quality, undated, four-color brochure, which is used for several years in conjunction with a rate and date sheet insert that is updated annually. Other camps print a new brochure annually. Some camps simply send out an announcement with an application form — but that happens less and less frequently in this competitive age.

To be effective, a brochure must be targeted to a specific audience and seldom can speak to multiple audiences effectively. If a variety of audiences are to be reached or significantly different programs are to be marketed, several smaller brochures, rather than one extensive one, may be more effective. Each brochure requires careful consideration. For example, type size may not be important in the development of a brochure aimed at youth, but adults prefer at least ten-point type for ease of reading.

A brochure need not be expensive to be attractive and effective, but it does need to look professional. A camp director may not have experience in this area and therefore should seek the help of a volunteer from the design and printing professions or hire assistance. In the camper recruitment material for parent consumption, there must be clear definition of age and maturity of staff, type of program and instruction, refund policy, health and age requirements, and values; materials directed to the camper will deal more with fun, adventure, specific program activities, and peer relationships. On the other hand, a brochure promoting group rental of facilities will emphasize comfort, types of facilities available, beauty of the setting, appropriate seasonal pictures, good food, and value. Information about environmental education opportunities or challenge course programs should also emphasize the program outcomes and goals and contribution to the group's purpose or curriculum.

Words should be used sparingly; pictures and open space should make up a large part of content. It is better to use good artwork than poor photographs, though a good picture always speaks best. Although four-color materials are very attractive, a color stock paper with one-color ink and the use of screening or reverse tools can also produce an attractive brochure at a lower cost. In a limited-budget situation, a self-mailer brochure that uses an enrollment card on one page while leaving space on the back cover for an address label and postage imprint might be considered.

Incentives

Incentives to returning campers who sign up by a given date and to staff or campers who sign up or recommend new campers can stimulate interest. These incentives range from pennants or T-shirts to cash discounts on camper fees or bonuses on staff salaries. Obviously, volunteer referral and genuine enthusiasm are preferable.

Visual Presentations

No matter how good a brochure is, the full visual and emotional impact of the camp experience cannot be captured on paper. That is more effectively revealed in the voice of a person who has been there along with pictures illustrating the camp experience. Video presentations, color slides, and Power Point presentations are tools that can combine both of those elements. There are advantages as well as disadvantages to each of these in various settings.

Again the principle of quality prevails, for it is better to do something simply and do it well than to produce a highly technical video that is poorly done. Therefore, a camp director will do well to start with good slides and either a firsthand, or taped, narration until the time, budget, and expert assistance to move to the next level is possible.

With the availability of volunteers with home video cameras or experience in developing Web pages, it is difficult not to immediately take advantage of an offer to help one develop this tool. To be effective, such efforts need to be carefully planned, scripted, photographed, and tightly edited. It is better to take the extra time and money and do it right when so much hinges upon telling the story effectively.

Try to limit your audiovisual show for public use to eight minutes. That is a short time, but viewers' minds wander when it goes much longer. Supplement the show with ten to fifteen minutes of personal presentation, which may include a presentation by a camper or staff member. The prospective audience must be determined first, and the presentation must be designed to address, captivate, and sell that audience.

Developing a Web site takes a totally different approach and also requires particular skills so that it attracts attention. As more and more camps develop Web sites, it becomes critical to stand out from among the many other camps on the Web. Some camps post photos from a day's activities on the Web site regularly during the summer.

Though many camps are utilizing videos or compact discs in place of brochures, a live person offering a visual presentation is certainly preferable to achieve a face-to-face sale. Where used as a brochure, the video or CD has the advantage of multiple showings and the potential involvement of many friends and neighbors. On the other hand, no matter how well made such a presentation is, the sales world knows it is best when someone is there to make the sale — to ask the prospect to enroll and sign on the dotted line. Where this is not possible (e.g., mailing a video/CD or visiting a camp's Web site), there needs to be a clear way in which the viewer can get more information, as well as be contacted by a staff member as soon as possible.

Outside Referrals

A plan to secure referrals from social agencies, judiciaries, churches, and synagogues can be valuable. Many camps rely on referrals from social workers, agencies, the court system, or their own membership. In these cases, early contacts with the people responsible for such referrals are important so that the director can establish a good relationship with changing personnel at the agency and develop a plan for working together. A clear understanding of the ability of the camp to serve people with certain problems and the plan for payment is essential in this arrangement.

Camper Referral Services

Camper referral services will list a number of camps and refer prospective campers who inquire about a camp or camps that meet the requirements the parents and children have set forth. Some agencies charge the camp a percentage (ten to fifteen percent) of the camp fee of children who actually enroll. Other agencies, particularly not-for-profit agencies, which are there to serve a specific population, will refer campers as a service to the parent, with no charge to the camp.

Public Displays

Displays with quantities of brochures in public locations can stimulate interest in camp. Choose carefully the locations where the demographic profile of the camp's potential customer would shop, stop, or browse. Generally, this cannot be afforded except with a relatively inexpensive brochure. However, an attractive display with pictures or a self-contained slide show and return postcards to request a brochure can lower the cost and narrow the prospects.

Advertising

Camper Fairs

Camper fairs are events where a large number of camps are invited to set up individual booths to interpret their camp for one day. The camp is normally charged a fee. The event is publicized and advertised broadly, and large numbers of people flow through a fair for its duration. A booth must have a lively visual and aggressive but personable staff to distinguish it from the many others in the lineup.

Magazines, Newspapers, and Other Media Advertising

Media advertising requires an attractive, professionally designed ad and, to be effective, must be run on a regular basis during the peak period for enrollments. Advertising on the radio or television certainly requires professional advice and development to be effective. Though many radio stations offer free time for spot announcements to not-for-profit organizations, the spots often run at odd hours. In each medium, regular repetition of the ad is vital.

To advertise in any and every publication is not a wise use of funds. Diane Meckler of the *New York Times* states, "An advertising campaign is not an end unto itself in securing enrollments, but a means for securing prospects who can then be turned into enrollments. [When] you have defined the target audience geographically, by your cost and by your specialty, you are ready to choose the right [medium] for your advertising campaign."[10]

Web Pages

A Web page can give basic information about the camp in a fashion to entice the reader to e-mail or call for further information. Because Web pages exist for a variety of camps, it is important to identify the unique characteristics and mission of your camp. Pictures, illustrations, and testimonials will liven up the copy and will appeal to the reader.

Billboards

Attractive, professionally designed billboards can attract attention to the camp. However, location, timing, and duration of exposure are critical ingredients. The cost factor is a consideration. Even if space is donated, the cost of design and printing is significant.

Posters

Posters must be eye-catching and should include tear-off blanks to request more information or the placement of brochures nearby.

Direct Mail

There are businesses that sell lists of names and addresses based upon the specifications given by the customer. For example, a camp may wish to purchase labels for families (1) of a certain income, (2) in certain zip codes, and (3) with children in a certain age range. The camp presents the company with three specifications that they are to meet, and the company provides a set of labels accordingly.

At this point, reference to the earlier market analysis will indicate the neighborhoods, schools, zip codes, or organizations from which more campers and groups have previously enrolled. It will usually prove much more effective to market in areas where sales have been made previously than to pioneer totally new territory. It takes less time and budget because of built-in recommendations and contacts, where people have already been receptive to the camp's message.

With the volume of bulk mail received by the public at large, such a mailing must be eye-catching and have a response gimmick to make it pay for itself. As a rule, one may expect an inquiry rate of about four percent of the number mailed with a one percent sign-up.

Publicity and Public Relations

Public Presentations

B ecause various service clubs and community organizations are often looking for a program, a presentation of the camp's video or slide show along with a verbal interpretation can be a different way of spreading the word about the value of the camp experience. Parents of campers, staff members, and volunteers often have relationships with churches, synagogues, or schools (both public and private) that can make possible presentations to interested individuals. Though the presentations may not be designed for camper recruitment, the programs can help others know about the camp.

News Stories

C amp is rich with human interest stories. One need only make sure that a staff member has the responsibility of providing enough details to interest a reporter of a local newspaper or magazine or radio/TV station. Though camp season may offer the most obvious opportunities, special events during the rest of the year may also stimulate stories.

Bringing Groups to the Camp

A rranging a time during the camp season for people in the local community nearest camp to visit the camp can be invaluable in developing strong community understanding and ties.

Though many camps offer facilities for rental in periods other than the summer, the rental groups and participants in outdoor education programs are often looked upon as a separate program or entity. Actually, if time and energy are spent, these groups can be ideal conduits for camp promotion. These organizations offer a natural marketing target. The nature of a rental group may enable the marketing approach to be tailored in a fashion that may generate interest in specific programs or facilities. Perhaps benefits of individual participation in camp can also benefit the group, thus stimulating the support and interest of the leader of the group.

When rental groups arrive at the camp, there should be a clear plan of check-in and orientation. The orientation should include not only facility locations and directions, but also information about mealtimes, safety regulations, and how to obtain help in case of an emergency. Though much of this information will have been presented to the group in writing, it should still be presented in person, if at all possible. Helping people feel at home and comfortable is the beginning of a good experience and the continuation of marketing.

Such an orientation provides the opportunity to explain about other camp programs and to indicate that materials are available at a given location. Attractive displays including brochures will stimulate interest on the part of some participants. A self-contained video or slide show could be set up in one corner of the dining hall or in a lounge area.

Again, developing a plan for marketing that selects which of these marketing devices will be used and in what fashion is important. The selection of the tools to be used will depend upon many factors: amount of funds available, the number of new campers desired, the camp's philosophy and message, and the audience to be addressed. It is always better to do a few things well than to use many tools and use them poorly.

Registration Forms

Regardless of whether the camp is enrolling individuals or groups, a registration form will be needed. It should be carefully designed in light of its intended use before, during, and after the campers or groups are at camp. Whether it is a card, a sheet, or a half sheet should be determined by how it is to be filed and how often it will be handled. The format of the form will also be influenced by whether the information will be transferred to a computer file. It should be remembered that the information gathered on the registration form will provide the beginning of the camp's database of campers and groups. Consequently, careful thought should be given to what data will be helpful for comparative purposes a year hence.

Actual information on the application blank for individual campers may include

- Address of camper (zip code sorts may reveal some of your best markets)

- Home phone number

- Birth date

- School and grade (specify either the grade at the time of enrollment or the grade for the following fall)

- Parents' and guardians' names and emergency contacts

- Work address and phone numbers of each parent and guardian

- Height and weight

- Religious affiliation (particularly if special arrangements are made for attending religious services out of camp)

- Name of a friend the camper wishes to have in the same living group

- Where the camper learned about camp

- Other organizational programs or activities in which the camper participates

- Any physical, psychological, or mental disabilities that may require special attention

- Gender

- Any previous camping experience

- Cancellation and refund policy

In addition, there is usually a paragraph that the parent or guardian signs giving permission for the child to be enrolled in camp for the given session, stating that he or she will pay the camper fee. In the case of adult campers, there should be a paragraph that the person signs stating the session for enrollment and that he or she will pay the given fee. A paragraph may include

- A release for the camp to use any photos taken of the camper at camp

- A statement concerning family income, if the child qualifies for financial assistance through any local, county, state, or federal program

- Information about the family's or individual's health insurance carrier (if the camp is not providing health and accident insurance on the camper or if the family's insurance is used as the primary or secondary insurance)

- A medical and surgical release statement (in some communities, this statement must now be notarized as a requirement of the local hospital)

- Information about to whom, if anyone other than the admitting parent, a minor camper is to be released

- Any special dietary requirements

Actual information on the registration form for groups may include

- The name of the organization or group, and its office address and phone number

- The name of the responsible adult who will be in charge of the group at the time of their arrival

- The name, address, and phone number of the person making the reservation

- The number of persons who will be present, including some breakdown by sex and general age grouping

- Where the group learned about the camp

- The planned arrival and departure times

- What services will be covered in the contract (e.g., meals, staff for program, equipment, linens, room setup, special menus)

- The conditions for the use of any equipment and facilities such as swimming area, as well as who is responsible for such items as first aid, supervision, behavior, program

- The rate that the group will be charged

- The amount of deposit required, the minimum fee, and cancellation policies relating to refunds and deadlines

- Any rules that the group leadership must agree to in advance on behalf of the group (e.g., rules concerning alcoholic beverages, controlled substances, or firearms)

Some camps, by their special nature, have rather specific entrance requirements or limitations necessitated by the owner's purpose and program. Those entrance requirements should be clearly spelled out in the promotional materials and on the registration form. The registration form should elicit all the information necessary to determine if an applicant meets those requirements. All camps have some requirements even though they may be only a given sex or minimum age.

In some cases it may be essential to collect specific information to determine the suitability of the activities at camp for the camper or to ensure the placement of the camper in the appropriate level of activities.

The Americans With Disabilities Act of 1990 requires that all camps, except those operated by religious groups and private clubs, make their programs and facilities accessible to individuals with disabilities. Religious groups and private clubs are exempted only when serving their own members and then only if they are not receiving any federal funding or food or milk commodities from the U.S. Department of Agriculture.

To determine appropriate accommodations, it is permissible to ask that disabilities be identified on registration forms. It is important, however, that the information requested about a camper's health and disabilities be used only to identify appropriate health care and to better serve the camper, not to screen out campers. It will be helpful to indicate to parents that the goal of the camp is to provide the best camp experience possible. Wording to this effect may also be added to letters that accompany health forms where parents are asked to identify any disabilities or health problems the prospective camper has. Privacy of health information and records is discussed in chapter 12.

Some camps may find that they are unable to serve campers with certain disabilities. The Americans With Disabilities Act obligates camps to make reasonable accommodations to include individuals with disabilities in their programs, so long as the accommodations are readily achievable and do not create an undue burden on the organization or fundamentally alter the basic experience the camp is designed to provide. "For example, it would appear to fundamentally alter a wilderness backpacking experience conducted in mountainous rocky terrain where there are no paths, if persons in wheelchairs were included on the trip."[11]

Camps must also be concerned with the level of safety provided to the individual and every other camper in the program. "The ADA expressly states that a public accommodation may exclude an individual, if that individual poses a direct threat to the health or safety of others that cannot be mitigated by appropriate modifications in the camp's policies or procedures, or by the provision of auxiliary aids. [Camp directors] will be permitted to establish objective safety criteria for the operation of their camps. However, any safety standard must be based on objective requirements rather than stereotypes or generalizations about the ability of people with disabilities to participate in an activity."[12] Therefore, decisions about participation should be on an individual basis.

Registration forms may also include an agreement to participate. Ed Schirick, President of Schirick and Associates Insurance Brokers, suggests that "there is a growing trend toward acceptance [of agreements to participate or waivers]. This is especially true when the individuals have been 'properly' informed of the risks and understand what might happen to them if they participate in the activity. The basis of this is a reaffirmation by the courts, in some states, of the common law doctrine of assumption of risk."[13] Obviously, such statements should be developed in consultation with the camp's attorney, but they can never remove the responsibility of the host to the guest. See chapter 11 for more information about waivers and liability releases.

The third step, after identifying the message and selecting the tools to be used, is to develop a plan of implementation. A plan should outline each of the steps to accomplish the goals and should place those steps in calendar form for a twelve-month period with a deadline for each.

Joanna Warren Smith recommends that "the best way to convey consistent attention to detail and excellence at every level of your program is to put your ideas on paper and publish a year-round marketing strategy. . . . Plan mailings, phone calls, and newsletters. Be realistic about necessary preparation time. Be clear about the personalized follow-up that every inquiry demands. Through this tracking you can see what is working, what is not, and where you have too much and not enough."[14] The emphasis here is on approaching marketing on a twelve-month basis, calendaring each segment of the plan, and reviewing regularly the progress of the plan.

It is to the director's advantage in planning, buying supplies, and employing staff, to start camper enrollment as early as possible. It takes time to develop a pattern of early enrollment but it can be gradually encouraged. On the other hand, certain weather changes or seasons do encourage thoughts about camp, for example, the arrival of warm days in the spring or a vacation period when the youngsters are around the house a great deal.

The camp director cannot possibly accomplish these steps alone. It is wise to enlist the assistance of staff, former staff, former campers, parents of campers, and committee members. This enlistment will provide a variety of energetic and enthusiastic persons who, given the proper information and training, can spread the camp's story much more effectively than one person can. Most of this process can be accomplished through volunteers, though it may be necessary to employ one or two persons to carry out more time-consuming or specialized portions of the plan. The next step is to implement the plan and to check repeatedly whether the plan is proceeding on schedule. Even the best volunteers need follow-up calls and pep talks from time to time.

Planning for the succeeding year will require evaluation of how well the plan worked and how it should be changed. There is more on evaluation in chapter 16.

Checkpoints

1. Clarify your camp's identity.

2. Do a market analysis of your camp.

3. Locate all materials previously used for camp promotion. Study them in light of the camp's identity and your market analysis. Ask an unbiased outside expert to critique them or check out your competition's marketing materials.

4. List the steps that you can take in light of your market analysis; arrange them in order of importance.

5. Develop a market plan for your camp, calendared for one year.

6. Implement and follow through with the market plan.

Related Standards

Accreditation Standards for Camp Programs and Services: OM-12, 19–21 HW-5, 7, 17, 23; "Additional Professional Practices": Item 16

[1] Armand Ball. 1982. "On the Ball." *Camping Magazine*, Vol. 54, No. 3, February. p. 2.

[2] Dr. Dwight Jewson, Strategic Frameworking, Inc.,Vashon, Washington, May 31, 2003.

[3] Parents Are Listening More to Kids." *USA Today*. January 24, 1990.

[4] Edward L. Hayes. 1989. "Positioning Your Ministry in the Market Place." *Journal of Christian Camping*, Vol. 22, No. 3, May/June. p. 10. Reprinted with permission from CCI/USA.

[5] "Survey Says ... ." 2001. *Christian Camps and Conference Journal*, Vol. 5 No. 5, September-October. pp. 30-33.

[6] Dr. Dwight Jewson. 1978. "The Promotional Aspect of Camp Marketing." *Camping Magazine*, Vol. 50, No. 6, May. p. 17.

[7] Douglas B. Herron. 1997. *Marketing Not-for-profit Programs and Services*. San Francisco: Jossey-Bass Publishers. p. 34.

[8] Herron. 1997. p. 34.

[9] Report of Maguire Associates, Inc., Concord, MA, for the American Camping Association Private Independent Camps, 1990.

[10] Diane Meckler. 1988. "Marketing." *Camping Magazine*, Vol. 61, No. 1, September/October. p. .

[11] Marge Scanlin. 1992. "Better Camping for All: A Beginning Look at the Americans With Disabilities Act." *Camping Magazine*, Vol. 64, No. 3, February. p. 31.

[12] Scanlin. 1992. p. 31.

[13] Ed Schirick. 1990. "Risk Management." *Camping Magazine*, Vol. 62, No. 5, March. p. 9.

[14] Joanna Warren Smith. 1997. "Out-of-the-Box Marketing Strategies." *Camping Magazine*, Vol. 70, No. 5, September/October. p. 25.

Business & Finance

Continuing success in camping is obviously dependent upon sound business procedures . . . the camp business administration is just as surely a long-term means of accomplishing our camp objectives as are other phases of camp operation, such as program, staff recruiting, and property upkeep.[1]

The fiscal management of the camp is too often the last consideration of many camp directors whose primary concerns lie with campers and program. To others, the bottom line is the starting point, and program considerations wait on the financing. Actually, the philosophy, program, marketing, and finances are so interdependent that each one is ineffectual without the other.

Where the camp director chooses to give significant personal attention to the program of the camp when groups are on site, there may need to be a support system in place to oversee the camp's operations and fiscal affairs. Often camp directors retain the direct supervision of program because of their interest and find an assistant who serves as business manager. A business manager typically supervises all or some of the operational systems of the camp (e.g., office, business, food service, transportation, property and site management, health service). Other staffing arrangements may divide functions differently, depending on the interest and skills of the camp director and other personnel and on the organizational structure of the camp.

The director should assign day-to-day financial responsibilities to one staff person at camp and should provide that person with a precise job description. Lines of responsibility and accountability should be clear to all staff. The maintenance of up-to-date, accurate records is essential, so some training and experience is necessary for this job. A business manager with some accounting experience is ideal; in addition, some camps will have a bookkeeper in the camp or main office.

Accounting Practices

The specific accounting and budgetary practices of camps will vary greatly according to the volume of financial transactions and the sophistication of the operator's organization. Camps that are part of a larger organization will find that the systems the camp is expected to follow are already in place. Other camps will have the opportunity of setting up their own systems; in most cases, those systems will be tied to a computer program. Today even the smallest camps have access to a computer and a simple bookkeeping system. However, with or without a computer, the basic principles are the same and need to be understood from the outset:

- A budget of projected income and expenses should be established.

- All income must be documented and verified.

- All monies (cash receipts and checks) should be deposited promptly.

- Internal controls should be established.

- Expenditures should be made against approved invoices.

- Regular summaries of financial activity, preferably monthly, should be planned. During more active times, weekly summaries should be scheduled.

- A system that identifies high and low points of cash flow should be developed so that low points may be adequately planned for.

- The books should be audited annually, by some person not on the staff.

Advice from a certified public accountant or other knowledgeable source should be secured on the following matters (in some cases, a bookkeeping service will be able to answer your questions):

- Choice of a cash or accrual system of bookkeeping

- Tax reports required by local, state, and federal governments

- Generally Accepted Accounting Principles (GAAP) as defined by the Financial Accounting Standards Board (FASB)[2]

- Financial records to be kept, including journals and receivables, payables, and payroll, the length of time different records should be kept, and the value of computer records versus paper copy

Annual Audit

If you are setting up a new financial system or reevaluating a system already in place, an Operational Financial Risks Worksheet (*see illustration 14.1*) will be of help in identifying office procedures to manage and safeguard financial resources.

Illustration 14.1 | *Operational Financial Risks Worksheet*

OPERATIONAL FINANCIAL RISKS WORKSHEET

Operational financial risks are those where property, equipment, and/or money might be damaged or lost. Considerations to effectively manage and safeguard the financial resources include identifying the financial controls needed and determining procedures to control or reduce the risks.

Oversight of the financial operations includes audits, preparation of financial statements, preparation of and monitoring of the annual budget and cash flow projections, and monitoring of actual cash flow, etc. Person responsible _____

Petty Cash
1. Amount of cash available _____ Maximum an individual may request _____
2. Person responsible for maintaining _____ Reconciling _____
3. Person with access to petty cash _____ How is cash secured? _____
4. Explain reimbursement requirements from petty cash _____
5. Person authorizing payments _____ How is petty cash replenished? _____

Cash Receipts
1. Person handling checks received by mail _____
   How and when are checks endorsed and recorded (numbered receipts reconciled with cash received)?
   _____
2. How often are deposits made _____ By _____
3. Procedure for giving checks/cash to staff or volunteers _____
4. Person with access to checks/cash _____
5. How are checks/cash secured on-site? _____ Off-site? _____
6. Policy on third-party checks _____

Cash Disbursements
1. Does the procedure include use of prenumbered checks? _____ And a system to secure and account for unused checks? _____
2. Person authorized to sign checks _____
   Is there a limit over which a second signature is required? _____
3. Are purchase orders and receiving documents required for payment? _____
   Person authorizing payment _____ Are invoices canceled after payment? _____
4. Explain the refund policy _____
5. Person with authority to purchase or commit camp funds _____
   Are there limits to this authority? _____
6. Person responsible for entering into a contract on the camp's behalf _____
7. When is bidding required? _____
   What is considered for comparison, (e.g., quantity, quality, delivery availability and time, cost, size or minimum order requirements, etc.)? _____
8. What expenses are reimbursable and at what rate? _____
   Documentation requirements _____

Reconciliation and Analysis
1. Are bank statements reconciled monthly _____ By _____
2. Explain the policy on payroll and benefits accrual _____
   Person responsible for analyzing _____
3. Person responsible for reviewing receivables _____
   Is there a policy on write-offs of accounts receivables? _____
4. Person responsible for generating a monthly list of outstanding unpaid invoices _____

Inventory of Equipment and Supplies
1. Person responsible for program supplies _____ Person with access _____
   How are program supplies secured? _____
2. Person responsible for office supplies _____ Person with access _____
   How are office supplies secured? _____
3. Person responsible for food supplies _____ Person with access _____
   How are food supplies secured? _____
4. Person responsible for sale merchandise _____ Person with access _____
   How is sale merchandise secured? _____

Tax Liability
1. Is sales tax being collected and remitted on selling of supplies? _____ By _____
2. Person responsible for remitting payroll tax forms, filling 990s, paying into unemployment funds, and making provisions for any contingencies that might encumber the future operation _____

Where camps are part of larger organizations, the organization will have already chosen a cash or accrual system of bookkeeping. In an independent camp, that choice is one the director should make in consultation with the accountant. A *cash system* recognizes cash when received and disbursed and treats all monies received and expended in a given period of twelve months as the operating funds. An *accrual system* recognizes income when earned and expenses when incurred regardless of when cash is actually received or paid and seeks to attribute the income and expenses to the actual twelve months of operation they affect, thereby accruing or accumulating and applying income and expense for the next year's operation to the next year's budget.

Financial Statements

There are three important financial statements for camps. The first important statement to be considered is a *statement of activities* or *income statement*, which shows the income and expense activity in a given month. This statement should be reviewed on a monthly basis for management control purposes. The director may want this statement to show columns for that month and also for the year to date, the budgeted amount, and the actual numbers for the same month the previous year. This provides a checkpoint for the director (and board, if

---

Illustration 14.2 *Statement of Activities*

ANNUAL NONPROFIT STATEMENT OF ACTIVITIES AND STATEMENT OF CHANGES IN NET ASSETS

	Unrestricted	Temporarily Restricted	Permanently Restricted	Total
ANNUAL STATEMENT OF ACTIVITIES				
Revenues, Gains, and Other Support				
Contributions				
Fees				
Income on investments				
Other				
Net assets released from restrictions				
Program restrictions				
Equipment acquisition restrictions				
Expired restrictions				
Total revenues, gains, and other support				
Expenses and Losses				
Program A — Summer				
Program B — Environmental Education				
Program C — Rentals				
Management and general office				
Fund raising				
Total expenses and losses				
Change in Net Assets				
ANNUAL STATEMENT OF CHANGES IN NET ASSETS				
Net assets at beginning of year				
Net assets at end of year				

Illustration 14.3   *Income Statement*

FOR-PROFIT INCOME STATEMENT

	Monthly Actual	Monthly Actual Last Year	Year To Date	Annual Budget
REVENUES				
Camper fees				
Special fees				
Investment income				
Sales				
Miscellaneous				
Total Revenues				
EXPENSES				
Salaries and benefits				
Food				
Utilities				
Equipment				
Taxes and insurance				
Repairs				
Depreciation and amortization				
Transportation expenses				
Program expenses				
Training expenses				
Office expenses				
Total Expenses				
NET INCOME				

there is one) to adjust certain expense items if income is not living up to expectations or if some expense accounts are running over expectations. At the end of the year, the not-for-profit's statement of activities provides a summary of all income and expenses by accounts for the year and indicates a net gain or loss for the year. For-profit organizations generally call these income statements. See *illustration 14.2* for an example of a not-for-profit's statement of activities and *illustration 14.3* for an example of a for-profit's income statement.

In addition to a statement of activities, the second important camp financial statement is a *balance sheet* or, under new not-for-profit terminology, a *statement of financial position*.[3] This statement summarizes the net assets and liabilities of the camp and is a key to the long-range financial health of the camp. *Illustration 14.4* shows a sample not-for-profit statement of financial position. *Illustration 14.5* provides a sample format for such a balance sheet statement for a for-profit organization. The annual operations either add to or detract from the positive side of this equation. For instance, a deficit in a year's operation uses any surplus funds that are on hand from previous years or causes obligations against property. The goal of every camp, even the not-for-profit operation, is to provide a growth in the assets of the camp to ensure that people will be served in the future. In the case of the for-profit camp, this investment usually is a good portion of the owner's assets, which are to provide income or security at the time of retirement. Both statements identify the actual bottom line of the camp's assets or investments.

Illustration 14.4 *Statement of Financial Position*

NONPROFIT STATEMENT OF FINANCIAL POSITION

ASSETS

Cash and cash equivalents

Account and interest receivable

Inventories and prepaid expenses

Contributions receivable

Short-term investments

Assets restricted to investment in land,
 buildings, and equipment

Land, buildings, and equipment

Long-term investments

Total Assets

LIABILITIES AND NET ASSETS

Accounts payable and accrued expenses

Grants payable

Notes payable

Long-term debt

Total Liabilities

NET ASSETS

Unrestricted

Temporarily restricted

Permanently restricted

Total Net Assets

Total Liabilities and Net Assets

Illustration 14.5 *For-Profit Balence Sheet*

FOR-PROFIT BALANCE SHEET

ASSETS

Current Assets

Cash and cash equivalents (investments)

Accounts receivable

Inventories

Prepaid expenses

Total Current Assets

Facilities

Land

Building

Furniture

Subtotal Facilities

Accumulated Depreciation and Amortization (minus)

Total Facilities

Total Assets

LIABILITIES AND OWNER'S EQUITY

Liabilities

Accounts payable and accrued expenses

Deferred income

Total Current Liabilities

Long-term Liabilities

Mortgage payable

Total Long-term Liabilities

Owner's Equity

Capital stock

Retained earnings

Total Owner's Equity

Total Liabilities and Owner's Equity

The third important financial statement is a *cash flow statement*. Under the new rules of the Financial Accounting Standards Board, not-for-profit organizations are required to prepare a cash flow statement as for-profit organizations have done traditionally. These statements identify the changes in cash flow during the year. The cash flow statement shows the difference between the beginning and ending operating accounts. The increases or decreases are shown in the various lines on the statement of financial position, ultimately showing a net change in cash position at year end. Not-for-profit organizations should seek the assistance of their own certified public accountant to work out the correct format and records. See *illustration 14.6* for a list of elements to include in a cash flow statement, as well as a sample statement in *illustration 14.7*.

Illustration 14.6 — *Cash Flow Statements*

ELEMENTS TO INCLUDE IN CASH FLOW STATEMENTS

NONPROFIT

Cash Flow from Operating Activities
Change in Net aAsets
  Adjustment to reconcile change in net assets to
    net cash used by operating activities
  Depreciation
  Increase in accounts and interest receivable
  Decrease in inventories and prepaid expenses
  Increase in contributions receivable
  Increase in accounts payable
  Decrease in grants payable
  Contributions restricted for long-term investment
  Interest and dividends restricted for long-term
    investment
Total Cash Used by Operating Activities

Cash Flow from Investment Activities
  Purchase of equipment
  Proceeds from sale of investments
  Purchase of investments
Net Cash Used by Investment Activities

Cash Flow from Financing Activities
  Proceeds from contributions restricted for:
    Investment in endowment
    Investment in plant
  Other financing activities
  Interest and dividends restricted for reinvestment
  Payments of annuity obligations
  Payments on notes payable
  Payments on long-term debt
Net Cash Used by Financing Activities

Net Decrease in Cash and Equivalents

Cash and Cash Equivalents at Beginning of Year

Cash and Cash Equivalents at End of Year

FOR-PROFIT

Cash Flow from Operating Activities
Net Income
  Adjustments to reconcile net income to cash used
    by operating activities
  Depreciation expense
  Increase or decrease in accounts receivable
  Increase or decrease in inventories
  Increase or decrease in prepaid expense
  Increase or decrease in other current assets
  Increase or decrease in accounts payable
  Increase or decrease in accrued expenses
  Increase or decrease in taxes payable
  Increase or decrease in other current liabilities
Total Cash Flow from Operating Activities

Cash Flow from Investment Activities
  Proceeds from sales of investments
  Purchase of investments
  Purchase of equipment
Total Cash Flow from Investment Activities

Cash Flow from Financing Activities
  Short-term debt
  Long-term debt
  Capital stock
  Other equity
Total Cash Flow from Financing Activities

Net Change in Cash

Cash and Cash Equivalents Beginning of Year

Cash and Cash Equivalents End of Year

Illustration 14.7 *Cash Flow Planning Chart*

SAMPLE CASH FLOW PLANNING CHART

Accounts	Annual Budget	January	February	March	April	May	June	July	August	September	October	November	December	TOTAL
INCOME														
111 Camper fees	$250,000	$ 5,000	$ 2,000											
112 Environmental education fees	100,000	10,000	8,000											
121 Horseback	10,000													
122 Bus fees	15,000													
until all are listed														
TOTALS	$375,000	$15,000	$10,000											
EXPENDITURES														
210 Full-time employees	$ 75,000	$ 6,250	$ 6,250											
220 Part-time employees	100,000	2,000	1,750											
230 FICA	10,500	490	470											
240 Unemployment compensation taxes	2,000	70	60											
250 Health insurance	8,000	600	600											
until all are listed														
TOTALS	$375,000	$20,200	$ 9,130											
DIFFERENCE	$ -0-	($ 5,200)	$ 870											

(Difference between income and expenses indicates cash excess or cash needed that month.)

Budgeting

As the Merriam-Webster dictionary puts it, a budget is simply a statement of the financial position of an administration for a definite period of time based on estimates of expenditures during the period and proposals for financing them.[4] The budget is also a reflection of the camp's mission and philosophy, since where one secures and spends money indicates the priorities of the operation.

Most budgets cover a twelve-month period, though not all budget cycles follow the calendar year. Some fiscal years or budget years are established differently to parallel the owner's financial and budgetary activity, which often follows program operation. Where there is a parent organization involved, the budget will need approval by the operating committee, board, or agency; this necessitates planning and adoption well in advance of the starting date of the fiscal year.

A budget is part of a planning process and reflects the setting of goals such as the number of participants to be recruited, the number of staff to be employed, the number and type of program activities that can be operated, and the ultimate balance sheet position the director desires. Because a budget reflects planning and goal-setting, it must be adjusted to actual experience as time progresses. If recruitment reports show that there are likely to be fewer campers or groups than budgeted, then not only is the income item for campers lessened but reductions in expenses must also be made to the same degree. Where budgets are approved by groups or people other than the owner and camp director, there should be an established system by which revisions are made and approved.

The Budget Process

The development of a list or chart of accounts, or categories of income and expenses, is the starting point in the budget process. In organizations, those accounts will be given to the camp, and the camp must fit its income and expenses into those existing descriptions. Where a camp has the opportunity to develop its own set of accounts, it is wise to list all the types of income sources and expenses, grouping them into logical account names. A sample list of accounts is shown in *illustration 14.8*. Many organizations, including most not-for-profits, desire or require that this list of accounts be grouped by different functions or areas of income and expense. This functional accounting is demonstrated in *illustration 14.9*.

Projecting Income and Expense

The safest method of budgeting is to project income conservatively and expenditures more liberally. Ideally, of course, the projections should be as realistic as possible; however, it is better to err on the side of overprojecting expenses than income.

In budgeting, the director should not project income from any more campers or groups

Illustration 14.8

SAMPLE LIST OF ACCOUNTS

INCOME

Acct.	Acct. Explanation
110	*Tuition Fees*
111	Camper
112	Environmental education
120	*Fees*
121	Horseback riding
122	Bus transportation
123	Arts/crafts
130	*Rental of Facilities*
131	Summer
132	Fall-Winter-Spring

Acct.	Acct. Explanation
140	*Sales*
141	Camper store (supplies, shirts)
142	Meals to visitors
150	*Miscellaneous*
160	*Contributions*
161	Individuals
162	Government grants
163	United Way
164	Other

EXPENDITURES

Acct.	Acct. Explanation
200	*Wages and Benefits*
210	Full-time employees
220	Part-time/seasonal employees
230	FICA
240	Unemployment compensation/taxes
250	Health/accident insurance
300	*Food Service*
310	Kitchen Food
320	Supplies
330	Campout/trail food
400	*Occupancy*
411	Gas
412	Electricity
413	Telephone
414	Water
415	Sewer
420	Maintenance supplies
430	Equipment repairs
450	Taxes
460	Property/liability insurance
470	Building repairs
480	Building construction
500	*Transportation*
510	Charters or rental/lease
520	Insurance
530	Gas/oil
540	Repairs
550	Licenses

Acct.	Acct. Explanation
600	*Program*
610	Equipment
620	Supplies
700	*Training*
710	Organization dues
720	Books, films, materials
730	Conferences, workshops
740	Training travel
800	*Office*
810	Postage/UPS
820	Printing (stationery, envelopes, etc.)
830	Office supplies
840	Promotional printing
850	Promotional advertising
860	Promotional travel
900	*Board/Committee Expense*
910	Board meeting expense
920	Board training
930	Director/officer insurance
1000	*Designated Contributions*
1010	Campership grants
1020	Special projects

than were actually enrolled the previous year unless there is strong reason to believe additional campers will come (e.g., other camps in the area are no longer offering the same programs, the camp has increased promotion efforts). When increasing fees, and therefore budgeted income, consideration should be given to whether the increase will lead to any reduction in enrollment. Other income accounts should be compared to expenditures for those related activities or services (camp store, transportation to and from camp, special activities) to see if the fees are adequate to provide an acceptable margin of income beyond expenditures in each area. It is vital, if extra fees are charged for some activities, to include all the related costs of such activity in this comparison; for example, the salary and related costs for the personnel to

Illustration 14.9

ACCOUNTS BY VARIOUS FUNCTIONS

EXPENSES

Administration*

210	Full-time employees
220	Part-time/seasonal employees
230	FICA
240	Unemployment compensation
250	Insurance (health, worker's comp.)
420	Supplies
710	Organization dues
730	Conferences/workshops
810	Postage/UPS
820	Printing (stationery, envelopes, etc.)
830	Office supplies

Food Service

210	Full-time employees
220	Part-time/seasonal employees
230	FICA
240	Unemployment compensation
250	Insurance (health, worker's comp.)
310	Kitchen food
420	Supplies
320	Campout/trail food

Program

210	Full-time employees
220	Part-time/seasonal employees
230	FICA
240	Unemployment compensation
250	Insurance
420	Supplies
610	Equipment
700	Training

Promotion/Marketing

210	Full-time employees
220	Part-time/seasonal employees
230	FICA
240	Unemployment compensation
250	Insurance
413	Telephone — long distance
420	Supplies
810	Postage/UPS
820	Printing
850	Advertising
860	Travel

Fund-Raising**

210	Full-time employees
220	Part-time/seasonal employees
230	FICA
240	Unemployment compensation
250	Insurance (health, worker's comp.)
413	Telephone — long distance
420	Supplies
810	Postage/UPS
820	Printing
910	Campership grants
920	Allowance for uncollectible pledges

Occupancy

210	Full-time employees
220	Part-time/seasonal employees
230	FICA
240	Unemployment compensation
250	Insurance (health, worker's com.)
411	Gas
412	Electricity
413	Telephone
414	Water
415	Sewer
420	Supplies
430	Equipment purchases
440	Equipment repairs
450	Taxes/licenses
460	Insurance (building, liability, etc.)
470	Building repairs
480	Building construction
510	Charters/rental/lease vehicles
520	Insurance — vehicle
530	Fuel — vehicles
540	Repairs — vehicles

Volunteer Leadership

910	Meeting expense
920	Training
930	Director/officer insurance

*Where it is not possible to differentiate functions for certain expenses, a section labeled "administrative" can be added. Those expenses can then be totaled and divided among the other functions on the basis of a percentage based on income, facility, usage, or staff time.

Where camps have substantive operations other than summer camp or conferences (e.g., outdoor education, retreats, etc.), separate functional divisions may be established.

**Nonprofits only.

operate an activity should be added to the cost of materials and facilities when setting an activity's fees.

In projecting expenditures, one should identify the fixed costs of operation, or those that will not change as the number of campers or staff changes (e.g., property taxes, base utilities, office space, salaries and benefits of full-time employees). Expenses that are not fixed are considered variables (e.g., food for 50 campers versus 100 campers). Several projections may be necessary with these expenses based upon various levels of camper enrollment. There will be a point when the fixed expenses plus the variable expenses will balance with or exceed the projected income. This becomes the minimum target for budgeting and marketing. The director should always consider the most disastrous thing that could happen (e.g., price increases, need for extra staff, equipment breakdown and replacement). Large-expenditure items should be carefully documented. Salaries and food often account for as much as fifty to sixty percent of a camp budget and need to be analyzed carefully because a slight change in either item could substantially alter the budgeted expenditures.

Depreciating Buildings and Equipment

Many camps have been slow to include a budget line for appropriate depreciation of camp buildings and equipment. Each building and every piece of major equipment should be depreciated, or have its value reduced, on an agreed-upon schedule, after consultation with the camp's accountant and/or board. In an ideal situation, the amount depreciated in a given year is placed in a reserve account for the eventual replacement of the building or equipment. Not-for-profit camps have often avoided this issue by relying upon campaigns for charitable contributions to replace major structures. However, it is increasingly difficult for many sponsoring organizations to find major capital funds. With increasing financial pressures upon not-for-profit organizations, camps may need to be aggressive to get the attention of the organization's board for needed capital expenditures and ask the board to choose between setting up replacement reserves and committing to securing capital funds from other sources. In any case, each camp needs to develop a plan for replacement of buildings and equipment over appropriate time periods.

Final Budget Development

Only when a director has viewed the realistic expectation of income and expenses is he or she in a position to work toward final budget development. It is critical that all the expenses of camp operation be included in the budget. Particularly in the not-for-profit sector, certain expenses may have been covered in other budgets, or allowances may not have been made for depreciation; thus, the budget won't reflect the true cost of camp. For example, in some organizations the salary and related benefits of the year-round professional employee responsible for the camp and/or certain insurance or bookkeeping services may be carried in the overall organizational budget rather than the camp's budget. Even if they are covered under the organizational budget, the accurate amount of any such costs based upon the percentage of time devoted to the camp should be reflected in the camp's budget in order to really understand true costs. All these issues are important in producing an accurate picture of the camp's state of being for management purposes and for presentation to committees and boards and to the public.

Adjusting Expenses

If, at this point in the budget process, expenses exceed income, the director should review each expense account to see what can be pared down without endangering the program outcomes and goals of the camp or the health and safety of the campers. After the director has determined the essential expenses, the camper income that can be expected based upon past experience, other self-generated income (e.g., from the camp store, program and transportation fees), and possible outside funding available (e.g., subsidies, foundation grants, campership funds, contributions), a decision can be made whether any remaining difference should come from increased fees or from reduced expenditures, which may mean decreased program or personnel. Because camper fees need to be set early in the promotional year, decisions related to fees should be completed by early fall, which may not always coincide with the budget schedule for the fiscal year.

In determining income from campers' fees in a camp where some campers pay the full fee and others pay a reduced or no fee, it is important to show the source of income for any subsidy of camper fees in the income statement. The director must know the actual cost of the camp experience per camper, especially when he or she is seeking supplemental funds for campers who cannot pay the full fee. Donors often respond well to the concept of sending a needy camper to camp but may expect documentation of costs. Outside funding sources, including the United Way and most foundations, require such documentation as well.

Cash Flow

Just as important as whether one is meeting or exceeding budgetary plans is whether the cash received matches the cash needed to cover the expenses for the same time period. Developing a cash flow planning chart prior to the beginning of the fiscal year will assist the director in planning for cash shortages or overages. A sheet should be completed with the income accounts and descriptions in a vertical column to the left, followed by columns for an estimate of how much will be received or spent in each account for each month, plus a year-end total. See *illustration 14.9* for an example of a cash flow planning chart. The income and expense accounts are also totaled separately for a given month, providing a cash position. If there are several months in a row where the cash needs are higher than the income expected, then a plan must be developed to draw cash from reserves or from a bank loan. Similarly, if there are several months where there will be cash excesses, plans should be made for short-term investments during that period to gain interest income. Where there is flexibility, the cash flow planning chart also provides an opportunity to adjust the time table for certain expenditures.

Operational Systems

Purchasing

After a budget is approved, a plan of purchasing should be adopted that will give the director control over what is spent against each budgeted account. A purchase order system is the most common approach to purchasing. See *illustration 14.10* for one type of purchase order form. The basic principle of a purchase order plan is that a written order (normally in multiple copies) for each purchase is filled out and approved in advance of the

Illustration 14.10 *Purchase Order Form*

PURCHASE ORDER FORM
Camp Everyone
234 Same Street, Everyplace, NY 12345-6789
123-456-7890 • everyone@camp.com

Purchase Order No. _____ Date _____

To: _____

Ship: ❏ Parcel Post ❏ UPS ❏ Motor Freight ❏ Best Way

Quantity	Item Number	Description	Unit Cost

To arrive by _____ Date _____

Signature _____

purchase: one copy to the vendor from whom merchandise is being purchased, one copy for the bookkeeper (to compare to the invoice when it arrives), and one copy for the person making the purchase. Normally, purchase orders are prenumbered, providing a means of tracking for the purchaser and the vendor. If the purchase order is not given or mailed to the vendor, the purchase order number is usually given when the purchase is authorized by telephone. The principle of purchase orders can be followed, with some shortcuts, even in a small operation. No matter how this system is implemented, it is vital that the following steps be taken:

- Purchasing is limited to as few people as is possible.
- Purchase orders are approved in advance of ordering.
- Copies of the purchase orders are written for the vendor and the purchaser.
- A secure, agreed-upon price is obtained and included on the purchase order.

Purchasing should begin early in the year, and ample time should be given to investigate sources and compare prices and quality for value. The best discounts are secured through advance planning and purchasing. Use of the camp's cash flow planning chart will be invaluable in maximizing potential discounts from suppliers. It is important to order early to ensure delivery of items on time or in advance of the opening date of camp.

Payment System

A system of payment should also be worked out in advance. Most vendors expect payment within thirty days, although some will require payment in advance or on actual delivery. The method of payment should be understood at the time the order is placed and specified on the purchase order. A disbursement system or payment-for-goods system for a camp should include provisions for the following points:

- The time at which the person placing the order, or someone designated by that person, checks to make sure the merchandise or service has been delivered. When the merchandise arrives, each item should be checked as to quantity, type, and condition, and all items should be checked against those appearing on the purchase order.
- A careful check of the invoice for mathematical errors and inclusion or exclusion of proper tax and discounts, as well as a check to see that the bill includes only the items received.
- Payment upon receipt of approved invoice that either matches a purchase order already on file or has been approved by an appropriate staff member.
- Payment by check. When payment in cash is necessary, a receipt including all pertinent information and marked "PAID" should be secured.
- Checks should have at least two authorized signatories; checks larger than a predetermined amount should be signed by both individuals.

Cash Payments

Because of their rural locations and variety of day-to-day immediate needs, camps generally have more frequent cash payments than do many organizations. A careful procedure for cash expenditures should be worked out. People who have custody of cash should be bonded (insured).

A petty cash fund is the most common method of dealing with cash expenditures. A check for a set sum is issued at the beginning of the year, season, or period, and it is cashed.

The cash is kept in a locked box in the safe (if there is one) and handled by only one or two authorized and bonded individuals. Staff members may make authorized purchases and be reimbursed in cash from the fund upon presentation of a signed receipt, or cash may be advanced for purchases and an accounting made after the purchase. In the case of advances, the amount of cash advanced and the date should be recorded on a slip of paper that is signed by the person taking the cash. See *illustration 14.11* for a sample petty cash advance slip. Upon the return of a receipt for the amount spent and the proper change, the advance cash slip is discarded and the change and receipt are returned to the cash box.

The receipts and cash should be balanced regularly, depending on the volume of use: daily during periods of heavy cash receipts, weekly during less busy times. When the receipts become significant and available cash is dwindling, receipts should be attached to a written summary, assigned account numbers, and a check written to the cash box caretaker for the total amount, bringing the cash fund back up to the original amount. At the end of the fiscal year or season, any remaining cash should be redeposited in the main camp account.

Illustration 14.11 — *Petty Cash Advance Slip*

PETTY CASH ADVANCE SLIP

Date _____

Received $ _____ for _____

_____

Account No. _____ by _____
                                        Signature

Income Documentation

Careful accounting of all funds received is essential for accurate records and good public relations and for the protection of all concerned. A written record should be kept of each payment received. It is wise to be able to provide a receipt to each payee, although many individuals accept their canceled check as a receipt. The camp's record of the receipt is used for two purposes: crediting the payee's account and designating the deposit of that payment to the proper budget account. Receipt records should be maintained for seven years.

Receipts should be deposited with the bank or organizational office at regularly scheduled times. A daily deposit of such funds is preferable, but, in many camps, payments come in cycles (at the beginning of the period, for example). This schedule may necessitate a daily deposit at the beginning of a session, but only a weekly deposit during the balance of the period. By promptly depositing checks and cash, the director can avoid having substantial amounts of money in camp.

Most camps ask for payment of the entire camper fee in advance or upon arrival at camp. A billing system is usually necessary either to secure the advance payments or to follow up delinquent payments. Bills should specify the amount, the person served, the dates covered, and the services rendered, as well as any amounts already paid and the balance due.

Taxes

Although an accountant or an attorney is of great assistance for most financial matters, such expertise becomes essential in the area of taxes. The type of taxes applying to a specific camp will vary not only in the locality of the office and camp location but also in whether the camp is a for-profit or not-for-profit organization. Specific tax areas to be examined are payroll, real estate, personal property, and sales. Always get advice from the camp's CPA.

Camp Store and Camper Bank

In most camp situations, campers will need certain supplies (e.g., toothpaste, toothbrushes, stationery, stamps) other than those that the camp supplies as part of the fee. Campers are also anxious to have souvenirs or reminders of their camp experience (e.g., T-shirts, patches, pennants, postcards). The director should consider how such items may be sold to campers in a way that is consistent with the camp's philosophy and desired outcomes and goals.

Campers will arrive at camp with varying amounts of cash, whether or not the camp has items for sale. Most camps do not wish to have the camper go to commercial establishments off the campsite. The presence of cash in a camper's duffel or clothing may lead to losses and disputes. A plan to safeguard this cash as well as to disburse it, if items are to be sold to campers, should be developed and announced in advance of camp. Most camps have a plan for campers to deposit funds on arrival, allowing the camper to draw against those funds for necessary expenditures on personal items or for additional activity fees. The following processes should be considered in developing such a plan:

- Suggesting to parents and campers in advance the maximum and minimum amount of cash needed during the camper period.

- Indicating what essential items the campers may need to purchase.

- Listing programs that may require additional expenditures depending on the camper's interests and skill (e.g., craft supplies, trips, horseback riding, ammunition for riflery). If possible, it is best if these fees can be included initially in the camper fee or identified as an option in the payment of the fee plus extras.

- Identifying what items the camp may wish to make available to campers for purchase.

- Providing the camper with a receipt for cash deposited.

- Setting up a simple plan of accounting (i.e., charging against an individual's account for purchases, entering deposits, and providing a refund, if necessary, at the end of the period). Two sample systems are shown in *illustration 14.12*. The first is a checkbook that the camper uses to write a check for each purchase (providing him or her with a record of expenditures and the experience of keeping his or her own record). The second is a card held by the camp on which deposits and expenditures are recorded at the time the purchase and deposits are made.

Where camps serve groups, the problem of dealing with the individual's cash does not arise. However, the group may need advice on how to handle youth participants who may have money with them. A system for selling the various supplies should be established, and the group leader should be given information in advance about what is available at camp during the group's stay.

In developing a camp store, careful accounting practices should be established. The store operation should provide income to the camp over and above the cost of merchandise, cost of

Illustration 14.12 — Expenditure/Deposit Record

Balance forward $_____
Deposited $_____
Less Check No. _____
for $_____
Balance $_____

_____ 20_____ Check No. _____

Pay to Camp $_____._____

$ _____ Dollars

for _____

Signed _____ Cabin_____

Figure 1. Checkbook Type of Expenditure/Deposit Record

Name _____ Cabin _____

Date	Item Purchased	Cost	Department	Balance

Figure 2. File Card Type of Expenditure/Deposit Record

labor, and related overhead. It is unrealistic to expect to cover only the cost of the merchandise. Many camps have found this to be a significant source of income. The sale of items with the camp name and logo is also another method of public relations. It advertises the camp wherever that individual goes, and name recognition is important. It can also stimulate others to ask the individual about the camp and his or her experience there. Whether or not to have snacks for sale (e.g., ice cream, candy, chips) will depend on the camp's philosophy, parent desires, and so on. The camp may want to limit the number of snacks a camper can buy each day.

An appropriate location that will provide security, accessibility, and appropriate storage needs to be selected. The store should be a part of the program and not compete with it. The display of items with clearly marked prices will stimulate sales and save time when campers come to the store. Camp stores are usually open only at certain times that coincide with the program schedule. While one person should have the ongoing responsibility for the store, including the inventory of stock, ordering of additional supplies, and supervising of sales, additional people may be needed at busy times.

Camp Office

Many camps will have two offices: one in a home or city and another at camp. The camp office should be in a location that is easy to find when arriving at camp, and yet where noisy activities will not be distracting to those at work. Though the office should be the center of efficiency and accuracy in terms of records and administration, it should have a relaxed, congenial atmosphere. It often is the first "people impression" on the camp site and serves as the reception area for visitors, vendors, and often the parents of campers.

The telephone may serve a similar function of greeting people. Because many of the inquiries and questions from prospective campers and their parents come by telephone or e-mail, it is important that the person answering the phone or replying to camp e-mails reveal a pleasant personality and have many immediate answers to questions.

Staff

The size of the office staff will vary with the size of the camp, with larger camps having a combination receptionist and telephone operator, a bookkeeper, a secretary, and a business manager. Smaller camps may have only one person in addition to the camp director. At times, any camp office may be overly busy and harried, but it is important that people be willing to stop and deal graciously with the public — whether in person or on the phone.

Arrangement of the Office

Several factors should be considered in the construction or arrangement of the office. Sufficient storage for supplies and records is essential. Some privacy for the camp director, other administrators, and program personnel is also necessary since conferences with individual staff or campers may be of a confidential nature. A second door with direct access to the outside may provide more privacy. An area near the front door should have some chairs where people may wait. A counter here may assist in separating visitors from the work area and also give a space where it is convenient for a staff member to write or stand and provide information. A more than average number of electrical outlets with adequate power supply will be needed because of the variety and quantity of office equipment and desk lighting. Consideration of controlled access areas should also be made for the security of cash and records. Any desk with computers that need to access the Internet should have a phone line nearby.

Computerization

The computerization of the camp office has changed the way in which many functions are handled. Computer programs that allow the entire registration process of individuals or groups to be recorded on the computer are available; these programs create not only a registration record but also an accounts receivable, a billing mechanism, labels for mailings, a living-group assignment preference, and program-group sign-ups. The marketplace provides standard programs that can provide accounting, word processing, mailing list maintenance, mail merge, spreadsheets, and desktop publishing. At the same time, several companies have developed for camps special software that provides the program-group and living-group assignment process as well as the camp registration format. Christine Z. Howe identifies a variety of applications available as shown in *illustration 14.13*.[5]

On-line computers are now allowing even more convenient information transfer across the country and around the world. The popular on-line services allow access to the Internet. Some camps allow campers to register and receive mail via e-mail, and some camp directors are part of the Camp Professional Discussion Group or other groups that discuss current issues. This service provides new opportunities to communicate with parents and campers, with other camp directors, and with other businesses. Most camps are trying to make a computer available for staff to use for e-mails. Some have a computer in the staff lounge and set up schedules for use. This is particularly beneficial for international staff.

It is important that you devise a system to back up your database and other materials maintained on your computer regularly. During registration, a daily backup would be recommended.

Whether investing in a computer for the first time or simply adding new software, it is wise to investigate carefully the variety of options. Technology changes so rapidly and varies so much in applicability to different camp settings that it is wise to examine several hardware and/or software options and compare notes with other camp directors on problems and successes. New software should be implemented program by program because unforeseen problems inevitably slow the process and frustrate office personnel. For example, it is best to

Illustration 14.13 — *Selected Applications for Personal Computers*

SELECTED APPLICATIONS FOR PERSONAL COMPUTERS

ADMINISTRATION

Financial
Accounting
General ledger
Investments
Forecasting and decision support
Work load cost tracking
Utility management
Invoices and billing
Budget and revenue and expenditures

Personnel
Recordkeeping and employee rosters
Recordkeeping and volunteer rosters
Recordkeeping and client rosters
Payroll
Insurance
Performance standards and job descriptions

Word Processing — General
Permits and licenses
Mailing labels
Bulk mailing
Manuals and training materials
Printing
Graphics and mapping
Aggregate client data-participation
and demographics
Monthly reports

Research
Accident studies
Marketing
Long-range planning
Demand studies
Survey tabulation

Maintenance
Custodial cost tracking
Vandalism monitoring
Horticultural and irrigation management
Aquatics scheduling and management

SERVICE DELIVERY

Recordkeeping
Activity registration
Attendance reporting
Facility and site usage
Activity scheduling

Program Planning and Evaluation
Advertising and publicity
Activity master planning
Activity analysis
Activity tracking

Activities
Games — electronic and simulation
Arts and crafts
Music forms
Interactive stories and reading

LEISURE COUNSELING AND EDUCATION

Counseling
Recreational needs assessment
Interest inventories
Problem solving
Values awareness and clarification
Individual demographics
Communication and expression of thoughts
and feelings

Education
Development of positive self-concept through
mastery referral systems leisure matching
systems

implement the new accounting system or the word processing system first and to get the office staff familiar with the new system rather than to install all programs at once. Henderson and Bialeschki outline the following steps to be taken in getting started with computers:

- "Review the present operation for sizing. Determine how large your camp enrollments, budgets, and inventories are so you can more accurately decide which computer system you will need and what the benefits might be for its use.

- "Set goals and objectives and criteria for what a computer can do for you. . . . Do not buy a computer . . . and then try to decide how to use it. The applications must be determined first.

- "Find a vendor and locate software sources. It may be necessary to consult with more than one vendor to determine what the best buy is and who will provide the most support services.

- "Design an implementation schedule to determine how you will begin to use the computer and its software. It is impossible to do everything at once, so you must decide systematically how you will begin to use the equipment.

- "Begin implementing applications with a continual approach for evaluating and adding potential software."[6]

However, there is no question that, even in the smallest operation, the proper computer system can provide a long-term solution to many traditional problems and time-consuming functions in the camp setting. It is critical to have either a very knowledgeable person on the staff who can troubleshoot or a convenient and helpful supplier who makes a commitment to be a resource to the camp through the conversion process. In any case, the question of the type of supplier support is critical; the firm's reputation, references, maintenance contract fees, and troubleshooting response should be checked thoroughly.

Maintaining Records

The checkbook and bank deposit slips should be balanced with the monthly bank statement upon receipt. If the finance office is staffed by multiple individuals, the appropriate checks and balances between employees need to be established and followed. Records should be kept in a fireproof container and should be retained by the camp or organization for at least five years. Backup computer records can help to reconstruct financial histories but should not be considered equal to or replacements for the primary paper documents.

Record retention requirements vary from state to state, but, in general, the following records should be kept for the minimum time shown (see *illustration 14.14*).[7] The director should give careful thought to minimum record retention and should obtain legal counsel.

Gerald G. Newborg suggests four values to be considered in retention:
- "Administrative value relates to the need of the office or agency in carrying out its work.

- "Legal value adheres to essentially any record which provides documentation for a legally enforceable right or obligation. These values may be embodied in state or federal law, state or federal regulations, or in local ordinances.

- "Fiscal value . . . records which document financial transactions.

- "Archival value . . . is permanence . . . [and] enduring."[8] Each camp will determine its own records of historical and enduring value.

Illustration 14.14 *Recommendations for Record Retention*

RECOMMENDATIONS FOR RECORD RETENTION

TYPE OF RECORD	MINIMUM RETENTION
Accident/incident reports	Adults, 7 years
	Minors, 2 years beyond age of majority
Accident/incident reports/claims	30 years
Accounts payable ledgers/schedules	7 years
Accounts receivable ledgers/schedules	7 years
Annual reports*	Indefinitely
Audit reports	Indefinitely
Bank reconciliations	1 year
Camper registration forms*	Adults, 6 years
	Minors, 2 years beyond age of majority
Camper health records (including treatments)*	Adults, 6 years
	Minors, 2 years beyond age of majority
Cash books	Indefinitely
Charters, constitution, bylaws, incorporation records	Indefinitely
Charts of accounts	Indefinitely
Checks (canceled)	4 years
Checks (exceptions: payments such as taxes, property purchases, special contracts, etc.)	Indefinitely
Contracts and leases (expired)	7 years
(current)	Indefinitely
Correspondence (routine)	1 year
(general)	3 years
(legal and important matters)	Indefinitely
Deeds, mortgages, and bills of sale	Indefinitely
Depreciation schedules	Indefinitely
Duplicate deposit slips	1 year
Employee personnel records**	3 years after termination
Employee health records (including treatments)*	30 years
Employment applications (not hired)	3 years
Expense analyses/expense schedules	7 years
Financial statements (end-of-year)	Indefinitely
Fire inspection reports*	6 years
Forms used, dated file copies*	Indefinitely
General and private ledgers with end-of-year trial balances	Indefinitely
Insurance policies (expired)	3 years

The policy of the organization or camp on recordkeeping and record retention should be developed on the basis of law, the rule of reason, and the risk involved. Such a policy should be in writing and available to the people who file and maintain these records. In developing a retention policy, the period for retention should be clearly defined by tying the specified retention period to the beginning or end of a calendar or fiscal year.

Fund-Raising

It is the unusual not-for-profit camp that does not rely on some contribution income to operate the camp. Many independent camps have moved to not-for-profit foundations to

Illustration 14.14 *Recommendations for Record Retention,* *continued*

TYPE OF RECORD	MINIMUM RETENTION
Insurance records (current accident reports, claims, policies, etc.)	Indefinitely
Internal audit reports*	Depends
Internal reports	3 years
Inventories of products, materials, supplies	7 years
Invoices to customers	7 years
Invoices from vendors	7 years
Licenses (federal, state, local)*	Dispose of after receiving new license
Journals	Indefinitely
Minutes of directors', stockholders' meetings	Indefinitely
Notes receivable ledgers/schedules	7 years
Occupational injury/illness records	5 years
Payroll records and summaries	3 years
Petty cash vouchers	3 years
Physical inventory tags	3 years
Property appraisals	Indefinitely
Property records including costs, depreciation reserves, blueprints, and plans	Indefinitely
Purchase orders (except primary copy)*	1 year
(primary copy)*	7 years
Safety inspection reports*	8 years
Securities transactions	3 years
Stock and bond certifications (canceled)	6 years
Stock and bond records	Indefinitely
Subsidiary ledgers	7 years
Tax returns and worksheets	Indefinitely
Time books/records	7 years
Travel expense reports*	3 years
Vouchers for payments	7 years
Withholding tax statements*	4 years

*These record retention timelines are not from the American Society of Association Executives, but from miscellaneous other sources. In many cases, American Society of Association Executives did not offer a suggested retention policy on these items.

**When a minor is involved, records should be kept at least four years beyond the year when the age of majority is reached. This requirement, along with other record retention requirements, should be checked with your state requirements.

ensure the continued operation after the present owners are gone. Other independent camps have utilized an arrangement with the American Camping Association by which friends and parents make contributions to that association, a 501(c)(3) organization, in the name of a particular camp and the gifts are used to fund campers who cannot afford their full camp fee. This means that almost every camp director is faced with the prospect of mastering another skill — that of fund-raising.

Each state has developed regulations that affect fund-raising. Therefore, it is important to consult with the camp's attorney and accountant to understand the applicable laws and regulations.

Determining the Use of Funds

If funds are to be raised for the camp, their overall use should be carefully evaluated. These funds might be used in the following ways:

- To help alleviate the cost of the camp experience for every camper, thus lowering the fee for all

- To lower the cost of the camp experience for particular campers who cannot pay the usual fee

- To cover capital expenditures, such as land development, building facilities, extensive large equipment purchases, or major renovation

- To experiment with new programs that might eventually offer a year-round program or diversification

- To improve the wage and benefit package for staff, thus enabling the director to recruit better qualified staff

In other words, the camp director and board (if there is one) must consider carefully the purpose of the fund-raising, for there must be a clearly felt need resulting in a clearly stated purpose. It may be that there are varying needs, ranging from keeping the fees lower than average to replacing buildings or equipment. Before lumping all the needs together, consideration should be given to the types of fund-raising. It may be helpful at this stage to consider an outside consultant to assist in the creation of a financial development program that provides a foundation and pattern for fund-raising over a period of time.

Basic Principles

Some basic principles should be followed in fund-raising regardless of the type of fund-raising activity:

- Seek professional fund-raising counsel to conduct a feasibility study and conduct the campaign or train the camp director.

- Establish a clearly stated purpose for the funds.

- Recruit capable volunteers to raise the funds.

- Provide a training program for the volunteers.

- Develop attractive, succinct, and clear descriptive materials.

- Acknowledge every gift and recognize the giver in some fashion.

- Use the funds for the purpose for which they are raised and report to the giver.

- Maintain careful accounting of all gifts, including pledges. Under new accounting rules, pledges are considered to be income in the year they are made, not the year they are paid.

Annual Giving

Annual giving is one type of fund-raising in which an approach is made annually to one's constituency. In this type of fund-raising activity, a specific period is set aside each year for the effort, and a volunteer leadership is secured either from the board, committee, or alumni group. An organization with subchairs and workers is developed similar to the diagram shown in *illustration 14.15*. A list of prospective givers is developed from the records of the camp: parents of campers, former campers and staff, foundations, board or committee personnel, and vendors.

The annual giving campaign or event lends itself best to providing funds for the ongoing operating budget of the camp through direct subsidy or the provision of camperships for needy youth. Some camps have used it to replace budgeting depreciation reserves. After a person has committed to the camp with a charitable gift, it becomes simpler to go back to them each year, as long as a good acknowledgment and information program is in place.

A variety of methods may be used to approach potential annual givers.

- **Direct mail.** A letter and material describing the needs with an addressed and stamped envelope for returning a contribution.

- **Telethon.** A group of trained volunteers come together in a location where there are multiple telephone lines, call prospective givers, and take pledges by telephone. A confirmation letter and a return envelope are then sent to those pledging.

- **Personal approach.** A volunteer approaches a prospective giver, explaining the needs and asking for a contribution. This is always the most effective method.

- **Public gathering.** A presentation is made at some type of special event sponsored by the camp, and return envelopes and pledge cards are distributed after a public appeal.

- **Fund-raiser.** An activity is developed that will render its profits to the cause by the tickets sold or money collected through other activities.

Capital Campaigns

Capital campaigns are another type of fund-raising. In contrast to annual giving, this is done less frequently, generally every five to ten years, depending on the size of each campaign. The constituency to be approached is the same as for annual giving, but it can also be extended to businesses in the area and certain foundations that consider capital projects. Again, a volunteer organization is developed, not dissimilar to that of the annual campaign. This type of campaign depends upon having individual volunteers approaching potential givers individually.

In capital campaigns, professional counsel is especially important. It is not wise to embark on such a campaign if there is not some certainty that the goal can be reached. A professional consultant may complete a feasibility study that will examine the willingness of potential large givers to contribute to the campaign, uncover individuals who are willing to serve in leadership roles, and assess the potential capability of the camp to raise funds. A capital campaign is especially dependent upon securing one or two large gifts equal to twenty percent of the goal and sixty to seventy percent of the goal from large givers. Therefore, the

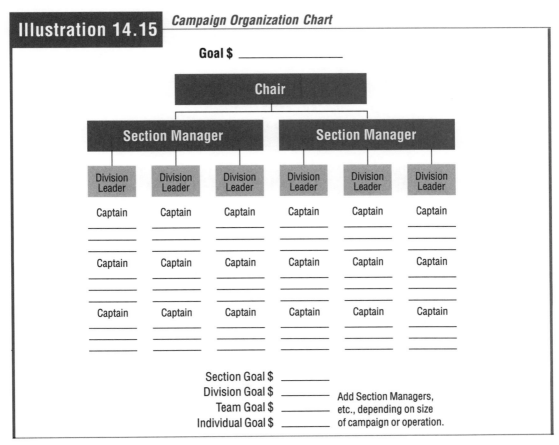

Illustration 14.15 *Campaign Organization Chart*

Goal $ _____

Chair

Section Manager | Section Manager

Division Leader | Division Leader | Division Leader | Division Leader | Division Leader | Division Leader

Captain | Captain | Captain | Captain | Captain | Captain

Captain | Captain | Captain | Captain | Captain | Captain

Captain | Captain | Captain | Captain | Captain | Captain

Section Goal $ _____
Division Goal $ _____ Add Section Managers,
Team Goal $ _____ etc., depending on size
Individual Goal $ _____ of campaign or operation.

identification, cultivation, and assessment of potentially large givers are a vital part of this type of fund-raising. In addition, professional counsel should lay out the steps and give advice in a smaller campaign or be a resident consultant for the period of a major campaign.

Endowment Development

Endowment development is another type of fund-raising and requires a quite different approach from the capital or annual support campaigns. Though one-time campaigns, similar in organization to the capital campaign, can be run for endowment purposes, they are not as customary for camps as for universities, hospitals, and other organizations. Encouraging supporters to remember the camp in their wills and insurance or through trusts requires a program of cultivation and education, which may not show results immediately, as does the capital campaign format.

Although it is possible to approach prospects who have not given to the camp and interest them in planned giving, those people who have given to the camp through annual support efforts or capital campaigns are usually the best prospects for the endowment effort. Because these people are known to the camp and the camp reports to them through mailings somewhat regularly, it is possible to begin to develop an awareness of the various instruments used in planned giving without initially asking for a gift. The use of planned-giving instruments affects the estate of a person and, in many cases, has helpful tax implications. Therefore, any decision usually requires more consideration, consultation, and often the advice of an attorney, trust officer, or accountant.

A program of endowment development should be carefully charted, with the strong commitment of the committee or board related to the camp. Professional guidance from a person knowledgeable about endowment development efforts should be sought initially. Only not-for-profit 501(c)(3) organizations can provide the tax benefits that make this method of fund-raising attractive to many people.

Fund-Raising Personnel

To develop effective fund-raising efforts takes considerable time, training, and expertise. The camp director should carefully evaluate his or her willingness to allot the amount of time from his or her schedule, or another staff member's schedule, for this purpose. Even when an outside consultant is brought in to help with the fund-raising, it will still require time from the camp director. Fund-raising cannot be done effectively if done half-heartedly, poorly, or without professional planning. On the other hand, most not-for-profit organizations cannot survive without an effective program of fund-raising.

It may be helpful to seek outside fund-raising counsel to help develop a plan for the total financial development and to assist in the actual fund-raising efforts. The experience and competence of the fund-raising counsel should be explored carefully by checking references with previous or present clients.

Checkpoints

1. Outline the budgeting process for the camp.

2. Describe the three basic types of fund-raising and the principles that affect all good fund-raising.

3. Who may purchase for the camp? By what methods? Who checks the order when it is received and approves payment?

4. Who handles cash at camp? Are they bonded? What check is there on the cash received?

5. Is there a study of the expenses and income related to the camp store that shows what margin of income over expenses is being achieved?

6. Describe the steps in moving into a computerized operation.

7. When was your record retention policy last reviewed?

Related Standards and Guidelines

Accreditation Standards for Camp Programs and Services,
"Additional Professional Practices": Item 18

Guidelines for Conference and Retreat Centers: II-3–4

[1] John A. Ledlie. 1961. *Managing the YMCA Camp*. New York: Association Press (YMCA of the USA). p. 125.

[2] *Financial Accounting Standards Board*, P.O. Box 5116, Norwalk, CT 06856-5116.

[3] Kathy J. Tyson. 1994. "Accounting Alert." *Camping Magazine*, Vol. 66, No. 5, May/June. p. 44.

[4] *Merriam-Webster's College Dictionary*, 10th edition. 1993. Springfield, MA: Merriam-Webster, Inc.

[5] Christine Z. Howe. 1984. "Change, Computers, and the Camp Administration." *Camping Magazine*, Vol. 57, No. 1, September/October. p. 17.

[6] Karla Henderson and M. Deborah Bialeschki. 1983. "Computer Consciousness." *Camping Magazine*, Vol. 55, No. 7, May. p. 16.

[7] American Society of Association Executives. 1992. *Association Management*, Vol. 44, No. 9, September. pp. 50–51.

[8] Gerald G. Newborg. 1989. "Record Retention and Disposition Schedules." *Technical Leaflet 107*. Nashville, TN: American Association for State and Local History.

Volunteers

It seems to me that the first and foremost reason that volunteers dedicate so much of their personal lives to chosen projects . . . is that they believe in the organization's mission. In leadership training we call this "alignment" with the mission and vision of the organization.[1]

Few camps operate without some volunteer assistance — whether it is on the staff, on a board or committee, or from former staff, parents, or campers who refer others to the camp. A volunteer is any person who gives his or her services to the camp without any compensation. The growth and nurturing of volunteers is an art that every camp director needs to develop. Volunteers spread and enhance the mission of a camp and stimulate enthusiasm unmatched by staff.

One's first reaction is that volunteers should be cultivated because they save the camp money if they serve as staff members, work around camp, or take on roles ordinarily paid for. Another reaction is that volunteers bring in money because they become fund-raisers or recruiters of campers. Either or both may be true, but first and foremost, volunteers should be cultivated because they are an outgrowth of the spirit and philosophy of the camp. It is a tribute to a camp that former campers or staff and parents of either may wish to share the experience of the camp with others. However, to be most effective and to gain the greatest personal satisfaction from the experience, volunteers also need some structure and professional leadership.

Some principles of any volunteer service should be kept in mind. The volunteer must perceive a need. The need may be stimulated or sold by the professional, but it must challenge the volunteer or rekindle earlier positive experiences or felt needs. That need must parallel the individual's motivation, which varies from person to person. Clary, Snyder, and Ridge state that "people volunteer to satisfy personal and social needs and goals. . . . The first step toward successful recruitment is considering the audience from which recruiting will take place so that the relevant motivations of potential volunteers can be identified."[2]

Volunteers should be guided to the type of activity in which they will be most effective. Success is important in any task, particularly when one is giving energy, time, and money to accomplish the task. It is not wise to assign or recruit volunteers randomly.

A written job description should be prepared for the task and shared with the volunteer. In a face-to-face interview, the volunteer should be asked if he or she has a problem with any of the functions, as it may be useful to adjust some portions of the task. Along with the job description there should be a targeted time for accomplishment and evaluation.

The volunteer should be informed of the ground rules: personnel policies, limits of authority, budget limitations, or whatever other limits there may be.

The volunteer should be given adequate assistance in accomplishing the task — whether it be funds, tools, manpower, or the director's own time to consult.

Supervision should be provided as needed. This includes observation by the supervisor and regular conferences to gain insights into the assigned task.

The performance of the volunteer should be appraised upon completion of the task. There should be public recognition of the volunteer.

Legal Ramification

In recent years, court cases have centered on the legal definition of *volunteerism. Corpus Juris 2d,* a legal encyclopedia, defines the volunteer as: "one who does or undertakes to do that which one is not legally or morally bound to do, and which is not in pursuance or protection of any interest . . . one who enters into service of his own free will; one who gives his service without any express or implied promise of remuneration . . . ; one who has no interest in his work, but nevertheless undertakes to assist therein."[3]

The definition of a pure volunteer is very narrow and somewhat different from a gratuitous volunteer. Volunteers may be differentiated by a two-part test concerning whether the person is subject to the control of the organization and whether the person receives any benefit from the job performed. The pure volunteer performs a task when and how he or she prefers for no benefit whatever. The gratuitous volunteer performs the task at a time or in a manner prescribed by the organization and/or receives some benefit from the organization. The pure volunteer may not be able to expect the same sort of legal safeguards that a gratuitous volunteer may expect where the organization takes on some control or responsibility for the volunteer. Because camps may use both types of volunteers, it is important to understand this difference.

A number of court cases illustrate some of the problems for the organization in gratuitous volunteer service. For example, in *Bond v. Cartwright Little League, Inc.,*[4] the Little League solicited help from volunteers to remove some large lights it had purchased from a municipal baseball field. A volunteer started up one of the 100-foot poles and fell forty feet, injuring himself. The Arizona Supreme Court reasoned that the volunteer was not a pure volunteer because the Little League "set the time and place as well as the manner in which the lights were to be removed and had control over the volunteer."

In the North Dakota Supreme Court case *Olson v. Kem Temple, Ancient Arabic Order of the Mystic Shrine*, a volunteer was denied financial recovery when he fell off a small stepladder and was injured because the stepladder is considered a "simple tool."[5] The court reasoned that "where the tool or appliance is simple in construction and a defect therein is discernible without special skill or knowledge, and the employee is as well qualified as the employer to detect the defect and appraise the danger resulting therefrom" there could be no recovery.

In the Washington Court of Appeals case *Baxter v. Morningside, Inc.*,[6] a volunteer driver for a charitable organization was in an accident negligently causing injury to several people. The court held that the organization was liable for the volunteer driver's actions because it "controlled or could have controlled the physical conduct and performance of the volunteer driver."[7]

In 1985 the Supreme Court decided in *Tony and Susan Alamo Foundation v. Secretary of Labor*[8] that workers for the foundation who received room and board were not true volunteers because "they were working with the expectancy of some remuneration." Therefore, the court held that volunteer workers were subject to the provisions of the Fair Labor Standards Act (FLSA), which included the minimum wage. It has been suggested that this decision has "created a new category which might be called the 'quasi-volunteer' who, though functioning like a volunteer, is afforded the 'protection' of the Act, because there is some identifiable expectation of compensation."[9] The Alamo case involved two elements for the not-for-profit foundation: a commercial activity and the payment of room and board, both unrelated to its exempt purpose. So Grange and LeSourd point out that, in a camp setting, the room and board are provided as conditions of employment; that is, because of their job in working with campers and being in the camp setting, it is to the benefit of the camp to provide the meals and lodging. This has yet to be tested in court.

Several principles arise from these cases that camp directors should take into consideration:

- No remuneration should be given that is not for the convenience of the camp. For example, lodging is provided a camp counselor as a convenience to the camp because the person could not effectively do the job without living at the camp. Therefore, it is for the convenience of the employer.

- No remuneration should be given that is not a part of the responsibility undertaken. For example, to provide meals and lodging to a person whose home is a mile down the road from camp and the person only instructs an activity one or two hours a day is really beyond the responsibility undertaken.

- If the camp asks that a specific task be undertaken at a given place and time, then the camp should provide safeguards and give supervision to the activity.

- The same care and training should be required of volunteers as with employees who undertake potentially liable services, such as driving.

- Volunteers should be urged to inspect equipment carefully before using it, though that in no way relieves the camp of ordinary care and upkeep of that equipment.

Volunteers as Staff

Many not-for-profit organizations utilize volunteers either as the majority or total of the camp staff. A volunteer director is recruited for a one- or two-week period, and then he or she recruits staff to work during that session or sessions. In other camps, the core program staff is employed, and volunteers are recruited as counselors or assistants in other functions. Throughout this book, no differentiation has been made between the volunteer and employed staff member. Generally speaking, the principles involved in the selection, retention, orientation, training, and supervision of employed staff should also apply to volunteer staff. This means that the camp director or organization should

- Select volunteer staff carefully, following the same type of screening methods discussed earlier, including an application and references. Where certifications are needed, they should be required of volunteer staff.

- Have a written agreement with those staff members that states
  - The person is a volunteer and not a paid employee.
  - Room and board are provided as a convenience of the employer.
  - The camp assigns sleeping space and duties to the volunteer.
  - No fringe benefits provided a regular employee are provided the volunteer.
  - Volunteer services can be terminated by either party at any time.
  - A training period, before the campers arrive, will be provided.
  - Supervision will be provided during the camp periods.
  - There will be an evaluation and recognition at the end of the period.

There are certainly differences between volunteer-staffed camps and camps with paid staff, and the camp director needs to assess those differences carefully. For example, training may have to occur on several weekends during the spring or early summer because the volunteers cannot give another week prior to the camp period. More supervision may be needed in certain program areas because of the limited time for training and orientation of volunteers.

It should be pointed out that the practice of giving honorariums or scholarships rather than wages to someone considered a volunteer and exempting that person from minimum wage or FICA provisions would probably not hold up under the court definitions of a pure volunteer or gratuitous employee.

Volunteer Committees and Board

In not-for-profit camps, a governing board or committee of the organization's board works with the employed or volunteer camp director. The relationship between the committee and board and the director can be a most creative and exciting experience, or it can deteriorate into a struggle for power. Peter Drucker suggests that the potential for friction between the board and the executive "has forced an increasing number of not-for-profits to realize that neither board nor CEO is 'the boss.' They are colleagues, working for the same goal but each having a different task."[10]

Early in his or her employment, the camp director should try to understand the structure of the particular organization for which he or she works. The director should seek answers to the following questions:

- Who is the chief elected officer of the organization?

- What is the elected governing body and its policy function?

- What is the body to which the camp committee or board reports, if any?

- What are the types of policies the camp committee or board has under its jurisdiction?

- What is the organization's staff role as it relates to these committees or boards?

- What is the stated purpose of the organization, especially its "exempt purpose" (i.e., the purpose for which it is granted exemption from certain taxes)?

- What are the job descriptions of board members and officers?

Obviously, no two organizations operate in exactly the same way. Therefore, generalizations made in this chapter must be adapted to the specific camp's situation. The chart in *illustration 15.1* gives an overview of the roles often assumed by committees or boards and by the director of a camp.

A set of bylaws that govern the actions of the board and its subcommittees should be in place. This is a legal document that outlines the way in which the organization elects officers and members and the manner in which meetings of the board and organization must be held. It is an important document to understand, and the employed director has a legal responsibility to help ensure that the elected officials adhere to the bylaws of the organization. Bylaws may be changed, and the method of change is usually specified in the bylaws.

The volunteer support system should never be viewed as an unnecessary step in administration; it can be the greatest advantage the not-for-profit organization has. The volunteer committee member can be a vital checkpoint of community or organizational reaction, as well as an additional staff member. However, few volunteers are simply interested in another committee position or in having their names listed. If they commit themselves to membership on a committee or board, they expect to perform useful and meaningful services. To simply be figure heads is degrading and demoralizing and, in the ultimate analysis, deadly to a camp and its sponsoring organization.

Illustration 15.1 — *Responsibilities in Volunteer Organizations*

RESPONSIBILITIES WITHIN THE VOLUNTEER ORGANIZATION

Operator Responsibilities	Shared Responsibilities	Camp Director Responsibilities
■ See that the camp is operated in harmony with the organization's overall mission and goals	■ Keep minutes of decisions and meetings	■ Recommend and implement policy
■ Set policy for the camp	■ Assist in site development and maintenance	■ Recruit and train the staff of the camp (full-time, part-time, and volunteer)
■ Recruit a capable administrator for the camp and provide adequate support services	■ Raise capital funds	■ See that the camp site is maintained in good condition and alert board or committee to needs
■ Provide resources (site, capital, community support)	■ Raise supplemental (contributed) funds	■ Develop a budget and provide a careful and honest accounting of income and expenditures
■ Approve an annual operating budget with overall financial policies and direction	■ Be responsible for meeting the applicable local, state, and federal laws	■ Be responsible for meeting the applicable local, state, and federal laws
■ Be responsible for meeting the applicable local, state, and federal laws	■ Promote the camp and recruit campers	■ Recruit campers
■ Set admission requirements (age, membership, sex)	■ Monitor good standards of operation in health, safety, and personnel	■ Develop, implement, and evaluate camp program
■ Develop overall program goals and direction	■ Evaluation	■ Ensure good standards of operation in health, safety, and personnel
■ Be responsible to the community		
■ Supervise the administrator		

John Pearson, former executive director of Christian Camping International/USA, suggests that "the care and feeding of a board member will be much easier if the director can participate in the board member selection process. Camp boards are selected through a variety of election procedures. The alert camp director, however, will request that the nominating committee consult with him before the nominees are recruited."[11]

After the recruitment process is completed, each new board member should be involved in a group or individual orientation session and given a copy of the bylaws, the policy manual, and a job description. When a meeting of the camp committee or board is scheduled, the camp director should make certain that

- The agenda is developed with the chairperson in advance of the meeting.

- The written reports on subjects to be discussed are clear and concise and, when possible, have been circulated in advance of the meeting.

- The decisions or actions to be considered are outlined clearly.

- The members who are expected to report have the data or information they need.

- The room and setting are ready for a comfortable and informal meeting.

The director's next step is to involve the volunteer in a task over and above attendance at the committee or board meeting. The assignment of a task by the chairperson to a subgroup often moves that subgroup to action; at this point, the camp director should be an aide to that group, helping them outline the steps to be taken and assisting as needed. It is of particular value to have the committee members visit the camp, especially during sessions, so that the program and objectives can be personalized. Workdays, weekends, and special program events will also provide opportunities for volunteer leadership and contribution.

A careful and accurate record of committee proceedings, with particular attention to actions taken, should be maintained in the office or headquarters of the camp. Though the secretary may be an elected or appointed position, the camp director has responsibility for assisting and making sure that the minutes of all meetings are circulated to appropriate people and kept in a permanent file in the office, preferably bound. The policies adopted by the committee or board should be pulled from minutes and placed in some appropriate sequence or order in a notebook, which is then given to each member of the committee or board.

Orientation of new committee or board members should be a part of the ongoing procedures of the committee or board. A regular set of materials, including the policy manual of the group as well as past minutes, should be given each new member, along with a verbal orientation to the way in which the group works.

A plan of volunteer recognition should be established early in the year. The material aspect of the recognition is not as important as the sincerity and public expression of appreciation.

If an award or symbol of recognition is presented, it should be chosen on the basis of its appropriateness to the task and service given and be of a permanent nature. Ordinarily, volunteers should take the public leadership in recognizing other volunteers.

There are also legal ramifications for those volunteers who agree to serve on a managing committee or board of a not-for-profit organization. Generally, a board member is not held liable individually for either the directives of the board or the negligence of an employee. If legal action against directors does occur, it is on the basis that the board or an individual failed to take action or that some action taken was inadequate or irresponsible. Although the specific laws in each state may differ, there are three major categories of violations of their fiduciary responsibility. They are mismanagement, or failure to follow fundamental management principles; nonmanagement, or failure to use existing opportunities for good management; and self-dealing, or personally benefiting from the decisions of the board (not disclosing a conflict of interest). The basic principle is that the board must make sure that its decisions are informed and reasonable.

For the director working with a board, George Webster and Hugh Webster suggest six guidelines as the result of *Smith v. Van Gordkum* in the Delaware Supreme Court:

1. "Make decisions deliberately and without undue haste or pressure.

2. "Be as thoroughly and completely prepared as possible before making a decision. Make sure the board receives and reviews, in advance, materials pertaining to any major decision.

3. "Become actively involved in deliberations during the board meeting. Comment as appropriate on written materials.

4. "Keep written records of board preparation and deliberation. It is necessary to create a paper trail showing compliance with procedural requirements.

5. "In the case of any major transaction, review all basic legal documents and all analyses by experts.

6. "Ensure that, at a minimum, in-house experts, and at best, accountants and lawyers, prepare independent evaluations of important issues."[12]

Other Roles

One function that camp committees and boards in today's climate must expect to undertake is that of fund-raising. Fund-raising is a volunteer function, even though it deserves professional leadership and assistance. The actual fund-raising should be done by a volunteer and recognized by the board or committee.

Many camps are fortunate in having volunteers who are also able and willing to be involved directly in program or work events. These volunteers will often organize and lead groups to camp for work or activity weekends, implement much of the promotion of camp and recruitment of campers, and come to camp for a specific work project.

The relationship between the volunteer and staff member can be most creative and satisfying when they share a common purpose and both feel a sense of contribution and worth. As the staff member is an extension of the policy-making group, so may the volunteer become an extension or arm of the staff member.

Checkpoints

1. Does the camp have a written agreement with volunteers?

2. Does the camp have a regular program orientation and training for all volunteers — both at the staff and committee/board level?

3. Is there a diagram or outline of the volunteer structure? If not, develop one for your own understanding and use.

4. Who is the lay person responsible for overall organization direction?

5. What are the specific responsibilities of the camp committee/board and its subgroups?

6. In what ways that are not used now could your camp use volunteers?

Related Standards and Guidelines

Many of the standards and additional professional practices refer to policies, and to the degree that a volunteer board or committee may be responsible for setting policy, those standards would need to be considered.

Accreditation Standards for Camp Programs and Services: HR-1–21, OM-2; "Additional Professional Practices": Items 25–29

Guidelines for Conference and Retreat Centers: II-34–36

[1] George Burns. 1989. "How to Keep Volunteers Coming Back." *Journal of Christian Camping*, Vol. 21, No. 5, September. p. 6. Reprinted with permission from CCI/USA.

[2] E. Gil Clary, Mark Snyder, and Robert Ridge. 1992. "Volunteers' Motivations: A Functional Strategy for the Recruitment, Placement, and Retention of Volunteers." *Not-for-profit Management & Leadership*, Vol. 2, No. 4, Summer. p. 341.

[3] Robert A. Christenson. 1982. "What You Should Know About the Legal Definition of a Volunteer." *Voluntary Action Leadership*, Fall. p. 17.

[4] 536 p. 2d 697, 1975. Citations such as this one may be used to look up the complete text of the legal cases mentioned in this chapter. Take the citation to a law library and ask for assistance; law firms and local bar associations often have law libraries.

[5] 43 N.W.2d 385, 1950.

[6] 521 P. 2d 948, 1974

[7] Christenson. 1982. p. 17.

[8] 105 S.Ct.1953, 1985.

[9] George (Chip) R. Grange II and Nancy Oliver LeSourd. 1989. "Volunteers: Court Decisions vs. Cost Effective Help." *Journal of Christian Camping*, Vol. 21, No. 5, September/October. p. 8. Reprinted with permission from CCI/USA.

[10] Peter F. Drucker. 1989. "What Business Can Learn from Not-for-profits." *Harvard Business Review*, July/August. p. 91.

[11] John Pearson. n.d. *The Director and The Camp Board: A Creative Partnership*. Wheaton, IL: Christian Camping International, United States Division. p. 39. Reprinted with permission from CCI/USA.

[12] George D. Webster and Hugh K. Webster. 1994. "Avoiding Personal Liability: How to Minimize the Risks of Board Service." *Association Management, Leadership*. p. L–57.

Evaluation & Reporting

Chapter 16

*Evaluation comes at the **end** of the relationships, training and program processes. It is also the **beginning** of new relationships, improved training, and more exciting and purposeful programming. Strategic planning is a circular process which begins and ends with evaluation.*

Evaluation

In an era when the consumer is demanding more value for money spent, the competition for services in the recreation and education fields continues to grow. Parents are demanding that camps do more to meet expectations concerning their children's experiences. To meet the increasing competition, a camp director can improve quality by establishing a process of evaluation for every part of the camp operation. Dozens of questions need to be asked. Was this a successful season? Did we achieve our outcomes and goals? Did this year's staff do a better job than last year's? Is there a way to improve the food without increasing costs? Which was the most popular program? Did we meet our financial budget this season? How did this season's enrollment compare to last season's? Which staff members should be hired for next season?

Evaluation can be regarded as the process of examining the camp operation to see that every part of the predetermined plan is functioning according to the performance standard necessary for accomplishing established outcomes and goals. Henderson defines evaluation as "the systematic collection and analysis of data to address criteria and make judgments about the worth or improvement of something."[1]

Henderson and Bialeschki further suggest that "evaluation includes all strategies and technologies that are used to determine the value and worth of programs, facilities, administrative procedures, and staff within organizations. . . . The two major reasons for evaluation are accountability and decision making."[2]

One does not wait for a problem to surface before considering an evaluation plan. The advantages of a plan of systematic evaluation of all segments of an operation can be numerous. A comprehensive plan of evaluation can help the director to determine

- Whether desired outcomes and goals have been met
- Whether campers enjoyed camp
- Any shortcomings in various segments of the operation
- The effectiveness of staff performance
- The financial efficiency of the business operation
- The value of various camp program activities
- The effectiveness of administrative staff as well as the director
- What is working and what is not working
- Quality control measures
- Areas to be considered in planning for the future

Determining Criteria

In order to evaluate objectively, the director must establish criteria against which to examine performance. The more precise or specific the criteria, the better are the chances for useful information at the end of the evaluation process. There are a variety of sources for establishing the basic performance criteria:

- The desired outcomes and goals of the organization and/or camp
- Governmental regulations
- Standards of an accrediting body
- Standards of the sponsoring organization, if any
- Expectations of parents, campers, or customers
- A plan of work or a strategic planning document

More than one set of criteria may need to be established. For example, to evaluate the camp food service on the basis of governmental regulations or standards and not take into consideration the expectations of parents and campers cannot provide the full information needed.

If the evaluation effort is the result of identification of an existing problem, the focus for evaluation will be more quickly determined and the criteria more easily isolated. Taking the previous example further, if the existing problem relates to too much leftover food after meals, then examination of standards or regulations will be meaningless, whereas the examination of the expectations of campers and staff may reveal useful information.

If the director is following a comprehensive plan of evaluation, all or most of the listed sources may be considered in the development of the criteria. It is recognized that establishing objective criteria will be easier in some areas of operation, for example, "a balanced budget," than in others, such as "a camper having fun."

Who administers the evaluation can also affect the outcomes and/or the credibility of the resulting report. Though more costly than internal evaluation, sometimes it is more important to have a completely unbiased evaluation from an outside consultant concerning an operational area where problems are creating significant internal or external concerns. The accreditation visit of the American Camping Association is one example of an external evaluation that carries with it an internal evaluation component. It provides a test against established industry standards and a public recognition of minimum compliance. A consultant may assist in analyzing areas not possible to be covered by standards or regulations or may give the evaluation process a sense of credibility that is important only to the immediate camp community (e.g., board, staff, present or potential contributors).

An ongoing plan of evaluation can be accomplished internally with staff and volunteers, as long as objective criteria are set and appropriate methods are chosen and administered properly.

Gathering Data

Before beginning to gather data, a director needs to identify the principal areas to be considered in the evaluation process: site and facilities, program, personnel performance, administrative practices, marketing, the camper. Some of these areas, such as personnel performance, require continuous data collection, while others, such as site and facilities, may require only an annual review.

Before selecting methods or instruments, the difference in quantitative and qualitative data should be considered. Quantitative data exists or is converted into numbers from answers such as yes or no. Such data are often most helpful in determining whether the desired outcomes and goals have been met. Obviously, financial records, enrollment statistics, maintenance records, and attendance reports can provide quantitative data by the use of a variety of instruments.

Quantitative data relies most often on

- Questionnaires — self-administered or administered in person or by telephone
- Tests — self-administered or in group setting
- Records — financial, maintenance, historical, and so on
- Observations — from predetermined checklists
- Physical evidence — leftovers, wear and tear, and so on

Qualitative data deal most often with words and their meanings in a given context. Here open-ended questions provide clues and new information not easily gained through yes-no answers. The use of qualitative data is most often helpful in looking at processes and describing what happens in given situations.

Qualitative data relies most often on

- Interviews — open-ended questions, in person or by telephone

- Questionnaires — with open-ended questions

- Focus groups — trained leader asking open-ended questions

- Observation — with field notes

- Records — minutes, historical, publications, and so on

- Experiential — camper logs, narratives, testimonials, letters, and so on

Some expertise is required in the collection and use of both kinds of data and in the selection and use of various available instrument(s). It is wise to seek outside guidance in the development of instruments. The very wording of a question, whether open-ended or requiring a yes or no answer, can greatly affect the outcome of the inquiry.

Because quantitative data are most often reduced to yes-no-don't know answers or numbers relative to degree of agreement (1-2-3-4-5), computer statistical packages can be helpful in sorting the various factors under consideration.[3]

At this point, the director must carefully analyze the following factors:

- How will the information desired be secured in statistical format — yes-no, numbers?

- How much manpower is available?

- What is the ease of tally?

- What is the cost?

- What degree of training is required?

- What type of sample — everyone, selective, random — will be used?

- How will the data collected be interpreted?

- Who is the information for — public, staff, board, parents?

- Can data be secured without intruding?

Having analyzed these questions, the director is in a position to choose whether qualitative or quantitative data are needed and what instruments will best provide that information.

If for some reason it is not possible or practical to collect information from all parties, the type of sample to be used must be examined with a person knowledgeable in statistics and randomization.

To be sure that every part of the operation is included, the director should first develop a list of each component of the camp operation. One way to begin is to list these components, one to a line on the left side of a sheet of lined paper. To the right of these, draw columns and label them: camper, program staff, counselors, administrative board, committee, and so on — whatever groups will participate in the evaluation process. Then each of the components listed should be examined and the appropriate columns on the right checked to indicate the group or groups that participate in each phase of camp life. From this completed chart, the director can then consider the instruments most appropriate to each group and area. (*See illustration 16.1.*) Particular consideration should be given to the following areas of evaluation.

(See illustration 16.1.)

Illustration 16.1 — *Evaluation Checklist*

EVALUATION CHECKLIST

Group to Evaluate Elements

Elements Requiring Evaluation	Administrative Staff	Board Members	Campers	CITs	Committee Members	Counselors	Kitchen Staff	Parents/Campers	Program Staff
1. Archery		■			■	■			
2. Arts and crafts									
3. Cabin cleanup									
4. Camp promotion									■
5. Canoeing instruction		■			■	■			
6. Evening program — all-camp									
7. Evening program — unit		■			■	■			
8. Health service									
9. Indian lore		■			■	■			
10. Maintenance									
11. Meal time									
12. Nature hikes		■			■				
13. Office — registration									
14. Office — business, records			■	■		■		■	
15. Out-of-camp trips									
16. Overnights		■			■	■			
17. Riflery									
18. Staff training		■						■	
19. Swimming — free time		■			■	■			
20. Swimming — instruction		■			■	■			
21. Transportation		■			■				
22. Waterskiing		■							

Staff Evaluation of Overall Operation

A questionnaire may provide the most objective information in this situation, but a dialogue with the staff can reveal concerns not easily identified through a questionnaire. A group dialogue by staff should be led by someone who is very objective and has the trust of the group. If the director can establish a reputation for openness to suggestions and ideas throughout the season, staff may be quite willing to respond to questions about the operation. It would be quite natural to set aside an afternoon or a day after campers depart for a group evaluation. The director or discussion leader should give staff members an opportunity to react to each camp area and to make observations about the season and suggestions for the next season. If the director and other administrative staff can keep from being defensive and simply make notes as the discussion moves along, such a meeting may reveal attitudes as well as founded observations.

If the departure schedule or size of the staff makes such an approach inadvisable, a questionnaire may be developed. To be most effective, such a form should use a simple method allowing for quick answers, so that the person can check or circle a choice of answers for each question. It is also effective to include one or two open-ended questions, near the end of the form, that will elicit more extended comments. If signing the form is optional, staff members can be honest without feeling that they might be jeopardizing their chance to return for another season.

Program Evaluation

Because the camp program is the channel through which desired outcomes and goals are realized, it should be subjected to careful assessment to determine whether desired outcomes and goals are being met and where changes should be made. Prior to camp, a method should be devised for and specific staff given the responsibility of gathering data on individual programs throughout the period. These data will be used for the end-of-season evaluation. The plan may include a carefully designed checklist for staff to record data on the program from their own observations and from discussions with counselors and campers who participate in a particular program.

Depending on the age and experience of the campers, securing a valid program evaluation from them may be more difficult. If a natural evaluation of an experience can occur informally (e.g., on an overnight, on a canoe trip, in a group activity), it can provide qualitative information. A living-group counselor is often the most effective leader of any camper evaluation, except where it deals with the counselor's own performance. If a spontaneous evaluation occurs, there should be a form or some other method of documentation the counselor can use to relay the information to the administration.

Use of video cameras or tape recorders in an evaluation session where campers participate can be a valuable tool. Certainly the group should agree to the use of such devices. However, it takes a very experienced leader to move the group to relaxed and non-self-conscious responses when recording or taping.

Some camper experiences and situations lend themselves to a recounting in personal logs or journals. This activity helps the camper to focus on his or her experiences daily, as well as aiding the camper in understanding the changes during the time frame covered by the experience. This exercise becomes an avenue of self-evaluation for the camper. Sometimes campers will share their journals with the counselor or director. Some camps have had the privilege of publishing excerpts from such journals with the camper's consent.

An evaluation questionnaire may also be helpful. However, handing each camper a form to check off on the last day of camp may diminish the feelings of the moment. Use of a form by the counselor with the living group earlier in the day may be better. Another alternative is to mail the camper a form with a return envelope after the camper returns home.

Alternatively, the director can request evaluations from parents after the camper has returned home. Parents may be able to voice the camper's feelings effectively as well as to evaluate any changes. To encourage responses, the questionnaire needs to be carefully designed and be as brief as it is consistent in securing the necessary information. Providing a stamped, self-addressed envelope and making a signature on the form optional will probably increase the percentage of return.

Where there are particular program activities run or supervised by particular staff members, these staffers should be provided with an opportunity to evaluate their effectiveness — either in an interview or with a questionnaire. There should also be an opportunity for making recommendations for future changes in the program. Obviously, staff members most closely associated with a particular activity should have the best viewpoint for appraising the procedures and methods used.

General questions about programs or activities, such as those that follow, will help staff members think about effectiveness:

- Does the program or activity consider the needs and interests of the campers as well as their stage of development?

- Does the program or activity provide for individual differences in skill and maturity?

- Does the program or activity stress the values of participation: group loyalty, tolerance, concern for others?

- Does the program or activity allow for self-expression or creativity?

- Does the program or activity enable campers to realize a sense of achievement through participation?

- Does the program or activity promote the development of leadership skills?

- Does the program or activity offer progression to higher skill levels?

Some organizational factors should be assessed in considering the framework of a particular program or activity. Was consideration given to the optimal size and makeup of the program group? Was the area where the activity took place adequate? Was the equipment adequate, in good repair, and available in sufficient numbers for the group size? Was the activity conducted within safe guidelines?

Administrative Services Evaluation

All administrative services should be appraised throughout the season and reviewed not only by those responsible for the operation but also by other staff outside each operation as well.

Camp property, facilities, and equipment need to be reviewed not only for purposes of safety and good maintenance but also with an eye to possible improvements. The suggestions of participants, parents, and staff regarding changes should be considered.

The food service operation should be examined regarding factors such as food quality, cost per meal, sanitation, efficiency of management and organization, and maintenance of happy relationships with campers and staff as they move in and out of the dining area during mealtimes.

The health and safety and risk management program should be measured. Can the daily routine for treating people at the health center be improved? Do some activities have a high accident rate? How can injuries be reduced? On out-of-camp trips, are all health and safety precautions taken? Can the procedures at the waterfront be improved to offer a better check on swimmers?

Hospitality Services Evaluation

In a conference/retreat center or where a camp rents facilities to others, questionnaires should be devised to enable guests, group leaders, and staff to comment on housing, equipment, food, staff, hospitality, service, health and safety concerns, grounds, and facilities. Different questions should be asked of the secondary customers (i.e., guests) from those asked the primary customer (i.e., organizations or leaders). Responses can prove to be a valuable tool in marketing as well as in improving services.

Staff Performance Appraisal

A major part of the evaluation process is the appraisal, at all levels, of employed and volunteer camp staff. This process is discussed in full in chapter 8.

Evaluation of the Director

Often the camp director has the most difficult time getting a direct critique of his or her job performance. There should be a way devised for staff and volunteers to share reactions to the director's performance. Sometimes direct verbal feedback is a possibility, but most often, a questionnaire (which does not have to be signed) is given to staff and volunteers to be returned to a neutral person. Open-ended questions usually elicit the most helpful comments. A sample form is shown in *illustration 16.2*. The use of such a form may be helpful to the director's supervisor, which could be an agency executive director, camp administrator, owner, or personnel committee of an operating board, since such an annual evaluation and feedback is beneficial to a director.

Evaluation of Boards or Committees

In camps that have governing committees or boards, it is important both to the director/ administrator and the chief elected officer to have regular times to check the effectiveness of their work with that body. It is also important for the volunteer governing body to evaluate its own operation. Sometimes this can be done in an informal dialogue in a retreat setting, where time is not as pressed as in regular meetings and methods can be used to secure qualitative input. Where such an approach is not possible, a checklist, such as that shown in *illustration 16.3*, may provide a more objective evaluation.

Similarly, volunteers need feedback as to their performance and participation. Performance appraisal of volunteer staff members is covered in chapter 9.

Evaluation of Campers

The evaluation of campers varies greatly from camp to camp. Many camps keep careful records of each child's program participation and relationship to peers. This information is often helpful in placing the camper in a living group another year and may be useful in planning activities at the beginning of the next season.

Ideally, the evaluation of campers should go back to the developmental goals of the age group served and the outcomes directed to those developmental goals. At the end of the season, the degree to which the camp experience has met those outcomes and goals is one true test of the camp experience. Having focused staff on those developmental goals during staff training and referred staff back to them during supervisory conferences, it is logical that the level of achievement of those outcomes and goals be measured. These results can be most helpful in responding to parents and also in assessing changes needed in program operations for the next season.

Two nationwide research projects (Nationwide Camp Evaluation Project, 1993-1996, and the National Inclusive Camp Practices, 1997-2000) used qualitative data and comparative case studies to reveal camper growth. In these studies, counselors and parents believed that "the vast majority of examples . . . described an improvement in camper performance associated with the camp experience. A summative analysis of all interview comments received from campers and parents revealed that increased independence (self-reliance) was the predominant growth outcome for the case-study campers."[4] Such programs require involving

Illustration 16.2 *Director Evaluation Form*

DIRECTOR EVALUATION FORM

Director's name _____ Date _____

Scale

5 = superior performance; consistently goes beyond expectations; demonstrates appreciable growth

4 = consistently meets expectations; shows personal initiative; shows progress in personal growth and competency

3 = meets minimal expectations most of time; little personal initiative or personal growth; performs to level of abilities

2 = achieves at a level lower than abilities; occasionally meets minimal expectations; shows no growth

1 = fails to meet expectations; performs below level of ability; no discernible growth; performance unacceptable

0 = no knowledge

	0	1	2	3	4	5
1. Demonstrates vision regarding camp's objectives and long-range plans						
2. Sets high standards for the committee, staff, and campers						
3. Sees that high standards are met in: maintenance and improvement of sight; selection and training of staff; health and safety of campers and staff						
4. Has good physical health and stamina						
5. Demonstrates personal interest in: each staff member; campers; committee members and volunteers						
6. Communicates well with: staff; campers; committee members and volunteers; public						
7. Demonstrates fairness in working with people						
8. Keeps well informed on all aspects of operation						
9. Effectively delegates responsibility and related authority						
10. Maintains effective program of evaluation: of program; of staff; by campers and parents						
11. Maintains a team-building approach						
12. Inspires confidence and trust						
13. Has pleasant personality and gets along well with people						
14. Is effective in marketing approach						

1. Demonstrates vision regarding camp's objectives and long-range plans
2. Sets high standards for the committee, staff, and campers
3. Sees that high standards are met in:
   - maintenance and improvement of sight
   - selection and training of staff
   - health and safety of campers and staff
4. Has good physical health and stamina
5. Demonstrates personal interest in:
   - each staff member
   - campers
   - committee members and volunteers
6. Communicates well with:
   - staff
   - campers
   - committee members and volunteers
   - public
7. Demonstrates fairness in working with people
8. Keeps well informed on all aspects of operation
9. Effectively delegates responsibility and related authority
10. Maintains effective program of evaluation:
    - of program
    - of staff
    - by campers and parents
11. Maintains a team-building approach
12. Inspires confidence and trust
13. Has pleasant personality and gets along well with people
14. Is effective in marketing approach

Other comments:

Signed _____

Illustration 16.3 *Evaluation for Boards and Committees*

VOLUNTEER COMMITTEES AND BOARDS EVALUATION FORM

This document is designed to obtain your evaluation of our board's (committee) effectiveness. Circle the number on the rating scale that corresponds to your evaluation of the board in each category. Number 1 indicates poor performance and number 5 excellent performance as illustrated by the statements nearest those numbers.

1. CLARITY OF ROLE AND FUNCTION

Lacks. We're fuzzy about our responsibilities.　　1　2　3　4　5　　Present. We distinguish clearly between policy determination and management functions. We know what we are about.

2. LEADERSHIP

Dominated by one or a few persons. Other resources within the board are never used.　　1　2　3　4　5　　Shared among members according to abilities and insights. All resources are used.

3. IMPORTANT ISSUES

Not addressed, but "swept under the rug" or dealt with outside of the board.　　1　2　3　4　5　　Consistently on the agenda for open consideration, debate, and decision.

4. PREPARATION

Lacks. We're consistently caught off guard without adequate information, facts, and documentation.　　1　2　3　4　5　　Outstanding. Committees and staff do excellent preliminary work. Members are well informed and understand the pros and cons of all decisions.

5. COMMUNICATION OF IDEAS

Poor. We don't listen. Ideas are ignored.　　1　2　3　4　5　　Good. We listen and try to understand one another's ideas. Ideas are well presented and acknowledged.

6. RESPONSIBLE PARTICIPATION

Lacks. We reflect our own biases. We "grind our own axes" and watch from "outside."　　1　2　3　4　5　　Present. We're sensitive to the need to reflect for our camp and its clientele. Everyone is "on the inside participating."

7. FREEDOM OF PERSONS

Stifled. Conformity is explicitly or implicitly fostered. Members are often manipulated.　　1　2　3　4　5　　Enhanced and encouraged. Creativity of persons and their individuality is respected.

8. CLIMATE OF RELATIONSHIPS

One of hostility or suspicion or indulgent politeness or fear of anxiety.　　1　2　3　4　5　　One of mutual trust and genuineness. Atmosphere is relaxed and friendly.

9. DECISION MAKING

Superficial. We're a "rubber stamp" body. Decisions are crammed down our throats.　　1　2　3　4　5　　Participative. All data is available and all opinions are aired, with resultant ownership of decisions that are made.

10. ACTION AGREEMENTS

Not reached. We don't set target dates or plan for follow through.　　1　2　3　4　5　　Reached. We agree on next steps and set target dates for review.

11. FISCAL ACCOUNTABILITY

Lacks. We don't consider the cost of an action before it is taken.　　1　2　3　4　5　　Present. We carefully consider financial implications of proposals before approval.

12. CONTINUITY

Lacks. Each meeting seems to "start from scratch."　　1　2　3　4　5　　Present. We build on previous work in an efficient manner.

13. PRODUCTIVITY

Low. We're proud and happy, just coasting along. Meetings are irrelevant and a waste of time and money.　　1　2　3　4　5　　High. We are digging hard and earnestly at work in important tasks. We create and achieve at each meeting.

Please list any additional suggestions or ideas you have for increasing the effectiveness of this board. Particular attention to items you rated 1 or 2 is greatly appreciated.

a professor or staff person skilled in program evaluation techniques to help design the instrument and plan for evaluation in addition to clarifying program desired outcomes and goals and involving the approval of the governing organization, if there is one.

In keeping parents in touch with the camper's progress, some camps use a regular report form for parents at the end of the season, whereas others require counselors to write progress reports to parents at regular intervals. Camps with shorter sessions require the progress reports at the end of the session the camper attended. Whatever the form or time frame, the evaluation should be approached with concern for objectivity and balance. Counselors need to understand that they see the camper in isolation from his or her familiar environment, which means that their observations may be one-sided or limited in scope. In addition, these records are sometimes necessary for reports to an agency that referred the camper or that has an ongoing relationship with the camper.

In many instances, the most effective form of evaluation is that done in one-on-one conversation with the camper. Helping a camper see him- or herself through the eyes of others is an important outcome for many camps. If that is an outcome, then it can only be reached in an open and trusting living situation. Counselors need careful training and sensitivity in order to give campers a positive experience of self-evaluation. The process should begin with discussing with each individual camper, as well as with the group, individual goals for the camp period. Their conversations with campers should begin on a positive note and emphasize positive achievements toward that camper's goals, but the areas in which a camper can improve should also be pointed out honestly and discussed.

The best evaluation of a camper happens when the camper can be led into a realistic self-evaluation. If the focus of conversations and observations can be on how the camper perceives his or her achievement, skill level, behavior, or response to others, it is more likely to become a part of his or her ongoing life experience.

Accreditation

The program of accreditation pioneered by the American Camping Association is designed to measure the performance of a particular camp or conference center against a list of standards of operation in many areas. The accreditation program features a visit by trained professionals. Preparation for the visit may extend over a period of months. The ACA standards, developed over a period of more than sixty years and now accepted nationally as industry standards, can also be used as a tool for self-evaluation. A great deal is said for having a pattern against which the director can measure the camp. Involvement of administrative staff, as well as any operating committee or board, can also be most useful.

Illustration 16.4

APPLICABLE TOOLS TO VARIOUS AREAS OF EVALUATION

Group to Evaluate Elements

Areas of Evaluation	Observations	Questionnaires	Interviews	Records	Focus Groups	Physical Evidence	Experiential	Tests
1. Campers	C/N		O	P		X		
2. Facilities and equipment	C	Y	O	R	X	X		
3. Financial	C	Y		X		Y		
4. Marketing		Y/O	O	X	X	X		
5. Personnel appraisal								
▪ Director	C/N	Y/O	O		X			
▪ Staff	C/N	Y/O	O					
▪ Volunteers	C/N	Y/O	O					
6. Personnel selection		Y/O	O	X		X	X	
7. Program	C/N	Y/O	O		X	X		
8. Support services								
▪ Food service	C/N	Y/O	O	X	X	X	X	
▪ Health service	C/N	Y/O	O	X	X			

Key

C	= Checklist	R	= Repairs/maintenance
N	= Field notes	X	= Applicable
O	= Open ended	Y	= Yes/No
P	= Program		

Finances

Though monthly financial reports give a clue to the financial operation, the year-end report provides an opportunity for a variety of evaluations. This report will be of the greatest interest to the camp director, business manager, and a governing board. It should include the cost per meal served, the cost per camper day, cost-effectiveness analysis, a cost-benefit analysis by specific services or program activities, and a comparison of income and expenditures by category over a five-year period.

Illustration 16.4 provides a chart showing the instruments most applicable to the various areas of evaluation covered earlier. Though other instruments are available, these are the most commonly used in the camp operation.

Reporting — The Judgment Phase

The final step, after the criteria have been determined and the data gathered, is to make judgments about the meaning of the data in relationship to the camp operation. In a single proprietorship, the data gathered lands on one desk and the judgments are made there. In most cases, however, multiple individuals are involved in the judgment process; this will require reports describing the data and conclusions.

In interpreting quantitative data, the director must not be too quick to simply assume that the highest numerical sums necessarily provide the proper judgment. Rather, the frequencies must be examined to see if particular portions of the data skew the results in some fashion. Establishing a mean or average and a median (the position at which there is an equal number above and below) in the data will help the director discover if the two are relatively close. If there is a substantial difference, the data may need to be examined more closely for anything unusual that is skewing the results. If the quantitative data becomes this complex, many camp directors may wish to consult with someone who has training in statistical analysis for assistance in interpreting the data.

In interpreting qualitative data, Henderson suggests that, early in the organization of data, the director will "continually reexamine the data. 'Negative evidence,' which means you will be trying to make sure everything fits your categories, will be sought." Here the evaluator looks to see whether there is any evidence that does not fit. Further, she suggests that the director look "for multiple sources of evidence to draw conclusions . . . that interpretations come from being intimately familiar with the data. Therefore, the evaluator . . . read(s) the data over and over."[5]

The director must carefully examine the data for information that he or she did not necessarily seek because there are often unexpected insights that come from evaluation. This information may be more valuable than much of the data that was sought. Look for negative impacts as well as positive experiences.

After the data have been examined again and again and basic conclusions and inconclusive areas have been identified, the director can write a report outlining the areas studied, criteria identified, sample used, instruments chosen, data collected, and resulting conclusions and recommendations for action. The use of this report will vary with the audience to whom it is addressed, with considerably more detail offered to the decisionmakers than to parents or campers. Each audience requires a different approach.

Reporting to the Corporate Board

Most camps have a governing group that expects reports at the conclusion of the camp season. These reports can take many forms but are most often directed to the camp director's supervisor or a governing committee or board. This report should certainly highlight the events of the summer, giving the group a sense of the program, outcomes, and goals achieved, as well as the values derived from the experience. The use of comments from camper logs or parental letters can be helpful in sharing this feeling.

In addition to communicating the programmatic aspects of camp, it is vital that the results of the evaluation process be shared with the governing group. Summaries of the data with comparative data from previous summers will give perspective to the facts. Furthermore, the director may wish to make recommendations for improvements and steps for the next season growing out of the evaluation process. This approach helps the governing body focus discussion on the major concerns and alternatives to the recommendations.

Such a report should summarize the criteria, the methods used to collect the data, any instrument used in the process, and the resulting data. Following this narrative, a list of conclusions and resulting recommendations may be presented. If the report is quite long, an executive summary plus the conclusions and recommendations may be used for wider distribution. These reports should be retained in the camp's files, along with the raw materials collected in the process.

Reporting to Parents and Participants

The report to the parents and participants often emphasizes the overview of the season with comments on camper activities and projects. Pictures and stories will make such reports more interesting and readable. It should be kept in mind that the report parents receive is an important tool in developing loyalty and interest in the camp for another season and many times developing a case for future contributions of money or services.

Many camps publish a yearbook or annual calendar that tells the season's story in pictures and words for the campers and staff. Here emphasis is given to the good times had by all, with pictures of as many different campers and staff as possible. Not only is this an instrument for next year's recruitment, but it also provides a tool that might be shared with friends.

The size and layout of the camp's report will depend partially on the funds available. In any case, the report should be designed to be an attractive, interpretative tool.

Reporting to Alumni

Developing an updated list of camper and staff alumni is valuable for sharing information about the camp. Certainly a report of each season should be shared with the alumni group. This report goes beyond the sort of report sent to parents and is not as detailed as the report to the governing body. The report for alumni might be a summary of the major events of the camp season with an enclosure concerning the major decisions the camp is facing in the near future.

Here the report is designed to maintain the interest of the alumni, assuring them of the continuing allegiance to the philosophy of the camp and stimulating interest in ways the alumni can further serve the camp through contributions of money and services.

Checkpoints

1. Were evaluations done in previous seasons? If so, have you found copies in the files?

2. What type of evaluations would have been helpful to you as you began planning for your first season?

3. Using *illustration 16.1* as a basis, develop your own chart listing the areas of the camp program and the people who should be involved in the evaluation of each area.

4. Develop an overall evaluation plan that will provide information identified in question 2.

5. What information would your governing committee or board like to have at the end of the season?

6. Review your evaluation plan to see if it will provide that information.

7. What sort of evaluation from your staff will be most helpful?

8. How do you help your campers begin the process of self-evaluation?

9. Have you set up a system to evaluate the camp program against the developmental outcomes of the each age group? If not, how do you do so?

Related Standards and Guidelines

Accreditation Standards for Camp Programs and Services: OM-2, 3, 5;
  "Additional Professional Practices": 15, 23

Guidelines for Conference and Retreat Centers: II-29–30

[1] Karla A. Henderson with M. Deborah Bialeschki. 1995. *Evaluating Leisure Services: Making Enlightened Decisions*. State College, PA: Venture Publishing, Inc.

[2] Karla A. Henderson and M. Deborah Bialeschki. 1993. "Camp Was Great, But the Water Was Too Cold." *Camping Magazine*, Vol. 65, No. 5, May/June. pp. 31–32.

[3] Henderson with Bialeschki. 1995. p..

[4] Steve Brannan , Ed.D., and Ann Fullerton, Ed.D. 1999. "Case Studies Reveal Camper Growth." *Camping Magazine*, Vol. 72, No. 1, January-February. pp. 22-–25.

[5] Henderson with Bialeschki. 1995. p..

Becoming a Professional

The impetus for an educational experience naturally should come from camp directors. This would not only be the best guarantee of its productiveness, but would also reflect a high degree of genuinely professional consciousness on the part of camp directors.[1]

All the answers are not in this volume because no one has all those answers. The camp director must find many answers on his or her own — through experience, through peer relationships, through research, through study, through workshops and conferences. The quotation from Hedley Dimock at the beginning of this chapter is as true today as when it was written over fifty years ago.

Camping as a Profession

The subject of the camp director as a professional has been an issue since the early part of this century, but the discussion has intensified during the past four decades. In our society, the term professional has been so greatly overused that, at times, the only commonality among its many uses is that it differentiates between a paid and an unpaid person — though today we have coined the expression "professional volunteers." Originally the word was used to talk about law, medicine, and religious vocations, but it has been broadened in modern times.

It is recognized that many people come into the camping and conference/retreat center field for a few years only, before taking other positions in other human service organizations. Many people in other professions, such as education, spend their summers as well as part of the school year involved in the camp field. However, a significant number of directors are individuals who spend their lives in the camp field — as camp directors, administrators, consultants, and teachers. To these people, there is a strong feeling that being a camp or conference/retreat center director is a profession worthy of note.

A work group at the ninth Character Education in Camping Seminar at George Williams College identified seven marks of a profession. These are paraphrased here but are taken from that seminar report:[2]

1. A profession rests upon "*a social function, distinct from other functions, that is basic, important and relatively permanent.*" This is most obvious in medicine, the ministry, engineering, and law. Camping is so young, as compared to these professions, that it is a bit premature to espouse our social function, much less equate 130 plus years as permanency.

2. A profession has a "*distinctive or specialized body of knowledge,*" a theory that ties together many disciplines that represent a unique body apart from other fields. As identified in this text, many disciplines must be mastered in this field, but what makes that body of knowledge unique from education, perhaps the closest profession to camping?

3. A profession "*demands a specialized or professional preparation, in addition to general education, for its practitioners.*" This means that the body of knowledge is so complex and large that it cannot be mastered on the job, as in a craft. This is one of the differences between a carpenter and an architect. Standards for specialized education are set, and only those individuals who meet them are eligible for admission to that profession. An effort was made, in this regard, through an American Camping Association Certified Professional program, but after a number of years of granting certification it became apparent that the field was far from accepting this as an eligibility requirement to practice in the field. The program was discontinued pending additional study.

4. A profession functions collectively through people "*joining together for mutual betterment and growth and to provide a service to the public.*" These were once called guilds or societies but today are known as associations. The functions include

- Formulating the conditions for entrance into the profession, as mentioned previously in the discussion of the first mark of a profession.

- Developing a code governing ethical practices of those in the field, as it relates to the "relationships between the practitioner and the other practitioners, and the practitioner and the public." The American Camping Association has established a code for camp directors, which does set some basic ethical practices for the field. This code is included in appendix F and deserves study by every camp director because it contains basic ethical practices.

- Stimulating the "discovery of new knowledge and practice pertinent to the profession." Researching and publishing articles on various aspects of the field's practice is a recognized way of advancing the body of knowledge in a field and one's professional contribution. Dr. Betty van der Smissen and Dr. Judy Brookhiser developed a bibliography of research in the field in 1982.[3] ACA's Web site has a place to search research documents and bibliographies and updated this comprehensive bibliography of research. In 1999, Paul Marsh did a meta-analysis of twenty-two studies completed on the influence of camp experiences on youth self-constructs.[4]

- "Facilitating the interchange and dissemination of" knowledge in the field throughout the entire profession. This function is the obligation and effort to update continually the field and to provide new input into the body of knowledge. It is being done today by camp directors who write for such journals as *Camping Magazine*, the *Christian Camp & Conference Journal*, and the *Journal of Experiential Education*, and who author books in the field. Such interchange and dissemination of knowledge has happened in Christian Camping International, the American Camping Association, and the International Association of Conference Center Administrators. It follows that, when the camp director becomes part of one or all of those bodies, he or she moves toward being a professional.

5. A profession "*formulates and applies standards that govern the practice of the profession in the community.*" This goal has been met in our field through the standards of the American Camping Association, which have been developed over more than sixty years and are now the accepted standards for the industry in the United States. However, we are still some distance from having all camps or conference/retreat centers meet those standards or from having all states recognize accreditation as essential for licensing.

6. A profession is "*motivated by a social spirit and purpose. Social values presumably transcend individual and economic values in a profession.*" In other words, the reason for camps to exist is to serve the public, and that becomes an essential ingredient of any professional organization or association that brings together camp directors. The challenge, therefore, is to keep individual directors and their associations focused on growth of the camp director and service to the public, rather than mutual protection societies. There will always be pressures to move toward the mutual protection society rather than toward the protection of the public, and the voices of professionals in the field must keep their associations on course.

7. A profession "*implies a personal standard of workmanship characterized by both sincerity and intellectual integrity. The professional person seeks to maintain high standards of competence, to keep abreast of changing conditions and of new knowledge and techniques, and to embody the new learnings in his practice.*" This requirement means that a professional has an obligation to update his or her knowledge in the field continually. A professional holds oneself out to the public as being up-to-date on the current and best practices in one's field. Herein, the director must move beyond his or her own camp or organization to exchange information and to dialogue with fellow professionals around key issues and development.

An examination of the seven marks of a profession gives us evidence that some requirements have been fulfilled while others have not. Therein is the challenge for the future. Hedley S. Dimock, in speaking to this issue, wrote: "A professional . . . will submit himself to the rigid discipline of straight thinking, to a constant search for new knowledge and better techniques that should be embodied in practice. In this quest for higher standards of workmanship, he will ally himself with other camp directors and personnel through camping associations or similar organizations. He will accept his share of collective responsibility to discover and disseminate knowledge through research and publications, to raise the standards of camping generally, and to interpret to the public the objectives and standards of the modern camp. He will work within the planning structure of the community to make camping experience available for the larger number of persons who need this experience."[5]

Expanding One's Education

There are at least six areas of educational endeavor that will enable a camp director to gain more knowledge and keep current with developments in the field.

For camp directors, the American Camping Association has devised a Professional Development Plan that is depicted in *illustration 17.1*. The first course in the plan is a New Director's Orientation that gives an overview of all aspects of the job for new seasonal and assistant directors, as well as late hires, and is offered at the local section level.

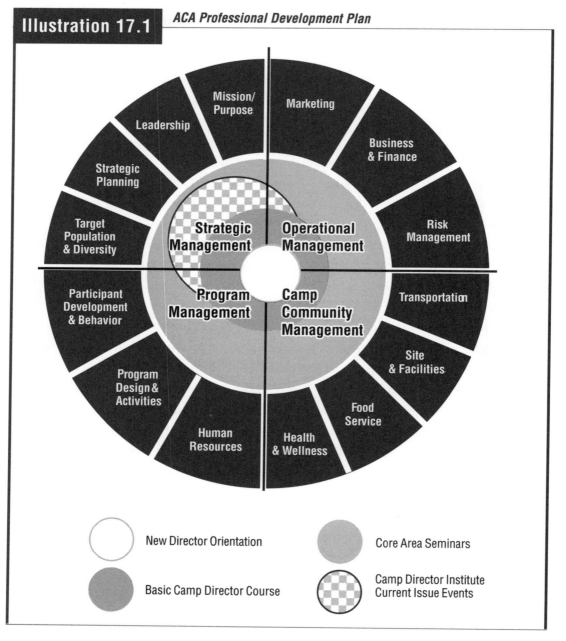

Illustration 17.1   *ACA Professional Development Plan*

○ New Director Orientation

● Basic Camp Director Course

● Core Area Seminars

▣ Camp Director Institute Current Issue Events

The second course is the Basic Camp Director's Course (BCDC), which is the best comprehensive introduction to the management of camps and covers thirteen of the fourteen core areas. Primarily designed for camp directors with less than six years of experience, the course is offered in conjunction with American Camping Association national, regional and sectional conferences. Selected resource lists targeted to each core area are available in appendix J.

Camp Director Institutes are designed for experienced directors who have completed the BCDC and have at least three years of experience as a director with overall responsibility for the operation and management of a camp or conference center or six years of experience as a director.

Christian Camping International, the American Camping Association, and the International Association of Conference Center Directors offer a variety of workshops, courses, and conferences, which will assist the camp director in areas in which he or she feels deficient and will help him or her keep abreast of current practices. The annual and regional conferences of the organizations provide a wealth of such information. A variety of other organizations offer courses, workshops, and conferences that will benefit camp directors in certain areas. Many of these organizations are listed in appendix C. In addition, a number of colleges and universities offer courses in camp administration or related subjects through their schools of physical education or recreation and leisure studies.

Participation in a local section of American Camping Association and/or the Christian Camping International provides an opportunity to meet fellow camp directors and to develop relationships that will allow sharing and problem solving together. The American Camping Association's Web site (*www.ACAcamps.org/education/calendar.htm*) provides details regarding local section educational opportunities, as well as on-line courses.

Participation in the accreditation process of the American Camping Association is one of the best educational tools available. The Standards Course and a study of the *Accreditation Standards for Camp Programs and Services, 1998 edition* (or use of the *Guidelines for Conference and Retreat Centers, 2003 edition*) is an ideal way to start, whether or not the camp is seeking accreditation. Of course, actual participation in the accreditation of one's camp is an exciting and grueling educational experience, well worth the time, effort, and money. Further, completion of the course for standards visitors and participating in accreditation visits to other camps is a way for camp directors to expand their horizons and to understand the broader field of camping.

Personal reading and study cannot be dismissed as being any less important than the items listed previously. The professional journals in the field should be read regularly, and journals in related fields should be perused as the occasion allows. The American Camping Association offers a Web site with a Knowledge Center, on-line courses, and a catalog of publications in the field that is updated regularly. Even though a camp director may be distant from conferences and workshops and able to make them only every few years, computers and books with pertinent information are always close at hand.

All the costs for the preceding activities are business-related and should be borne by the camp, where possible. However, where not borne by the camp, they may be itemized for personal tax deductions.

A professional portfolio is a career planning tool to help camp directors analyze their competencies and document their professional development experiences. A sample can be downloaded from the ACA Web site. It contains information commonly included in a resume including such items as

- Career goals

- Previous job experience

- Completed degree programs

- Courses, seminars, and workshops specific to the camping industry

- Participation in other educational events

- Self-study experiences

- A regularly updated needs assessment

- ACA leadership and volunteer experiences

- Other experiences relevant to the profession

Finally, there is an opportunity for every camp director to add to the body of knowledge in the field of camping. One of the exciting aspects of the camping field is that there is an opportunity to experiment and explore more efficient ways of operating camps and conference/retreat centers as well as to develop new methods of helping people grow outdoors. As a director, you can be one who studies, experiments, documents, and adds to that body of knowledge. But whatever you do, may your work in the camping field not only aid those participants and staff in your program but also ensure that future generations will continue to benefit from this unique human experience.

Checkpoints

1. Which of the seven marks of a profession do you think accurately reflects the camping profession?

2. How does the Code of Ethics apply to your work or your camp?

3. What is your plan for professional development?

Related Standards and Guidelines

Accreditation Standards for Camp Programs and Services: HR-1

Guidelines for Conference and Retreat Centers: II – 31–33

[1] Hedley S. Dimock. 1948. "Camping and the Future." IX in a series, *Character Education in the Summer Camp*. New York: Association Press (YMCA of the USA). p. 59.

[2] Dimock. 1948. pp. 24–26.

[3] Betty van der Smissen and Judy Brookhiser, Editors. 1982. *Bibliography of Research in Organized Camping, Environmental Education, Adventure Education, and Interpretative Services*. Martinsville, IN: American Camping Association.

[4] Paul Marsh. 1999. "What Does Camp Do for Kids? A Meta-analysis of the Influence of the Organized Camping Experience on the Self-constructs of Youth" (Master's thesis, Indiana University).

[5] Dimock. 1948. p. 269.

Appendix A:
Sample Job Descriptions

Position Title: Program Director

Responsible to: Camp Director

General Responsibility: To be responsible for the camp program and to assist in staff training

Qualifications:

- At least twenty-one years of age, preferably at least twenty-five years of age
- At least two years of college, preferably a graduate
- Extensive experience as a group counselor or staff member in camp setting; experience at programming in a camp setting preferred
- Emotionally mature and willing to accept responsibility
- Believe in the individual worth of the camper
- Able to work with a minimum of supervision

Specific Responsibilities:

- Assist the camp director in planning and carrying out precamp and in-service staff training
- Be responsible for all camp programs provided for the camper
- Directly supervise and appraise the unit counselors, nature specialist, arts and crafts specialist, aquatics specialist, equine specialist, and tripping specialist
- Maintain proper records as required by the camp director
- Coordinate, with assistant director and maintenance supervisor, matters of interest in areas of overlapping responsibility while always seeking the best solution for campers and the camp
- Review program budget and search for ways to increase services offered within budgetary constraints; be prepared to defend proposed programming budget changes
- Be responsible for the health and welfare of campers

Essential Functions:

- Be able to train the staff
- Visually observe the assigned staff in performance of their duties, as well as the behavior of campers in their care, and be able to provide guidance as needed
- Visually identify hazards in the camp operation and respond appropriately
- Be able to work and communicate well with a variety of age groups

Position Title: Site Manager

Responsible to: Camp Director

General Responsibility: To oversee and maintain all properties of the camp

Qualifications:

- High school diploma required, with some college or technical school work beyond high school preferred
- Experience in carpentry, plumbing, electrical, and general maintenance repairs
- Experience in supervising work of others
- Ability to get along well with people

Specific Responsibilities:

- Oversee and maintain all properties according to annual work plans and schedules
- Live on the camp site and act as site manager of camp property
- Hire occasional helpers and subcontractors for projects and ongoing maintenance
- Supervise any employee assigned to maintenance area of camp
- Make recommendations for budgeted repairs and maintenance during budget preparation period; outline costs and detail
- Recommend maintenance and improvements that are beyond budgeted amounts; develop cost figures and details
- Direct volunteer groups who come to camp for work weekends and projects
- See that all major equipment and vehicles are maintained and housed appropriately
- Order maintenance supplies and check delivery; forward approved invoices to the camp director
- Welcome rental groups when asked by camp director and check them out at time of departure; check facilities for damage or unusual disarray
- See that all repair requests are completed or responded to within 48 hours
- Be responsible for the health and welfare of campers

Essential Functions:

- Be able to drive all camp owned vehicles
- Have the necessary physical strength to carry out maintenance and repairs (e.g., to lift heavy objects, to dig, to load and unload trucks, to carry out assigned repairs)
- Visually identify hazards throughout the camp property, and respond appropriately
- Visually identify repairs and cleaning that need to be accomplished throughout the camp property
- Be able to make the appropriate repairs

Position Title: Food Service Supervisor

Responsible to: Camp Director

General Responsibility: To oversee the food service and dining area of the camp

Qualifications:

- A minimum of two years documented experience and training in food service management; previous camp experience preferable
- Emotionally mature
- Ability to manage and supervise subordinates
- Ability to relate well to children and other adults

Specific Responsibilities:

- Supervise all kitchen activities
- Enforce all health standards and regulations established by the Department of Health plus those deemed necessary by the camp director
- Supervise the serving of all meals
- Plan all menus according to healthful nutrition standards two weeks in advance for checking by the camp director
- Order all food and kitchen supplies; maintain costs within the prescribed budget
- Provide for special food needs such as cookouts, snacks, and special events, as well as for persons with special needs
- Participate in the total camp program when appropriate and as long as primary duties are not neglected
- Be responsible for the health and welfare of campers

Essential Functions:

- Ability to operate gas, electrical, and mechanical equipment in the food service area
- Maintain accurate records (e.g., menus, food orders, inventories)
- Visual ability to determine the cleanliness of the entire kitchen and dining room, and ability to supervise corrective action as needed
- Physical strength to lift heavy pots and pans and to move food and supplies
- Ability to assess the condition of food upon preparation and in storage
- Ability to provide supervision to kitchen staff

Appendix B:
Risk Management Checklist for Camp Personnel

Staff Recruitment

- Clear organizational chart showing who supervises whom
- Established ratios (in writing) for
  - supervisor to supervisee
  - counselor to campers
  - program leaders to campers (may vary due to risks)
- Job description in writing
  - general responsibilities
  - specific responsibilities
  - essential functions
  - qualifications
  - revised (in writing) any time duties change or at least annually
- Written policies on remuneration
  - time off
  - insurance coverage
  - meals/lodging credit toward minimum wage, if any
  - minimum wage
  - wages
- Written job performance and appraisal processes

Screening

- Application
  - no gender questions unless required for a specific job (e.g. cabin counselor)
  - no marital status questions (may ask about housing needs for family in resident camp)
  - no race or national origin questions
  - no religion questions unless required for a specific job (e.g. religious education)
  - no disability questions (unless basis of essential functions of job)
  - no specific age questions (may ask if over a specific age)
  - references (at least three)
    - specific to position skills
    - specific to work with children
    - volunteer supervisors
    - employers
  - criminal background check
  and/or
  - volunteer disclosure statement
  - application updated by returning staff
- References checked
  - form includes reference to work with children (if applicable)
  - form includes reference to child abuse
  - form includes reference to specific skill required for position
  - mailed to each reference

- telephone call to references not received or questionable with written notes on call
- Interviews
  - face-to-face
  - telephone, when face-to-face not possible

  or
  - second hand, when face-to-face not possible
  - questions outlined for interview in advance
  - notes taken during interview
  - specific questions around child abuse
  - specific questions around drug use
  - specific questions around discipline
- Employment agreement
  - reviewed by legal counsel

Training

- Staff or employee manual
  - statement of philosophy, mission, goals
  - personnel policies
  - sexual harassment policy
- Precamp training
  - written schedule
  - specific sessions on
    - human development relative to age groups
    - risk management
    - disciplinary policy and practice
    - rules and regulations
    - training specific to each job's functions
  - hazards and known risks
  - abuse identification
  - abuse of camper to camper, staff to camper
  - abuse prevention
- Documented
  - as to who led sessions
  - content of sessions
  - length of sessions
  - who attended (sign-up sheet)
- Training provided for late hires or late arrivals (documented)
- Tools required by job
  - provided
  - training given in use and care
  - protective devices, with training given in use of
- In-service training
  - documented
    - dates
    - material covered
    - length of sessions
    - who led
    - who attended

Supervision

- Each employee given information as to supervisor
- Plan for supervision

- observation
- formal conferences
- informal conferences
- written reprimands signed by supervisor
- performance appraisal system
- Training provided supervisors
    - uniform performance appraisal system
    - observation methods and recording
    - appropriate/inappropriate staff behavior and consequences
    - conference formats, recording, techniques
- Plan for termination
    - documented
    - exit interview

Other

- OSHA
    - OSHA 101 form
    - OSHA 200 form
    - OSHA poster
    - MSDS sheets
- Personnel files
    - application
    - interview notes
    - notes on references contacted by telephone
    - voluntary disclosure statement
    or
    - criminal background check
    - exit interview, if terminated
    - job description, plus any documented changes
    - employment agreement
    - time cards, if applicable
    - attendance record
    - references
    - supervisory notes
    - any written reprimands
- Master file for each year of
    - staff/employee manual
    - staff training outline/documentation
    - supplemental training
    - list of staff by positions
    - counselor/camper housing assignments
    - health records
    - incident reports
    - health and safety bulletins
    - emergency plans
    - completed OSHA forms
- Staff health and accident records kept separate from personnel files

Appendix C:
Organizational Resources

Adventure Programs/Challenge Courses

American Mountain Guides Association
P.O. Box 1739
Boulder, CO 80302
303-271-0984
fax: 303-271-1377
www.amga.com

Association for Challenge Course Technology
P.O. Box 255
Martin, MI 49070-0255
269-685-0670
fax: 269-685-6350
e-mail: acct@net-link.net
www.acctinfo.org
(newsletter, conference)

Association for Experiential Education
2305 Canyon Boulevard, Suite 100
Boulder, CO 80302
303-440-8844
fax: 303-440-9581
e-mail: info@aee.org
www.aee.org
(journal, conferences, publications, accreditation program, and manual)

Experience Based Learning (EBL)
5075 Wilderness Trail
Rockford, IL 61114
815-637-2969
fax: 815-637-2964
www.ebl.org

National Outdoor Leadership School (NOLS)
284 Lincoln Street
Lander, WY 82520
800-710-NOLS (6657)
fax: 307-332-1220
www.nols.edu
(training programs)

Outward Bound National Office
100 Mystery Point Road
Garrison, NY 10524
845-424-4000
fax: 845-424-8286
e-mail: info@obusa.com
www.outwardbound.com

Project Adventure
701 Cabot Street
Beverly, MA 01915
978-524-4500
fax: 978-524-4505
e-mail: info@pa.org
www.pa.org
www.adventurebusiness.com
(publications, training, ropes courses)

Wilderness Education Association
900 East 7th St.
Bloomington, IN 47405
812-855-4095
fax: 812-855-8697
e-mail: wea@indiana.org
www.weainfo.org
(training, certification)

Aquatics

American Canoe Association
7432 Alban Station Boulevard, Suite B232
Springfield, VA 22150-2311
800-929-5162
703-451-0141
fax: 703-451-2245
www.aca-net.org
(journal, newsletter, books, maps, certification programs)

American Red Cross
2025 E Street NW
Washington D.C. 20006
800-797-8022
202-303-4498
fax: 202-303-0044
www.redcross.org
(certification, publications on swimming,
boating, and first aid)

American Whitewater
1424 Fenwick Lane
Silver Spring, MD 20910
866-BOAT4AW
fax: 301-565-6741
www.americanwhitewater.org

Aquatics International
Hanley-Wood, LLC
6222 Wilshire Blvd., Suite 600
Los Angeles, CA 90048-5123
888-999-5631 x 4983
fax: 323-801-4986
www.aquaticsintl.com

Boy Scouts of America
(National Office)
1325 Walnut Hill Lane
P.O. Box 152079
Irving, TX 75015-2079
972-580-2000
www.scouting.org

Canadian Red Cross
170 Metcalfe St. Ste 300
Ottawa, Ontario, K2P 2P2 Canada
613-740-1900
fax: 613-740-1911
www.redcross.ca

Ellis and Associates, Inc.
3506 Spruce Park Circle
Kingwood, TX 77345
281-540-9404
800-742-8720
www.jellis.com
(safety inspections, lifeguard training, design
and safety consultation for new aquatic facilities)

Lifesaving Society — Canada
11759 Groat Road
Edmonton, AB T5M 3K6
Canada
780-415-1755
fax: 780-427-9334
e-mail: experts@lifesaving.org
www.lifesaving.org

National Association of Underwater Instructors (NAUI)
P. O. Box 89789
Tampa, FL 33689-0413
800-553-6284
813-628-6284
fax: 813-628-8253
e-mail: nauihq@nauiww.org
www.naui.org
(training programs, certification)

National Organization for Rivers
212 W. Cheyenne Mountain Blvd.
Colorado Springs, CO 80906
www.nationalrivers.org
719-579-8759
fax: 719-576-6238
www.nationalrivers.org
(publications)

PADI Americas (Scuba Diving Instructors)
30151 Tomas Street
Rancho Santa Margarita, CA 92688
949-858-7234
800-729-7234
fax: 949-858-7264
www.padi.com
(training programs, certification)

Royal Life Saving Society (RLSS) — Australia
National Branch
P.O. Box 525
Drummoyne NSW 1470
Australia
61-02-9181-5444
61-02-9181-5080
e-mail: info@rlssa.org.au
www.rlssa.org.au
(water-safety education, instructor's manuals)

Lifesavers—Royal Life Saving Society (RLSS) — United Kingdom
River House, High Street
Broom, Warwickshire B50 4HN
United Kingdom
44-1-789-773994
fax: 44-1-789-773995
e-mail: membership@rlss.org.uk
www.rlss.org.uk
(water-safety education, instructor's manuals)

Scuba Schools International
2619 Canton Court
Fort Collins, CO 80525-4498
970-482-0883
fax: 970-482-6157
www.ssiusa.com

**U.S. Coast Guard
Office of Boating Safety**
2100 Second Street SW
Washington D.C. 20593-0001
202-267-2229
800-368-5647
TTY: 800-689-0816
e-mail: uscginfoline@gcrm.com
www.uscgboating.org
(magazine and other, publications)
www.uscg.mil

U.S. Sailing Association
15 Maritime Drive
P.O. Box 1260
Portsmouth, RI 02871
800-USSAIL1
401-683-0800
fax: 401-683-0840
e-mail: info@ussailing.org
www.ussailing.org

U.S.A. Water Ski
1251 Holy Cow Road
Polk City, FL 33868
863-324-4341
fax: 863-325-8259
e-mail: usawaterski@uswaterski.org
www.usawaterski.org
(coaching clinics, nationwide clubs, kids' club,
certification)

YMCA of the U.S.A.
101 North Wacker Drive, 14th Fl.
Chicago, IL 60606
800-872-9622
312-977-0031
fax: 312-977-1134
www.ymca.net

Health, Wellness and Safety including First Aid/CPR

American Academy of Pediatrics
141 Northwest Point Blvd.
Elk Grove Village, IL 60007-1098
847-434-4000
847-434-8000
e-mail: webeditor@aap.org
www.aap.org
(professional association, advocacy, research,
publications)

**American Association for Leisure and
Recreation/Council on Outdoor Adventure,
Education and Recreation**
1900 Association Drive
Reston, VA 20191
703-476-3400
800-213-7193
fax: 703-476-9527
www.aahperd.org/aalr
(journal and other, publications, conferences)

American Heart Association
7272 Greenville Avenue
Dallas, TX 75231-4596
800-AHA-USA-1 (800-242-8721)
www.americanheart.org/cpr
(publications, research, courses)

American Safety and Health Insitute
4148 Louis Ave.
Holiday, FL 34671
800-682-5067
www.ashinstitute.com
(certification, first aid)

Association of Camp Nurses
8630 Thorsonveien NE
Bemidji, MN 56601
218-586-2633
fax: 218-586-8771
www.campnurse.org
(workshops, conferences, publications, research,
consulting)

Centers for Disease Control (CDC)
1600 Clifton Road Northeast
Atlanta, GA 30333
404-639-3311
404-639-3534
800-311-3435
www.cdc.gov
(publications, research, statistical information,
training)

Medic First Aid International
500 S. Oanebo Ave.
Eugene, OR 96402
541-344-7099
800-800-7099
fax: 541-344-7429
(first aid/CPR, certification)

National Fire Protection Association
1 Battergmarch Park
Quincy, MA 02169-7471
617-770-3000
fax: 617-770-0700
e-mail: library@nfpa.org
www.nfpa.org
(publications)

National Safety Council
1121 Spring Lake Drive
Itasca, IL 60143-3201
800-621-7619
630-285-1121
fax: 630-285-1315
e-mail: info@nsc.org
www.nsc.org
(publications)

NSF International
P.O. Box 130140
Ann Arbor, MI 48113-0140
800-673-8010
fax: 734-769-0109
e-mail: info@nsf.org
www.nsfconsumer.org
(information on food and drinking water safety,
including food service equipment, plumbing
products, and water treatment)

**President's Council on Physical Fitness
and Sports**
HHH Building, Room 738H
200 Independence Avenue Southwest
Washington, D.C. 20201
202-690-9000
fax: 202-690-5211
www.fitness.gov
(awards)

SOLO
P.O. Box 3150
Conway, NH 03818
603-447-6711
603-447-2310
www.soloschools.com
(wilderness, medical certification)

Wilderness Medicine Associates
189 Dudley Rd.
Bryant Pond, ME 04219
207-665-2702
888-945-3633
www.wildmed.com
(education, search and rescue, outdoor
leadership, prehospital medicine)

**Wilderness Medicine Institute - National
Outdoor Leadership School (NOLS)**
284 Lincoln Street
Lander, WY 82520
800-710-NOLS (6657)
fax: 307-332-1220
www.nols.edu/wmi
(training programs)

Horseback Riding

**American Association for Horsemanship
Safety**
Headquarters and Training Center
P.O. Box 39
Fentress, TX 78622
512-488-2220
fax: 512-488-2319
www.horsemanshipsafety.com
(certification, seminars, workshops)

Certified Horsemanship Association
5318 Bullard Road
Tyler, TX 75703-3612
800-399-0138
fax: 903-509-2474
e-mail: horsesafety@aol.com
www.cha-ahse.org
(certification, job placement, insurance program,
group buying program, camp riding-program
guidelines)

Horsemanship Safety Association, Inc.
P.O. Box 2710
Lake Placid, FL 33862-2710
800-798-8160
fax: 863-699-5577
e-mail: hsanews@aol.com
(publications, certification)

**National American Riding for the
Handicapped Association (NARHA)**
P.O. Box 33150
Denver, CO 80233
800-369-7433
fax: 303-252-4610
www.narha.org

U.S. Pony Clubs, Inc.
Kentucky Horse Park
4041 Iron Works Pike
Lexington, KY 40511-8462
859-254-7669
fax: 859-233-4652
e-mail: uspc@ponyclub.org
www.ponyclub.org
(newsletter and other publications, clinics)

Target Sports

Civilian Marksmanship Program
P.O. Box 576
Port Clinton, OH 43452
419-635-2141
fax: 419-635-2802
www.odcmp.com
(camp riflery programs)

National Field Archery Association
31407 Outer I-10
Redlands, CA 92373
800-811-2331
fax: 909-794-8512
e-mail: nfaa-archery@aol.com
www.nfaa-archery.org
(magazine, youth archery program)

National Rifle Association of America
11250 Waples Mill Road
Fairfax, VA 22030
800-336-7402
www.rraha.org
(range operations, safety standards, teaching marksmanship)

USA Archery (National Archery Association)
1 Olympic Plaza
Colorado Springs, CO 80909
719-866-4576
fax: 719-632-4733
www.usarchery.org
(certification, training)

Youth Organizations

Boys and Girls Clubs of America
1230 West Peachtree St. NW
Atlanta, GA 30309-3494
404-487-5700
fax: 404-815-5727
www.bgca.org

Boy Scouts of America
(National Office)
1325 Walnut Hill Lane
P.O. Box 152079
Irving, TX 75015-2079
972-580-2000
www.scouting.org
(educational programs, character building)

Camp Fire USA
4601 Madison Avenue
Kansas City, MO 64112-1278
816-756-1950

fax: 816-756-0258
www.campfire.org

Child Welfare League of America
440 First St. NW, Third Floor
Washington, D.C. 20001-2085
202-638-2852
fax: 202-638-4004
www.cwla.org

**4-H – National Headquarters
CCREES/USDA**
1400 Independence Ave. SW
Washington, D.C. 20250
www.4h-usa.org

Girl Scouts of the U.S.A.
420 Fifth Avenue
New York, NY 10018-2798
800-478-7248
212-852-8000
www.girlscouts.org

JCC Association
15 East 26th Street
New York, NY 10010-1579
212-532-4949
fax: 212-481-4174
e-mail: info@jcca.org
www.jcca.org

YMCA of the U.S.A.
101 North Wacker Drive
Chicago, IL 60606
800-872-9622
fax: 312-977-1134
www.ymca.net

YWCA of the U.S.A.
1015 18th St. NW, Suite 100
Washington, D.C. 20036
202-467-0801
fax: 202-467-0802
www.ywca.org

Other Professional Organizations

American Camping Association, Inc.
5000 State Road 67 North
Martinsville, IN 46151-7902
765-342-8456
fax: 765-342-2065
e-mail: bookstore@ACAcamps.org
www.ACAcamps.org
(*Camping Magazine*, catalog
of publications, accreditation, conferences)

Canadian Camping Association

P.O. Box 74030
Peppertree P.O.
Edmonton, AB T5K 2S7, Canada
877-427-6958
780-427-6605
fax: 780-427-6695
e-mail: info@ccamping.org
www.ccamping.org
(journal, provincial conferences, accreditation)

Christian Camping International/USA

P.O. Box 62189
Colorado Springs, CO 80962-2189
719-260-9400
fax: 719-260-6398
e-mail: cciusa@cciusa.org
www.cci.gospelcom.net
(journal, newsletter, and other publications, conferences)

International Association of Conference Centers North America

234 North Lindbergh Blvd.
St. Louis, MO 63141
314-933-8575
fax: 314-993-8919
e-mail: info@iacconline.org
www.iacconline.org
(conference, publications, personnel referral)

International Association of Conference Center Administrators

1685 S. Colorado Blvd., S-357
Denver, CO 80222-4011
e-mail: info@iacca.org
www.iacca.org
(magazine, directory, workshops, conferences)

National Association of Therapeutic Wilderness Camps

698 Dinner Bell
Ohiopyle Rd.
Ohiopyle, PA 15470
724-329-0229
e-mail: info@natwc.org
www.natwc.org

National Recreation and Parks Association

22377 Belmont Ridge Road
Ashburn, VA 20148
703-858-0784
fax: 703-858-0794
www.nrpa.org
(journal, and other publications, conventions)

Other Program Resources

Adventure Cycling Association

P.O. Box 8308
Missoula, MT 59802
800-755-2453
406-721-1776
fax: 406-721-8754
www.adv-cycling.org

American Bicycle Association

P.O. Box 718
Chandler, AZ 85244
480-961-1903
fax: 480-961-1842
www.ababmx.com

American Hiking Society

1422 Fenwick Lane
Silver Spring, MD 20910
301-565-6704
fax: 301-565-6714
www.americanhiking.org

Bicycle Federation of America

1506 21st Street NW
Washington, D.C. 20009
202-463-6622
www.cyclery.com

Bicycle Helmet Safety Institute

4611 Seventh St. S.
Arlington VA 22204-1419
703-486-0100
e-mail: info@helmets.org
www.helmets.org

Environmental Protection Agency

Ariel Riso Bldg.
1200 Pennsylvania Ave. NW
Washington, D.C. 20640
202-272-0167
www.epa.gov
(President's Environmental Youth Awards—PEYA; Environmental Explorer's Club)

National Association of Rocketry

P.O. Box 177
Altoona, WI 54720
800-262-4872
www.nar.org

National Audubon Society
700 Broadway
New York, NY 10003
212-979-3000
fax: 212-979-3188
e-mail: education@audubon.org
www.audubon.org
(magazine)

National Speleological Society, Inc.
2813 Cave Avenue
Huntsville, AL 35810-4431
256-852-1300
e-mail: nss@caves.org
www.caves.org

National Wildlife Federation
11100 Wildlife Center Drive
Reston, VA 20190-5362
800-822-9919
www.nwf.org
(magazines and other publications)

OBIS (Outdoor Biology Instruction Strategies)
Delta Education, Inc.
P.O. Box 915
Hudson, NH 03051
800-442-5444
510-642-1016
www.1hs.berkeley.edu/obis
(publications)

U. S. Amateur Baseball Association
P.O. Box 55633
Seattle, WA 98155
425-776-7130
e-mail: usba@usaba.com
www.usaba.com

U. S. A. Gymnastics
Pan American Plaza
201 S. Capitol Ave. #300
Indianapolis, IN 46255
1-800-345-4719
317-237-5050
fax: 317-237-5069
e-mail: admin@usa-gymnatics.org
www.usa-gymnastics.org

U. S. Golf Association
P.O. Box 708
Far Hills, NJ 07931
908-234-2300
fax: 908-234-9687
www.usga.org

**Target Populations
Diversity/Accessibility**

Access By Design
3909 Buena Vista Dr.
Loveland, CO 80538
970-635-9843 phone/fax
www.access-by-design.com

American Association of People with Disabilities
258 Main St., Ste. 203
Milford, MA 01757
866-241-3200
fax: 508-634-5427
e-mail: mail@aapd.com
www.aapd.com

Americans With Disabilities Act (ADA)
U. S. Department of Justice
950 Pennsylvania Ave. N.W.
Washington, D. C. 20530-0001
Technical Information Line: 800-514-0301
TTY: 800-514-0383
www.usdoj.gov/crt/ada

National Center for Accessibility
2805 E. 10th St., Suite 190
Bloomington, IN 47408-2698
812-856-4422
TTY: 812-856-4421
fax: 812-856-4480
e-mail: nca@indiana.edu
www.ncaonline.org

U. S. Access Board
1331 F St. NW #1000
Washington, D.C. 20004-1111
800-USA-ABLE (892-2253)
TTY: 800-993-2822
fax: 800-892-0081
www.access-board.gov

Appendix D:
International Resources

These agencies currently provide assistance to camps desiring international counselors for summer programs. For specific information, communicate directly with the agencies.

BUNACAMP
P.O. Box 430
Southbury, CT 06488
203-264-0901
800-GO-BUNAC (462-8622)
fax: 203-264-0251
www.bunac.org

Camp America
River Plaza
9 West Broad Street
Stamford, CT 06902
800-727-8233
fax: 203-399-5590
e-mail: dregan@aifs.com
www:campamerica.aifs.com
dregan@aifs.com

Camp Counselors U.S.A.
2330 Marinship Way, Suite 250
Sausalito, CA 94965
415-339-2728
800-999-CAMP (2267)
fax: 4150339-2744
www.campcounselors.com

International Camp Counselor Exchange Program
38 West 88th Street
New York, NY 10024
212-787-7706
fax: 212-780-9283
www.chez.com/icep

International Camping Fellowship, Inc.
1844 Ravenscliffe Road
Huntsville, ONT P1H 2N2
Canada
705-789-5612
fax: 705-789-6624
e-mail: info@campingfellowship.org
www.campingfellowship.org

YMCA International Camp Counselor Program
5 West 63rd Street
New York, NY 10023-9197
888-477-9622
fax: 212-727-8814
e-mail: ips@ymcanyc.org
www.ymcaiccp.org

Appendix E:
Governmental Resources

Essential Area	Federal Government Agency	State Agency/Department (if applicable)
Business & Finance		
Business Development	Small Business Administration (SBA) www.sba.gov Minority Business Development Agency www.mbda.gov	
Foreign Funds	Export-Import Bank of the U.S. www.exim.gov	
Loans	Small Business Administration (SBA) www.sba.gov/	
Taxes Nonprofit and Income	Internal Revenue Service (IRS) www.irs.gov/	Revenue (Taxation, Assessor)
Taxes Real Estate, Bed, Recreation, Sales		Revenue (Taxation, Assessor)
Licenses/Permits		Health & Sanitation (except Colorado and Michigan, where Social Services; New Hampshire, where Water Supply & Pollution; and New Mexico, where Environmental Improvement Agency
Food Services		
Food Safety	United States Department of Agriculture (USDA) www.usda.gov/ USDA Food Safety and Inspection Service www.fsis.usda.gov	Local Health Department
Special Milk Program		Education
Summer Feeding Program		Education
Surplus Commodities		Education
Health & Wellness		
Health	Department of Health & Human Services (DHHS) www.hhs.gov/ Centers For Disease Control (CDC) www.cdc.gov/	Health (Environmental Resources, Environmental Health, Health & Sanitation)
Medication Management	Food and Drug Administration (FDA) www.fda.gov	Local Health Department
Septic Tanks Water Systems	Centers For Disease Control (CDC) www.cdc.gov/	Health (Environmental Resources, Environmental Health, Health & Sanitation)
Human Resources		
Child Labor Regulations, Work Permit	Department of Labor (DOL) www.dol.gov/	Labor
Employment Practices	Department of Justice – Civil Rights Division www.usdoj.gov/civilliberties.htm Equal Employment Opportunity Office Office of American Disabilities Act www.ada.gov	Civil Rights
Employment Services	Department of Labor (DOL) /www.dol.gov/	Labor, Employment Security
FICA	Department of Health & Human Services (DHHS) www.hhs.gov/ Social Security Administration (SSA) www.ssa.gov/	Employment Security
International Staff	Immigration and Naturalization Service www.ins.gov	
Medicare & Medicaid Services	Centers for Medicare and Medicaid Services www.cms.hhs.gov	Labor
Minimum Wage Overtime	Department of Labor – Wage & Hour Division www.dol.gov/	Labor

Occupational Safety & Health Act	Department of Labor – Occupational Safety & Health Office – www.osha.gov	Labor
Unemployment Compensation (FUTA/SUTA)	Department of Labor www.dol.gov/	Labor, Employment Security
Worker's Compensation	Department of Labor www.dol.gov/	Industrial Board (Labor)
Leadership	Small Business Administration www.sba.gov	
Marketing	Small Business Administration www.sba.gov	
Mission & Outcomes	Small Business Administration www.sba.gov	
Participant Development & Behavior	Department of Health and Human Services www.hhs.gov	
Program Design & Activities		
Boating Operator's License Inspections Licenses	Coast Guard (if in USCG jurisdiction) www.uscg.mil/	Department of Natural Resources
Conservation & Environmental Education	Environmental Protection Agency www.epa.gov	Department of Natural Resources/Fish & Game/Forestry/ Environmental Protection
Firearms	Bureau of Alcohol, Tobacco, Firearms & Explosives www.atf.treas.gov	
Fish	Department of Interior – Fish & Wildlife Services www.doi.gov/	Department of Natural Resources – Fish & Game/Environmental Protection
Flying Programs	Federal Aviation Administration (FAA) www.faa.gov	
Hunting	Department of Interior – Fish & Wildlife Services www.fws.gov/	Department of Natural Resources – Fish & Game/Environmental Protection
Radio	Federal Communications Commission (FCC) www.fcc.gov	
Sports & Fitness	President's Council on Physical Fitness and Sports www.fitness.gov	
Risk Management		
OSHA	Department of Labor (OSHA) www.osha.gov/	Labor, OSHA
Site & Facilities		
Accommodations (ADA) Dining Facility Housing Restrooms	Department of Justice – Civil Rights Division www.usdoj.gov/ Office of American Disabilities Act www.ada.gov Department of Transportation www.dot.gov/ Federal Communications Commission www.fcc.gov/ Architectural & Transportation Barriers Compliance Board www.access-board.gov/	Civil Rights
Building Codes Electrical Inspections Plumbing		City/County/State Building Departments
Environment (pollution, spills, etc.)	Environmental Protection Agency www.epa.gov	Environmental Protection
Fire		Fire Marshall/Department
Forestry	Department of Agriculture – Forest Service www.usda.gov/	Department of Natural Resources
Public Lands	Department of Interior – National Parks Service www.nps.gov/ Department of Agriculture – Forest Service www.fs.fed.us/ Corps of Engineers www.usace.army.mil/ Department of Interior – Bureau of Land Management www.blm.gov/nhp/facts/index.htm	City or County Park Department State Parks Department City or County Forest Preserves
Soil Conservation/Erosion	Department of Agriculture – Forest Service www.fs.fed.us/	Department of Natural Resources
Water	Environmental Protection Agency www.epa.gov/	Health
Strategic Planning	Small Business Administration www.sba.gov	
Target Population & Diversity		
Camper Assistance Funds	Department of Health & Human Services (DHHS) www.hhs.gov/	Public Welfare
Persons with Disabilities	Department of Justice, Office of American Disabilities Act www.ada.gov	Civil Rights
Transportation		
Vehicles Registration Licenses Operator's Licenses Inspections	Department of Transportation www.dot.gov/ National Highway Traffic Safety Administration www.nhtsa.dot.gov/	Department of Motor Vehicles

Alphabetical List of Selected Federal Agencies	Contact Information
Agriculture – Food Programs	www.usda.gov
Americans with Disabilities Act	www.ada.gov
Bureau of Alcohol, Tobacco, Firearms and Explosives	www.atf.treas.gov
Bureau of Land Management	www.blm.gov/nhp/facts/index/htm
Center for Disease Control	www.cdc.gov
Centers for Medicare and Medicaid Services	www.cms.hhs.gov
Corps of Engineers	www.usace.army.mil/
Environmental Protection Agency	www.epa.gov
Equal Employment Opportunity Commission	www.eeoc.gov
Export-Import Bank of the U.S.	www.exim.gov
Federal Aviation Administration	www.fcs.gov
Federal Communications Commission	www.fcc.gov
Federal Emergency Management Agency	www.fema.gov
Food and Drug Administration	www.fda.gov
Forest Service	www.fs.fed.us/
Health and Human Services	www.hhs.gov/
Immigration and Naturalization Service	www.ins.gov
Interior	www.doi.gov
Internal Revenue Service	www.irs.gov
Justice	www.usgof.gov
Labor	www.dol.gov
Minority Business Development Agency	www.mbda.gov
National Highway Traffic Safety Administration	www.nhtsa.gov
National Park Service	www.nps.gov
National Transportation Safety Board	www.ntsb.gov
Occupational Safety and Health Administration	www.osha.gov
President's Council on Fitness and Sports	www.fitness.gov
Small Business Administration	www.sba.gov
Social Security Administration	www.ssa.gov
Transportation	www.dot.gov
U.S. Customs Service	www.customs.treas.gov
U.S. Fish and Wildlife Service	www.fws.gov

Appendix F:
ACA Code of Ethics

Exemplary Ethical Practices for All Members of the American Camping Association

A Code of Ethics identifies those behaviors and attitudes the profession believes to be minimum acceptable commitments to the well being of others. It is not possible for a code to identify or include all such practices or concepts. The existence of a Code of Ethics cannot guarantee that all persons will behave in ways deemed ethical by all other persons. A code is built on a commitment to integrity, truthfulness, and fairness to all persons. To that end, the members of the American Camping Association agree, by their membership, to uphold the following:

1. I shall conduct myself in a manner consistent with the association's mission to serve organized camps, affiliated programs, and the public by promoting better camping for all.

2. I shall recognize my responsibility for the welfare of others in my care.

3. I shall abide by and comply with the relevant laws of the community.

4. I shall be a member in the proper ACA classification as currently defined by the ACA National Board of Directors; and I shall disclose my affiliation with ACA only in a manner specifically permitted by the association.

5. I shall speak for the association only when specifically authorized to do so and will otherwise make clear that my statements and actions are those of an individual member.

6. I shall respect the confidences of ACA members, camps, and other constituents within the camp community; however, I shall accept responsibility to pass on to the appropriate ACA official, information I deem reliable that will help protect the camp community against unethical practices by any individual.

Exemplary Ethical Practices for Camp Owners, Directors, and Executives

The association recognizes the camp owner, director, and executive as the primary professional persons assuming the greatest responsibility for actual camp practices. Therefore, in addition to the Code of Ethics for all members, any member operating a camp accredited by or affiliated with the American Camping Association agrees to subscribe to the following:A Code of Ethics identifies those behaviors and attitudes the profession believes to be minimum acceptable commitments to the well being of others. It is not possible for a code to identify or include all such practices or concepts. The existence of a Code of Ethics cannot guarantee that all persons will behave in ways deemed ethical by all other persons. A code is built on a commitment to integrity, truthfulness, and fairness to all persons. To that end, the members of the American Camping Association agree, by their membership, to uphold the following:

1. I shall conduct myself in a manner consistent with the association's mission to serve organized camps, affiliated programs, and the public by promoting better camping for all.

2. I shall recognize my responsibility for the welfare of others in my care.

3. I shall abide by and comply with the relevant laws of the community.

4. I shall be a member in the proper ACA classification as currently defined by the ACA National Board of Directors; and I shall disclose my affiliation with ACA only in a manner specifically permitted by the association.

5. I shall speak for the association only when specifically authorized to do so and will otherwise make clear that my statements and actions are those of an individual member.

6. I shall respect the confidences of ACA members, camps, and other constituents within the camp community; however, I shall accept responsibility to pass on to the appropriate ACA official, information I deem reliable that will help protect the camp community against unethical practices by any individual.

7. I shall endeavor to provide an environment conducive to promoting and protecting the physical and emotional well being of the campers and staff.

8. I shall seek to instill in my staff and campers a reverence for the land and its waters and all living things, and an ecological conscience which reflects the conviction of individual responsibility for the health of that environment.

9. I shall follow equal opportunity practices in employment and camper enrollment.

10. I shall endeavor to employ persons based upon factors necessary to the performance of the job and the operation of the camp.

11. I shall be truthful and fair in securing and dealing with campers, parents/guardians, and staff.

12. I shall provide a written enrollment policy for all camper/family applicants including fees, payment schedules, discounts, dates of arrival and departure, together with a clearly stated refund policy.

13. I shall provide for each staff member a written job description and employment agreement including period of employment, compensation, benefits, and exceptions.

14. I shall promptly consult with parents or guardians of any camper or minor staff member as to the advisability of removing him/her from camp should it be clear that he/she is not benefiting from the camp experience or the camper's or minor staff member's actions have created this need.

15. I shall make arrangements with the parents or guardians for the return of their camper(s) or minor-age staff member(s).

16. I shall pay the correct national and section fees as established by the ACA National Board of Directors and the ACA Section Board of Directors.

17. I, or my agent, will promptly respond to any and all complaints received by me and make a good faith effort to resolve all such complaints in accordance with generally accepted good business practices and the ACA Code of Ethics.

Adopted 2-26-95, Revised 3/2/97; Revised 2/25/00; Revised 2/23/02
ACA Council of Delegates

Appendix G

Best Practices for International Staff in American Camping Association Camps

The availability of international staff is made possible by a number of organizations that arrange what are formally designated as cultural exchange programs by U.S. Department of State. Over the last several decades, the use of such international staff has evolved from a value-added opportunity into a vital resource for many American summer camps. As this trend continues, we must take care not to lose sight of the cultural exchange aspect of these programs.

Additionally, as an industry we are bound to protect the resources on which the summer camp experience depends. We unite to address environmental, educational, legal and financial issues. We set standards to which we hold ourselves accountable, and we understand the moral and ethical aspects of conducting an enterprise that is essentially human in nature. It is reasonable, therefore, that we identify and engage in best practices as we employ counselors and support staff from abroad. Moreover, following such practices is consistent with our mission of ". . . enriching the lives of children and adults through the camp experience."

The organizations that work with the camp community to provide international staff recruit and screen young people from other countries to work at American camps under the J-1 cultural exchange visa program. There has been a substantial increase in the number of international staff working in camps in the U.S. in the last five years, and because a number of issues and trends emerged ACA joined with camp directors and international staffing agencies to isolate the basics that are expected of participating camps. See *illustration G.1*. In addition, they enumerated exemplary practices(i.e., those practices beyond the basics that display a higher degree of commitment to the education and welfare of internationals and the tenets of cultural exchange).

Leaders in the international staffing agencies agreed that, regardless of which agency a camp utilizes or which type of camp is seeking staff, the success of the cultural exchange experience for the camp and for the staff member depends on a number of identified "best practices."

We encourage you to post illustration G.1 on a bulletin board as a reminder to all staff.

Sponsoring agencies would be happy to help you strengthen your international staffing or to put you in touch with camp directors already effectively using international staffing. For further information, contact the following agencies:

BUNAC
P.O. Box 430
Southbury, CT 06488
800-462-8622 or 203-264-0901
fax: 203-264-0251
www.bunac.org

Camp America
River Plaza
9 West Broad Street
Stamford, CT 06902-3788
phone: 800-727-2437
fax: 203-399-5595
www.aifs.org/camp

Camp Counselors U.S.A.
2330 Marineship Way, Suite 250
Sausalito, CA 94965
800-999-2267 or 415-339-2728
fax: 415-339-2744
www.campcounselors.com

International Camp Counselor Program-YMCA
5 West 63rd Street, 2nd Floor
New York, NY 10023-9197
888-477-9622 or 212-727-8800
fax: 212-727-8814
www.ymcaiccp.org

International Counselor Exchange Program
38 West 88th Street
New York, NY 10024-2502
phone: 212-787-7706
fax: 212-580-9283
www.chez.com/icep

Best Practices

For International Staff in American Camping Association Camps

The following "best practices" have been identified as those that directly contribute to the success of the cultural exchange experience for the camp and for the staff member.

Sponsoring Agency and Administrative Concerns

Expected practices of directors:

- Understand that the purpose of the J-1 visa program is for cultural exchange
- Establish a strong relationship with sponsoring agency
- Provide decent wages and access to money owed (Note that checks are hard for internationals to cash. Offer help with that process!)
- Be aware of the insurance coverage of the agency and whether Workers' Compensation coverage is needed
- Have a crisis plan in place for dealing with injury to, arrest, or death of an international

Exemplary practices of directors:

- Feature cultural programming in camp
- Show international programs and staff in camp marketing materials

Hiring Process

Expected practices of directors:

- Be able to define why the camp wants to include internationals on their staff (other than filling vacancies)
- Interview the potential applicant on the phone prior to hiring
- Be thorough in evaluating candidates and selecting staff
- Spend at least as much time in hiring process as you do with American staff
- Provide clear expectations of staff while at camp

Exemplary practices of directors:

- Able to articulate how inclusion of international staff fits into their camp philosophy
- Avoid stereotyping nationalities by demonstrating a willingness to hire international staff from all countries and use them in all positions

After hiring — Prior to Camp

Expected practices of directors:

- Talk to the staff member by phone before camp
- Provide advanced information by mail or e-mail including policies, handbook, organizational chart, map, weather, what to bring, camp Web site, orientation/training schedule, job descriptions, camper profile, rules and regulations, mission/purpose, time off policies, transportation to town options, e-mail of mentor/buddy, local attractions/local community info, etc.

- Paint a realistic picture of the camp and establish expectations, i.e., help with understanding of rural community differences, sleeping accommodations, typical menus.

Exemplary practices of directors:

- Provide opportunities for effective networking with former international staff in their country, e.g., share e-mail addresses of former camp staff

Arrival and Pre-camp

Expected practices of directors:

- Provide comfortable/efficient transportation to camp from orientation site

- Arrange for welcoming staff on arrival

- Be sensitive to time and cultural adjustments needed

- Provide adequate housing that is welcoming and clean, including linens and bedding

- Active effort to integrate groups of staff

- Be sensitive to language issues

- Training reflects understanding in dealing with cultural differences B sexual practices, hygiene, sexual harassment, fashions, etc.

- Provide responsible education/orientation B training for understanding and competence

- Be sensitive to food issues, allergies, cultural and religious practices B e.g., lactose intolerance, pork

Exemplary practices of directors:

- Demonstrate a real attitude of "I care about you and want you to have a successful summer."

- Utilize a contact/liaison on camp staff who understands international issues

- Develop a buddy/mentor system

During the Summer

Expected practices of directors:

- Provide positive feedback and reinforcement

- Continue to acknowledge and work with language differences

- Help arrange transportation on time off

- Continue to partnership with agency on "problems"

- Be sensitive to financial issues — e.g., cashing checks

- Provide secure place for papers and valuables

- Treat all staff as adults; treat support staff equal to program staff

- Have trained/competent supervisors

- Provide for open communication between the director and international staff

- Provide Internet access — e-mail
- Demonstrate a real VALUING of international staff and acceptance of cultural differences
- Provide ongoing training and support
- Provide at least some cultural programming as a part of the camp's activities
- Be sensitive to health issues — doctors, dentists, medications, etc.
- Encourage staff to obey the rules of the program and return to home country after the summer
- Support the rules governing the J-1 program which restricts switching staff between support and counseling roles
- Develop a program of training and support to solve a problem, using fair termination policy as a last resort and only after consultation with the sponsoring agency
- Provide opportunities for out of camp recreational or area tourist experiences
- Make provision for international staff to do their laundry
- Give access to camp activities and facilities
- Provide adequate time off
- Treat American and international staff equally especially in number of hours required to work

Exemplary practices of directors:

- Have outstanding cultural programming
- Provide multinational opportunities showing diversity in camp
- Feature some international staff and programming in the camp video
- Identify and work with local family or alumni sponsors to integrate staff into the local community
- Provide international staff with an equal shot at key positions and leadership opportunities
- Help with transportation post-camp

Appendix H:
Sample Personnel Hiring Log

Sample Personnel Hiring Log

Applicant's name _____

Position sought _____

Application Information

Date application received _____

Certifications Received   Date

_____   _____
_____   _____
_____   _____
_____   _____
_____   _____

Criminal Background Checks

Date criminal background records check requested from:

Local _____   State _____   Federal _____

Date criminal background information received from:

Local _____   State _____   Federal _____

and/or Volunteer Disclosure Form received _____

References and Employment

Date requests for references sent _____   Dates references received: _____

    Reference #1 _____

    Reference #2 _____

    Reference #3 _____

	Date Past Employment Requested	Verification Received
Employer #1	_____	_____
Employer #2	_____	_____
Employer #3	_____	_____
Employer #4	_____	_____

Personal Interview

Person doing interview _____

Date interview completed _____

Job Offer

Date employment agreement sent _____

Date signed agreement received _____

Other Information Requested After Hire

Date health records received _____

Date I-9 received _____

Date W-2 received _____

Reasonable accommodations requested

Other Notes

_____

_____

_____

_____

_____

_____

_____

Appendix I:
Outdoor Living Skills

Be a Part of Shaping the Future

As camping professionals and outdoor educators, do your campcraft, hiking, and nature awareness programs and practices measure up to current concerns about the environment? Are the campers bored? Then take those blues away and make them green. With the OLS program, campers learn to make responsible decisions while participating in activities such as hiking, cookouts, overnights, games, and nature exploration. They also learn to understand the impact of such activities on the environment.

Great Outdoor Program for Youth

- Customize the program for your campers; earn patches in a few days or over several summers.
- Build a sense of accomplishment and keep your campers coming back.
- Start where you'll be challenged — this well-organized program allows you to begin at any level.

Level-One Participant Requirements

(This is a sample of the requirements for level one; most include group planning and interaction.)
- Plan a half-day hike. Know what to wear and what to take.
- Pack for and go on a half-day hike.
- Plan a lunch that won't spoil. Properly dispose of your trash.
- Play a game that helps you understand ecology.
- Do an activity using your senses.

An Excellent Resource for Precamp Training

- Plan your staff training.
- Learn how to work with all ages of campers.
- Update your nature program with current environmental concerns.
- Learn methods and tips for working with groups.
- Use sample training modules.
- Meet U.S. Forest Service guidelines for minimum-impact camping.

Adult Cards Document Skills

Program Leader Course is for staff or volunteers who work directly with campers. The course will include minimum-impact camping and outdoor skills needed to offer the OLS program to campers. Program Leader cards provide documented training in outdoor living skills activities. This course addresses ACA 1999 standards PD-1, PD-2, PD-3, PD-7, and PD-9.

Instructors Course is for ACA members and nonmembers who are 18 years old or older, with camping experience and outdoor skills. The course covers adult education and training methods, and has a complete session-by-session curriculum for training Program Leaders and counselors. The manual also explains how to administer the OLS program in a camp.

Training

The OLS program can be used by any group. If you would like more information on training, check out the OLS Workshops on the Professional Development Calendar at ACA's Web site: www.ACAcamps.org. Training schedules can be found in section newsletters and *Camping Magazine*; or contact an ACA section or the ACA national office, 765-342-8456, ext. 320, or e-mail aca@aca-camps.org.

Appendix J:
Selected Resources

Human Resources/Staffing

Books

Brandwein, Michael. 1999. *Training Traffic Staff*. Lincolnshire, IL: Michael Brandwein.

Coutellier, Connie and Henchey. Kathleen. 2000. *Camp is for the Camper: A Counselor's Guide to Youth Development*. Martinsville, IN: American Camping Association.

Eitington, Julius E. 1996. *The Winning Trainer*. Houston, TX: Gulf Publishing.

Patterson, John C. 1998. *Staff Screening Tool Kit: Keeping the Bad Apples Out of Your Organization*. Washington, DC: Nonprofit Risk Management Center.

Videos

American Camping Association. *So You Want to Be a Supervisor: An Educational Package to Train Camp Supervisory Staff*. 1996. Martinsville, IN: American Camping Association.

Ditter, Bob. *To Tell the Truth*. 1990. Martinsville, IN: American Camping Association.

Site and Facilities

Books

Burch, Monte. *Pole Building Projects*. 1993. Pownal, VT: Storey Books.

Forster, Gary. *This Old Camp: Camp Property Management*. 1994. Colebrook, CT: Camp Jewell YMCA.

Goltsman, Gilbert, Wohlford and Kirk. *The Accessibility Checklist: An Evaluation System for Buildings and Outdoor Settings*. Berkeley, CA: MIG Communications.

Lucchetti, Robert C. *Lightly on the Land: The SCA Trail-Building Maintenance Manual*. 1996. Seattle, WA: The Mountaineers.

Marketing

Books

Bade, Nicholas E. *Marketing Without Money for Small and Midsize Businesses.* 1999. Willoughby, OH: Halle House Publishers.

Clark, Silvanna. *Taming the Recreation Jungle:100 Ways to Improve the Quality of Recreation Programs.* 1993. Seattle, WA: Book Partners, Inc.

Herron, Douglas B. *Marketing Nonprofit Programs and Services.* 1997. San Francisco, CA: Jossey-Bass, Inc., Publishers.

Risk Management

Books

American Camping Association. *Accreditation Standards for Camp Programs and Services.* 1998. Martinsville, IN: American Camping Association.

Coutellier, Connie. *Management of Risks and Emergencies.* 1993. Kansas City, MI: Camp Fire, Inc.

Jackson, Peggy M.; White, Leslie T.; and Herman, Melanie L. *Mission Accomplished: A Practical Guide To Risk Management for Nonprofits.* 1997. Washington, DC: Nonprofit Risk Management Center.

Videos

American Camping Association. *Camp White Cloud Goes to Court–Video and Leader's Guide.* 1994. Martinsville, IN: American Camping Association.

American Camping Association. *So You Want to Be a Supervisor?* 1996. Martinsville, IN: American Camping Association.

CDs

American Camping Association. *The Complete Resource Pack: Includes RP I, RP II, and 20 new items.* 2003. Martinsville, IN: American Camping Association.

Health and Wellness

Books

Forgey, William. *Wilderness Medicine: Beyond First Aid, Fifth Edition.* 2000. Guilford, CT: Globe Pequot.

Erceq, Linda Ebner and Pravda, Myra. *The Basics of Camp Nursing.* 2001. Martinsville, IN: American Camping Association.

Leadership

Books

Covey, Stephen R. *Seven Habits of Highly Effective People.* 1989. New York, NY: Simon and Schuster.

Graham, John. *Outdoor Leadership: Techniques, Common Sense and Self-Confidence.* 1997. Seattle, WA: The Mountaineers.

Hunsacker, Phillip L. and Alessandra, Anthony J. *The Art of Managing People.* 1986. New York: Simon and Schuster, Inc.

Business and Finance

Books

Finney, Robert G. *Essentials of Business Budgeting.* 1995. New York, NY: American Management Association.

Tyson, Eric and Schell, Jim. *Small Business for Dummies.* 1998. Foster City, CA: IDG Books Worldwide.

CDs

American Camping Association. *2003 Camp Benchmarks: Program, Staffing, and Financial Profiles.* 2004. Martinsville, IN: American Camping Association

Food Service

Books

Reath, Jim. *A Recipe File for Camps.* 1998. Muskegan, MI: Jim Reath.

Shugart, Grace and Molt, Mary. *Food for Fifty.* 1997. Upper Saddle River, NJ: Prentice-Hall.

Spain, Viki Kappel. *Food Service Manual: Lessons in Group Food Service.* 2003. Martinsville, IN: American Camping Association

Transportation

Books

Rypkema, Pam. *Avoiding a Crash Course: Auto Liability. Insurance, and Safety for Nonprofits.* 1995. Washington, DC: Nonprofit Risk Management Center.

Mission/Philosophy

Books

Hill, Amie and Herman, Richard. *The Interlocken Differences: Four Decades of Experiential Learning and Community.* 1998. Dubuque, IA: Kendall/Hunt Publishing Company.

Nolan, Timothy; Goldstein, Leonard; and Pfeiffer, William. *Plan or Die: 10 Keys to Organizational Success.* 1993. San Diego, CA: Pfieffer and Company.

Sales, Amy L., and Saxe, Leonard. *How Godly Are Thy Tents: Summer Camps As Jewish Socializing Experiences*. 2003. Waltham, MA: Brandeis University

Youth Development/Behavior

Books

Beker, Jerome; Magnuson, Doug; Magnuson, Connie; and Beker, David. *What Do I Do Now?* 1996. Martinsville, IN: American Camping Association.

Ditter, Bob. *Life-Lines and Safety-Nets, A Staff Resource and Training Booklet.* 1994. Boston, MA: Little Fox Productions, Ltd.

Pastore, Michael. *Dynamite Counselors Don't Explode.* 1993. Dayville, CT: Zorba Press.

Pipher, Mary. *Reviving Ophelia: Saving the Selves of Adolescent Girls.* 1995. New York, NY: Ballantine Books.

Pollack, William. *Real Boys.* 1998. New York, NY: Henry Holt & Company.

Thompson, Ph.D., Michael and Kindlon, Ph.D., Dan. *Raising Cain: Protecting the Emotional Life of Boys.* 2000. New York, NY: Ballantine Books.

Target Populations/Diversity

Books

Barbarash, Lorraine. *Multicultural Games.* 1997. Champaign, IL: Human Kinetics.

Chappelle, Sharon; Bigman, Lisa; and Hillyer, Francesca. *Diversity in Action.* 1998. Covington, GA: Adventure, Inc.

Kasser, Susan L. *Inclusive Games.* 1995. Champaign, IL: Human Kinetics.

Roswal, Glenn; Dowd, Karen J.; and Bynum, Jerry. *Including People with Disabilities in Camp Programs: A Resource for Camp Directors.* 1997. Martinsville, IN: American Camping Association.

Strategic Planning

Books

Allison, Michael and Kaye, Jude. *Strategic Planning for Nonprofit Organizations.* 1997. New York, NY: John Wiley & Sons.

Bryson, John. *Strategic Planning for Public and Nonprofit Organizations: A Guide to Strengthening and Sustaining Organizational Achievement.* 1995. San Francisco, CA: Jossey-Bass Publishers.

Program Design and Activities

Books

American Camping Association. *The Outdoor Living Skills Instructor's Manual.* 2002. Martinsville, IN: American Camping Association.

Scheder, Catherine M. *Outdoor Living Skills Program Manual; An Environmentally Friendly Guide.* based on *Take a New Bearing* by Phyllis Ford. 2002. Martinsville, IN: American Camping Association.

Henderson, Karla A. and Bialeschki, M. Deborah. *Evaluating Leisure Services: Making Enlighted Decisions.* 1995. State College, PA: Venture Publishing, Inc.

Kasser, Susan L. *Inclusive Games.* 1995. Champaign, IL: Human Kinetics.

Milford, Susan. *Kids' Nature Book: 365 Indoor/Outdoor Activities and Experiences.* 1996. Charlotte, VT: Williamson Publishing.

Morton, Annie; Prosser, Angie; and Spangler, Sue. *Great Special Events.* 1991. State College, PA: Venture Publishing, Inc.

Priest, Simon and Gass, Micheal A. *Effective Leadership in Adventure Programming.* 1997. Champaign, IL: Human Kinetics.

Volunteers

Books

Carner, John. *Boards that Make a Difference.* 1990. San Francisco, CA: Jossey-Bass Publishers.

Isley, Paul J. *Enhancing the Volunteer Experience.* 1990. San Francisco, CA: Jossey-Bass Publishers.

Levin, Mark. *The Gift of Leadership.* 1997. Columbia, MD: B.A.I., Inc.

BAND-AID

Index

personal interaction with campers, marketing and, 240–242
personality strengths/limitations, interview and, 118–119
personnel, 83. See also staff
    benefits, 94–96
    fund-raising, 282
    health service, 200–203
    job descriptions, 89–96
    job responsibilities, 84
    maintenance, 170–171
    performance outcomes, 28
    policies, 96–99
    risk management and, 176
    salary, 94–96
    staff-to-camper ratio, 84–85
    supervisory lines, 85–88
personnel files, employment agreement and, 123
Petty Cash Advance Slip, 270
philosophy
    definition, 23
    development, 24
physical disabilities, growth and development and, 44–45
physical evidence, evaluations and, 297
physical facility. See facility
physical skills, outdoor activities, 77
physical stress, 158
physicians. See health service
Pinelands Camps, 2
placement services, recruiting and, 102
population
    special, program design and, 74–76
    targeting, 35–39
posters as advertisement, 247
post-staff-training interview, counselor/supervisor, 146–147
precamp training, 130–131
    abuse information, 133–134
    documentation, 137
    experiential training, 131–132
    scheduling, 132–133
    supervisory staff, 135–137
    variety among sessions, 134–135
preinterview
    camp information, 117
    job description, 116–117
    organization chart, 117
    questions you may/may not ask, 117
preparation of participants
    groups, 55
    individuals, 53–55
present staff, recruiting and, 101–102

professional associations, 4
professional camp directors, ACA Professional Development plan, 314
professional camp directors, 311–313
    education, 314–316
program, organizational designs and, 64
program design
    activities
        arts, 77
        land sports and games, 76
        outdoor-oriented, 77
        social recreation, 78
        special events, 77
        spiritually oriented activities, 78
        water sports and games, 77
    beyond summer, 73–74
    centralized, 63
    decentralized, 63
    emphases, 70–72
    group living, 72
    operating procedures
        activity level appropriateness, 79–80
        emergency procedures, 80
        equipment, 79
        information to include, 78
        leadership and, 79
        safety procedures, 80
    organizational designs, 64
    progression and, 71
    special populations, 74–76
program development. See also program design
    activities, identifying potential, 61
    benefits of programs, 59–60
    developmental needs, 60–61
    goals
        assessing, 60
        reviewing, 61
    implementation, 62
    influencing factors, 61
    interests, 60–61
    mission/purpose, 60
    operating procedures, 62
    outcomes, 28
        assessing, 60
        reviewing, 61
    philosophy, 60
    program design, 62, 63–66
    promotion, 62
    refinement, 62
    resources of campers, 62
    staff training, 62
program evaluation, 300–302
program organization
    activities, all-camp, 69

bus program and, 69
individuals, 67–68
instruction, 68–69
interest groups, 68
living groups, 67
schedule sample, 66
sections, 69
units, 69
progression in programs, 71
promotional materials, 242
    brochures, 244
    flyers, 244
    incentives, 244
    outside referrals, 245–246
    prospective campers/groups, 243
    public displays, 246
    visual presentations, 245
property insurance, 182–183
psychological abuse, 48
psychological conditions, developmental needs and, 48–52
public relations, 248–249
purchasing system, 268–269
purpose statement, 26–27

Q

qualitative data, evaluations and, 297–298
Quebeck Camping Association, 4
questionnaires, evaluations and, 297
questions asked during interview, 117
    general to specific, 120
    leading questions, 119
    open-ended, 119–120
    self-appraisal, 120

R

record keeping
    computer records, 210
    evaluations and, 297
    health records, 193–194
        accident/incident reports, 210
        computer records, 210
        Health Examination Form sample, 213
        health examination forms, 209
        histories, 209
        inventories, 210
        logs, 209–210
            sample, 215
        OSHA-required records, 210
        permissions, 209
        screenings, 209
            sample form, 214
    incident reports, 195
    market analysis and, 233–235